M000305882

HARCOURT

Math

GEORGIA EDITION

Harcourt

Visit *The Learning Site!*
www.harcourtschool.com

Source for Georgia Performance Standards for Mathematics: Georgia Department of Education

Printed in the United States of America

ISBN 13: 978-0-15-347155-1

ISBN 10: 0-15-347155-7

6 7 8 9 10 032 15 14 13 12 11 10 09 08 07

Senior Author
Evan M. Maletsky
Professor of Mathematics
Montclair State University
Upper Montclair, New Jersey

▶ Mathematics Advisor
Margaret W. Faircloth
K–12 Mathematics Consultant
Georgia Presidential Award for
Mathematics
Macon, Georgia

Authors

Angela Giglio Andrews
Math Teacher, Scott School
Naperville District #203
Naperville, Illinois

Jennie M. Bennett
Houston Independent School District
Houston, Texas

Grace M. Burton
Professor, Watson School of Education
University of North Carolina at Wilmington
Wilmington, North Carolina

Lynda A. Luckie
K-12 Mathematics Coordinator
Gwinnett County Public Schools
Lawrenceville, Georgia

Joyce C. McLeod
Visiting Professor
Rollins College
Winter Park, Florida

Vicki Newman
Classroom Teacher
McGaugh Elementary School
Los Alamitos Unified School District
Seal Beach, California

Tom Roby
Associate Professor of Mathematics
University of Connecticut
Storrs, Connecticut

Janet K. Scheer
Executive Director
Create A Vision
Foster City, California

Program Consultants and Specialists

Elsie Babcock
*Director, Mathematics and
  Science Center
Mathematics Consultant*
Wayne Regional Educational
  Service Agency
Wayne, Michigan

William J. Driscoll
Professor of Mathematics
Department of Mathematical
  Sciences
Central Connecticut State
  University
New Britain, Connecticut

Lois Harrison-Jones
*Education and Management
  Consultant*
Dallas, Texas

Dr. William O. Lacefield, III
*Associate Professor of
  Mathematics Education*
Tift College of Education
Mercer University
Atlanta, Georgia

Rebecca Valbuena
*Language Development
  Specialist*
Stanton Elementary School
Glendora, California

UNIT 1

Understand Whole Numbers and Operations

1 PLACE VALUE AND NUMBER SENSE

Technology Link

Harcourt Mega Math:
  Chapter 1, pp. 2, 5, 15
  Chapter 2, pp. 34, 40, 47, 53
The Harcourt Learning Site:
www.harcourtschool.com
Multimedia Math Glossary:
www.harcourtschool.com/mathglossary

2 ADD AND SUBTRACT WHOLE NUMBERS 26

UNIT WRAPUP

UNIT 2

CHAPTERS 3-4

Data and Graphing

Technology Link

Harcourt Mega Math:
   Chapter 3, p. 72
   Chapter 4, pp. 80, 83
The Harcourt Learning Site:
www.harcourtschool.com
Multimedia Math Glossary:
www.harcourtschool.com/mathglossary

4 ANALYZE AND GRAPH DATA 78

UNIT WRAPUP

UNIT 3
CHAPTERS 5-6

Multiplication and Division Facts

Technology Link

Harcourt Mega Math:
  Chapter 5, pp. 115, 119
  Chapter 6, pp. 129, 130, 137
The Harcourt Learning Site:
www.harcourtschool.com
Multimedia Math Glossary:
www.harcourtschool.com/mathglossary

UNIT 4
CHAPTERS 7-9

Multiply by 1- and 2-Digit Numbers

Technology Link

Harcourt Mega Math:
  Chapter 7, pp. 153, 157
  Chapter 8, pp. 168, 172
  Chapter 9, pp. 185, 192
The Harcourt Learning Site:
www.harcourtschool.com
Multimedia Math Glossary:
www.harcourtschool.com/mathglossary

UNIT 5
CHAPTERS 10–11

Divide by 1- and 2-Digit Numbers

Technology Link

Harcourt Mega Math:
Chapter 10, pp. 208, 217
Chapter 11, p. 234
The Harcourt Learning Site:
www.harcourtschool.com
Multimedia Math Glossary:
www.harcourtschool.com/mathglossary

DIVIDE BY 2-DIGIT NUMBERS 228

UNIT WRAPUP

UNIT 6 Geometry and Fractions

CHAPTERS 12–15

 Technology Link

Harcourt Mega Math: *Chapter 12, pp. 255, 258, 262*
  Chapter 13, pp. 273, 274, 277, 282, 286
  Chapter 14, p. 301
  Chapter 15, pp. 311, 315, 317
Harcourt Learning Site:
www.harcourtschool.com
Multimedia Math Glossary:
www.harcourtschool.com/mathglossary

UNIT 7 Measurement

CHAPTERS 16–17

 Technology Link

Harcourt Mega Math:
Chapter 16, pp. 333, 343
Chapter 17, p. 361
The Harcourt Learning Site:
www.harcourtschool.com
Multimedia Math Glossary:
www.harcourtschool.com/mathglossary

UNIT 8 Decimals

CHAPTERS 18–21

Technology Link

Harcourt Mega Math: *Chapter 18, pp. 380, 384*
  Chapter 19, pp. 405, 406, 410
  Chapter 20, p. 420
  Chapter 21, pp. 434, 438
The Harcourt Learning Site:
www.harcourtschool.com
Multimedia Math Glossary:
www.harcourtschool.com/mathglossary

Using Math In
Georgia
▶ Building Success Now

You use decimals when you compare times of track and field events. ▼

▲ You use weight when you shop for fruits and vegetables.

You use computation skills when you spend money. ▶

You will use the mathematics that you learn in **Harcourt Math** every day. The skills you learn will help you **build success** both now and in the future.

▶ Building Success for the Future

◀ An air-traffic controller analyzes data during the takeoffs and landings of aircraft.

Hartsfield-Jackson Atlanta International Airport

Georgia Institute of Technology, Atlanta, Georgia

An architect uses angles, plane figures, and solid shapes when designing homes and buildings.
▼

▲ A medical researcher uses decimal numbers when reading and recording laboratory results.

Georgia International Convention Center, College Park, Georgia

For CRCT preparation, see the CRCT Test Prep at the end of each chapter and the CRCT Practice at the end of this Pupil Edition.

Multiplication Facts

![Georgia state icon] **Concepts/Skill to Maintain** Multiplication and division of whole numbers

You can use repeated addition, the Commutative Property, an array, and an area model to practice multiplication facts.

REPEATED ADDITION

$6 \times 2 = $ ▨

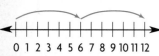

0 1 2 3 4 5 6 7 8 9 10 11 12

Start with 6. Add as many sixes as the second number.
$6 + 6 = 12$

So, $6 \times 2 = 12$.

THE COMMUTATIVE PROPERTY

$2 \times 6 = $ ▨

2×6 is the same as 6×2.
Use $6 \times 2 = 12$.

So, $2 \times 6 = 12$.

ARRAY

$6 \times 8 = $ ▨

There are 6 rows with 8 in each row.
So, $6 \times 8 = 48$.

AREA MODEL

$8 \times 9 = $ ▨

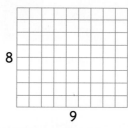

8

9

So, $8 \times 9 = 72$.

▶ Practice

Find the product.

1. 2×2 **2.** 4×3 **3.** 3×9 **4.** 9×5

5. 5×8 **6.** 7×4 **7.** 6×7 **8.** 4×9

9. 7×2 **10.** 2×8 **11.** 8×8 **12.** 7×7

13. $\begin{array}{r} 3 \\ \times 4 \\ \hline \end{array}$ **14.** $\begin{array}{r} 1 \\ \times 8 \\ \hline \end{array}$ **15.** $\begin{array}{r} 9 \\ \times 6 \\ \hline \end{array}$ **16.** $\begin{array}{r} 5 \\ \times 4 \\ \hline \end{array}$

17. $\begin{array}{r} 6 \\ \times 3 \\ \hline \end{array}$ **18.** $\begin{array}{r} 5 \\ \times 7 \\ \hline \end{array}$ **19.** $\begin{array}{r} 2 \\ \times 1 \\ \hline \end{array}$ **20.** $\begin{array}{r} 6 \\ \times 6 \\ \hline \end{array}$

Division Facts

 Concepts/Skill to Maintain Multiplication and division of whole numbers

You can use repeated subtraction, a model, a related multiplication fact, or a related division fact to help practice division facts.

REPEATED SUBTRACTION

$8 \div 2 = \blacksquare$

Use a number line. Start at 8. Count back by twos until you reach 0. Count the number of times you subtract 2. You subtract 2 four times.

0 1 2 3 4 5 6 7 8

So, $8 \div 2 = 4$.

MODEL

$28 \div 4 = \blacksquare$

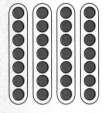

28 counters can be divided into 4 groups of 7 counters each.

So, $28 \div 4 = 7$.

RELATED MULTIPLICATION FACT

$35 \div 5 = \blacksquare$

Think of a related multiplication fact.
$5 \times 7 = 35$

So, $35 \div 5 = 7$.

RELATED DIVISION FACT

$35 \div 7 = \blacksquare$

Think of a division fact that you know.
$35 \div 5 = 7$

So, $35 \div 7 = 5$.

▶ Practice

Find the quotient.

1. $6 \div 2$ **2.** $21 \div 3$ **3.** $8 \div 4$ **4.** $18 \div 2$

5. $28 \div 7$ **6.** $9 \div 1$ **7.** $42 \div 6$ **8.** $36 \div 9$

9. $15 \div 5$ **10.** $56 \div 7$ **11.** $72 \div 8$ **12.** $49 \div 7$

13. $4\overline{)20}$ **14.** $6\overline{)36}$ **15.** $5\overline{)25}$ **16.** $2\overline{)12}$

17. $3\overline{)27}$ **18.** $9\overline{)81}$ **19.** $8\overline{)24}$ **20.** $5\overline{)40}$

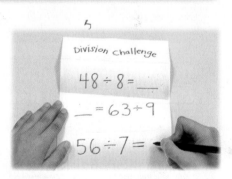
Division Challenge
$48 \div 8 =$ ___
___ $= 63 \div 9$
$56 \div 7 =$

Place Value and Number Sense

≡FAST FACT • SCIENCE

The Smithsonian National Museum of Natural History in Washington, D.C., has a collection of over 40 million plant and animal fossils and rock samples.

INVESTIGATION Look at the numbers in the table. What are other ways that you can write these numbers?

Using Data
NATURAL HISTORY MUSEUM COLLECTIONS

Museum	Number of Animal Fossils
Carnegie Museum of Natural History, Pittsburgh, Pennsylvania	543,000
Field Museum, Chicago, Illinois	405,400
Florida Museum of Natural History, Gainesville, Florida	636,700

CHECK WHAT YOU KNOW

Use this page to help you review and remember important skills needed for Chapter 1.

✔ READ AND WRITE NUMBERS TO THOUSANDS

Write each word form in standard form.

1. ninety

2. six thousand, seven

3. nine hundred seventy

✔ PLACE VALUE

Write the value of the blue digit.

4. 24,638

5. 1,002

6. 53,692

7. 48,361

✔ ORDER NUMBERS TO THOUSANDS

Write the numbers in order from least to greatest.

8. 684; 680; 689

9. 3,564; 3,278; 3,782

10. 4,037; 4,370; 3,407

✔ BENCHMARK NUMBERS

Estimate the number of beads in each jar.

Jar A has 10 beads.

Jar B has 50 beads.

11.

10 or 50?

12.

25 or 50?

13.

50 or 100?

14.

20 or 70?

VOCABULARY POWER

REVIEW

digit [di′jət] *noun*

One meaning of *digit* is "a finger or toe." What is the mathematical meaning of *digit*? Write a sentence using *digit* to show your understanding of the word.

PREVIEW

period

millions

benchmark

pictograph

 GO ON-LINE

www.harcourtschool.com/mathglossary

Understand Place Value

 M4N1.a. Identify place value names and places from hundredths through one million. *also* **M4P3.a., M4P3.b., M4P3.c., M4P3.d., M4P4.a., M4P4.b.**

Quick Review

1. $55 - 10$ 2. $21 + 10$

3. $877 - 100$ 4. $163 + 100$

5. $3,218 + 1,000$

▷ Learn

IT'S DEEP! The deepest-living starfish was collected from a depth of 24,881 feet in the western Pacific Ocean in 1962.

What is the value of the digit 2 in 24,881?

Remember

A digit is one of the ten symbols 0, 1, 2, 3, 4, 5, 6, 7, 8, or 9 used to write numbers.

Ten thousands	Thousands	Hundreds	Tens	Ones
2	4,	8	8	1
$2 \times 10,000$	$4 \times 1,000$	8×100	8×10	1×1
20,000	4,000	800	80	1

Think: Multiply the digit by its ← place value to find the value of each digit.

So, the value of the digit 2 is 20,000.

MATH IDEA The value of a digit depends on its place-value position in the number.

Changing a given digit in a number changes the value of the number.

Technology Link

More Practice: Harcourt Mega Math The Number Games, *Tiny's Think Tank*, Level A

Examples

> **Ⓐ** 58,937 to 59,937   increased by 1,000
>
> **Ⓑ** 58,937 to 68,937   increased by 10,000
>
> **Ⓒ** 58,937 to 88,937   increased by 30,000
>
> **Ⓓ** 58,937 to 57,937   decreased by 1,000
>
> **Ⓔ** 58,937 to 48,937   decreased by 10,000
>
> **Ⓕ** 58,937 to 28,937   decreased by 30,000

▲ The Japan Marine Science and Technology Center's *Shinkai 6500* collects ocean data from any depth down to 21,325 feet.

• Which digit in the number 13,872 would be changed to form 19,872? How would the value of 13,872 change?

1. **Explain** how to find the value of the digit 7 in the number 76,308.

Write the value of the digit 4 in each number.

2. 27,345
3. 74,960
4. 83,412
5. 14,873

Compare the digits to find the change in value.

6. 8,947 to 3,947
7. 82,756 to 82,716
8. 14,583 to 16,583

▶ **Practice and Problem Solving** ⟨ Extra Practice, page 22, Set A ⟩

Write the value of the digit 8 in each number.

9. 53,489
10. 97,806
11. 86,239
12. 68,391

Compare the digits to find the change in value.

13. 62,895 to 32,895
14. 93,714 to 99,714
15. 38,047 to 38,097
16. 49,807 to 49,207
17. 51,386 to 11,386
18. 29,471 to 29,671

Change the value of the number by the given amount.

19. 37,842 increased by 1,000
20. 37,842 decreased by 1,000
21. 63,172 increased by 600
22. 24,597 increased by 4,000
23. 71,408 decreased by 20,000
24. 52,496 decreased by 70

Complete.

25. $24{,}180 = 20{,}000 + \blacksquare + 100 + 80$
26. $5{,}2\blacksquare6 = 5{,}000 + 200 + 30 + 6$

27. **NUMBER SENSE** In a 4-digit number, the first two digits are both 2. The sum of the ones and tens digits is 14. What numbers are possible?

28. ✎ **Write About It** If you add a ten thousands digit that is 2 times the ones digit to the number 2,794, what is the new number? Explain.

⌐Maintain Skills ⌐

29. 4×5
30. 8×3
31. 14×7
32. $54 \div 9$
33. $25 \div 5$
34. $32 \div 8$

⌐CRCT Test Prep ⌐

35. ⟨ M4N1.a. ⟩ What is the value of the digit 7 in the number 57,406? (p. 2)

A. 70,000
C. 700
B. 7,000
D. 7

Place Value Through Hundred Thousands

 M4N1.a. Identify place value names and places from hundredths through one million. *also* **M4N1.b., M4P3.a., M4P3.b., M4P3.c., M4P3.d.**

▷ **Learn**

EARTH TO MOON The least distance from Earth to the moon is 225,792 miles.

To show this number, a column for hundred thousands has to be added to the place-value chart.

┌──── PERIOD ────┐

THOUSANDS			ONES		
Hundreds	**Tens**	**Ones**	**Hundreds**	**Tens**	**Ones**
2	2	5,	7	9	2

Each group of three digits is called a **period**. Commas separate the periods. Each period has ones, tens, and hundreds in it. The number 225,792 has two periods, *ones* and *thousands*.

⚡ **MATH IDEA** Place-value and period names help you read and write numbers.

Standard Form: 225,792

Word Form: two hundred twenty-five thousand, seven hundred ninety-two

Expanded Form: 200,000 + 20,000 + 5,000 + 700 + 90 + 2

Examples

Standard Form	Word Form	Expanded Form
Ⓐ 40,915	forty thousand, nine hundred fifteen	40,000 + 900 + 10 + 5
Ⓑ 607,304	six hundred seven thousand, three hundred four	600,000 + 7,000 + 300 + 4

Quick Review

Write the place value of the digit 3.

1. 49,031   **2.** 35,477

3. 2,386   **4.** 693

5. 83,904

VOCABULARY
period

1. **Explain** how its period helps you identfiy the place value of the digit 9 in 952,700. In 1969, the *Apollo 11* astronauts traveled 952,700 miles.

Write each number in two other forms.

2. two hundred five thousand, sixty-one

3. 916,359

▷ **Practice and Problem Solving** (Extra Practice, page 22, Set B)

Write each number in two other forms.

4. three hundred thousand, ninety-six

5. four hundred sixteen thousand, two hundred ten

6. 40,705

7. $60,000 + 3,000 + 40 + 8$

Complete.

8. $52,376 = $ fifty-two _?_, three hundred _?_ = ■ $+ 2,000 + 300 + 70 + $ ■

9. $90,000 + ■ + 80 = 90,58■ = $ ninety thousand, five _?_ eighty

Write the value of the blue digit.

10. 534,908

11. 980,571

12. 143,296

13. 278,105

14. 357,841

15. 493,560

16. 782,046

17. 609,428

18. If five hundred thousand, twenty-six is increased by three thousand, what is the new number in standard form?

19. I am 900 more than the greatest possible 4-digit even number that can be made using the digits 1, 4, 2, 5. What number am I?

20. Write the word form of the number that is 1,000 more than 23,548.

Technology Link

More Practice: Harcourt Mega Math The Number Games, *Tiny's Think Tank,* Level A

Maintain Skills

21. 7×9

22. 5×6

23. 2×8

24. 4×4

25. 8×5

26. 9×3

CRCT Test Prep

27. (**M4N1.b.**) What is the standard form for the number $9,000 + 40 + 6$? (p. 4)

   A. 90,046   C. 9,046

   B. 9,406   D. 946

Place Value Through Millions

 M4N1.a. Identify place value names and places from hundredths through one million. *also* **M4N1.b., M4P4, M4P4.c.**

▷ **Learn**

READ ALL ABOUT IT! Newspapers keep people informed of local, national, and world events. The first newspaper was written in Germany in the 1600s.

Look at this story. It contains about 200 words. If there are 5 stories of this size on one page, about how many words are on the page?

Think:
200 + 200 + 200 + 200 + 200 = 1,000

So, there are about 1,000 words on a page.

With 1,000 words on a page,
    10 pages have 10,000 words.
  100 pages have 100,000 words.
1,000 pages have 1,000,000 words.

The period to the left of *thousands* is **millions** .

			← PERIOD →					
MILLIONS			THOUSANDS			ONES		
Hundreds	Tens	Ones	Hundreds	Tens	Ones	Hundreds	Tens	Ones
		1,	0	0	0,	0	0	0

Write: 1,000,000   **Read:** one million

One million is a large number. If you read 100 words a minute, it would take you almost 7 days nonstop to read 1,000,000 words.

More About Millions

You can use place value and period names to help you read and write numbers in the millions.

The world's largest ball of twine is found in Cawker City, Kansas. As of September 2001, it contained over 83,264,496 inches of twine.

Look at this number on the place-value chart.

▲ The ball of twine weighs 17,320 pounds. That's more than the weight of 6 cars!

PERIOD								
MILLIONS			THOUSANDS			ONES		
Hundreds	Tens	Ones	Hundreds	Tens	Ones	Hundreds	Tens	Ones
	8	3,	2	6	4,	4	9	6

Standard Form: 83,264,496

Word Form: eighty-three million, two hundred sixty-four thousand, four hundred ninety-six

Expanded Form: 80,000,000 + 3,000,000 + 200,000 + 60,000 + 4,000 + 400 + 90 + 6

Examples

Standard Form	Word Form	Expanded Form
Ⓐ 54,060,900	fifty-four million, sixty thousand, nine hundred	50,000,000 + 4,000,000 + 60,000 + 900
Ⓑ 100,207,054	one hundred million, two hundred seven thousand, fifty-four	100,000,000 + 200,000 + 7,000 + 50 + 4

▶ Check

1. Tell how many periods an 8-digit number has.

Write the value of the blue digit.

2. 7,943,120

3. 8,450,203

4. 68,549,227

Write each number in word form.

5. 7,643,120

6. 16,452,003

7. 608,049,227

LESSON CONTINUES ▶

Write the value of the blue digit.

8. 7,534,908   **9.** 98,745,300   **10.** 2,980,871

11. 4,371,568   **12.** 36,420,156   **13.** 512,604,397

Write each number in word form.

14. 5,769,042   **15.** 882,831,001   **16.** 42,168,339

Use place value to find each missing number. Explain.

17. 6,758,324; 6,768,324; ■;
6,788,324

18. 9,537,461; 9,537,561; ■;
9,537,761

19. 2,408,693; 2,409,694; ■;
2,411,696

20. 4,657,839; 4,657,939; ■;
4,658,139

21. Write the word form of the number that is
1,000,000 more than 5,670,891.

22. Write 2,097,341 in expanded form.

23. Write 8,000,000 + 100,000 + 70,000 + 3,000 +
900 + 50 + 6 in word form.

Complete.

24. 7,523,■46 = 7,000,000 + 500,000 + 20,000 +
3,000 + 800 + 40 + 6

25. 7,903,264 = seven __?__ , nine hundred three __?__ , two
hundred sixty-four

26. **? What's the Question?** Mrs. Diaz wrote the number
46,152,780. The answer is 6,000,000. What is
the question?

27. What number is twice the value of the
ten thousands digit in 423,008?

28. ▤**FAST FACT** • **SCIENCE** Saturn
takes about 10,760 days to orbit the
sun. Is it correct to read this number
as ten million, seven hundred sixty?
Explain.

29. **? What's the Error?** Carl said that 24,613,351 is one million more than 14,613,351. Describe his error.

30. **Vocabulary Power** What does the *place value* of a digit tell you? How does switching the positions of the digits in the number 52 affect that number's value?

Maintain Skills

31. 25×6 **32.** $270 \div 9$

33. 32×12 **34.** $126 \div 6$

35. A rectangular rug is 5 feet long and 2 feet wide. What is the area of the rug?

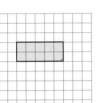

CRCT Test Prep

36. **M4N1.b.** What is one million, thirty-seven thousand, five in standard form? (p. 6)

A. 1,370,005   C. 1,037,005
B. 1,037,500   D. 1,000,375

37. **M4N1.a.** In which number does the digit 6 have a value of 6,000? (p. 4)

A. 62,135   C. 34,608
B. 56,154   D.   609

Problem Solving   Thinker's Corner

ROMAN NUMERALS Our *numeration system* uses Arabic numerals, or digits (0, 1, 2, . . .), to write numbers. The Romans used the symbols in this chart to name numbers.

I	V	X	L	C	D	M
1	5	10	50	100	500	1,000

A Add when the symbols are alike or when the symbols' values decrease from left to right. A numeral cannot be added more than three times in a row.

$$LXIII = 63$$
$$50 + 10 + 1 + 1 + 1 = 63$$

B Subtract when a symbol's value is less than the value of the symbol to its right.

$$XIX = 19$$
IX represents $10 - 1 = 9$
$$10 + 9 = 19$$

Write the Roman numerals as Arabic numerals.

1. XIV   **2.** XXXIX   **3.** XLI   **4.** XC   **5.** LXVIII

6. **REASONING** Find the missing numbers.
III, VI, IX, XII, ■, ■, XXI.

7. Write 35, 44, and 62 as Roman numerals.

Benchmark Numbers

M4P5. Students will represent mathematics in multiple ways.
also **M4P3.a., M4P3.b., M4P3.c., M4P3.d.**

▶ **Learn**

SIZE IT UP! For a number to have meaning, it should be related to something you already know.

The Washington Monument is 555 feet tall. That is about the same as 25 two-story houses stacked on top of each other.

MATH IDEA A **benchmark** is a known number of things that helps you understand the size or amount of a different number of things.

You can use a benchmark when you are estimating a number of items that would take a long time to count.

VOCABULARY

benchmark

Examples

A Use the benchmark to decide which is the most reasonable number of nickels in the full jar.

100   1,000   10,000

Benchmark: 500 nickels

The full jar holds about 2 times the benchmark amount.

2 × 500 = 1,000

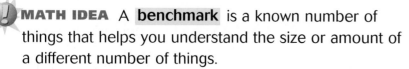

500 nickels

The most reasonable number of nickels in the full jar is 1,000.

B Use the benchmark to decide what is a reasonable number of beans in the full jar.

Benchmark: 50 beans

The full jar holds about 8 times the benchmark amount.

8 × 50 = 400

50 beans

A reasonable number of beans in the jar is 400.

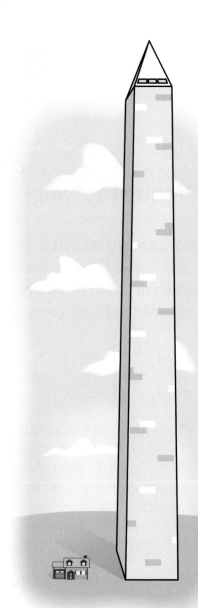

• In Example B, why is 4,000 not a reasonable number?

1. **Explain** whether the number of students in your class is a good benchmark for the number of students in your school.

Use the benchmark to decide which is the more reasonable number.

2. beads in the jar

20 beads   80, 200, or 800

3. gallons of water in the tank

 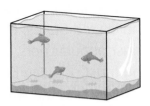

20 gallons   40; 200; or 2,000

▶ **Practice and Problem Solving**   Extra Practice, page 22, Set D

Use the benchmark to decide which is the more reasonable number.

4. pretzel sticks in the jar

100 pretzels

50, 250, or 500

5. beads in the vase

20 beads

200; 400; or 2,000

6. Emily has 6 dolls, and Dana has 11. If Laura has 8 more dolls than Emily and Dana combined, how many dolls does Laura have?

7. 📖 **Write About It** Explain when you would use a benchmark number.

Maintain Skills

Write the value of the blue digit.

8. 7,138

9. 92,487

10. 52 × 7

11. 255 ÷ 3

CRCT Test Prep

12. **M4N1.a.** What number is 3,452 increased by 1,000? (p. 2)

A. 4,452   C. 3,462

B. 3,552   D. 2,552

Problem Solving Skill
Use a Graph

M4D1.b. Investigate the features and tendencies of graphs. *also* **M4P1.a.,
M4P1.b., M4P1.c., M4P1.d., M4P2.a., M4P2.b., M4P2.c., M4P2.d., M4P3.a.,
M4P3.b., M4P3.c., M4P3.d.**

PRIZED PETS Betty, Marcia, and Ed want to
know which pets are the most popular in
the United States. Betty thinks cats are the
most popular pets. Marcia thinks dogs are
the most popular. Ed's choice is fish. How
can you find out who is correct?

A **pictograph** is a graph that uses pictures
to show and compare information. You can
use a pictograph to compare the estimated
numbers of kinds of pets in the United States.

Quick Review

1. 210 + 37   2. 364 − 122
3. 97 + 103   4. 527 + 81
5. 2,230 − 1,023

VOCABULARY
> pictograph

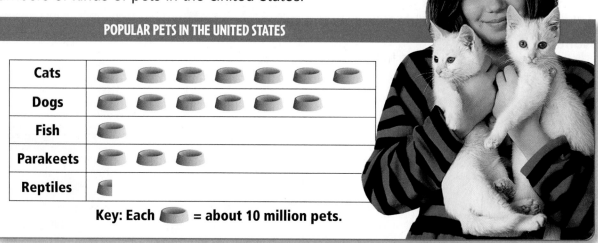

POPULAR PETS IN THE UNITED STATES

Cats	🥣 🥣 🥣 🥣 🥣 🥣 🥣
Dogs	🥣 🥣 🥣 🥣 🥣 🥣
Fish	🥣
Parakeets	🥣 🥣 🥣
Reptiles	🥣

Key: Each 🥣 = about 10 million pets.

Look at the pictograph. Cats are shown with the most symbols, 7.
Since each symbol stands for 10,000,000 pets, there are about
70 million pet cats.

So, Betty is correct. Cats are the most popular pets in the
United States.

Talk About It

• About how many pets are dogs?

• The number of reptiles is shown with one half of a symbol.
About how many pets are reptiles?

• **What if** the number of reptiles were about 15 million?
How many symbols would be used?

USE DATA There are more than 62,000,000 pet dogs in the United States. The graph shows how some of their birthdays were celebrated.

DOG BIRTHDAY CELEBRATIONS

Special treat	🎉 🎉 🎉 🎉 🎉
Cake	🎉 🎉
New toy	🎉 🎉
New bone	🎉
Trip to the park	🎉

Key: Each 🎉 = about 1 million celebrations.

1. Find the number of dogs who got birthday cake. How did you find this number?

2. What celebration happened the least number of times?

USE DATA For 3–4, use the cat food sales graph.

3. During which week were the most bags of cat food sold?

 A Week 1 **C** Week 3
 B Week 2 **D** Week 4

4. In which weeks were fewer than 500 bags of cat food sold?

 F Weeks 1, 2
 G Weeks 1, 4
 H Weeks 2, 4
 J Weeks 1, 3

Mixed Applications

5. **MULTISTEP** Haley gave 23 jelly beans to Phil and twice as many jelly beans to Lila. Now she has 31 jelly beans left. How many jelly beans did Haley start with?

6. **ALGEBRA** Tom is 4 years younger than Jan but 2 years older than Sue. If Jan is 15, how old is Sue?

7. In two hours, 639 people rode to the top of the Sears Tower. During the first hour, 257 people went to the top. How many people rode to the top during the second hour?

8. **REASONING** Yvonne arrived at the party after Irma. Diana arrived before Irma but after Ann. In what order did they arrive at the party?

9. I am less than 80 and greater than 60. The sum of my digits is 8. I am odd. What number am I?

10. Gloria spent $5.08 for milk and eggs. The eggs cost $1.49. How much did the milk cost?

Place Value: Compare Numbers

M4N1.a. Identify place value names and places from hundredths through one million. *also* **M4P4.a., M4P4.b., M4P4.c., M4P5.b., M4P5.c.**

▶ **Learn**

RIVER RUN The Missouri River is 2,315 miles long, and the Mississippi River is 2,348 miles long. Which river is longer?

One Way Use a number line to compare the lengths of the rivers. Compare 2,315 and 2,348.

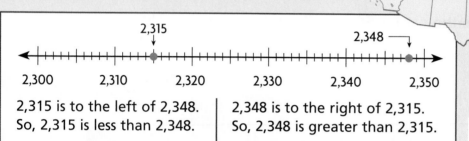

2,315 is to the left of 2,348. So, 2,315 is less than 2,348.	2,348 is to the right of 2,315. So, 2,348 is greater than 2,315.
2,315 < 2,348	2,348 > 2,315

So, the Mississippi River is longer.

Another Way Use base-ten blocks to compare numbers. Compare 348 and 362.

Compare the values of the blocks in each place-value position from left to right. Keep comparing until the values are different.

> **Remember**
>
> < means "is less than."
> > means "is greater than."
> = means "is equal to."

	hundreds	tens	ones
Model 348.			
Model 362.			

There is the same number of hundreds. 4 tens is less than 6 tens.

So, 348 < 362.

Compare Using Place Value

A place-value chart can help you compare two numbers by comparing the digits in each place-value position.

Compare 2,340,083 and 2,331,760.

MILLIONS			THOUSANDS			ONES		
Hundreds	Tens	Ones	Hundreds	Tens	Ones	Hundreds	Tens	Ones
		2,	3	4	0,	0	8	3
		2,	3	3	1,	7	6	0

Example

STEP 1

Start with the first place on the left.
Compare the millions.

2,340,083
↓   2 = 2
2,331,760

There is the same number of millions.

STEP 2

Compare the hundred thousands.

2,340,083
↓   3 = 3
2,331,760

There is the same number of hundred thousands.

STEP 3

Compare the ten thousands.

2,340,083
↓   4 > 3
2,331,760

4 ten thousands is greater than 3 ten thousands.

So, 2,340,083 > 2,331,760.

 MATH IDEA To compare numbers, start at the left, and compare the digits in each place-value position until the digits differ.

Technology Link

More Practice: Harcourt Mega Math Fraction Action, *Number Line Mine,* Level B

▶ Check

1. **Make** a model or draw a picture to compare 1,358 and 1,427 using base-ten blocks.

Compare using the number line. Write the greater number.

3,200   3,210   3,220   3,230   3,240   3,250

2. 3,224 or 3,242   3. 3,218 or 3,240   4. 3,234 or 3,229

Compare. Write <, >, or = for each ●.

5. 2,346 ● 2,338   6. 521,878 ● 52,878   7. 52,457 ● 67,623

8. 254,908 ● 254,908   9. 9,531 ● 4,631   10. 478,765 ● 479,112

LESSON CONTINUES ▶

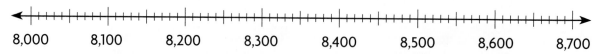
Compare using the number line. Write the greater number.

```
◄─┼┼┼┼┼┼┼┼┼┼┼┼┼┼┼┼┼┼┼┼┼┼┼┼┼┼┼┼┼┼┼┼┼┼┼┼┼┼┼┼┼┼┼┼┼┼┼┼┼┼┼┼┼─►
   8,000     8,100     8,200     8,300     8,400     8,500     8,600     8,700
```

11. 8,110 or 8,340   **12.** 8,600 or 8,060   **13.** 8,413 or 8,314

Compare. Write <, >, or = for each ●.

14. 2,475 ● 2,475

15. 13,056 ● 13,156

16. 255,136 ● 25,116

17. 301,876 ● 3,018,760

18. 1,670 ● 1,670

19. 410,000 ● 414,000

20. 3,911,067 ● 3,911,007

21. 50,320,943 ● 9,503,209

22. 5,000,371 ● 500,371

23. 82,245,235 ● 82,245,535

Find all of the digits that can replace each ■.

24. 9■7,536 < 957,549

25. 3,■96,517 < 3,695,815

26. 84,41■,811 < 84,413,604

27. 24,■62 > 24,701

Are the two numbers equivalent? Write *equivalent* or *not equivalent.*

28. 153,890 and one hundred fifty-three thousand, eight hundred ninety

29. 2,000,000 + 400,000 + 50,000 + 600 + 7 and 2,450,670

30. thirty-eight million, forty-nine and 30,000,000 + 8,000,000 + 40 + 9

USE DATA For 31–33, use the table.

31. Which river is longer, Amazon or Nile?

32. Which Asian river has a length greater than 3,500 miles?

33. ✎ Write a problem that compares two rivers from the World Rivers table.

WORLD RIVERS		
River	**Continent**	**Length (in mi)**
Amazon	South America	4,000
Chang	Asia	3,964
Huang	Asia	3,395
Nile	Africa	4,160

34. Vocabulary Power When you *compare* two items, you tell how they are alike and different. What do you do when you compare two numbers? Give an example.

35. REASONING Which is greater, the number that is 1,000 less than 13,495, or the number that is 10,000 less than 23,495? Explain.

36. Chris and his father drove 876 miles on a weekend. They drove 416 miles of that on Sunday. Did they drive farther on Saturday or on Sunday?

37. **?** **What's the Error?** Sarah said that 6,850 is greater than 48,500 because 6 > 4. Describe her error. Tell which number is greater.

Maintain Skills

Write the value of the digit 4.

38. 41,389

39. 59,486

40. Write the number that is 1,000 greater than 7,236

41. Write 34,506 in word form.

42. Complete.
40,000 + ■ + 50 = 40,850

CRCT Test Prep

43. **M4N1.b.** What is the standard form of 50,000,000 + 30,000 + 4? (p. 6)

A. 15,034,000   C. 50,030,004
B. 15,304,000   D. 50,300,400

44. **M4N1.a.** What is the value of the change from 34,891 to 36,891? (p. 2)

A.   200   C.   20,000
B. 2,000   D. 200,000

Problem Solving — Thinker's Corner

ALGEBRAIC THINKING You can use what you know about <, >, and = to describe other number relationships.

> ≠ means "is not equal to."
> ≤ means "is less than or equal to."
> ≥ means "is greater than or equal to."

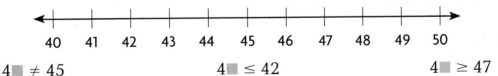

| 4■ ≠ 45 | 4■ ≤ 42 | 4■ ≥ 47 |

40, 41, 42, 43, 44, 46, 47, 48, and 49 are *not equal to* 45.

So, you can replace ■ with 0, 1, 2, 3, 4, 6, 7, 8, or 9.

40, 41, and 42 are *less than or equal to* 42.

So, you can replace ■ with 0, 1, or 2.

47, 48, and 49 are *greater than or equal to* 47.

So, you can replace ■ with 7, 8, or 9.

Find all of the digits that can replace each ■.

1. 360 ≠ 36■

2. 52■ ≤ 525

3. 4,■15 ≥ 4,715

4. 17,6■8 ≤ 17,648

5. 8,396 ≠ 8,39■

6. 29,024 ≥ 29,0■4

Place Value: Order Numbers

M4N1.a. Identify place value names and places from hundredths through one million. *also* **M4P4.a., M4P4.b.**

▶ **Learn**

LOTS OF LAND The map shows the land area, in square miles, of Illinois, Iowa, and Wisconsin. Place the states in order from least to greatest land area.

One Way Use a number line to show the order.

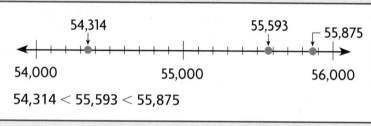

54,314 < 55,593 < 55,875

WISCONSIN
54,314 sq mi

ILLINOIS
55,593 sq mi

IOWA
55,875 sq mi

So, the order is Wisconsin, Illinois, Iowa.

Another Way Use place value to order numbers. Order 437,243; 469,872; and 435,681 from least to greatest.

STEP 1	STEP 2	STEP 3
Start with the first place on the left. Compare the hundred thousands. 4̲37,243 ↓ 4̲69,872 4 = 4 ↓ 4̲35,681 There is the same number of hundred thousands.	Compare the ten thousands. 4̲3̲7,243 ↓ 4̲6̲9,872 3 < 6 ↓ 4̲3̲5,681 Since 3 < 6, 469,872 is the greatest.	Compare the thousands digits in the other two numbers. 43̲7̲,243 ↓ 5 < 7 43̲5̲,681 So, the order from least to greatest is 435,681; 437,243; 469,872.

• Explain how you would order 68,195; 681,095; and 61,958 from least to greatest.

Use Models

New York, Virginia, and Massachusetts all have coastlines on the Atlantic Ocean. Use base-ten blocks to model the numbers in the table and place the states in order from longest to shortest coastline.

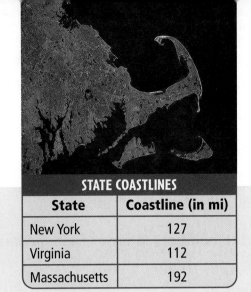

STATE COASTLINES	
State	Coastline (in mi)
New York	127
Virginia	112
Massachusetts	192

Example Compare.

Model the three numbers using base-ten blocks. Then compare the values of the blocks in each place-value position from left to right.

New York	Virginia	Massachusetts
127	112	192

STEP 1

Compare the hundreds.

There is the same number of hundreds.

STEP 2

Compare the tens.

The model for 192 has the most tens, so it is the greatest number.

STEP 3

Compare the tens in 127 and 112.

The model for 127 has more tens, so it is greater than 112.

So, the states in order from longest to shortest coastline are Massachusetts, New York, Virginia.

Check

1. **Draw** a picture of base-ten blocks to show how to order 2,617; 2,716; and 2,672 from *least* to *greatest*.

Write the numbers in order from *least* to *greatest*.

2. 7,969; 7,964; 7,975

7,950 7,955 7,960 7,965 7,970 7,975 7,980

3. 9,131; 9,155; 9,138

9,130 9,135 9,140 9,145 9,150 9,155 9,160

Write the numbers in order from *greatest* to *least*.

4. 35,000; 35,225; 34,350

5. 870,000; 877,000; 807,000

LESSON CONTINUES ▶

Write the numbers in order from *least* to *greatest*.

6. 12,139; 12,117; 12,109; 12,123

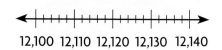
12,100 12,110 12,120 12,130 12,140

7. 36,397; 36,457; 36,384; 36,419

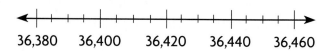
36,380   36,400   36,420   36,440   36,460

8. 190,209; 191,210; 190,201

9. 1,234,410; 1,234,402; 1,434,320

Write the numbers in order from *greatest* to *least*.

10. 16,432; 16,905; 7,906

11. 119,234; 119,819; 1,119,080

12. Order the numbers in the box from greatest to least. Then, underline the numbers greater than 625,000 and less than 650,000.

> 648,279   628,341   642,978
> 682,437   624,879   612,443

For 13–14, write the number represented by each letter. Then, write the *greatest* and *least* numbers.

13.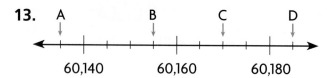
60,140   60,160   60,180

14.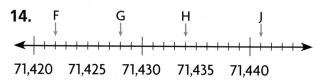
71,420   71,425   71,430   71,435   71,440

Write all of the digits that can replace each ■.

15. 358 < 3■3 < 370

16. 1,012 < 1,■20 < 1,200

17. 5,328 < ■,680 < 5,690

18. 82,913 < 8■,086 < 83,096

19. 4,526,109 > 4,526,■17 > 4,526,010

20. 3,942,687 > 3,942,6■3 > 3,942,670

21. I am a number between 149,900 and 150,000. My tens digit is 7 more than my ones digit. The sum of my tens and ones digits is 9. What number am I?

22. **? What's the Error?** Paul ordered the populations of three states from least to greatest. His work is shown below. Describe his error. Write the states in the correct order.

23. Jamal bought 3 packages of hamburger buns. If each package contains 8 buns, how many buns did he get?

24. ✎ **Write a problem** comparing three or more numbers. Use facts from your science book.

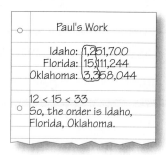
Paul's Work

Idaho: 1,251,700
Florida: 15,111,244
Oklahoma: 3,358,044

12 < 15 < 33
So, the order is Idaho, Florida, Oklahoma.

25. Name the Great Lakes in order from greatest area to least area.

26. Which lakes have areas greater than Lake Erie's area?

27. Which lakes have areas less than 10,000 square miles?

AREAS OF THE GREAT LAKES (in square miles)	
Lake	Area
Erie	9,910
Huron	23,000
Michigan	22,300
Ontario	7,340
Superior	31,700

Maintain Skills

Find the product or quotient.

28. 13×5

29. 27×2

30. $99 \div 3$

31. $225 \div 5$

32. A 5-digit number has two 8's and three 7's. No two digits next to each other are the same. Write the number in standard form.

CRCT Test Prep

33. **M4N1.a.** What is the value of the digit 5 in 54,287? (p. 2)
   A. 5
   B. 50
   C. 5,000
   D. 50,000

34. **M4N1.a.** What is the value of the digit 3 in 3,720,980? (p. 6)
   A. 3,000
   B. 30,000
   C. 3,000,000
   D. 30,000,000

Problem Solving Thinker's Corner

PICO, CENTRO, NADA In Venezuela, people play a number game called *Pico, Centro, Nada.*

Think of a 2-digit number. Have your partner try to guess the number. With each incorrect guess, give one of these clues:

- *Pico* means that one digit is correct, but it's in the wrong place.
- *Centro* means that one digit is correct, and it's in the correct place.
- *Nada* means that neither digit is correct.

1. When one number for each player is found, work together to compare the numbers using $<$, $>$, or $=$.

2. When four numbers have been found, list the numbers in order from *least* to *greatest.*

VENEZUELA

Extra Practice

Set A (pp. 2–3)

Write the value of the digit 6 in each number.

1. 7,056   **2.** 15,608   **3.** 60,789   **4.** 16,340

Set B (pp. 4–5)

Write each number in two other forms.

1. 482,907   **2.** 500,128   **3.** 961,542   **4.** 271,964

Write the value of the blue digit.

5. 137,568   **6.** 739,062   **7.** 561,342   **8.** 906,723

Set C (pp. 6–9)

Write the value of the blue digit.

1. 13,749,568   **2.** 4,739,062   **3.** 397,561,342   **4.** 458,906,723

Set D (pp. 10–11)

Use the benchmark to decide which is the more reasonable number.

1. table tennis balls in bucket B

A   B

10 balls   100; 1,000; or 10,000

2. sunflower seeds in bird feeder B

A   B

300 seeds   600; 3,000; or 30,000

Set E (pp. 14–17)

Compare. Write <, >, or = for each ●.

1. 47,569 ● 47,650   **2.** 594,031 ● 594,010   **3.** 731,598 ● 703,892

Set F (pp. 18–21)

Write the numbers in order from *least* to *greatest*.

1. 160,502; 160,402; 163,500   **2.** 7,450,343; 7,429,203; 7,492,393

Review/Test

✓ CHECK VOCABULARY AND CONCEPTS

Choose the best term from the box.

1. A graph that uses pictures to show and compare information is a __?__. (p. 12)

2. Each group of three digits is called a __?__. (p. 4)

✓ CHECK SKILLS

Write each number in two other forms. (pp. 4–5, 6–9)

3. $20,000 + 80 + 3$ **4.** $200,057$ **5.** $4,902,746$ **6.** $48,360,105$

Write the value of the blue digit. (pp. 2–3, 4–5, 6–9)

7. $8,451$ **8.** $29,710$ **9.** $652,700$ **10.** $4,136,729$

11. Which is the most reasonable number of beads in the full jar, 70, 350, or 700? (pp. 10–11)

12. Which is the most reasonable number of gallons of water in barrel B, 3, 30, or 300? (pp. 10–11)

10 beads

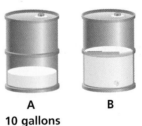

A   B

10 gallons

Compare. Write <, >, or = for each ⬤. (pp. 14–17)

13. $15,980$ ⬤ $15,754$ **14.** $780,256$ ⬤ $783,130$ **15.** $1,895,006$ ⬤ $1,392,950$

16. Write 25,908; 25,616; and 25,972 in order from *least* to *greatest*. (pp. 18–21)

17. Write 3,791,808; 3,759,204; and 3,090,910 in order from *greatest* to *least*. (pp. 18–21)

✓ CHECK PROBLEM SOLVING

For 18–20, use the graph. (pp. 12–13)

18. Which animals have lifespans longer than 20 years?

19. About how many years does the grizzly bear live?

20. About how many years longer does the Asian elephant live than the grizzly bear?

ANIMAL LIFESPANS	
Gorilla	🐾 🐾
Asian elephant	🐾 🐾 🐾 🐾
Polar bear	🐾 🐾
Grizzly bear	🐾 🐾 🐾

Key: Each 🐾 = about 10 years.

Chapter CRCT Test Prep

NUMBERS AND OPERATIONS

1. **M4N1.b.** In 2000, the population of Fulton County, GA, was 816,006 residents. What is the expanded form of 816,006?

   A. 816 + 6

   B. 8,000 + 100 + 60 + 6

   C. 800,000 + 1,000 + 600 + 6

   D. 800,000 + 10,000 + 6,000 + 6

2. **M4N1.a.** Which number has 5 in the ten-thousands place and 2 in the tens place?

   A. 3,754,023

   B. 3,724,053

   C. 3,524,093

   D. 3,154,293

3. **M4N1.a.** What is the value of the digit 7 in 1,723,614?

   A. 700

   B. 70,000

   C. 100,000

   D. 700,000

4. **M4N1.b.** If four hundred thirteen thousand, two hundred three is increased by six thousand, what is the new number in standard form?

   A. 413,203

   B. 413,209

   C. 419,203

   D. 473,203

NUMBERS AND OPERATIONS

5. **M4N1.b.** What number completes the number sentence below?

   $$30,000 + 8,000 + 400 + 5 = \square$$

   A. 30,845

   B. 38,045

   C. 38,405

   D. 38,450

6. **M4N1.a.** What is the value of the digit 3 in 64,732?

   A. 3

   B. 30

   C. 300

   D. 3,000

7. **M4N1.b.** What is the standard form for 5,000,000 + 300,000 + 90,000 + 1,000 + 20 + 4?

   A. 5,391,240

   B. 5,391,204

   C. 5,391,024

   D. 539,124

8. **M4N1.b.** What is the word name for 60,740?

   A. sixty-seven thousand, forty

   B. sixty thousand, seven hundred forty

   C. sixty thousand, seven hundred four

   D. sixteen thousand, forty

Chapter CRCT Test Prep

NUMBERS AND OPERATIONS

9. **M4N1.a.** Which statement is TRUE?

   A. $3,458 < 3,548$

   B. $3,458 > 3,548$

   C. $3,548 > 3,584$

   D. $3,584 < 3,548$

10. **M4N1.a.** Which list shows the numbers in order from least to greatest?

    A. 17,408; 17,840; 17,804

    B. 17,408; 17,804; 17,840

    C. 17,804; 17,408; 17,840

    D. 17,840; 17,804; 17,408

11. **M4N1.b.** What is the word name for $200,000 + 10,000 + 50 + 7$?

    A. twenty-one thousand, fifty-seven

    B. two hundred thousand, one hundred fifty-seven

    C. two hundred ten thousand, fifty-seven

    D. two milllion, one hundred fifty-seven

12. **M4N1.b.** One of the runways at Hartsfield-Jackson Atlanta International Airport is eleven thousand, eight hundred eighty-nine feet long. What is the standard form for this number?

    A.   1,189

    B.   11,809

    C.   11,889

    D. 11,800,089

DATA ANALYSIS

Use the bar graph below to answer question 13.

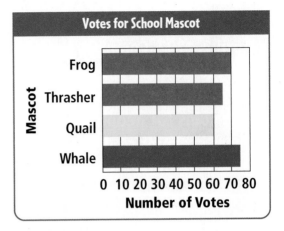

13. **M4D1.a.** Which data set was used to make the bar graph?

    A. frog: 75
       thrasher: 60
       quail: 65
       whale: 70

    B. frog: 70
       thrasher: 60
       quail: 65
       whale: 75

    C. frog: 70
       thrasher: 60
       quail: 60
       whale: 80

    D. frog: 70
       thrasher: 65
       quail: 60
       whale: 75

CHAPTER 2
Add and Subtract Whole Numbers

≡FAST FACT • SOCIAL STUDIES

On April 2, 1792, Congress created the United States Mint. The United States Mint's primary mission is to produce enough coins for people to use. It produces six coins of different values, sizes, and weights.

INVESTIGATION The weight of one dime plus the weight of what other coin is equal to the weight of one dollar? The weights of which two coins can be combined to equal the weight of a half dollar? What other equivalent weight combinations can you find?

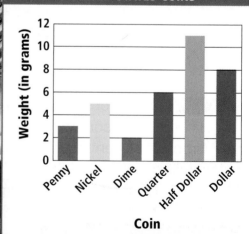

Using Data

APPROXIMATE WEIGHTS OF UNITED STATES COINS

Weight (in grams) vs Coin

Coin	Weight (in grams)
Penny	3
Nickel	5
Dime	2
Quarter	6
Half Dollar	11
Dollar	8

CHECK WHAT YOU KNOW

Use this page to help you review and remember important skills needed for Chapter 2.

TWO-DIGIT ADDITION AND SUBTRACTION

Find the sum or difference.

1. $\begin{array}{r} 13 \\ +24 \end{array}$

2. $\begin{array}{r} 58 \\ -29 \end{array}$

3. $\begin{array}{r} 36 \\ -14 \end{array}$

4. $\begin{array}{r} 52 \\ +11 \end{array}$

5. $\begin{array}{r} 78 \\ -43 \end{array}$

6. $\begin{array}{r} 73 \\ -19 \end{array}$

7. $\begin{array}{r} 65 \\ +36 \end{array}$

8. $\begin{array}{r} 42 \\ +68 \end{array}$

9. $\begin{array}{r} 90 \\ -28 \end{array}$

10. $\begin{array}{r} 81 \\ +26 \end{array}$

11. $23 + 37 + 42 = \blacksquare$

12. $42 + 31 + 63 = \blacksquare$

13. $87 - 59 = \blacksquare$

14. $64 - 29 = \blacksquare$

NUMBER PATTERNS

Write the next three possible numbers in the pattern.

15. 10, 20, 30, 40, ■, ■, ■

16. 25, 30, 35, 40, ■, ■, ■

17. 30, 26, 22, 18, ■, ■, ■

18. 99, 88, 77, 66, ■, ■, ■

VOCABULARY POWER

REVIEW

thousand [thou′zənd] *noun*

The word *thousand* comes from a combination of old Germanic words for *swollen (teue)* and *hundred (hundt)*. Does calling a thousand a "swollen hundred" make sense? Why or why not?

PREVIEW

- sum
- difference
- round
- expression
- variable

www.harcourtschool.com/mathglossary

Use Mental Math Strategies

M4N7.d. Use mental math and estimation strategies to compute.
also M4P1.a., M4P1.b.

▶ **Learn**

THINK IT THROUGH The **sum** is the answer to an addition problem. The **difference** is the answer to a subtraction problem. Sometimes you don't need paper and pencil to compute. You can compute mentally.

One Way   *Break Apart* Strategy

You can add or subtract tens and ones separately.

Examples

A   Find the sum. 58 + 26   Think: 58 = 50 + 8
                                                    26 = 20 + 6

Add the tens.   50 + 20 = 70

Add the ones.   8 + 6 = 14

Add the sums.   70 + 14 = 84

So, 58 + 26 = 84.

B   Find the difference. 46 − 25   Think: 46 = 40 + 6
                                                     25 = 20 + 5

Subtract the tens.   40 − 20 = 20

Subtract the ones.   6 − 5 = 1

Add the differences.   20 + 1 = 21

So, 46 − 25 = 21.

More Examples

C   Find the sum. 139 + 248
         100 + 200 = 300
            30 + 40 = 70
               9 + 8 = 17
      300 + 70 + 17 = 387

D   Find the difference. 97 − 52
         90 − 50 = 40
           7 − 2 = 5
        40 + 5 = 45

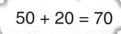

50 + 20 = 70

8 + 6 = 14

70 + 14 = 84

• Explain how to use this strategy to find 567 − 241.

More Strategies

Another Way   *Make a Ten* Strategy

You can change one number to a multiple of 10 and then adjust the other number.

Subtraction is easier if the number you are subtracting is a multiple of 10. If you increase the number you are subtracting, you must add the same amount to adjust the answer.

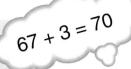

$67 + 3 = 70$

$24 - 3 = 21$

$70 + 21 = 91$

Examples

E Find the sum. $67 + 24$

$67 + 3 = 70$	**Think:** Add 3 to 67 to get 70.
$24 - 3 = 21$	Subtract 3 from 24 to adjust the sum.
$70 + 21 = 91$	Add $70 + 21$.

F Find the difference. $186 - 29$

$29 + 1 = 30$	**Think:** Add 1 to 29 to get 30.
$186 + 1 = 187$	Add 1 to 186 to adjust the difference.
$187 - 30 = 157$	Subtract $187 - 30$.

• What if you subtract 4 from 24 in Example E? How could you find $67 + 24$ mentally?

You also can adjust the sum or difference after changing one number.

More Examples

G Find the difference. $75 - 38$

$38 + 2 = 40$

$$\begin{array}{r} 75 \\ -\ 40 \\ \hline 35 \\ +\ 2 \\ \hline 37 \end{array}$$ Add 2 to 35 to adjust the sum.

H Find the sum. $284 + 476$

$284 + 6 = 290$

$$\begin{array}{r} 290 \\ +\ 476 \\ \hline 766 \\ -\ 6 \\ \hline 760 \end{array}$$ Subtract 6 from 766 to adjust the difference.

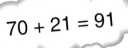

▶ Check

1. **Explain** how to find $83 - 37$ mentally.

2. **Write** an addition problem. Find the sum by breaking apart the numbers.

LESSON CONTINUES ▶

For 3–10, add or subtract mentally. Tell the strategy you used.

3. 85 − 17   **4.** 72 + 28   **5.** 83 − 19   **6.** 95 + 28

7. 68 + 25   **8.** 52 − 27   **9.** 74 + 32   **10.** 76 − 28

Practice and Problem Solving Extra Practice, page 54, Set A

For 11–22, add or subtract mentally. Tell the strategy you used.

11. 78 − 15   **12.** 16 + 28   **13.** 26 − 12   **14.** 47 + 23

15. 27 + 48   **16.** 75 − 36   **17.** 38 + 85   **18.** 91 − 66

19. 62 − 29   **20.** 34 + 58   **21.** 44 − 17   **22.** 63 + 39

Find the sum or difference.

23. 168 − 59   **24.** 249 + 87   **25.** 216 + 79   **26.** 152 − 75

27. 261 + 88   **28.** 431 − 232   **29.** 441 + 263   **30.** 284 − 192

31. 758 − 453   **32.** 576 − 391   **33.** 713 + 428   **34.** 674 + 332

USE DATA For 35–38, use the table.

35. Which animal has a length of about 60 feet?

36. How many feet longer is the blue whale than the crocodile?

37. Which two animals have the greatest difference in length? Which have the least difference?

38. **? What's the Question?** The answer is 90 feet.

39. On Friday, there were 2,999 people at the aquarium. On Saturday, there were 1,465 people. Use mental math to find how many people were at the aquarium during the two days. Explain your strategy.

40. **FAST FACT • SCIENCE** The Central Florida Zoo covers 109 acres. The National Zoo, in Washington, D.C., covers 163 acres. If the Central Florida Zoo bought another 55 acres for expansion, which zoo would be larger? How much larger?

LENGTHS OF SEA ANIMALS (in feet)	
Animal	**Length**
Blue whale	110
Whale shark	59
Asian saltwater crocodile	32
Atlantic giant squid	20
Japanese spider crab	9

41. Rex has 6 horses, 10 cows, 5 goats, and 4 cars. He puts the cows, goats, and cars in the barn. How many of his animals are in the barn?

42. Lisa's dog weighs 45 pounds. Reggie's dog weighs 27 pounds. How much more does Lisa's dog weigh than Reggie's dog?

Maintain Skills

43. 3×5 **44.** 10×6

45. Which is greater, 1 foot or 1 yard?

46. What digit is in the hundreds place in 77,045?

47. What is the perimeter of the rectangle?

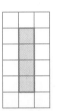

CRCT Test Prep

48. **M4N1.a.** What number has four more hundreds than the number 7,232? (p. 2)

A. 11,832   C. 7,272
B. 7,632   D. 7,236

49. **M4N1.b.** Fifteen thousand, four hundred ten people attended a basketball game. What was the attendance in standard form? (p. 4)

A. 150,410   C. 14,010
B. 15,410   D. 10,410

Problem Solving Thinker's Corner

COMPATIBLE NUMBERS Two numbers that add up to sums such as 10 or 100 are **compatible numbers.** Compatible numbers make mental math easy.

The Order Property of Addition says that numbers can be added in any order and the sum remains the same. Use the Order Property of Addition to add compatible numbers.

> HINT: These pairs of compatible numbers have a sum of 100.
>
> **10 and 90**
> **20 and 80**
> **30 and 70**
> **40 and 60**
> **50 and 50**

Find the sum. $68 + 230 + 32 + 170$

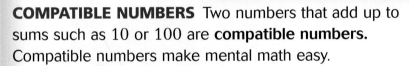

HINT: Look for compatible numbers.

$68 + 230 + 32 + 170 = 68 + 32 + 230 + 170$
$$= 100 + 400 = 500$$

So, the sum is 500.

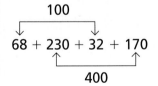

Use compatible numbers to find each sum.

1. $175 + 25 + 61 + 39 = \blacksquare$

2. $82 + 18 + 60 + 40 = \blacksquare$

3. $78 + 250 + 122 + 48 = \blacksquare$

4. $302 + 168 + 32 + 175 = \blacksquare$

2 Round Numbers

M4N2.a. Round numbers to the nearest ten, hundred, or thousand. *also* M4N2.b., M4P4.

▶ **Learn**

NEW NEIGHBORS In 2000, an average of 70,817 immigrants came to the United States each month. A reporter wants to **round** this number to the nearest ten to make it easier to understand. What is this number rounded to the nearest ten?

One Way

Use a number line to round numbers.

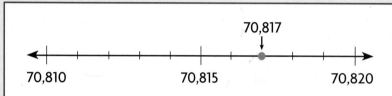

70,817

70,810   70,815   70,820

Think: 70,817 is closer to 70,820 than to 70,810.

So, 70,817 rounded to the nearest ten is 70,820.

Another Way

Use these rules to round numbers.

To round a number:	Round 70,817 to the nearest hundred.

To round a number:
- Find the place to which you want to round.
- Look at the digit to its right.
- If the digit is *less than 5,* the digit in the rounding place stays the same.
- If the digit is *5 or more,* the digit in the rounding place increases by 1.
- Change all digits to the right of the rounding place to zero.

Round 70,817 to the nearest hundred.

70,817 is between 70,800 and 70,900.

place to be rounded ⟶ 70,817 ⟵ Look at the tens digit.

Since 1 is less than 5, the digit 8 stays the same. So, 70,817 rounded to the nearest hundred is 70,800.

Round to the Nearest Thousand

Many immigrants from around the world live in Georgia. According to the 2000 U.S. Census, 8,257 people in Georgia speak Japanese at home.

Round the number of people who speak Japanese at home to the nearest

| thousand. | 8,257 | → | 8,000 |
| hundred. | 8,257 | → | 8,300 |

▲ You can learn about Japanese culture at the Japan Fest held in Atlanta.

Examples

A Round 39,742 to the nearest hundred.

39,742 is between 39,700 and 39,800.

place to be rounded → 39,742   Look at the tens digit.

Since 4 is less than 5, the digit 7 stays the same. So, 39,742 rounded to the nearest hundred is 39,700.

B Round 39,742 to the nearest thousand.

39,742 is between 39,000 and 40,000.

place to be rounded → 39,742   Look at the hundreds digit.

Since 7 is greater than 5, the digit 9 is increased by 1. So, 39,742 rounded to the nearest thousand is 40,000.

• When rounding, you change some digits to zero. Explain how you know which digits to change.

 Check

1. **Explain** how to round 9,999 to the nearest thousand.

2. **Find** the least and greatest numbers that round to 16,000.

Round each number to the nearest thousand.

3. 50,822   4. 5,104   5. 12,531   6. 9,523

Round each number to the place value of the blue digit.

7. 28,749   8. 403   9. 17,482   10. 7,962

LESSON CONTINUES

Round each number to the nearest thousand.

11. 4,385	**12.** 77,179	**13.** 6,531	**14.** 62,435
15. 59,822	**16.** 5,104	**17.** 36,531	**18.** 4,523

Round each number to the place value of the blue digit.

19. 749	**20.** 1,403	**21.** 22,482	**22.** 962
23. 27,841	**24.** 5,639	**25.** 43,602	**26.** 5,926
27. 4,837	**28.** 84,609	**29.** 5,408	**30.** 97,813
31. 9,721	**32.** 52,403	**33.** 7,454	**34.** 61,073

35. List all of the numbers that, when rounded to the nearest ten, are 500.

36. Which number rounds to six thousand, eight hundred: 6,864 or 6,849?

37. On the place-value chart, my thousands period is seventeen. My ones period is $500 + 20 + 3$. What number am I? Round me to the nearest thousand.

Technology Link

More Practice: Harcourt Mega Math Fraction Action, *Number Line Mine*, Level C

USE DATA For 38–41, use the table.

38. Which state had fewer than 1,000 immigrants admitted in 2003?

39. Which state's number of immigrants has the digit 2 in the thousands place?

40. Is the number of immigrants admitted to Georgia closer to 10,000 or to 11,000?

41. What number is 2,000 greater than the number of immigrants admitted to Alabama?

42. REASONING Write a number that never repeats a digit and rounds to 7,000.

43. ✍ **Write About It** Explain how to round 9,685 to the nearest thousand.

IMMIGRANTS ADMITTED, 2003	
State	**Immigrants**
Alabama	1,693
Florida	52,969
Georgia	10,805
Mississippi	730

44. ≡**FAST FACT** • **SOCIAL STUDIES** In 2003, a total of 19,781 people emigrated to the state of Virginia. Round this number to the nearest thousand.

45. Rachel is making 3 fruit tarts. She has 15 strawberries. She puts the same number of strawberries in each tart. How many strawberries are in each tart?

Maintain Skills

46. Which digit is in the hundreds place in 18,570?

47. What number is 100 greater than 5,332?

48. What is the product of 2 and 8?

49. Which is the best estimate of the length of a pencil, 7 inches or 7 feet?

CRCT Test Prep

50. **M4N1.b.** What number is one hundred fifty thousand, two hundred ten in standard form? (p. 4)
A. 150,201   C. 152,010
B. 150,210   D. 250,210

51. **M4N1.a.** Which number is between 476,891 and 674,198? (p. 4)
A. 468,981   C. 676,819
B. 647,918   D. 746,189

Problem Solving LiNKÜP . . . to Reading

STRATEGY • COMPARE When you **compare** two or more things, you look at how they are alike. When you **contrast** two or more things, you look at how they are different.

Look at the chart below. The chart compares and contrasts information about five Georgia counties. Can you think of other ways to compare and contrast the counties?

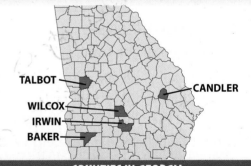

COMPARE	CONTRAST
Candler and Irwin each have more than 9,000 people.	Irwin has a greater area than Candler.
All of the counties have an area between 200 and 400 square miles.	Talbot has a greater area but a smaller population than Wilcox.

COUNTIES IN GEORGIA		
County	Population (2001)	Area (to nearest sq mi)
Baker	4,074	249
Candler	9,577	249
Irwin	9,931	363
Wilcox	8,577	383
Talbot	6,498	395

1. Look at the information about Irwin and Wilcox counties. How do the counties compare? How do they contrast?

2. Round each area to the nearest hundred. Compare and contrast the numbers. How does this change the data? What conclusion about rounding can you make from your answer?

Estimate Sums and Differences

 M4N7.d. Use mental math and estimation strategies to compute. *also* **M4N2.d.**

▶ **Learn**

PET POWER The table shows the results of a survey by the North Adams Animal Shelter. About how many people have either dogs or cats, but not both?

One Way Use rounding.

> Estimate. 34,221 + 38,899
>
> Round each number to the nearest thousand.
>
> $$\begin{array}{rcr} 34{,}221 & \rightarrow & 34{,}000 \\ +\,38{,}899 & \rightarrow & +\,39{,}000 \\ \hline & & 73{,}000 \end{array}$$
>
> So, about 73,000 people have either dogs or cats.

Another Way Use front-end estimation.

> Estimate. 34,221 + 38,899
>
> Add the value of the front digits.
>
> $$\begin{array}{rcr} 34{,}221 & \rightarrow & 30{,}000 \\ +\,38{,}899 & \rightarrow & +\,30{,}000 \\ \hline & & 60{,}000 \end{array}$$
>
> So, about 60,000 people have either dogs or cats.

- Which way, rounding or front-end estimation, do you think gives an estimate that is closer to the actual sum? Explain.

PET HOUSEHOLDS

Pet	Number
Cat only	34,221
Dog only	38,899
Cat & dog	6,520
Tropical fish	4,872
Bird	1,036

Examples

Ⓐ Estimate. 5,372 + 1,497

Round each number to the nearest hundred.

$$\begin{array}{rcr} 5{,}372 & \rightarrow & 5{,}400 \\ +\,1{,}497 & \rightarrow & +\,1{,}500 \\ \hline & & 6{,}900 \end{array}$$

The sum is about 6,900.

Ⓑ Estimate. 45,017 + 21,700

Use front-end estimation.

$$\begin{array}{rcr} 45{,}017 & \rightarrow & 40{,}000 \\ +\,21{,}700 & \rightarrow & +\,20{,}000 \\ \hline & & 60{,}000 \end{array}$$

The sum is about 60,000.

Estimate Differences

You can use rounding or front-end estimation to estimate the difference of whole numbers.

One Way   Use rounding.

Estimate. 86,017 − 35,572

Round to the nearest thousand.

$$
\begin{array}{rcr}
86{,}017 & \rightarrow & 86{,}000 \\
-\,35{,}572 & \rightarrow & -\,36{,}000 \\
\hline
 & & 50{,}000
\end{array}
$$

So, the difference is about 50,000.

Another Way   Use front-end estimation.

Estimate. 4,892 − 1,431

Subtract the value of the front digits.

$$
\begin{array}{rcr}
4{,}892 & \rightarrow & 4{,}000 \\
-\,1{,}431 & \rightarrow & -\,1{,}000 \\
\hline
 & & 3{,}000
\end{array}
$$

So, the difference is about 3,000.

Once you have found an estimate, you can adjust it to make it *closer to* the actual sum or difference.

More Examples

C Estimate. 7,593 − 3,145

Round to the nearest thousand.

$$
\begin{array}{rcr}
7{,}593 & \rightarrow & 8{,}000 \\
-\,3{,}145 & \rightarrow & -\,3{,}000 \\
\hline
4{,}448 & & 5{,}000
\end{array}
$$

Find a closer estimate by rounding to the nearest hundred.

$$
\begin{array}{rcr}
7{,}593 & \rightarrow & 7{,}600 \\
-\,3{,}145 & \rightarrow & -\,3{,}100 \\
\hline
4{,}448 & & 4{,}500
\end{array}
$$

So, a closer estimate is 4,500.

D Estimate. 22,720 + 34,378

Add the value of the front digits.

$$
\begin{array}{rcr}
22{,}720 & \rightarrow & 20{,}000 \\
+\,34{,}378 & \rightarrow & +\,30{,}000 \\
\hline
57{,}098 & & 50{,}000
\end{array}
$$

Find a closer estimate by including the value of the remaining digits.

2,720 + 4,378 is about 7,000.

50,000 + 7,000 = 57,000

So, a closer estimate is 57,000.

▶ Check

1. **Explain** why a front-end estimate of a sum will never be greater than the actual sum.

Estimate the sum or difference by using rounding.

2. $\begin{array}{r} 279 \\ +\,645 \\ \hline \end{array}$

3. $\begin{array}{r} 7{,}939 \\ -\,4{,}209 \\ \hline \end{array}$

4. $\begin{array}{r} 65{,}461 \\ +\,23{,}780 \\ \hline \end{array}$

5. $\begin{array}{r} 47{,}813 \\ -\,25{,}379 \\ \hline \end{array}$

LESSON CONTINUES ▶

Estimate the sum or difference by using front-end estimation.

6. 257 −123	**7.** 1,936 + 7,483	**8.** $13,024 + $58,417	**9.** 90,111 − 23,187

Adjust the estimate to make it closer to the exact sum or difference.

10. 9,876 + 6,291 = 16,167
   Estimate: 10,000 + 6,000 = 16,000

11. 87,908 − 33,110 = 54,798
   Estimate: 80,000 − 30,000 = 50,000

▶ **Practice and Problem Solving**   Extra Practice, page 54, Set C

Estimate the sum or difference by using rounding.

12. 123 +381	**13.** $40,717 + $74,910	**14.** 28,183 − 12,275	**15.** 8,600 − 4,908

Estimate the sum or difference by using front-end estimation.

16. 9,584 − 6,102	**17.** 8,037 + 4,047	**18.** 71,234 − 12,736	**19.** $96,254 + $15,224

Adjust the estimate to make it closer to the exact sum or difference.

20. 4,962 − 1,852 = 3,110
   Estimate: 5,000 − 2,000 = 3,000

21. 51,099 + 45,724 = 96,823
   Estimate: 50,000 + 40,000 = 90,000

22. 8,482 + 6,079 = 14,561
   Estimate: 8,000 + 6,000 = 14,000

23. 38,852 − 16,487 = 22,365
   Estimate: 30,000 − 10,000 = 20,000

USE DATA For 24–26, use the table.

24. About how many golden retrievers and cocker spaniels are registered in all?

25. About how many more German shepherds than poodles are there?

26. About how many beagles and poodles are registered in all?

27. REASONING Write two numbers that have an estimated sum of 10,000. Use the digits 2, 3, 4, and 5 in each number.

28. ✎ **Write About It** Write a problem that you can solve by using the estimate 7,000 + 5,000 = 12,000.

TOP U.S. DOG BREEDS

Breed	Number Registered
German shepherd	79,076
Golden retriever	68,993
Beagle	56,956
Poodle	56,803
Cocker spaniel	45,305

29. John and Sara both estimated the sum 5,512 + 2,501. John used rounding and got 9,000. Sara used front-end estimation and got 7,000. Whose estimate do you think is closer to the exact sum? Explain.

30. Vocabulary Power When we say that two things are *different*, we mean that they are unlike in some way. What does finding the *difference* between two numbers show about those numbers?

Maintain Skills

31. What is the value of the digit 3 in 4,036?

32. Which unit would be used to measure the area of a playground, yard or square yard?

33. Tina has 6 plates of cookies to sell at the bake sale. Each plate has 8 cookies. How many cookies in all does she have to sell?

CRCT Test Prep

34. **M4N1.b.** What is two hundred eighty-six in expanded form? (p. 4)

A. 200 + 86   C. 200 + 80 + 6
B. 280 + 6   D. 2,000 + 800 + 6

35. **M4N2.a.** What is 2,851 rounded to the nearest hundred? (p. 32)

A. 3,000   C. 2,800
B. 2,900   D. 2,000

Problem Solving Thinker's Corner

CLOSER ESTIMATES Another way to estimate is to find two estimates that an exact sum is *between*.

About how many Maine coon and Siamese cats are registered in the United States?

TOP REGISTERED PEDIGREE CAT BREEDS	
Breed	**Number**
Persian	25,524
Maine coon	4,539
Siamese	2,131

STEP 1

Find an *underestimate,* or an estimate that is a little *less than* the exact sum, by rounding *down* to the next hundred.

$$
\begin{array}{rcr}
4{,}539 & \rightarrow & 4{,}500 \\
+\,2{,}131 & \rightarrow & +\,2{,}100 \\
\hline
 & & 6{,}600 \leftarrow \text{underestimate}
\end{array}
$$

STEP 2

Find an *overestimate,* or an estimate that is a little *more than* the exact sum, by rounding *up* to the next hundred.

$$
\begin{array}{rcr}
4{,}539 & \rightarrow & 4{,}600 \\
+\,2{,}131 & \rightarrow & +\,2{,}200 \\
\hline
 & & 6{,}800 \leftarrow \text{overestimate}
\end{array}
$$

So, the actual sum 4,539 + 2,131 is *between* 6,600 and 6,800.

Find an underestimate and an overestimate for each sum.

1. 6,576 + 3,990   **2.** 2,849 + 17,365   **3.** 35,909 + 40,498

LESSON
4 Add and Subtract

M4N2.d. Represent the results of computation as a rounded number when appropriate and estimate a sum or difference by rounding numbers. *also* M4N1, M4N2, M4N3, M4N4, M4N5, M4N6, M4N7, M4N7.a., M4P2.a., M4P2.b., M4P2.c., M4P2.d., M4P4.c.

 Learn

GREAT LAKES! The area of Lake Erie is 9,910 square miles. The area of Lake Ontario is 7,340 square miles. What is the combined area of the two lakes? What is the difference in their areas?

Quick Review

1. 460 + 218
2. 355 − 145
3. 175 + 250
4. 796 − 445
5. 804 + 257

Example 1
Find the sum. 9,910 + 7,340

Estimate. 10,000 + 7,000 = 17,000

STEP 1	**STEP 2**	**STEP 3**	**STEP 4**
Add the ones.	Add the tens.	Add the hundreds. Regroup 12 hundreds.	Add the thousands.
9,910 +7,340 0	9,910 +7,340 50	¹9,910 +7,340 250	¹9,910 +7,340 17,250

So, the combined area of the two lakes is 17,250 square miles. The answer is close to the estimate, so 17,250 is reasonable.

 Technology Link
More Practice: Harcourt Mega Math The Number Games, *Tiny's Think Tank*, Levels B and C

Example 2
Find the difference. 9,910 − 7,340

Estimate. 10,000 − 7,000 = 3,000

STEP 1	**STEP 2**	**STEP 3**	**STEP 4**
Subtract the ones.	Regroup hundreds. Subtract the tens.	Subtract the hundreds.	Subtract the thousands.
9,910 −7,340 0	9,9̸10 −7,340 70	9,9̸10 −7,340 570	9,9̸10 −7,340 2,570

So, the difference in their areas is 2,570 square miles.
The answer is close to the estimate, so 2,570 is reasonable.

Example 3

Find the difference. 7,100 − 1,315

STEP 1

Subtract the ones.

Regroup 1 hundred as 9 tens 10 ones.

$$\begin{array}{r} \overset{0\;\overset{9}{\cancel{1}}\;10\,10}{7,\cancel{1}\cancel{0}\cancel{0}} \\ -\,1,3\,1\,5 \\ \hline 5 \end{array}$$

STEP 2

Subtract the tens.

$$\begin{array}{r} \overset{0\;\overset{9}{\cancel{1}}\;10\,10}{7,\cancel{1}\cancel{0}\cancel{0}} \\ -\,1,3\,1\,5 \\ \hline 8\,5 \end{array}$$

STEP 3

Subtract the hundreds.

Regroup 7 thousands as 6 thousands 10 hundreds.

$$\begin{array}{r} \overset{\overset{10}{6}\;\overset{9}{0}\;\overset{}{\cancel{1}}\;10\,10}{7,\cancel{1}\cancel{0}\cancel{0}} \\ -\,1,3\,1\,5 \\ \hline 7\,8\,5 \end{array}$$

STEP 4

Subtract the thousands.

$$\begin{array}{r} \overset{\overset{10}{6}\;\overset{9}{0}\;\overset{}{\cancel{1}}\;10\,10}{7,\cancel{1}\cancel{0}\cancel{0}} \\ -\,1,3\,1\,5 \\ \hline 5,7\,8\,5 \end{array}$$

STEP 5

Add to check.

$$\begin{array}{r} 5,7\,8\,5 \\ +\,1,3\,1\,5 \\ \hline 7,1\,0\,0 \end{array}$$

So, the difference is 5,785.

• In Step 1, why is it necessary to regroup 1 hundred?

▶ Check

1. **Explain** how you know when it is not necessary to regroup in subtraction.

2. How can you use addition to check a subtraction problem?

Find the sum or difference. Estimate to check.

3.
$$\begin{array}{r} 899 \\ +267 \end{array}$$

4.
$$\begin{array}{r} 674 \\ -406 \end{array}$$

5.
$$\begin{array}{r} 8,902 \\ -5,730 \end{array}$$

6.
$$\begin{array}{r} 9,201 \\ +\,1,321 \end{array}$$

7. $615 - 243$

8. $5,425 + 1,807$

9. $4,009 - 961$

10. $340 + 459 + 1,781$

Find the difference. Check your answer.

11.
$$\begin{array}{r} 400 \\ -287 \end{array}$$

12.
$$\begin{array}{r} 3,700 \\ -\,1,692 \end{array}$$

13.
$$\begin{array}{r} \$300 \\ -\,\$163 \end{array}$$

14.
$$\begin{array}{r} 2,100 \\ -\,594 \end{array}$$

Find the sum or difference. Estimate to check.

15. 798
− 127

16. $3,204
− $2,413

17. 409
762
+ 805

18. 5,762
5,243
+ 1,111

19. 2,409
+ 5,762

20. 5,320
− 1,375

21. 9,862
− 7,361

22. $3,228
+ $4,228

23. 409 + 952

24. $1,124 + $1,525 + $1,651 + $4,176

25. 6,230 − 4,651

26. 1,987 + 936

Find the difference. Check your answer.

27. 4,001
− 3,090

28. 6,008
− 4,009

29. $3,005
− $1,978

30. 5,004
− 859

31. 5,700
− 4,190

32. 7,001
− 3,090

33. 5,200
− 3,087

34. 8,600
− 6,123

35. 3,000
− 2,218

36. 8,000
− 2,319

37. 9,008
− 4,899

38. 1,000
− 919

Compare. Write <, >, or = for each ●.

39. 3,000 − 2,541 ● 4,200 − 3,756

40. 2,000 − 1,008 ● 2,100 − 1,097

For 41–42, find the missing digit.

41. 2,90■
− 1,894
1,007

42. 3,486
+ ■,964
9,450

USE DATA For 43–44, use the map.

43. The lengths of which two coastlines have a sum of about 4,000 miles? Find the actual sum.

44. About how many miles long are all the United States coastlines shown?

45. An arctic tern flew 9,230 miles to Antarctica. A sea turtle swam 1,400 miles to South America. How much farther did the arctic tern migrate than the sea turtle?

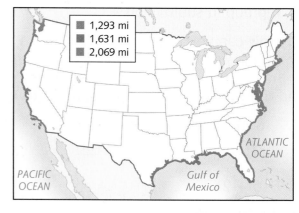

46. **MULTISTEP** A male walrus at the zoo weighs 1,390 kilograms. A female walrus weighs 268 kilograms less. How much do they weigh together?

47. 5×9 **48.** $105 \div 5$

49. What is the value of the digit 4 in 42,108?

50. Which measurement could be the height of the library door: 8 inches or 8 feet?

51. Use the decimal model to find $0.4 + 0.5$.

52. **M4N7.d.** The area of a yogurt shop is 1,954 square feet. The area of a pizzeria is 4,132 square feet. About how many square feet greater is the pizzeria than the yogurt shop? (p. 36)

   A. 1,000   C. 3,000
   B. 2,000   D. 4,000

53. **M4N7.d.** Which sum is the same as $43 + 25$? (p. 28)

   A. $40 + 22$ C. $40 + 28$
   B. $48 + 30$ D. $38 + 20$

Problem Solving — THiNKer's CorNer

ANOTHER WAY TO SUBTRACT ACROSS ZEROS Sometimes you can use other strategies you have learned to subtract across zeros.

To earn a free airline ticket on Aeromax Airlines, Foster needs to travel 40,000 miles. So far, he has traveled 7,165 miles. How many more miles must Foster travel to earn a free ticket?

Subtract. $40,000 - 7,165$

You have learned how to subtract across zeros by renaming. You can also change one number so that you can subtract without renaming and then adjust the difference.

Think: $40,000 = 39,999 + 1$

$$
\begin{array}{r}
39,999 + 1 = 40,000 \\
- 7,165 \quad\quad - 7,165 \\
\hline
32,834 + 1 = 32,835
\end{array}
$$

Add 1 to 32,834 to adjust the difference.

So, Foster needs to travel 32,835 more miles on Aeromax Airlines to earn a free ticket.

Change one number and adjust the difference to subtract.

  1. $50,000 - 6,732$ **2.** $30,000 - 4,578$ **3.** $6,000 - 89$

  4. Explain why you must add 1 to the difference in Exercise 1.

Problem Solving Skill
Estimate or Find Exact Answers

 M4N2.b. Describe situations in which rounding numbers would be appropriate and detemine whether to round to the nearest ten, hundred, or thousand. *also* **M4N7.d., M4P1.a., M4P1.b., M4P1.c., M4P1.d., M4P3.a., M4P3.b., M4P3.c., M4P3.d.**

UNDERSTAND ▶ PLAN ▶ SOLVE ▶ CHECK

DECISIONS, DECISIONS Coach Wilcox has $1,500 to order new baseball equipment. The table below shows the cost of some baseball equipment.

| BASEBALL EQUIPMENT PRICES ||
Equipment	Cost
Aluminum bleacher	$449
30 batting helmets	$719
Pitching machine	$589
Pair of foul poles	$799
7 catcher's chest protectors	$389

Examples

A Is there enough money to buy a pitching machine and a pair of foul poles?

Think: You can estimate to answer the question, so you can round.

$$\begin{array}{r} \$589 \\ +\ \$799 \end{array} \rightarrow \begin{array}{r} \$\ \ 600 \\ +\ \$\ \ 800 \\ \hline \$1,400 \end{array}$$ Round to the nearest hundred.

Since $1,400 < $1,500, there is enough money.

B If Coach Wilcox buys the pitching machine and poles, how much money will be left?

Think: You need an exact answer, so you cannot round.

Add to find the cost of the equipment.　Subtract to find the amount left.

$$\begin{array}{r} \$\ \ 589 \\ +\ \$\ \ 799 \\ \hline \$1,388 \end{array} \qquad \begin{array}{r} \$1,500 \\ -\ \$1,388 \\ \hline \$\ \ 112 \end{array}$$

So, there will be $112 left.

Talk About It

• At a baseball game, there were 16,514 fans for the home team and 12,809 for the visiting team. Tell whether you would round to the nearest ten, hundred, or thousand to find whether there were more than 30,000 fans at the game.

Problem Solving Practice

For 1–2, tell whether an estimate or an exact answer is needed. Solve.

1. Brianne bought a baseball hat and a pennant. How much change will she get from $20?

2. About how much money does Andy need to buy a baseball bat and baseball at the park?

3. The stadium shop sold 125 bats and 445 hats during the first game and 97 bats and 386 hats during the second game. Which question requires an exact calculation to answer?

   A Did the shop sell more bats or more hats?

   B About how many more hats than bats were sold during the second game?

   C How many hats were sold in all?

   D Did the shop sell more than 150 bats?

4. Which expression would be the best one to use to estimate by rounding the total cost of 2 hats and 2 bats?

   F $15 + $15 + $25 + $25

   G $10 + $10 + $10 + $10

   H $10 + $10 + $20 + $20

   J $20 + $20 + $20 + $20

Mixed Applications

5. At a college, 1,825 students signed up to play an indoor sport, and 2,984 signed up for an outdoor sport. Write an expression to show how many students signed up for a sport.

6. Of the students enrolled at the college, 1,408 are from Alabama, 1,450 are from Georgia, and 1,230 are from Louisiana. From which of these states do the most students come?

7. There are 9,470 students who live on campus. If there are 11,652 students in all, how many students do not live on campus?

8. In the football stadium, there are 66,322 seats. There are 2,974 people watching a practice game. How many seats are empty?

9. The School of Science bought a new telescope for $8,376. Write the number in word form.

10. **Write a problem** in which you need to find an estimated sum or difference.

Problem Solving

6 Expressions

M4A1.b. Represent unknowns using symbols, such as □ and △.
also **M4A1.c., M4N7.b., M4P2, M4P2.a., M4P2.b., M4P2.c., M4P2.d.**

 Learn

FANCY FLOWERS Sue had 12 flowers. Lily gave her 4 more flowers. Sue gave her teacher 3 of her flowers. How many does she have left?

You can write an expression to find the number of flowers Sue has left.

An **expression** has numbers and operation signs. It does not have an equal sign.

Think: 12 flowers plus 4 flowers, minus 3 flowers
↓   ↓   ↓   ↓   ↓
(12   +   4)   −   3

Find the value of $(12 + 4) − 3$.

$(12 + 4) − 3$ Add 12 and 4.
↓
$16 − 3$ Subtract 3 from 16.
↓
13

So, $(12 + 4) − 3$ is 13. Sue has 13 flowers left.

Parentheses tell which operation to do first. Expressions with the same numbers and operations can have different values, depending on where you place parentheses.

Quick Review

Add 15 to each number.

1. 460   **2.** 523

3. 196   **4.** 837

5. 728

VOCABULARY

expression

variable

Examples

A Find the value of $(9 − 5) + 2$.

$(9 − 5) + 2$ Subtract 5 from 9.
↓
$4 \quad + 2$ Add 4 and 2.
↓
6

So, the value of $(9 − 5) + 2$ is 6.

B Find the value of $9 − (5 + 2)$.

$9 − (5 + 2)$ Add 5 and 2.
↓
$9 − \quad 7$ Subtract 7 from 9.
↓
2

So, the value of $9 − (5 + 2)$ is 2.

• How is Example A different from Example B?

46

Expressions with Variables

Fergus planted 3 rows in his garden in the morning. In the afternoon, he planted some more rows. What expression can you write to show the total number of rows he planted?

You can use a variable to show the number of rows he planted in the afternoon. A **variable** is a letter or symbol that represents any number you don't know.

3 rows planted in the morning plus some more rows planted
↓   ↓   ↓
3   +   □

So, the expression showing the total number of rows is $3 + \square$.

How many rows did Fergus plant in all if he planted 4 rows in the afternoon? To find the value of the expression, replace □ with the number of rows planted in the afternoon.

$3 + \square$

$3 + 4$ ← Replace □ with 4 since he planted
↓   4 rows in the afternoon.
7

So, Fergus planted 7 rows in all.

Technology Link
More Practice: Harcourt Mega Math Ice Station Exploration, *Arctic Algebra*, Level G

More Examples

> **C** Find the value of $9 - \square$ if $\square = 2$.
>
> $9 - \square$ Replace □ with 2.
> ↓
> $9 - 2$ Subtract 2 from 9.
> ↓
> 7
>
> So, the value of the expression is 7.

> **D** Find the value of $8 + (\triangle - 2)$ if $\triangle = 6$.
>
> $8 + (\triangle - 2)$ Replace △ with 6.
> ↓
> $8 + (6 - 2)$ Subtract 2 from 6.
> ↓
> $8 + \quad 4$ Add 8 and 4.
> ↓
> 12
>
> So, the value of the expression is 12.

▷ Check

1. **Explain** when you need to use a variable when writing an expression.

LESSON CONTINUES ▶

Write an expression.

2. Eight people were at the party, and then 7 more arrived.

3. Mike had 21 toy cars. He gave 4 of them to a friend and then got 5 more.

4. There were 22 students in the class, but some were absent. Write an expression that shows the number of students present. Choose a variable for the unknown, and tell what it represents.

5. Chris had 18 cards. Then he bought some more but lost 7. Write an expression that shows the number of cards Chris has now. Choose a variable for the unknown, and tell what it represents.

Find the value of each expression.

6. $5 + 2 + 6$

7. $(8 - 7) + 1$

8. $6 - (3 + 2)$

Find the value of each expression if $\triangle = 6$ and $\square = 3$.

9. $\triangle + 9$

10. $(\triangle - 4) + 7$

11. $5 + (12 - \square)$

Practice and Problem Solving   Extra Practice, page 54, Set E

Write an expression.

12. The class collected 15 bags of trash and then collected 12 more bags.

13. A room had 25 desks. Five desks were added, and then 3 were removed.

14. Susan had 24 stamps. She used some of the stamps to mail letters. Write an expression that shows the number of stamps that Susan has now. Choose a variable for the unknown, and tell what it represents.

15. There were 4 pizzas at the party. Then the guests ate 3 of them and ordered some more. Write an expression that shows how many pizzas are left. Choose a variable for the unknown, and tell what it represents.

Find the value of each expression.

16. $17 - 9 - 6$

17. $(25 - 10) + 8$

18. $(62 - 40) + 31$

19. $29 + (15 - 8)$

20. $50 - (32 - 14)$

21. $38 - (12 + 23)$

Find the value of each expression if $\square = 12$ and $\triangle = 7$.

22. $50 - \square$

23. $\square + 10$

24. $(\triangle + 6) + \square$

Write words to match each expression.

25. $14 + 9$

26. $\triangle + (8 - 4)$

27. $80 - (47 - \star)$

28. Vocabulary Power The word *operation* is from a Latin word meaning "work." How do operations such as addition or subtraction "work" on numbers?

29. **? What's the Error?** David said that the value of $40 - (\triangle + 16)$ is 40 if $\triangle = 16$. Describe and correct his error.

30. A teacher donated 35 folders, 17 books, and 45 pencils to the school carnival. How many items did the teacher donate?

31. REASONING What whole numbers can □ and △ be if the expression 30 −(□ + △) has a value of 25?

Maintain Skills

32. In the number 14,683, which digit is in the tens place?

33. How many times as great is the value of the 4 in 40 than the value of the 4 in 1,400?

34. What is the length of the nail below to the nearest centimeter?

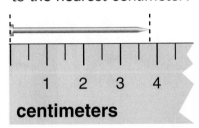

centimeters

CRCT Test Prep

35. **M4N7.d.** Subtract. Use mental math. (p. 28)

145 – 28

- A. 113
- B. 117
- C. 123
- D. 163

36. **M4N2.a.** What is 5,689 rounded to the nearest hundred? (p. 32)

- A. 6,000
- B. 5,800
- C. 5,700
- D. 5,600

Problem Solving LiNKUP . . . to Health

In 2005, MyPyramid replaced the Food Guide Pyramid to help Americans make healthier food choices. Andy found a poster showing nutritional guidelines for his age and activity level.

USE DATA For 1–2, use the MyPyramid poster.

1. Cereal and bread are two types of foods in the grains group. Andy ate 3 ounces of cereal for breakfast and 1 ounce of bread for lunch. Write an expression for the number of ounces of grains Andy needs to eat for dinner in order to have the recommended amount for the day. Find the value of the expression.

2. What expression could you write for the recommended number of servings from the milk group minus some number of cups of yogurt?

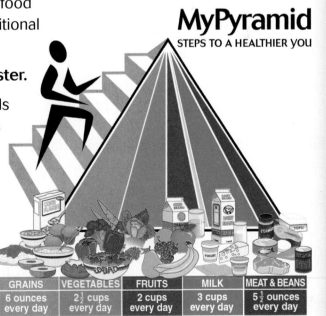

Mental Math: Number Sentences

M4A1.b. Represent unknowns using symbols, such as □ and △. *also* **M4A1, M4P3.a.,**
M4P3.b., M4P3.c., M4P3.d.

Quick Review

1. $17 + 35 = $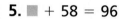
2. $24 + $ ■ $= 42$
3. $56 - 27 = $ ■
4. $49 - $ ■ $= 31$
5. ■ $+ 58 = 96$

▶ Learn

GOOD VIBRATIONS Richard had 12 CDs in his collection. He got some more CDs for his birthday. Now he has a total of 15 CDs. What number sentence can you write and use to find the number of CDs Richard received for his birthday?

You can write a number sentence to find how many CDs Richard received for his birthday.

12 CDs plus some CDs equals 15 CDs.
↓   ↓   ↓   ↓   ↓
12 +   ★   =   15

So, the number sentence is $12 + ★ = 15$. The variable ★ represents the number of CDs Richard received for his birthday.

A number sentence is true if the values on both sides of the equal sign are equal. You solve a number sentence when you find the value of a variable that makes the number sentence true. You can solve this number sentence using mental math.

$12 + ★ = 15$ **Think:** 12 plus what number equals 15?

$★ = 3$

Check: $12 + 3 \overset{?}{=} 15$ Replace ★ with 3.

$15 = 15 ✓$ The number sentence is true. The value of ★ is 3.

So, Richard received 3 CDs for his birthday.

Examples Find the number the variable represents.

Ⓐ $6 + △ = 10$ **Think:** 6 plus what number equals 10?

$△ = 4$

Check: $6 + 4 \overset{?}{=} 10$ Replace △ with 4.

$10 = 10 ✓$ The number sentence is true.

So, the value of △ is 4.

Ⓑ $□ - 8 = 3$ **Think:** What number minus 8 equals 3?

$□ = 11$

Check: $11 - 8 \overset{?}{=} 3$ Replace □ with 11.

$3 = 3 ✓$ The number sentence is true.

So, the value of □ is 11.

⚠ MATH IDEA You can use a variable to represent an unknown number when writing either number sentences or expressions.

1. **Explain** how you know when the value of a variable in a number sentence is correct.

Use mental math to find the number the variable represents. Check your answer.

2. $\square + 7 = 17$

3. $\star - 4 = 8$

4. $5 = 4 + \triangle$

5. $22 - \triangle = 10$

6. $6 = \square - 7$

7. $12 + \star = 14$

▶ **Practice and Problem Solving** (Extra Practice, page 54, Set F)

Use mental math to find the number the variable represents. Check your answer.

8. $\triangle + 12 = 20 - 3$

9. $8 + \square = 14$

10. $\square - 7 = 0$

11. $20 - \star = 11$

12. $10 - 8 = 7 - \square$

13. $15 = \triangle + 5$

14. $3 + \triangle = 3$

15. $13 - \star = 5 + 7$

16. $\square - 10 = 1$

17. Nadia has 21 CDs. Thirteen of the CDs are rock music, and the rest are classical music. She wrote the number sentence $21 - \square = 13$ to find how many of the CDs are country music. What is the value of $\square$?

18. **MULTISTEP** Alan had 43 video games. He gave 5 to Mindy. Then he got some video games from Max. Alan now has 47 video games. How many video games did he get from Max?

19. A post office sold 2,567 stamps on Monday and 1,614 stamps on Tuesday. How many more stamps were sold on Monday than on Tuesday?

20. ❓ **What's the Question?** Kathy has 8 pets: 2 dogs, 3 cats, and some birds. She used the number sentence $5 + \square = 8$. The answer is $\square = 3$.

Maintain Skills

21. In 2,053, what digit is in the ones place?

22. Multiply. 3×7

23. Divide. $50 \div 5$

24. Which unit is smaller, millimeter or kilometer?

CRCT Test Prep

25. M4N1.a. What number is 1,000 more than 35,921? (p. 2)

   A. 45,921   C. 36,921
   B. 44,921   D. 34,921

26. M4N1.a. Which number is less than 7,509? (p. 14)

   A. 7,590   C. 7,950
   B. 7,905   D. 7,095

Patterns: Find a Rule

M4A1.a. Understand and apply patterns and rules to describe relationships and solve problems. *also* **M4A1.b., M4A1.c., M4P3.a., M4P3.b., M4P3.c., M4P3.d., M4P4.a., M4P4.b.**

▶ **Learn**

NUMBER CRUNCHER When Mr. Wiley puts the number 12 into a number machine, the number 15 comes out. When he puts in 18, out comes 21, and when he puts in 24, out comes 27. What number comes out when he puts 30 into the machine?

INPUT	OUTPUT
12	15
18	21
24	27
30	

HINT: Look for a pattern to help you find a rule.

Pattern: Each output is 3 more than the input.

Rule: Add 3 to the input.

Input: 30   *Output*: 33

So, when Mr. Wiley puts in 30, out comes 33.

Examples Find a rule. Use the rule to extend the pattern.

Ⓐ

INPUT	OUTPUT
2	6
5	9
8	12
11	▣
14	▣

Rule: Add 4 to the input.

Test your rule on each pair of numbers in the table.

11 + 4 = 15   14 + 4 = 18

So, the next two numbers are 15 and 18.

Ⓑ

INPUT	OUTPUT
37	31
24	18
18	12
12	▣
6	▣

Rule: Subtract 6 from the output.

Test your rule on each pair of numbers in the table.

12 − 6 = 6   6 − 6 = 0

So, the next two numbers are 6 and 0.

Technology Link

More Practice: Harcourt
Mega Math Ice Station
Exploration, *Arctic
Algebra,* Level J

1. **Explain** why it is important to test the rule with all the numbers in the table.

Find a rule. Use the rule to extend the pattern.

2.

INPUT	6	15	18	23	28
OUTPUT	13	22	25	■	■

3.

INPUT	43	32	21	11	7
OUTPUT	37	26	15	■	■

► **Practice and Problem Solving**   Extra Practice, page 54, Set G

Find a rule. Use the rule to extend the pattern.

4.

INPUT	68	56	45	34	23	12
OUTPUT	57	45	34	23	■	■

5.

INPUT	39	47	55	60	67	75
OUTPUT	26	34	42	47	■	■

6.

INPUT	12	19	28	37	49	54
OUTPUT	■	■	48	57	69	74

7.

INPUT	15	30	20	37	28	43
OUTPUT	■	■	35	52	43	58

Use the rule to make an input/output table.

8. Add 8 to the input.

9. Subtract 6 from the input.

10. Add 12 to the input.

11. Subtract 10 from the input.

12. Add 21 to the input.

13. Subtract 14 from the input.

14. **MULTISTEP** The arena collects the same service charge for each ticket purchased. The total price for a $20 ticket is $22, and the price for a $25 ticket is $27. What is the total price for two $30 tickets?

15. ✎ **Write a problem** using a rule shown in this table. Then solve your problem to find the missing number.

INPUT	OUTPUT
$15	$8
$18	$11
$24	$17
$40	■

Maintain Skills

16. A blanket is 4 feet by 6 feet. What is the area of the blanket?

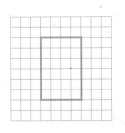

CRCT Test Prep

17. **M4N7.d.** On Friday, the Teen Scene Shop earned $3,679. On Saturday, the shop earned $5,302. What is the BEST estimate of the total sales for the two days? (p. 36)

A. $800   C. $8,000
B. $1,000   D. $9,000

Extra Practice

Set A (pp. 28–31)

Add or subtract mentally. Tell the strategy you used.

1. 98 + 46
2. 109 − 94
3. 246 + 176

Set B (pp. 32–35)

Round each number to the place value of the blue digit.

1. 399
2. 18,385
3. 4,581

4. 5,003
5. 39,210
6. 4,390

Set C (pp. 36–39)

Estimate the sum or difference.

1. $\begin{array}{r} 16,453 \\ -11,019 \\ \hline \end{array}$
2. $\begin{array}{r} 8,019 \\ +2,465 \\ \hline \end{array}$
3. $\begin{array}{r} 27,645 \\ -10,067 \\ \hline \end{array}$
4. $\begin{array}{r} 35,103 \\ +16,495 \\ \hline \end{array}$

Set D (pp. 40–43)

Find the sum or difference. Check your answer.

1. $\begin{array}{r} 625 \\ +292 \\ \hline \end{array}$
2. $\begin{array}{r} 9,004 \\ -5,762 \\ \hline \end{array}$
3. $\begin{array}{r} 2,435 \\ +2,576 \\ \hline \end{array}$
4. $\begin{array}{r} 8,000 \\ -4,934 \\ \hline \end{array}$

5. 1,452 + 984
6. 6,200 − 2,931
7. 2,073 + 8,465

Set E (pp. 46–49)

Find the value of each expression if $\triangle$ = 30 and $\square$ = 25.

1. 186 + $\triangle$ + 10
2. (96 − $\triangle$) + 3
3. $\square$ + (34 − 10)

Set F (pp. 50–51)

Find the number the variable represents.

1. 14 − $\square$ = 7
2. 13 = $\triangle$ + 4
3. $8 + $\square$ = $20

Set G (pp. 52–53)

Find a rule. Use the rule to extend the pattern.

1.

INPUT	12	20	31	45	65
OUTPUT	9	17	28	■	■

2.

INPUT	18	26	42	65	86
OUTPUT	■	■	49	72	93

Review/Test

✓ CHECK VOCABULARY AND CONCEPTS

Choose the best term from the box.

1. Sometimes you need an exact answer, while at other times, all you need is an _?_. (p. 44)

2. A letter or symbol that stands for an unknown is a _?_. (p. 47)

✓ CHECK SKILLS

Round each number to the place value of the blue digit. (pp. 32–35)

3. 43,719

4. 1,353

5. 91,203

6. 7,948

Find the sum or difference. (pp. 40–43)

7. 258 + 700

8. 8,586 − 486

9. 7,448 − 1,737

10. 5,000 + 3,718

Find the value of each expression if ★ = 108 and △ = 56. (pp. 46–49)

11. ★ − (20 + 12)

12. 251 + △ + 289

13. 44,876 − (317 − ★)

Find the number the variable represents. (pp. 50–51)

14. □ + 8 = 14

15. 23 − △ = 11

16. 9 = 15 − ★

17. Joaquin had 50 sports banners. He traded 32 of his banners for 15 new banners. Write an expression. How many banners does he have left?
(pp. 46–49)

18. Find a rule. Use the rule to extend the pattern. (pp. 52–53)

INPUT	47	54	62	84	96
OUTPUT	56	■	71	93	■

✓ CHECK PROBLEM SOLVING

Write whether an estimate or an exact answer is needed. Solve. (pp. 44–45)

19. The school cafeteria served 115 cartons of whole milk, 78 cartons of chocolate milk, and 35 cartons of orange juice. About how many drinks were served?

20. Ellie will win a prize if she sells 400 boxes of cookies this year. If she sold 113 in January, 107 in February, and 68 in March, how many more boxes does she need to sell to win a prize?

Chapter CRCT Test Prep

NUMBERS AND OPERATIONS

1. **M4N2.a.** The attendance at an Atlanta Symphony Orchestra concert was 1,681 people. Rounding to the nearest hundred, how many people attended the concert?

A. 1,600

B. 1,680

C. 1,700

D. 2,000

2. **M4N7.d.** By rounding to the nearest hundred, which subtraction has a difference of about 2,300?

A. $5,109 - 2,975$

B. $6,728 - 4,681$

C. $3,583 - 1,329$

D. $4,357 - 1,898$

3. **M4N2.d.** The distance from Atlanta, GA, to Seattle, WA, is 2,785 miles. The distance from Atlanta, GA, to Minneapolis, MN, is 1,135 miles. To the nearest hundred miles, what is the BEST estimate of how many more miles there are from Atlanta to Seattle than from Atlanta to Minneapolis?

A. 1,000 miles

B. 1,600 miles

C. 1,700 miles

D. 2,000 miles

ALGEBRA

4. **M4A1.c.** What is the value of $12 + (\Box - 3)$ if $\Box = 9$?

A. 0

B. 18

C. 21

D. 24

5. **M4A1.b.** The carousel at Zoo Atlanta has 38 wooden animal figures for children to ride. There are some children on the carousel now. Which expression BEST describes how many more children can ride the carousel?

A. $38 - \Box$

B. $\Box + 38$

C. $\Box - 38$

D. $38 \times \Box$

Use the table below to answer question 6.

In	Out
9	20
22	33
45	56
73	84

6. **M4A1.a.** What is the rule for the table?

A. Subtract 9.

B. Subtract 11.

C. Add 9.

D. Add 11.

Cumulative CRCT Test Prep

DATA ANALYSIS

Use the bar graph below to answer question 7.

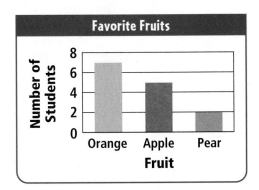

Favorite Fruits

7. **M4D1.a.** Joseph's class made a bar graph to show their favorite fruits. Which data set shows this?

   A. orange: 7, apple: 5, pear: 2

   B. orange: 7, apple: 6, pear: 2

   C. orange: 7, apple: 5, grape: 2

   D. orange: 7, apple: 4, pear: 2

Use the pictograph key below to answer question 8.

Key: Each 🕐 = 10 Minutes

8. **M4D1.a.** How many clock symbols would show that Randi practiced the piano for 25 minutes on Friday?

   A. 🕐 🕐

   B. 🕐 🕐 🕐

   C. 🕐 🕐 🕐 🕐

   D. 🕐 🕐 🕐 🕐 🕐

NUMBERS AND OPERATIONS

9. **M4N2.a.** In the late 1990s, Georgia had 4,635 miles of operating railroad track. What is that total rounded to the nearest hundred miles?

   A. 5,000 miles

   B. 4,700 miles

   C. 4,600 miles

   D. 4,000 miles

10. **M4N1.a.** What is the value of the blue digit in 1,673,075?

   A. 70,000

   B.   7,000

   C.   700

   D.   70

11. **M4N7.b.** What is the value of the expression?

$$25 - (13 + 1)$$

   A. 10

   B. 11

   C. 12

   D. 14

12. **M4N2.a.** Which number does NOT round to six thousand?

   A. 6,457

   B. 6,205

   C. 5,631

   D. 5,498

GPS/CRCT Vocabulary

ELA4R3 The student understands and acquires new vocabulary and uses it correctly in reading and writing. *also* **ELA4R3d.**

VOCABULARY

period   millions

benchmark

pictograph

sum

difference

variable

round   expression

MATCH GAME

MATERIALS *For each pair* Vocabulary Cards, Definition Cards

- Work with a partner.

- Mix up the cards, and place them face-down on the table.

- Take turns turning over two cards. If the vocabulary word and the definition match, place them face-up. If not, put them back face-down with the other cards.

- Play until all vocabulary matches have been made.

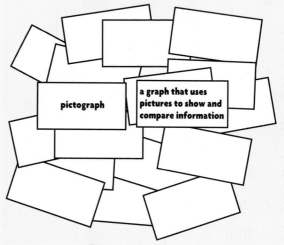

MATH WORD WORK

MATERIALS *For each student* drawing paper, markers or crayons

- Look at the vocabulary terms in the box at the top of the page.

- Select one word with which you are familiar that also has a nonmathematical meaning.

- Look up the word in the dictionary, and write the nonmathematical meaning on your paper.

- Draw a picture to illustrate the word's nonmathematical meaning.

WHAT AM I?

- On the top part of a sheet of paper, write a riddle using the definitions of four of the vocabulary terms. First, state the definition in your own words. Then write *What am I?* For example, *I am the period after thousands. What am I?*

- Write the vocabulary terms in random order at the bottom of your paper.

- Trade papers with a partner. Answer each riddle with one of the vocabulary terms.

I am the period after thousands. What am I?

WRITE IT UP

- For each vocabulary term, write a problem that has the vocabulary term in the question. Example: *Lisa's dog weighs 79 pounds. Her cat weighs 8 pounds. What is the difference between the two weights?*

- Trade papers with a partner, and solve each other's word problems.

- When you both have finished, check each other's work.

Georgia Tasks

M4N7.d. Use mental math and estimation strategies to compute. *also* **M4A1.c. M4N2.b., M4P1.a., M4P1.b., M4P1.c., M4P4.c.**

SS4G1a. locate major physical features of the United States to include, Atlantic Coastal Plain, Great Plains, Continental Divide, The Great Basin, Death Valley, Gulf of Mexico, St. Lawrence River, the Great Lakes. *also* **SS4E2**

Task A

THE COASTAL PLAIN

The Atlantic Coastal Plain in the United States is on the east coast. It starts at Cape Cod and ends at the Gulf of Mexico. Two parts of Georgia are coastal plain—the Atlantic Coastal Plain and the East Gulf Coastal Plain.

Screven County, Georgia, is on the coastal plain. Through the years, the population in the county has gone up and down. In 2000, it was about 15,400 people. In 1900, it was about 19,300. In 1950, it was about 18,000, and in 1990, it was about 13,800.

a. Make a table. Show the population data for Screven County from 1900 through 2000.

b. Tell how you organized your data. Why did you choose this way to organize it?

c. In 1850, there were about 6,800 people in Screven County. This number is rounded to the nearest hundred. Where in your table would you list this data? Describe what the exact population might have been.

Task B

BUYING A COMPUTER

The Stockwells saved $1,900 to buy a computer, monitor, and printer. The table shows the prices of items they might choose.

Computer		Monitor		Printer	
Brand A	$1,029	15-inch	$239	Ink jet	$289
Brand B	$1,179	17-inch	$379	Laser jet	$429

a. Estimate to find one possible choice of computer, monitor, and printer the Stockwells could buy with the money they have. Then find the actual total cost of these items.

b. How much of the $1,900 will be left if they purchase the items you suggested?

Maintain/Preview

Maintain

Write the value of the blue digit. (pp. 2–3, 4–5, 6–9)

1. 145,892

2. 8,360,745

3. 79,105,486

4. 402,379

Write the numbers in order from _least_ to _greatest._ (pp. 18–21)

5. 42,056; 42,605; 42,506

6. 183,294; 182,394; 182,493

Find the sum or difference. (pp. 40-43)

7. 6,391
  +2,547

8. 7,503
  +1,279

9. 5,000
  −3,295

10. 3,482
  − 735

Evaluate the expression for □ = 23. (pp. 46–49)

11. □ + 9

12. 24 − □

13. □ − 6

14. On Saturday, the cineplex sold 1,239 adult tickets and 784 children's tickets. To the nearest thousand, about how many tickets were sold on Saturday?
(pp. 36–39)

15. Shayna had 30 shells in her collection. She gave away 9 and collected some more. Write an expression that shows how many shells Shayna has now.
(pp. 46–49)

Preview

For 1–4, use the table. (Chapter 3)

1. How many different types of pets do the students have?

2. How many dogs do the students have?

3. How many more cats than birds do the students have?

4. How many pets do the students have in all?

Students' Pets	
Pet	**Number**
Dog	12
Cat	7
Bird	6
Fish	5

For 5–8, use the bar graph. (Chapter 4)

5. What is the title of the graph?

6. How many students are in the Drama Club?

7. Which club has the greatest number of members?

8. Which club has 15 members?

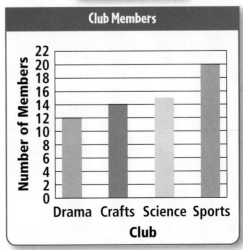

Collect and Organize Data

≡FAST FACT • SCIENCE The waters around the Florida Keys are home to more than 6,000 species of marine plants and animals.

INVESTIGATION The tally table lists the 5 most frequently sighted types of fish in the Florida Keys and shows how many of each type a diver saw during one dive. Choose a type of graph to display the data. Then make the graph.

Using Data

FISH SEEN DURING ONE DIVE

Type of Fish	Number Seen
Blue tang	◮◮ ◮ ◮◮ ⑀
Stoplight parrotfish	◮ ⑀⑀
Yellowtail snapper	◮◮ ◮◮ ⑁
Bluehead	⑁⑁
Sergeant major	◮ ⑀

CHECK WHAT YOU KNOW

Use this page to help you review and remember important skills needed for Chapter 3.

✓ READ PICTOGRAPHS

For 1–4, use the pictograph.

1. How many members of the Running Club are in fourth grade?

2. If 5 more third graders joined the Running Club, how many symbols would there be for third grade?

3. What is the total number of members in the Running Club?

RUNNING CLUB MEMBERS	
Third grade	🏃🏃🏃
Fourth grade	🏃🏃🏃🏃🏃
Fifth grade	🏃🏃🏃🏃🏃

Key: Each 🏃 = 2 members.

4. How many fifth-grade members are in the Running Club?

✓ TALLIES TO FREQUENCY TABLES

For 5–7, use the table.

5. Use the tally table to make a frequency table.

6. How many pieces of fruit were sold in Weeks 1 and 2?

7. How many more pieces of fruit were sold in Weeks 1 and 2 than in Weeks 3 and 4?

SCHOOL FRUIT STAND	
Week	Pieces of Fruit Sold
1	ℍℍ ℍℍ |||
2	ℍℍ
3	ℍℍ ||||
4	ℍℍ ||

VOCABULARY POWER

REVIEW

data [dā′tə] *noun*

Information collected about people or things from which conclusions can be drawn is known as *data*. There are many different ways to show collected data. Describe some of the ways that data can be displayed.

PREVIEW

survey

frequency

scale

interval

www.harcourtschool.com/mathglossary

Collect and Organize Data

M4D1. Students will gather, organize, and display data according to the situation and compare related features. *also* **M4P5.a., M4P5.b., M4P5.c.**

▶ Learn

TAKE YOUR PICK You are taking a **survey** when you ask different people the same questions and record their answers. Follow these rules to get the information you want:

• Make the questions clear and simple.

• Ask each person the questions only once.

• Use tally marks to record each person's answer, or response.

Jason and Susie each wrote a question to find the class's favorite color for School Spirit Day decorations. Compare the results of their surveys.

VOCABULARY

survey   frequency

Remember

In a tally table, tally marks are used to record data. The tally marks ⅧⅠ stand for 6.

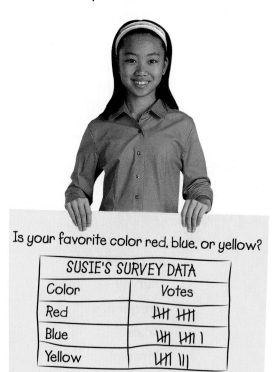

Is your favorite color red, blue, or yellow?

SUSIE'S SURVEY DATA	
Color	Votes
Red	ⅧⅠ ⅧⅠ
Blue	ⅧⅠ ⅧⅠ Ⅰ
Yellow	ⅧⅠ ⅢⅠ

What is your favorite color?

JASON'S SURVEY DATA

Color	Votes
Yellow	ⅢⅠ
Green	ⅧⅠ ⅧⅠ
Blue	ⅧⅠ Ⅰ
Red	ⅧⅠ Ⅰ
Orange	ⅢⅠⅠ

Both surveys ask about favorite colors, but Jason's allows more color choices. His survey allows any colors, such as orange or green. Susie's question allows only 3 color choices.

Frequency Tables

A frequency table helps you organize the data from a tally table. The **frequency** is the number of times a response occurs.

These tables show the numbers of loggerhead sea turtle nests found in four days on Fort Lauderdale Beach, Florida. Use them to find the day on which the most turtle nests were found and the total number of nests found.

LOGGERHEAD TURTLE NESTS FOUND	
Day	**Tally**
May 11	IIII
May 12	ⅢⅠ I
May 13	ⅢⅠ IIII
May 14	ⅢⅠ I

LOGGERHEAD TURTLE NESTS FOUND	
Day	**Frequency (Number of Nests Found)**
May 11	4
May 12	6
May 13	9
May 14	6

May 13 had the greatest frequency, so May 13 was the day on which the most turtle nests were found. Add the numbers in the frequency column to find the total number of nests found. Since $4 + 6 + 9 + 6 = 25$, the total number of nests found was 25.

 MATH IDEA Tables can be used to collect, organize, and display data.

 **Check**

1. **Write** a survey question, with choices, to find your classmates' favorite type of pizza.

Use Jason's and Susie's survey results on page 64. Tell whether each statement is *true* or *false*. Explain.

2. Susie's data show that more students prefer blue than red.

3. Jason's data show that red is the students' favorite color.

For 4–6, use this frequency table.

4. How many slices were sold during Hour 2?

5. By the end of Hour 3, how many slices had been sold?

6. How many more slices were sold during Hour 1 than during Hour 4?

Pizza Slices Sold	
Hour	**Frequency**
1	16
2	20
3	12
4	9

LESSON CONTINUES ▶

Gina asked her friends, "What is your favorite kind of party?" She put the data in a table.

FAVORITE KIND OF PARTY	
Party	**Votes**
Bowling	7
Skating	8
Movie	4
Pool	5

For 7–9, use the table to tell whether each statement is *true* or *false*. Explain.

7. Gina's data show that more friends prefer a bowling party than a pool party.

8. Gina's data show that a pool party is the least favorite choice.

9. Gina's data show that a skating party is the favorite party of the greatest number of her friends.

10. ✎ **Write About It** Write a survey question to find favorite fruits. Survey your classmates. Make a tally table and a frequency table for your data.

For 11–12, use the table.

11. How many tickets were sold during the 4 days?

12. On which two days were the most tickets sold?

SKATING TICKETS SOLD	
Day	**Tickets Sold**
Tuesday	5
Wednesday	18
Thursday	10
Friday	12

13. **MULTISTEP** Nancy planted a 4-year-old tree in the park in 1988. How old will the tree be in 2010?

14. **MULTISTEP** Mrs. Barker was 34 years old in 1998. How old was she in 1979?

For 15–17, use the bar graph.

15. Which cookie is the students' favorite?

16. How many more students chose chocolate chip cookies than raisin cookies?

17. **REASONING** How many students were surveyed in all?

18. **Vocabulary Power** A tally stick is an ancient stick that was used to record numbers. The stick was marked with notches to keep count or keep score. How is a tally stick similar to a tally table?

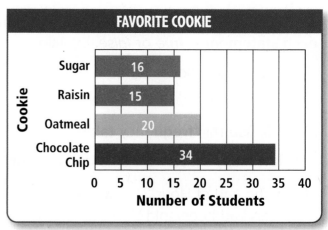

FAVORITE COOKIE

Cookie: Sugar 16, Raisin 15, Oatmeal 20, Chocolate Chip 34

Number of Students: 0 5 10 15 20 25 30 35 40

For 19–21, use the table.

19. How many bottles of juice were sold Monday and Tuesday?

20. How many more bottles of juice were sold on Thursday than Tuesday?

21. How many bottles of juice were sold in all?

JOE'S JUICE STAND	
Day	**Frequency**
Monday	140
Tuesday	197
Wednesday	259
Thursday	238

Maintain Skills

22. Use the model to find the sum 0.3 + 0.2.

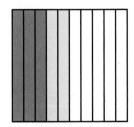

23. What digit is in the tens place in the number 5,639.8?

24. $4\overline{)64}$

25. $2\overline{)236}$

26. 3×8

27. 10×7

CRCT Test Prep

28. **M4A1.c.** Find the value of 17 − (5 + △) if △ = 8. (p. 46)
   - A. 4
   - B. 13
   - C. 20
   - D. 30

29. **M4N2.a.** Round 73,891 to the nearest thousand. (p. 32)
   - A. 70,000
   - B. 73,000
   - C. 73,900
   - D. 74,000

Problem Solving · Thinker's Corner

Taking a survey is a good way to predict how people will vote in an election. A random survey is one in which each voter has the same chance of being surveyed. A survey that is not random might ask the same question of a group of people with similar interests.

Angela and Paul are running for class president. Angela has promised more computer time if elected, and Paul has a lot of friends in the band.

KIM
Computer Club Members
Who would you vote for?
Angela 9 votes
Paul 1 vote

TOSHIO
Band Members
Who would you vote for?
Angela 2 votes
Paul 8 votes

SETH
Students at Lunch
Who would you vote for?
Angela 14 votes
Paul 20 votes

Use the survey results to answer each question.

1. Which group of people was probably chosen at random?

2. Explain why you think Kim's results were different from Seth's.

3. Who do you think will win the election? Tell why you think this.

Missing Information and Duplications in Data

M4D1.d. Identify missing information and duplications in data.
also M4P3.a., M4P3.c., M4P3.d., M4P4.c., M4P5.a., M4P5.b., M4P5.c.

▶ Learn

TELEVISION TIME Mr. Wallace surveyed five of his students to find out how many hours of television they watch each week.

Sam and Donnell each watch 5 hours of television each week, Kim watches 7 hours, and Al and Whitney each watch 10 hours. Al and Sam made graphs to show the results of the survey. What errors did Al and Sam make in their graphs?

Example 1
Compare the data in Al's graph with the data from the survey. Notice that 5 students were asked the question. Al's graph shows only 4 students. Which data is missing?
Al did not include the data about Donnell in his graph.

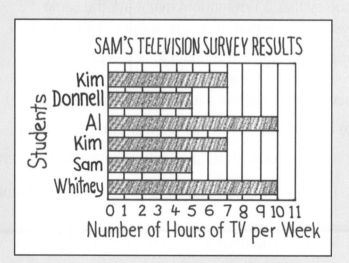

AL'S TELEVISION SURVEY RESULTS

Students: Al, Kim, Sam, Whitney
Number of Hours of TV per Week (0–11)

Example 2
Compare the data in Sam's graph with the data from the survey. Notice that 5 students were asked the question. Sam's graph shows 6 students. Which data was duplicated, or repeated?
Sam duplicated the data about Kim in his graph.

So, Al did not include some data in his graph, and Sam duplicated some data in his graph.

SAM'S TELEVISION SURVEY RESULTS

Students: Kim, Donnell, Al, Kim, Sam, Whitney
Number of Hours of TV per Week (0–11)

For 1-2, use Table 1.

1. **Explain** how you can find out whether the table correctly shows the data from Mr. Wallace's survey.

2. What error was made in the table?

3. Make a table that correctly shows the results of Mr. Wallace's survey.

TABLE 1 TELEVISION SURVEY RESULTS	
Student	Number of Hours of TV Per Week
Al	10
Donnell	5
Kim	7
Sam	5

▶ **Practice and Problem Solving** (Extra Practice, page 74, Set B)

For 4–6, use the graphs and Todd's test scores.

Todd's test scores: 92, 95, 96, 89, 92, 89, 84, 95, 84, 92

4. Does Graph 1 correctly show Todd's test scores? Explain.

5. Does Graph 2 correctly show Todd's test scores? Explain.

6. Explain how the graphs would change to correctly show Todd's test scores.

7. ✏ **Write About It** Explain the difference between a graph that is missing information and one that has duplication of data.

8. **ESTIMATION** The summer temperature in Savannah, GA, can be 92°F. The summer temperature in Anchorage, AK, can be 65°F. About how much warmer could it be in Savannah than in Anchorage?

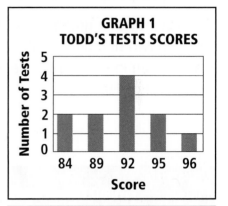

GRAPH 1
TODD'S TESTS SCORES

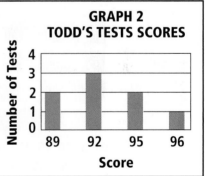

GRAPH 2
TODD'S TESTS SCORES

Maintain Skills

9. What is the value of the blue digit in 5,478?

10. Count the units to find the perimeter.

11. Multiply. 46 × 7

CRCT Test Prep

12. (M4A1.c.) Find the value of 7 + (9 − △) if △ = 4 (p. 46)

A. 2   C. 12
B. 5   D. 35

13. (M4N2.a.) Which is 7,098 rounded to the nearest hundred? (p. 32)

A. 7,100   C. 7,000
B. 7,090   D. 6,900

LESSON

3 Compare Graphs

M4D1.c. Compare different graphical representations for a given set of data. *also* **M4D1.a., M4D1.b., M4P2.a., M4P2.b., M4P2.c., M4P2.d., M4P3, M4P3.a., M4P3.b., M4P3.c., M4P3.d., M4P5.a., M4P5.b., M4P5.c.**

▶ Learn

RAISE THE BAR Graphs A and B show the same data. However, the graphs look different.

The **scale** of a graph is a series of numbers placed at fixed, or equal, distances. Both graphs have a scale of 0–50. The highest value of the scale should be greater than the greatest value of the data.

The **interval** of a graph is the difference between two numbers on the scale. Graph A's scale has an interval of 5. Graph B's scale has an interval of 10.

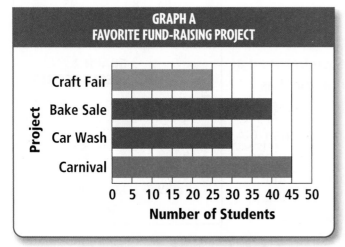

• Why is it easier to compare the bars in Graph A?

▶ Check

1. **Explain** why the lengths of the bars in Graph A and the lengths of the bars in Graph B are different.

For 2–3, explain how the lengths of the bars would change in Graph B above.

2. if the interval were 20

3. if the interval were 2

70

Quick Review

1. $349 + 690$

2. $921 - 487$

3. $14 + \blacksquare + 6 = 38$

4. 3×4 5. 5×8

VOCABULARY

scale   interval

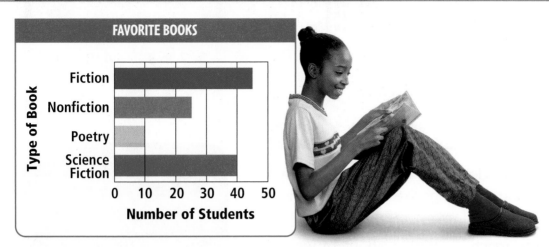

FAVORITE BOOKS

For 4–7, explain how the lengths of the bars would change in the graph above.

4. if the interval were 1

5. if the interval were 2

6. if the interval were 20

7. if the interval were 25

8. What book type is the favorite as shown in the graph above?

9. What is the scale of the graph above?

For 10–13, choose 5, 10, or 100 as the most reasonable interval for each set of data. Explain your choice.

10. 5, 16, 20, 11, 15

11. 15, 31, 48, 30, 69

12. 100, 200, 200, 450, 500, 300

13. 32, 50, 89, 60, 101

For 14–16, use the graph above.

14. Make a new graph with an interval of 5. Explain how the lengths of the bars changed.

15. Write a problem with an answer of 25, using the data from the graph.

16. **REASONING** Josef's choice had 15 more votes than nonfiction. Zoe's choice had the fewest votes. Ali's choice was different from Josef's and Zoe's, but it was not fiction. What did each student choose?

Maintain Skills

17. Kay takes the bus to work. Which unit of measure would Kay use to describe the distance she travels to work?

18. Jen has 15 marbles. Jim has 3 times as many marbles as Jen. How many marbles does Jim have?

CRCT Test Prep

19. **M4A1.b.** Which expression best shows this statement? (p. 46)
Claude had 9 eggs. He used some and then bought 12 more eggs.

A. $9 - \triangle + 12$ C. $9 + \triangle + 12$
B. $9 - \triangle - 12$ D. $\triangle - 9 - 12$

Problem Solving Skill
Use a Graph

M4D1.a. Represent data in bar, line, and pictographs. *also* **M4P1.a.,** **M4P1.b., M4P1.c., M4P1.d., M4P2.a., M4P2.b., M4P2.c., M4P2.d., M4P3.b.,** **M4P3.c., M4P4, M4P5.c.**

UNDERSTAND ⟩ PLAN ⟩ SOLVE ⟩ CHECK ⟩

FISH TALES You can determine the age of a fish by its scales, which have growth rings like trees. Each ring represents 1 year.

The life span of a French angelfish is about 14 years, and the life span of a queen parrotfish is about 5 years. The life span of a queen triggerfish is about 12 years, and the life span of a coney is about 4 years. Which two fish have the greatest difference in life spans?

You can make and use a pictograph to compare the life spans of the fish.

- Choose a title that tells about the graph.
- Label each row with the name of a fish.
- Look at the number of years each fish lives. Choose a key to tell how many each picture represents.
- Place the number of pictures you need next to the name of each fish.

The pictograph shows that the French angelfish has the longest lifespan. The coney has the shortest lifespan.

So, the French angelfish and the coney have the greatest difference in life spans.

Talk About It

- How can you use the pictograph to find the difference in life spans of the French angelfish and the coney?
- How can you use the pictograph to find the life span of the queen parrotfish?

LIFE SPANS OF FISH

Type of Fish	Life Span (in years)
French angelfish	🐟 🐟 🐟 🐟 🐟 🐟 🐟
Queen parrotfish	🐟 🐟 🐟
Queen triggerfish	🐟 🐟 🐟 🐟 🐟 🐟
Coney	🐟 🐟

Key: Each 🐟 = 2 years.

Technology Link

More Practice: Harcourt Mega Math The Number Games, *ArachnaGraph*, Level C

Problem Solving Practice

1. **What if** you wanted to add the bonefish to your pictograph? The bonefish has a life span of about 10 years. How many symbols would you use on your pictograph for this fish?

2. Use the pictograph on page 72. Order the names of the fish with the least life span to the greatest life span.

USE DATA For 3–4, use the pictograph.

3. How many trees were planted by the third, fourth, and fifth graders at Tate School?

   A 20   **C** 24
   B 23   **D** 25

4. If the sixth graders at Tate School planted 11 trees, how many symbols would be on the pictograph for the sixth grade?

   F $5\frac{1}{2}$ **H** 11
   G $6\frac{1}{2}$ **J** 22

TREES PLANTED BY TATE SCHOOL

NUMBER OF TREES

Third grade	🌲🌲🌲🌲
Fourth grade	🌲🌲🌲🌲🌲
Fifth grade	🌲🌲🌲🌲

Key: Each 🌲 = 2 trees.

Mixed Applications

5. Henri found that 986 people went to a movie on Friday, 1,453 people went on Saturday, and 1,622 went on Sunday. How many people went to the movie in all?

6. Scientists tagged 487 rainbow trout in a lake. They also tagged 321 brown trout. About how many more rainbow trout did they tag?

7. **MULTISTEP** There are 57 shirts. Twenty of them are blue, 12 of them are green, and the others are yellow. How many shirts are yellow?

8. **MULTISTEP** Rogers Elementary School has 286 students. Of those, 124 walk to school, and 28 ride their bikes. The rest of the students ride a school bus. How many students ride a school bus?

9. Carmen bought a shirt for $14.99. She bought a sweater for $25.39. About how much did Carmen spend?

10. There are 11 students going to the science museum. Each driver will take 3 students. How many drivers are needed to take the students?

Extra Practice

Set A (pp. 64–67)

Use the frequency table.

1. During which hour were the most cups of juice sold?

2. How many total cups of juice were sold?

3. What is the difference between the greatest number of cups of juice sold and the least number of cups of juice sold in 1 hour?

CUPS OF JUICE SOLD AT THE FESTIVAL	
Hour	**Frequency**
1	15
2	26
3	28
4	19

Set B (pp. 68–69)

Use the graph and the following data.

Bill listed the number of runs scored in his last ten games: 3, 6, 1, 1, 5, 3, 2, 1, 4, 3

1. Does the graph correctly show the number of runs scored in Bill's last ten games? Explain.

2. Make a new graph to show the data correctly.

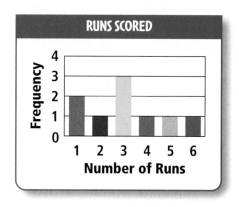

Set C (pp. 70–71)

Use the graph.

1. What is the scale of the graph? What is the interval?

2. How would the lengths of the bars change if the interval were 10? if it were 3?

3. Suppose Computer Games were added to the graph and 92 students chose it as their favorite activity. How could the scale and interval of the graph be changed to include the new data?

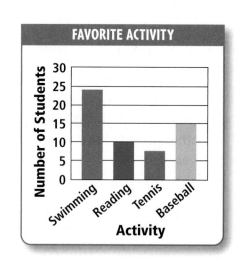

Review/Test

✅ CHECK VOCABULARY AND CONCEPTS

Choose the best term from the box.

1. You are taking a _?_ when you ask several people the same questions and record their answers. (p. 64)

2. The _?_ of a graph is a series of numbers placed at fixed, or equal, distances. (p. 70)

✅ CHECK SKILLS

For 3–4, use the frequency table. (pp. 64–67)

CANS OF FOOD COLLECTED	
Week	Frequency
1	10
2	12
3	14
4	18

3. How many cans were collected in all?

4. How many more cans were collected in Weeks 1 and 2 than in Week 4?

For 5–7, use the graph. (pp. 70–71)

5. What is the scale of the graph?

6. How would the bars change if the interval were 5?

7. Make a new graph with an interval of 20.

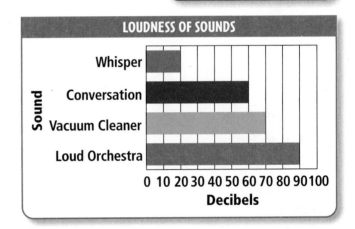

✅ CHECK PROBLEM SOLVING

For 8–10, use the table. (pp. 72–73)

8. The table shows the number of games won by a hockey team from 2003 to 2006. Use the data in the table to make a pictograph. Decide on a key, and give your pictograph a title.

9. Between which two years did the number of games won increase the most?

10. How many games did the Sharks win in all from 2003 to 2006?

SHARKS' WIN RECORD	
Year	Games Won
2003	35
2004	40
2005	30
2006	45

Chapter CRCT Test Prep

DATA ANALYSIS

Use the bar graph below to answer question 1.

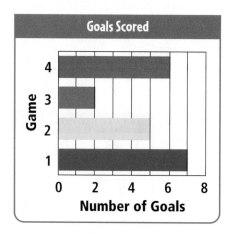

1. **M4D1.b.** What is the scale of the graph?

   A. 0 to 4

   B. 1 to 4

   C. 0 to 7

   D. 0 to 8

Use the pictograph key below to answer question 2.

Key: Each 🔵 = 2 Marbles

2. **M4D1.a.** How many marble symbols would show that Marty has 9 tri-color marbles?

   A. 4

   B. $4\frac{1}{2}$

   C. 9

   D. 18

DATA ANALYSIS

Use the bar graph below to answer question 3.

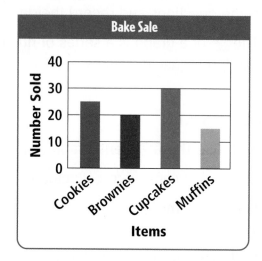

3. **M4D1.c.** How would the bars change if the interval were 5?

   A. The bars would be longer.

   B. The bars would be shorter.

   C. The bars would be wider.

   D. The bars would be thinner.

4. **M4D1.b.** Amy is making a bar graph using the data below.

   2, 2, 4, 8, 10, 14, 6, 6, 12

   Which interval is the MOST reasonable one for Amy to use?

   A. 1

   B. 2

   C. 6

   D. 10

Cumulative CRCT Test Prep

NUMBERS AND OPERATIONS

5. **M4N1.b.** What is three million, forty-two thousand, one in standard form?

   A. 342,001

   B. 3,042,001

   C. 3,402,001

   D. 3,420,001

6. **M4N2.a.** Which number is 13,517 rounded to the nearest thousand?

   A. 14,000

   B. 13,520

   C. 13,500

   D. 13,000

Use the table below to answer question 7.

Brooklyn Bridge	
Description	**Length (feet)**
Total length	5,989
Length of river span	1,596
Length of one cable	3,579

7. **M4N7.d.** About how much longer is the total length of the bridge than one of the cables?

   A. 2,000 feet

   B. 3,000 feet

   C. 4,000 feet

   D. 4,400 feet

ALGEBRA

8. **M4A1.a.** Sasha has a new job. She earns $3 on Monday. On each day after that, she earns $3 more than she did the day before. How much will Sasha earn on Friday?

Money Earned				
Mon	**Tue**	**Wed**	**Thu**	**Fri**
$3	$6	☐	☐	☐

   A. $9

   B. $10

   C. $12

   D. $15

9. **M4A1.b.** Jack has 45 baseball cards. Let ☐ represent the number of baseball cards Jack gives to Mae. Which expression represents how many baseball cards Jack has left?

   A. 45 + ☐

   B. 45 − ☐

   C. 45 ÷ ☐

   D. 45 × ☐

10. **M4A1.b.** Alicia had $15. She bought a movie ticket for $5 and spent some money on refreshments at the movies. Which expression shows how much money she has left?

   A. $15 − $5 + △

   B. $15 + $5 + △

   C. $15 − $5 − △

   D. $15 + $5 − △

Analyze and Graph Data

=FAST FACT • SCIENCE

Lightning flashes occur somewhere on Earth more than 100 times every second. Scientists measure the number of lightning flashes during storms.

INVESTIGATION The bar graph shows the greatest number of lightning flashes per square mile measured in each of 8 states during a storm. What conclusion can you draw from the graph? What other type of graph could you use to show the data? Explain your choice.

Using Data

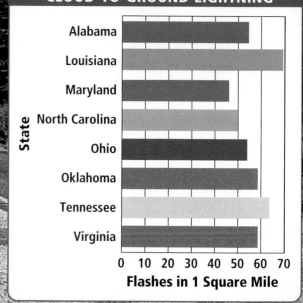

CLOUD-TO-GROUND LIGHTNING

State	Flashes in 1 Square Mile
Alabama	
Louisiana	
Maryland	
North Carolina	
Ohio	
Oklahoma	
Tennessee	
Virginia	

0 10 20 30 40 50 60 70

Flashes in 1 Square Mile

Use this page to help you review and remember important skills needed for Chapter 4.

✓ PARTS OF A GRAPH

For 1–3, use the first bar graph.

1. What is the title of this graph?

2. What label would you place at the bottom?

3. What label would you place at the left side?

✓ READ BAR GRAPHS

For 4–7, use the second bar graph.

4. Which way of going to school is used by the most students?

5. How many students ride to school in a car?

6. How many students were surveyed for this bar graph?

7. How many students go to school by car or by bicycle?

FAVORITE PLACES TO VISIT

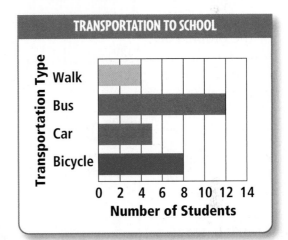

TRANSPORTATION TO SCHOOL

VOCABULARY POWER

REVIEW

graph [graf] *noun*

The word *graph* comes from the Greek word *graphein,* which means "to write." To the Greeks, writings also included drawings, carvings, and scratchings. How do these meanings relate to pictographs?

PREVIEW

- double-bar graph
- coordinate system
- ordered pair
- *x*-axis
- *y*-axis
- *x*-coordinate
- *y*-coordinate
- line graph
- trends

 GO ON-LINE www.harcourtschool.com/mathglossary

Make Bar and Double-Bar Graphs

M4D1.a. Represent data in bar, line, and pictographs. *also* M4P2.a., M4P2.b., M4P2.c., M4P2.d., M4P3.a., M4P3.b., M4P3.c., M4P3.d., M4P4.a., M4P4.b., M4P4.c., M4P5.a., M4P5.b., M4P5.c.

▶ **Explore**

Double-bar graphs are used to compare similar types of data. Make a double-bar graph that shows the data from the table.

VOCABULARY

double-bar graph

Activity

MATERIALS: bar-graph pattern, two different-colored crayons

STEP 1

Decide on a title, labels, and a scale for the graph. For these data, use a scale of 0–16 with an interval of 4.

MONTHLY SNOWFALL (in inches)			
City	Jan	Feb	Mar
Chicago	11	8	7
Cleveland	12	12	10

Technology Link

More Practice: Harcourt Mega Math The Number Games, *ArachnaGraph*, Levels C and D

STEP 2

Make the graph. Use one color for Chicago and another color for Cleveland. Make a key to show which color stands for each city.

MONTHLY SNOWFALL (in inches)

Inches / Month

Key: ■ Chicago ■ Cleveland

What scale and interval should I use for my Favorite Winter Activity graph?

• What does the graph show about the monthly snowfall in Chicago and Cleveland?

Try It

• Use the table to make a double-bar graph comparing the data for boys and girls.

FAVORITE WINTER ACTIVITY		
Activity	Boys	Girls
Sledding	77	60
Ice-skating	35	78
Skiing	75	70

▶ Connect

The data from the "Favorite Winter Activity" table on page 80 are shown in the two bar graphs below. The same labels, intervals, and scales are used for both graphs. A key is not needed when the data are graphed separately.

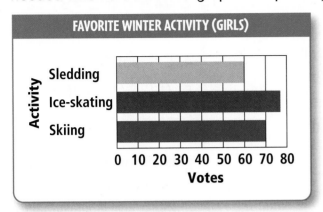

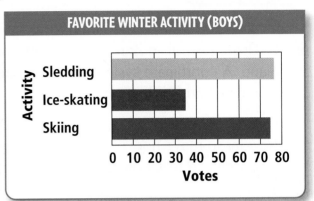

▶ Practice and Problem Solving

For 1–4, use the table.

1. Make a bar graph for each grade to compare the data for the two classes.

2. Make a double-bar graph to compare the data for the two classes.

3. Which graph makes it easier to compare the data for the two classes? Explain.

4. **REASONING** Conduct a survey of 40 fourth graders to determine their favorite events. Make a triple-bar graph using the data and the table above. What is the total number of third, fourth, and fifth graders surveyed?

FAVORITE WINTER OLYMPIC EVENT		
Event	Third Graders	Fifth Graders
Bobsledding	17	15
Ski jumping	14	16
Figure skating	9	10

5. **≡FAST FACT • SOCIAL STUDIES**
During the 2002 Winter Olympics, the United States won 10 gold medals, 13 silver medals, and 11 bronze medals. Germany won 12 gold, 16 silver, and 7 bronze medals. Make a double-bar graph to show the data.

Maintain Skills

6. What is the perimeter of the rectangle?

```
        10 ft
      ┌──────┐
4 ft  │      │  4 ft
      └──────┘
        10 ft
```

7. $6\overline{)75}$ 8. 9×8

CRCT Test Prep

9. **M4N1.a.** What is the value of the digit 6 in 48,602,751? (p. 6)

   A.   600
   B.   6,000
   C.   60,000
   D. 600,000

2 Use a Coordinate System

M4G3.a. Understand and apply ordered pairs in the first quadrant of the coordinate system. *also* **M4G3.b., M4G3.c., M4P3.a., M4P3.b., M4P3.c., M4P3.d.**

▶ **Learn**

A **coordinate system** is a method for locating points. Use an **ordered pair** (*x,y*) to name points in a plane. A coordinate system has an ***x*-axis** (a horizontal line) and a ***y*-axis** (a vertical line).

In an ordered pair such as (*x,y*), the ***x*-coordinate** tells how far to move horizontally along the *x*-axis. The ***y*-coordinate** tells how far to move vertically along the *y*-axis.

(5,9)
x-coordinate ⌐ ⌐ *y*-coordinate

Quick Review

Find the value of each expression.

1. 3 + □ if □ = 6
2. 24 − △ if △ = 3
3. ★ − 4 if ★ = 12
4. □ − 9 if □ = 11
5. (13 + △) − 8 if △ = 7

VOCABULARY

▸ **coordinate system   *y*-axis**

▸ **ordered pair   *x*-coordinate**

** *x*-axis   *y*-coordinate**

Example 1   A gardener used a coordinate system to locate where she planted each type of flower. What did she plant at (7,3)?

STEP 1

Start at 0. Count 7 units horizontally.

STEP 2

Then count 3 units vertically.

So, the gardener planted tulips at (7,3).

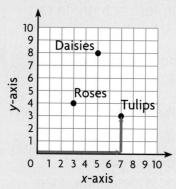

Example 2   What ordered pair tells where the roses are?

STEP 1

Start at the point labeled Roses. Look down at the *x*-axis. It is 3 units to the right of 0. The *x*-coordinate is 3.

STEP 2

Then look across at the *y*-axis. It is 4 units up from 0. The *y*-coordinate is 4.

So, the ordered pair (3,4) tells where the roses are.

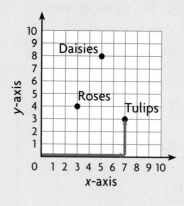

• What plane figure is shown if the points are connected?

1. **Explain** how to locate a point at (6,5).

2. **Name** the ordered pair that locates the daisies in the coordinate system on page 82.

Graph each ordered pair in a coordinate system.

3. (2,2)   **4.** (6,5)   **5.** (3,4)   **6.** (8,1)   **7.** (10,10)   **8.** (1,8)

Write the ordered pair for each object in the coordinate system.

9. tree

10. playhouse

11. swings

12. wading pool

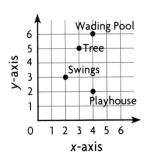

Technology Link

More Practice: Harcourt Mega Math The Number Games, *ArachnaGraph*, Levels G and H

▶ **Practice and Problem Solving**   Extra Practice, page 98, Set A

Graph each ordered pair in a coordinate system.

13. (1,5)   **14.** (1,3)   **15.** (5,1)   **16.** (4,9)   **17.** (0,7)   **18.** (4,1)

Write the ordered pair for each point in the coordinate system.

19. point A **20.** point B

21. point C **22.** point D

23. point E **24.** point F

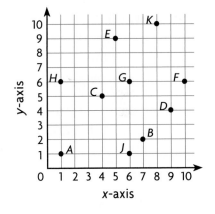

25. Which lettered points in the coordinate system form a square when connected? Which points form an isosceles triangle?

26. Susan graphed the points (2,1), (2,4), and (4,4) in a coordinate system. What point should she plot next if she wants the points to be the vertices of a rectangle?

Maintain Skills

27. What is the value of the blue digit in 93,410?

28. Which length is greater, 2 inches or 2 feet?

29. Paul has 48 trading cards. He puts them in piles of 5. How many cards are left over?

CRCT Test Prep

30. **M4A1.c.** Which expression has a value of 33 when ☐ = 11? (p. 46)

A. (32 + ☐) − 10

B. 42 + (☐ − 10)

C. (18 − 10) + ☐

D. 32 − (10 + ☐)

Read Line Graphs

M4D1.a. Represent data in bar, line, and pictographs. *also* M4D1.b., M4P3.a., M4P3.b., M4P3.c., M4P3.d.

▶ Learn

READ BETWEEN THE LINES You can show how data change over a period of time by using a **line graph**. You graph points on a line graph the same way you graph points in a coordinate system.

Example 1

Look at the graph. The line connecting the points shows the changes in snowfall amounts for each month. What is the snowfall amount for December?

STEP 1

Find the grid line labeled December. Follow that line up to the point (•).

STEP 2

Follow that grid line to the scale on the left to locate the snowfall amount for December.

So, the snowfall amount for December is 30 inches.

Example 2

Find the difference between the greatest and the least values of the data.

STEP 1

Look at the graph to find the greatest value and the least value.

30 inches ←greatest value

3 inches ←least value

STEP 2

Subtract the least value from the greatest value to find the difference.

$$\begin{array}{r} 30 \\ -\ 3 \\ \hline 27 \end{array}$$

So, the difference between the least and the greatest snowfall amounts is 27 inches.

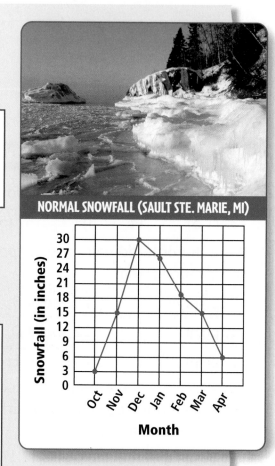

NORMAL SNOWFALL (SAULT STE. MARIE, MI)

In the Ski Club Membership line graph, you can see **trends**, or areas where the data increase, decrease, or stay the same over time. An increase in membership is seen between 2005 and 2006.

SKI CLUB MEMBERSHIP

For 1–4, use the line graph at the right.

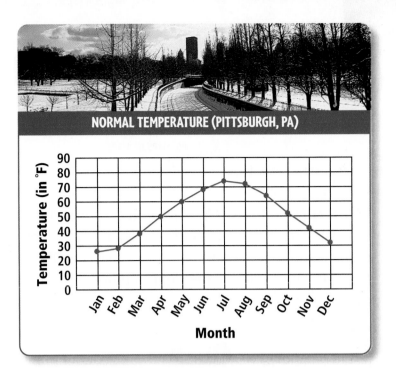

NORMAL TEMPERATURE (PITTSBURGH, PA)

1. **Name** the two months shown on the line graph between which the normal temperature increases from 39°F to 50°F.

2. What is the lowest normal temperature for Pittsburgh?

3. What month has the highest normal temperature?

4. Compare the February temperature to the June temperature.

Practice and Problem Solving | Extra Practice, page 98, Set B

For 5–7, use the line graph at the right.

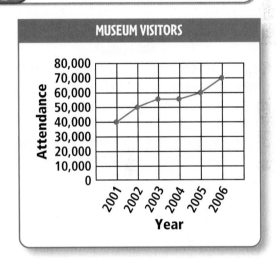

5. How many people visited the museum in the year with the lowest attendance?

6. About how many people visited the museum from 2001 through 2006?

7. Between which two years did the attendance stay about the same?

8. ✏️ **Write a problem** using the temperature data for Pittsburgh, PA.

Maintain Skills

9. Use the model to find the sum 0.24 + 0.17.

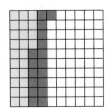

CRCT Test Prep

10. **M4N2.a.** There were 12,375 fans at a hockey game. What is the number rounded to the nearest thousand? (p. 32)

A. 12,000   C. 12,400

B. 12,300   D. 13,000

Make Line Graphs

HANDS ON

M4D1.a. Represent data in bar, line, and pictographs. *also* **M4G3.b., M4G3.c., M4P3.a., M4P3.b., M4P3.c., M4P3.d., M4P5, M4P5.b., M4P5.c.**

▶ Explore

LIGHTNING DISTANCE Have you ever wondered how far away from you a strike of lightning is? You can count seconds to find the distance. Use the Distance from Lightning table at the right to make a line graph.

Activity 1

STEP 1

Choose a scale and an interval for the time data. Write the scale numbers along the left side of the graph. Write the labels and title on the graph.

STEP 2

Plot a point to show each distance and the number of seconds until the thunder is heard. Connect the points from left to right.

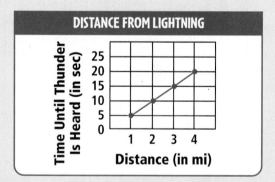

DISTANCE FROM LIGHTNING	
Distance (in mi)	Time Until Thunder Is Heard (in sec)
1	5
2	10
3	15
4	20

Try It

• You also can determine the distance lightning is from you in kilometers. Every three seconds equals one kilometer. Make a line graph of the data. Be sure to title and label your graph. Choose an appropriate interval and scale.

DISTANCE FROM LIGHTNING	
Distance (in km)	Time Until Thunder Is Heard (in sec)
1	3
2	6
3	9
4	12

► Connect

Each point on a line graph can be described by the horizontal and vertical labels. The first point on the graph at the right can be described as Monday and 1 cm.

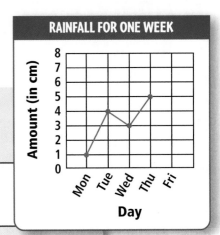

RAINFALL FOR ONE WEEK

Activity 2

Graph a point on the line graph for Friday and 2 cm.

STEP 1

Copy the graph. Find Friday on the horizontal scale, and go up until you reach 2 cm on the vertical scale.

STEP 2

Plot a point on your graph where these horizontal and vertical grid lines meet. Then connect the point for Thursday to the point for Friday.

► Practice and Problem Solving

For 1–2, make a line graph.

1.

STEVE'S PLANT					
Week	1	2	3	4	5
Height (in inches)	1	2	3	4	5

2.

LEON'S PLANT					
Week	1	2	3	4	5
Height (in inches)	0	1	3	5	6

3. Copy the graph at the right. Graph the following points: Monday and 4 cm, Tuesday and 3 cm, Wednesday and 5 cm, Thursday and 1 cm, and Friday and 0 cm.

4. **MULTISTEP** Look at the graph from Exercise 3. Is the rain total for Monday through Friday greater than or less than 10 cm?

5. ✏️ **Write About It** Explain how you can describe a point on a line graph.

RAIN IN MIAMI

Maintain Skills

6. Write an addition problem that you can use to find 5×4.

7. Which digit is in the thousands place in 30,792?

8. $9\overline{)270}$ 9. 7×8

CRCT Test Prep

10. **M4A1.b.** Which expression shows that Luisa bought 8 muffins and then ate some of them? (p. 46)

   A. $8 - \square$ C. $\square + 8$

   B. $\square - 8$ D. $\square - 8 - \square$

Analyze Graphs

M4D1.b. Investigate the features and tendencies of graphs.
also **M4P5.b., M4P5.c.**

Quick Review

Give the next number in the pattern.

1. 3, 5, 7, __

2. 4, 8, 12, 16, __

3. 11, 14, 17, 20, __

4. 25, 20, 15, 10, __

5. 64, 68, 72, __

LINE UP! The bar graph shows how many people are in five ticket lines at the cineplex. The manager wants to make all the lines the same length. How many people will be in each line then?

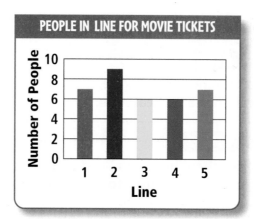

PEOPLE IN LINE FOR MOVIE TICKETS

Example 1

Use a model.

You can move people from longer lines to shorter lines so that there will be an equal number of people in each line. When one person moves from line 2 to line 3 and another person moves from line 2 to line 4, then all the lines have an equal number of people.

So, if each line has an equal number of people, there will be 7 people in each line.

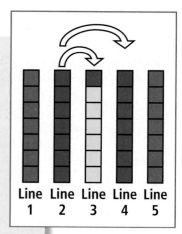

Line Line Line Line Line
1   2   3   4   5

Example 2

The pictograph below shows how many students saw four different types of movies. Which number of students occurs the most often in the data?

MOVIE ATTENDANCE	
Comedy	👤 👤 👤 👤
Spy movie	👤 👤 👤 👤 👤
Science fiction	👤 👤 👤 👤
Animated	👤 👤 👤

Key: Each 👤 = 6 students.

Each 👤 stands for 6 students. The graph shows that both the comedy and the science fiction movie had 24 students, the spy movie had 30 students, and the animated movie had 18 students.

So, the number 24 occurs the most often in the data.

Features of a Graph

The bar graph shows how many people were at five different movie screenings on Saturday. Which number shows the middle number of people who went to the movies on Saturday?

To find the middle number, first arrange the data in order from least to greatest:

125, 125, 140, 150, 175

Then find the number in the data with an equal number of items on either side of it.

Since there are two numbers to the left of 140 and two numbers to the right of 140, the middle number is 140. So, the middle number of people who went to the movies on Saturday is 140.

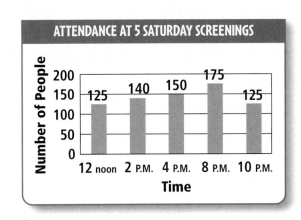

ATTENDANCE AT 5 SATURDAY SCREENINGS

MATH IDEA You can analyze data in graphs to find different types of information to help you draw conclusions and answer questions.

Check

1. **Explain** how to find the middle number for the number of people in line for movie tickets as shown in the bar graph on page 88.

   USE DATA For 2–3, use the bar graph on this page. For 4–5, use the pictograph on page 88.

2. What is the difference in attendance between the screenings that had the most people and the least people?

3. Which number occurs the most in the data?

4. How many more students saw a spy movie than a comedy?

5. **What if** the data from the graph is rearranged so an equal number of students went to see each of the different types of movies?

LESSON CONTINUES ▶

USE DATA For 6–9, use the line graph.

6. Drive-in theaters were popular years ago. What trend do you see in the number of drive-in theaters in Georgia?

7. How many more drive-in theaters were in Georgia in the 1970s than in the 1990s?

8. Estimate the difference between the greatest number and the least number of drive-in theaters in Georgia from 1950 through 2000.

9. Between which two years shown on the graph did the number of drive-ins change the most? Describe the change.

USE DATA For 10–13, use the bar graph.

10. What is the total number of drive-in theaters for the selected states?

11. How many drive-in theaters would be in each of the selected states if the total remained the same but each state had an equal number of theaters?

12. What is the middle number of drive-in theaters in the selected states?

13. How many more drive-in theaters are in Tennessee than in South Carolina?

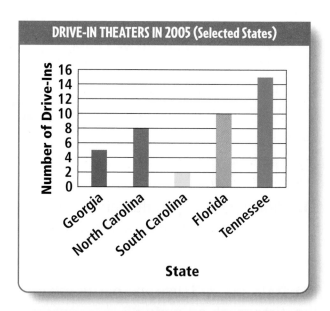

USE DATA For 14–17, use the pictograph.

14. What is the difference between the prices of the most expensive student ticket and the least expensive student ticket?

15. Which price occurs the most in the data?

16. What is the middle price for the data shown?

17. If Theater 3 raises the price of a student ticket by $3, then what would be the middle price for a student ticket?

PRICES OF STUDENT TICKETS AT THE CINEPLEX

Theater 1	$ $ $
Theater 2	$ $ $
Theater 3	$ $ $
Theater 4	$ $ $ $
Theater 5	$ $ $ $

Key: Each $ = $2.00

18. 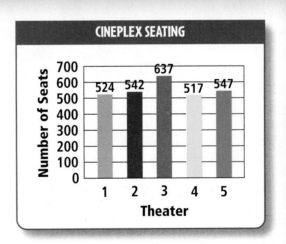 **Write a problem** with an answer of 3, based on the bar graph of Drive-In Movie Theaters in 2005 on page 90.

19. **Write About It** Explain how to find the middle number for a set of data.

Maintain Skills

20. What is the value of the digit 3 in 30,142?

21. 56 ÷ 2   **22.** 107 × 3

Write the correct unit.

23. Hector is 10 years old and about 5 _____ tall.

CRCT Test Prep

24. **M4A1.c.** What is the value of 15 + (9 − □) if □ = 4? (p. 46)

A. 24
B. 20
C. 10
D. 2

Problem Solving **LINKUP** . . . to Technology

STRATEGY · ORDER NUMBERS When you want to find the number that is in the middle of a data set, you must first order the numbers. You can use a spreadsheet program to order a list of data.

- Enter the data in two columns on a spreadsheet, and highlight all the data.

- Click *Data*. Then click *Sort*.

- You can then select a column by which to sort. To sort the list of data by number of seats, select Column B.

- Select whether you want to sort the list into *ascending* or *descending* order. To order from least to greatest, select *ascending*.

1. What is the middle number in the data?

2. Suppose that a Theater 6 had 610 seats and a Theater 7 had 562 seats. Use a spreadsheet to order the numbers, and find the middle number of the new data.

CINEPLEX SEATING

Theater	Number of Seats
1	524
2	542
3	637
4	517
5	547

	A	B	C
1	Theater 4	517	
2	Theater 1	524	
3	Theater 2	542	
4	Theater 5	547	
5	Theater 3	637	

Choose an Appropriate Graph

 M4D1.c. Compare different graphical representations for a given set of data. *also* **M4D1.b., M4P4.c., M4P5.b., M4P5.c.**

▶ **Learn**

NATURE NAP Some animals sleep most of the day, and others hardly sleep at all. Look at how Cindy and Elayna showed the data in the table. Which graph correctly displays the data?

HOURS OF SLEEP	
Animal	**Hours of Sleep in a Day**
Giraffe	4
Raccoon	13
Squirrel	14
Bear	8

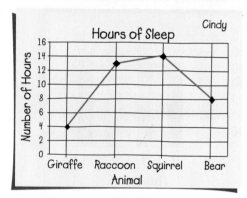

A line graph is used to show changes over time.

A bar graph is used to compare data about different groups.

The data show the number of hours different animals sleep each day. The line graph is not appropriate. The data do not show changes over time. So, Elayna's bar graph correctly displays the data.

• What other type of graph would be good for the data? Explain.

Bar Graph or Pictograph

The type of graph you choose usually depends on the type of information that you want to show.

Elsa recorded the number of dogs she groomed each week for nine weeks. She displayed the data in two different ways.

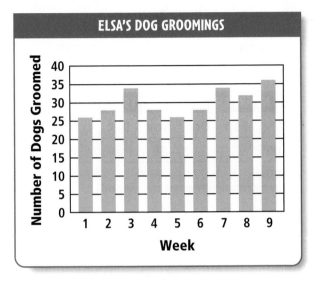

ELSA'S DOG GROOMINGS

Number of Dogs Groomed	Number of Times Groomed
26 dogs	🦴
28 dogs	🦴 🦴
32 dogs	🦴
34 dogs	🦴
36 dogs	🦴

Key: Each 🦴 = 2 times.

Elsa's pictograph shows the number of dogs groomed in one week, but the bar graph shows the week in which each number of dogs was groomed.

- **REASONING** Which display is better for finding how many times Elsa groomed 28 dogs? Explain.

▶ Check

1. **Choose** which display Elsa should use to show that she groomed the most dogs in Week 9. Explain your choice.

2. **Explain** the differences in the types of information shown in a bar graph, a pictograph, and a line graph.

For 3–6, write the type of graph you would choose.

3. to compare the speeds of five different animals

4. to show the votes that each candidate received in an election

5. to show your weekly math grades

6. to show your heights each year since birth

7. Lyn found that there were 9 cars, 4 vans, 6 bikes, and 1 bus on a street. Would a pictograph or a line graph be a better choice for Lyn's data?

8. The temperature was recorded each hour from 6 A.M. to 6 P.M. Would a bar graph or a line graph be a better choice to show the data?

9. ✍ **Write About It** Explain which display would be easier to use to find the middle number of dogs that Elsa groomed.

LESSON CONTINUES

For 10–17, write the type of graph you would choose.

10. to compare the favorite subjects of students in two fourth-grade classes

11. to show the number of soccer goals scored by each team member

12. to keep a record of plant growth

13. to show monthly temperatures

14. to show the favorite sports of students in fourth grade

15. to compare the favorite ice cream flavors of students in two classes

16.

RHONDA'S ALLOWANCE	
Activity	**Amount**
Movies	$5
Snack	$2
Skating	$3

17.

NUMBER OF NEW STUDENTS				
	Sep	**Oct**	**Nov**	**Dec**
2003	31	11	10	6
2004	18	22	2	10

For 18–21, use the bar graph and the pictograph.

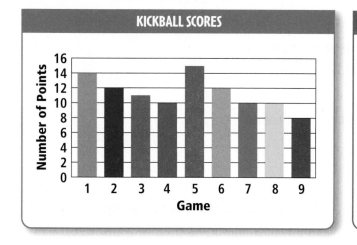

18. Which display shows how many points the team scored in the third game?

19. In which game did the team score more points than in the first game? How many more points were scored?

20. What is the team's middle score? What is the score that occurs the most?

21. In how many games did the team score more than 10 points?

22. Vocabulary Power A pictograph is a graph that shows data with pictures. The word *pictograph* also refers to an ancient drawing or painting on a rock wall. Tell how the two meanings are alike.

23. Collect data about the languages spoken by students in your class. Choose the best type of graph to display your data. Make the graph.

24. ✎ **Write About It** Write a question, and survey 20 students. Choose and make an appropriate display for the data. Tell why you chose that type of display.

25. NUMBER SENSE The least two-digit number that rounds to 100 is 50. What is the least three-digit number that rounds to 1,000? What is the greatest four-digit number that rounds to 1,000?

26. MULTISTEP A total of 2,615 concert tickets was sold from Monday through Wednesday. If 543 tickets were sold on Monday and 876 tickets were sold on Tuesday, how many more tickets were sold on Wednesday than on Tuesday?

Maintain Skills

27. What is the length of the battery to the nearest $\frac{1}{4}$ inch?

28. Each of Jo's 2 show dogs has won 7 blue ribbons. How many blue ribbons have the dogs won?

CRCT Test Prep

29. **M4N1.b.** What is three hundred eleven thousand, sixty-three in standard form? (p. 4)

   A. 300,011,063
   B.   311,163
   C.   311,063
   D.   301,163

Problem Solving THINKER'S CORNER

A scientist recorded notes about the lengths of animal tails. Help the scientist make inferences and predictions.

When you make an **inference,** you draw conclusions based on information you have.

When you make a **prediction,** you guess what might happen based on information you have.

1. Use the notes to make inferences and to complete the table.

2. Predict what the length of a baby African elephant's tail will be when the elephant is full-grown.

3. Tell why you made the prediction you did.

Notes

A. The tails of the red kangaroo, giraffe, and African buffalo are the same length.

B. The Asian elephant's tail is eight inches longer than the African elephant's tail.

C. The leopard's tail is four inches shorter than the Asian elephant's tail.

LENGTHS OF MAMMAL TAILS	
Mammal	Length (in inches)
?	51
?	43
?	59
?	43
?	43
?	55

Problem Solving Skill
Draw Conclusions

 M4D1.b. Investigate the features and tendencies of graphs. *also* M4P2, M4P2.a., M4P2.b., M4P2.c., M4P2.d., M4P3.a., M4P3.b., M4P3.c., M4P3.d., M4P4.c.

UNDERSTAND ➤ PLAN ➤ SOLVE ➤ CHECK

RAINY SEASON Bangladesh is located in Asia on the Indian Ocean. Sometimes the weather is very dry, and sometimes there are heavy rains. During the rainy—or monsoon—season, people often use waterways instead of roads for transportation.

You can use a graph to compare data. Use the data and what you know to answer questions and draw conclusions.

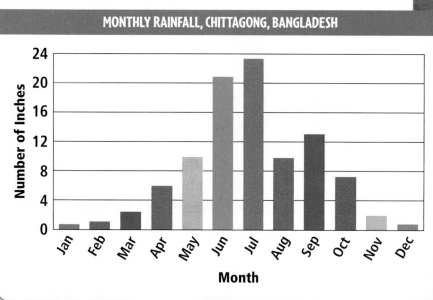

Which months of the year do you think make up the monsoon season?

Monsoon season is a time of very heavy rains. From April to October, Bangladesh usually receives over 5 inches of rain each month. During June and July, monthly rainfall can be greater than 20 inches.

So, June and July probably make up the monsoon season in Bangladesh.

• Estimate the yearly rainfall in Chittagong.

For 1–4, use the graph on page 96.

1. In which two months does Bangladesh receive the most rainfall?

2. In which two months does Bangladesh receive the least rainfall?

3. During which months are the roads in Bangladesh likely to be flooded?

4. Make a double-bar graph to compare the monthly rainfall in Chittagong with the monthly rainfall in your town.

For 5–6, use the graph.

Jennifer made a line graph to show the snowfall from November to March.

5. Which conclusion can you NOT make about the data?
  A More snow fell in January than in February.
  B The snowfall decreased from November to March.
  C Six more inches of snow fell in January than in December.
  D Eighteen inches of snow fell in December.

6. Between which two months was there the greatest change in the amount of snowfall?
  F November and December
  G December and January
  H January and February
  J February and March

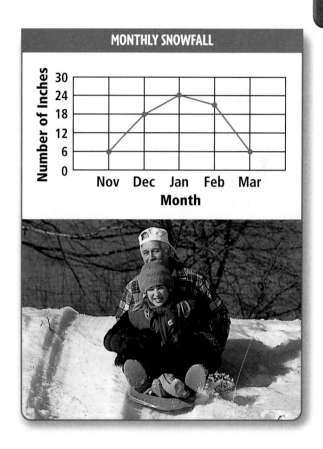

Mixed Applications

7. Mrs. Porter wants to buy one sticker for each of her 32 students. If stickers come in packs of 10, how many packs of stickers will she need to buy? Explain.

8. **REASONING** Write an expression with a value of 893, using only addition and subtraction, but do not use 3, 8, or 9 as digits.

9. **MULTISTEP** Mr. Milo is taking a trip of 731 miles. He travels 458 miles on Saturday and completes the trip on Sunday. How many fewer miles did he travel on Sunday?

10. ✷ **What's the Question?** Look at the Monthly Snowfall line graph. The answer is 18.

Extra Practice

Set A (pp. 82–83)

Write the ordered pair for the point in the coordinate system.

1. point *A*
2. point *B*
3. point *C*
4. point *D*
5. point *E*
6. point *F*

Set B (pp. 84–85)

For 1–3, use the graph.

1. During which week were the most people at the meeting? the fewest?

2. During which weeks were more than 6 people at the meeting?

3. Between which two weeks was there the greatest increase in the number of people at the meeting?

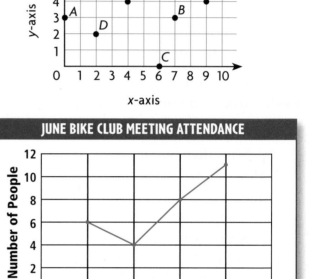

Set C (pp. 88–91)

For 1–2, use the graph.

1. What is the middle number of tomatoes picked during the 5 weeks?

2. What number of tomatoes was picked the most often during the 5 weeks?

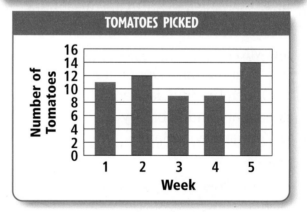

Set D (pp. 92–95)

For 1–4, write the type of graph you would choose.

1. to show your weights each year since birth

2. to show favorite sports seasons

3.

FAVORITE ACTIVITIES				
	Game	Playground	Movie	Puzzle
Boys	7	9	4	2
Girls	5	7	2	3

4.

LEAGUE ATTENDANCE					
Week	1	2	3	4	5
Members	29	21	27	30	24

Review/Test

✔ CHECK VOCABULARY AND CONCEPTS

Choose the best term from the box.

Vocabulary

double-bar graph

line graph

pictograph

coordinate system

1. A graph that uses a line to show how something changes over a period of time is a __?__. (p. 84)

2. A graph used to compare similar types of data is called a __?__. (p. 80)

Write the ordered pair for the point in the coordinate system. (pp. 82–83)

3. point A

4. point C

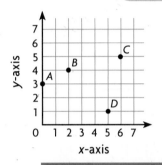

✔ CHECK SKILLS

For 5–6, use the line graph. (pp. 84–85)

5. The line graph shows how many people attended the school fair each year for 4 years. Between which two years did the attendance decrease the most?

6. Which year had the least attendance?

For 7–8, write the type of graph you would choose. (pp. 92–95)

7. to compare the favorite movies of two classes

8. to record the height of a tree during six months

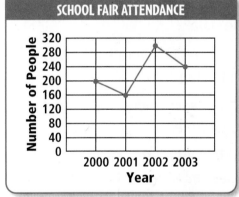

✔ CHECK PROBLEM SOLVING

For 9–10, use the Favorite Animals frequency table. (pp. 80–81, 96–97)

9. Make a double-bar graph to compare the data of the two grades.

10. Can you conclude that more first-grade students like both dogs and horses than do third-grade students? Explain.

FAVORITE ANIMALS		
Animal	First-Grade Students	Third-Grade Students
Cat	3	5
Dog	7	9
Fish	2	7
Horse	9	6

Chapter CRCT Test Prep

DATA ANALYSIS

Use the line graph below to answer question 1.

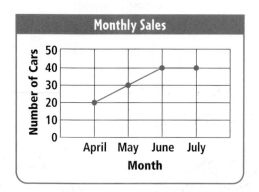

1. **M4D1.b.** Mia made a line graph to show car sales from April to July. Which conclusion can you make about the data?

   A. More cars were sold in April than in May.

   B. Car sales increased from April to June.

   C. Twenty more cars were sold in June than in July.

   D. Car sales in April and July were the same.

2. **M4D1.c.** Bill's school has five after-school clubs. What type of graph would be the BEST to display the number of girls and the number of boys in each club?

   A. bar graph

   B. double-bar graph

   C. line graph

   D. pictograph

GEOMETRY

3. **M4G3.c.** Which point is at (4,7) in the coordinate system?

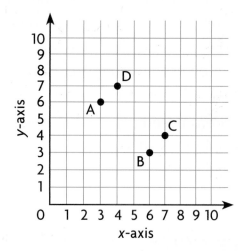

   A. point A

   B. point B

   C. point C

   D. point D

4. **M4G3.b.** What is the ordered pair for point C in the coordinate system?

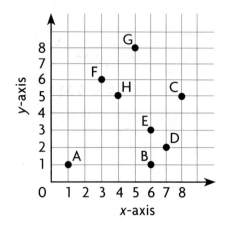

   A. (5,8)

   B. (8,5)

   C. (3,6)

   D. (6,3)

Cumulative CRCT Test Prep

ALGEBRA

5. (M4A1.b.) While fishing in Stone Mountain Lake, Josh caught 7 bass and 5 carp. He threw some fish back because they were too small. Which expression shows how many fish Josh kept?

A. $7 + 5 + \square$

B. $7 + 5 - \square$

C. $7 - 5 + \square$

D. $7 - 5 - \square$

6. (M4A1.a.) What is the rule for the table?

In	16	23	30	37
Out	7	14	21	28

A. Add 7.

B. Add 9.

C. Subtract 7.

D. Subtract 9.

7. (M4A1.c.) What is the value of the expression if $\square = 300$?

$$\square - (134 + 75)$$

A. 91

B. 241

C. 359

D. 509

NUMBERS AND OPERATIONS

8. (M4N7.d.) Rounded to the nearest hundred, which subtraction has a difference of about 2,500?

A. $8,380 - 5,595$

B. $7,279 - 4,509$

C. $5,681 - 3,214$

D. $4,975 - 2,263$

9. (M4N2.a.) Blackbeard Island Wildlife National Refuge has an area of 5,618 acres of forests, marshes, and beaches. What is its area rounded to the nearest hundred?

A. 5,600

B. 5,620

C. 5,700

D. 6,000

10. (M4N1.a.) What is the value of the digit 3 in 430,972?

A.　　30

B.　3,000

C.　30,000

D. 300,000

11. (M4N1.b.) What is the standard form for $20,000 + 5,000 + 300 + 90$?

A.　2,539

B. 20,539

C. 25,309

D. 25,390

GPS/CRCT Vocabulary

ELA4R3 The student understands and acquires vocabulary and uses it correctly in reading and writing.

VOCABULARY

survey	frequency
scale	interval
x-axis	*y*-axis
trends	

line graph

double-bar graph

coordinate system

ordered pair

x-coordinate

y-coordinate

MEET YOUR MATCH

MATERIALS *For each group* 2 Vocabulary Cards, Definition Cards

- Work in a small group made up of two teams. Give one team the definition cards and the other team the vocabulary cards.

- Members of the first team take turns reading a definition aloud. The other team finds and displays the matching vocabulary card.

- Have teams trade cards and repeat the activity.

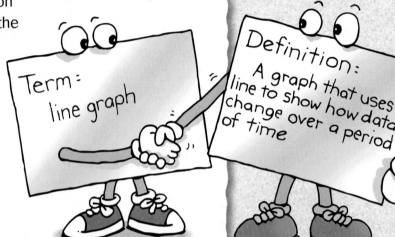

Term: line graph

Definition: A graph that uses a line to show how data change over a period of time

Letter Tally	
A	卌
B	I
C	I
D	I
E	III
F	
G	I
H	
I	IIII

MATH WORD WORK

- For each vocabulary term, make a tally table that shows the number of times each letter occurs in the word.

- Work with your group to make a frequency table that shows the number of times each letter occurs in all 13 words.

HAVE A CLUE

MATERIALS *For each pair* Vocabulary Cards

- Play this game with a partner.
- The first player chooses a vocabulary card without showing it to the other player.
- The first player gives a one-sentence clue about the vocabulary term.
- The second player guesses the vocabulary term. If the guess is not correct, then the first player gives other clues until the vocabulary term is guessed.
- Switch roles and play the game again.

> It has two numbers.

> It is used in a coordinate system.

> The order of the numbers is important.

ordered pair

10 QUESTIONS

MATERIALS *For each group* Vocabulary Cards, paper bag or small box

- Mix up the vocabulary cards, and put them in a paper bag or small box.
- Take a vocabulary card from the bag, and look at the word. Let the rest of the group try to guess the word by asking *yes*-or-*no* questions about it.
- No more than 10 questions can be asked. Make a tally on scratch paper.
- The first person to guess the word is the winner. The winner takes another vocabulary card from the bag, answers the questions, and makes the tally.

Georgia Tasks

M4D1.a. Represent data in bar, line, and pictographs. *also* **M4P4.a., M4P4.b., M4P4.c., M4P5.a., M4P5.b., M4P5.c.**

S4E4. Students will analyze weather charts/maps and collect weather data to predict weather events and infer patterns and seasonal changes.

Task A

FUN IN SAVANNAH

What would you like to do in Savannah? Listed below are just some of the activities you could enjoy. Use the list and the table shown at the right to complete the tasks below.

> **FUN THINGS TO DO IN SAVANNAH**
> Take a bus tour of historic Savannah
> Visit the museums   See a movie
> Shop at a mall   Go fishing
> Go boating   Go swimming

a. Make a bar graph to show the average monthly high temperatures.

b. Which would be your favorite month to visit Savannah? Name three activities you would want to do during your visit, based on the weather conditions for that month. Tell why you chose that month and those activities.

Average Monthly High Temperatures and Average Rainfall for Savannah		
Month	Average High Temperature	Average Rainfall (in inches)
Jan	58° F	4
Feb	62° F	3
Mar	70° F	4
Apr	77° F	3
May	84° F	4
Jun	88° F	6
Jul	91° F	6
Aug	88° F	8
Sep	85° F	5
Oct	77° F	2
Nov	70° F	2
Dec	62° F	3

Task B

FAVORITE ACTIVITIES

Caroline took a survey to find the favorite after-school activities of some of her classmates. She asked the students this question, "Would you rather go bike riding, play soccer, or play a video game?"

Favorite After-School Activity		
Activity	Boys	Girls
Bike Riding	⊮⊮ IIII	⊮⊮⊮⊮ I
Playing Soccer	⊮⊮⊮ II	⊮⊮⊮ III
Playing Video Game	⊮⊮⊮ I	⊮ III

a. Did Caroline ask a good survey question? Why or why not?

b. Caroline recorded the results of her survey in the table. Make a graph Caroline could use to display the data.

c. Write a question your classmates could answer by looking at the graph you drew.

Maintain/Preview

Maintain

For 1–3, use the bar graph. (pp. 70–71, 88–91)

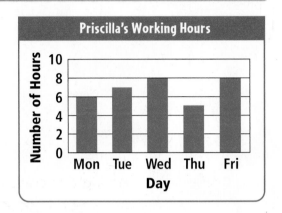

Priscilla's Working Hours

1. What is the scale of the graph?

2. How would the lengths of the bars change if the intervals were 4?

3. What is the middle number of hours that Priscilla worked?

For 4–5, write the type of graph you would choose. (pp. 92–95)

4. to show the height of a plant each week for 12 weeks

5. to show the number of votes each candidate received in an election

6. On her trip, Holly drove each day for 5 days. She drove 6 hours on the first day, 8 hours on the second day, 5 hours on the third day, and 9 hours on the fourth day. Can she make a graph to show this? Explain. (pp. 68–69)

7. The weights of Kyle's 5 cats are 13 pounds, 7 pounds, 6 pounds, 10 pounds, 8 pounds, and 10 pounds. Can he make a graph to show this? Explain. (pp. 68–69)

Preview

Use the array to find the value of the number sentence. (Chapter 5)

1.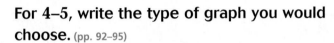

   □ rows of □ = □
   □ × □ = □

2. □ rows of □ = □
   □ × □ = □

3. □ rows of □ = □
   □ × □ = □

For 4–8, use the picture. (Chapter 5)

4. How many stars are there in all?

5. How many equal groups are there?

6. How many stars are in each group?

7. Write a related multiplication number sentence.

8. Write a related division number sentence.

Practice Multiplication and Division Facts

FAST FACT • SOCIAL STUDIES The New York Philharmonic was the first symphony orchestra in the United States. It was founded in 1842.

INVESTIGATION The graph shows the number of instruments in each section of an orchestra. How could you arrange the woodwind section into equal rows? Use manipulatives to show your arrangements.

Using Data

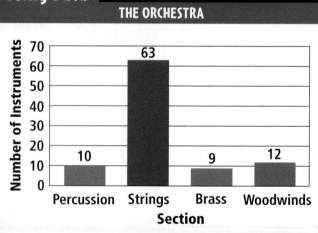

THE ORCHESTRA

Section	Number of Instruments
Percussion	10
Strings	63
Brass	9
Woodwinds	12

CHECK WHAT YOU KNOW

Use this page to help you review and remember important skills needed for Chapter 5.

✓ MEANING OF MULTIPLICATION

Use the array to find the value of each expression.

1.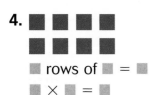

   ■ rows of ■ = ■
   ■ × ■ = ■

2.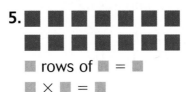

   ■ rows of ■ = ■
   ■ × ■ = ■

3.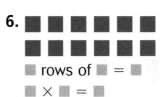

   ■ rows of ■ = ■
   ■ × ■ = ■

4.

   ■ rows of ■ = ■
   ■ × ■ = ■

5.

   ■ rows of ■ = ■
   ■ × ■ = ■

6.

   ■ rows of ■ = ■
   ■ × ■ = ■

✓ MEANING OF DIVISION

Answer the questions for each picture.

7. How many counters are there in all?

8. How many equal groups are there?

9. How many are in each group?

10. How many counters are there in all?

11. How many equal groups are there?

12. How many are in each group?

VOCABULARY POWER

REVIEW

factor [fak′tər] *noun*

A *factor* is a number that is multiplied by another number to find a product. *Part* is a synonym for *factor*. Describe how a factor is a part of a multiplication problem.

PREVIEW

inverse operations	Zero Property
fact family	Commutative Property
multiple	Associative Property
Identity Property	Distributive Property
	▶ product

GO ON-LINE www.harcourtschool.com/mathglossary

Mental Math: Multiplication Properties

M4N7.c. Compute using the commutative, associative, and distributive properties.
also M4A1.c., M4N7.d., M4P2, M4P4.a., M4P4.b., M4P5.b., M4P5.c.

▶ Learn

The answer to a multiplication problem is the **product**. Properties of multiplication can help you find products of two or more factors.

Quick Review

1. 4×3
2. 9×9
3. 10×8
4. 7×5
5. 12×4

VOCABULARY

Identity Property
Zero Property
Commutative Property
Associative Property
Distributive Property
▶ product

Properties

The **Identity Property** states that the product of 1 and any number is that number.

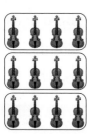

$1 \times 7 = 7$

The **Zero Property** states that the product of 0 and any number is 0.

$5 \times 0 = 0$

The **Commutative Property** states that you can multiply two factors in any order and get the same product.

$3 \times 4 = 12$ $\quad$ $4 \times 3 = 12$

The **Associative Property** states that you can group factors in different ways and get the same product. Use parentheses to group the factors you multiply first.

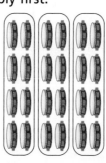 

$(4 \times 2) \times 3 = 24$ $\quad$ $4 \times (2 \times 3) = 24$

The **Distributive Property** states that multiplying a sum by a number is the same as multiplying each addend by the number and then adding the products.

 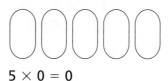

$2 \times 12 = 24$ $\quad$ $2(10 + 2) = (2 \times 10) + (2 \times 2) = 20 + 4 = 24$

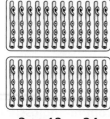

Use Mental Math Strategies

You can use mental math with the Commutative and Associative Properties to help solve multiplication problems.

Five members of the orchestra went to a music store. Each person bought 3 sheets of music. Each sheet of music cost $2. How much did the sheets of music cost in all?

Examples

A   Use the Commutative Property.

$$5 \times 3 \times 2 = 5 \times 2 \times 3$$
$$= 10 \times 3$$
$$= 30$$

B   Use the Associative Property.

$$(5 \times 3) \times 2 = 5 \times (2 \times 3)$$
$$= 5 \times 6$$
$$= 30$$

So, the sheets of music cost $30 in all.

You can use the Identity Property and the Zero Property along with the Commutative and Associative Properties.

Examples

A   Use the Identity Property.

$$1 \times 8 \times 9 = 1 \times (8 \times 9)$$
$$= 1 \times 72$$
$$= 72$$

B   Use the Zero Property.

$$7 \times 6 \times 0 = 7 \times (6 \times 0)$$
$$= 7 \times 0$$
$$= 0$$

For some multiplication problems, you can use the Distributive Property. Write the product as the sum of smaller products that are easy to find mentally.

Examples

A $6 \times 13 = 6 \times (10 + 3)$
$$= (6 \times 10) + (6 \times 3)$$
$$= 60 + 18$$
$$= 78$$

B $8 \times 14 = 8 \times (5 + 9)$
$$= (8 \times 5) + (8 \times 9)$$
$$= 40 + 72$$
$$= 112$$

• Show how you can find 6×13 by using a different pair of numbers whose sum is 13.

 MATH IDEA   Using the properties and other mental math strategies will help you multiply mentally.

1. **Name** two ways you can group $2 \times 5 \times 3$ to find the product. Are the products the same? Explain.

Use mental math to find the product.

2. 9×3 **3.** $6 \times 2 \times 5$ **4.** 7×14

▶ **Practice and Problem Solving**   Extra Practice, page 122, Set A

Use mental math to find the product.

5. 1×11 **6.** 8×2 **7.** 9×0

8. 4×15 **9.** $6 \times 3 \times 3$ **10.** 8×12

11. $6 \times 8 \times 0$ **12.** $9 \times 4 \times 2$ **13.** 3×17

Show two ways to group by using parentheses.
Find the product.

14. $5 \times 2 \times 3$ **15.** $9 \times 1 \times 5$ **16.** $3 \times 2 \times 6$ **17.** $9 \times 0 \times 12$

18. $2 \times 2 \times 3$ **19.** $5 \times 2 \times 5$ **20.** $4 \times 3 \times 4$ **21.** $2 \times 2 \times 6$

Write the missing number for each ▧. Then find the product.

22. $8 \times 4 = 4 \times ▧$ **23.** $2 \times 9 = ▧ \times 2$ **24.** $▧ \times 3 = 3 \times 5$

25. $6 \times ▧ = 5 \times 6$ **26.** $(9 \times 2) \times 3 = 9 \times (▧ \times 3)$ **27.** $4 \times 19 = 4 \times (10 + ▧)$

ALGEBRA   Write <, >, or = for each ●.

28. $10 \times (3 \times 1) \; ● \; 3 \times (3 \times 2)$ **29.** $1 \times 2 \times 3 \; ● \; 3 \times 1 \times 2$

30. $2 \times (2 \times 5) \; ● \; (2 \times 3) \times 5$ **31.** $9 \times (2 \times 3) \; ● \; 3 \times (6 \times 2)$

32. $1 \times (4 \times 7) \; ● \; 7 \times (4 \times 1)$ **33.** $3 \times (3 \times 2) \; ● \; (9 \times 1) \times 4$

34. Which multiplication property would you use to find 356×1? Explain and write the product.

35. **REASONING** Explain how the Associative Property can make it easier to find $(9 \times 2) \times 3$. Write the product.

36. **MULTISTEP** Emanuel practices the guitar for 3 hours each week. Lois practices the piano for 5 hours each week. How many more hours does Lois practice in 4 weeks than Emanuel?

37. Dennis has 3 cases of sports drinks. Each case has 4 different flavors. There are 3 bottles of each flavor in a case. How many bottles of sports drink does Dennis have?

38. MULTISTEP Mary Jane made 226 beaded bracelets and 59 beaded necklaces to sell at the crafts fair. After the fair, she had 98 bracelets and necklaces left. How may bracelets and necklaces did Mary Jane sell?

Maintain Skills

39. What digit is in the tenths place in 524.3?

40. Write a multiplication sentence for $9 + 9 + 9 + 9 = 36$.

41. 8×6

42. 5×7

43. $7\overline{)92}$

44. $6\overline{)240}$

CRCT Test Prep

45. **M4D1.c.** Which graph would BEST show the number of cars sold in one week by five different car dealers? (p. 92)

A. bar graph
B. double-bar graph
C. line graph
D. pictograph

Problem Solving   LiNKUP . . . to Reading

STRATEGY • CAUSE AND EFFECT Sometimes one action has an effect on another action. The **cause** is the reason something happens. The **effect** is the result.

Study Karen's party plans on the clipboard.

What if 4 more people come to Karen's party? Will this change her party plans?

Karen can make a table to help her plan.

Karen's Party Plans

29 people
8 tables
4 chairs at each table

CAUSE	EFFECT
4 more people come to the party.	There are more people at the party than I planned for.

Use the table to solve 1–3.

1. How many people are coming to the party?

2. What will happen because more people are coming?

3. Does she have enough chairs? Explain.

4. Felix bought 7 packs of water with 6 bottles in each pack for the fourth-grade field trip. He drank 2 bottles. If 38 students are going on the trip, will there be enough water? Make a table to solve.

Algebra: Relate Multiplication and Division

M4N4.a. Know the division facts with understanding and fluency.
also M4N7.a., M4P3.a., M4P3.b., M4P3.c., M4P3.d., M4P4, M4P4.a., M4P4.b.

Quick Review

1. 2×6 2. 4×3

3. 4×4 4. 8×2

5. 5×4

▷ Learn

HALFTIME NOTES The band played 6 songs during the halftime of the football game. Each song was 3 minutes long. How long did the band play?

$$6 \times 3 = \triangle$$
$$\downarrow$$
$$6 \times 3 = 18$$
$$18 = \triangle$$

So, the band played for 18 minutes.

VOCABULARY

inverse operations

fact family

Technology Link

More Practice: Harcourt Mega Math Ice Station Exploration, *Arctic Algebra*, Level E

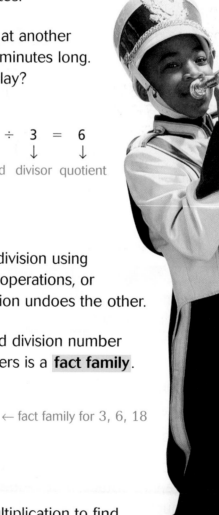

The band played for 18 minutes at another football game. Each song was 3 minutes long. How many songs did the band play?

$$18 \div 3 = \triangle$$

$$\underset{\text{factor}}{6} \times \underset{\text{factor}}{3} = \underset{\text{product}}{18}, \text{ so } \underset{\text{dividend}}{18} \div \underset{\text{divisor}}{3} = \underset{\text{quotient}}{6}$$

$$\triangle = 6$$

So, the band played 6 songs.

MATH IDEA Multiplication and division using the same numbers are opposite operations, or **inverse operations**. One operation undoes the other.

A set of related multiplication and division number sentences using the same numbers is a **fact family**.

$$6 \times 3 = 18 \qquad 18 \div 3 = 6$$
$$3 \times 6 = 18 \qquad 18 \div 6 = 3$$

← fact family for 3, 6, 18

▷ Check

1. **Explain** why you can use multiplication to find $24 \div 4$.

Find the value of the variable. Write a related number sentence.

2. $2 \times 4 = \square$ **3.** $12 \div 3 = \bigstar$ **4.** $28 \div 4 = \square$ **5.** $5 \times 3 = \triangle$

Practice and Problem Solving   Extra Practice, page 122, Set B

Find the value of the variable. Write a related number sentence.

6. $16 \div 2 = \triangle$ **7.** $20 \div 4 = \bigstar$ **8.** $3 \times 4 = \triangle$ **9.** $5 \times 4 = \square$

10. $6 \times 3 = \bigstar$ **11.** $6 \times 5 = \triangle$ **12.** $36 \div 4 = \bigstar$ **13.** $27 \div 3 = \square$

14. $\triangle \div 4 = 8$ **15.** $18 \div \square = 2$ **16.** $\bigstar \times 4 = 40$ **17.** $8 \times \square = 24$

Write the fact family for each set of numbers.

18. 2, 3, 6   **19.** 4, 7, 28   **20.** 3, 7, 21

21. Name 2 fact families that have only two number sentences. Explain.

USE DATA For 22–24, use the table.

22. **MULTISTEP** Michael collected baseball cards for 3 months. He collected 44 cards in the first month and 29 cards in the second month. How many cards did Michael collect in the third month?

23. Michael collected the same number of soccer cards in each of 4 weeks. How many soccer cards did he collect each week?

24. What is the total number of cards Michael collected?

25. 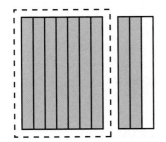 Write About It   Explain how you can use multiplication to solve a division problem. Give an example.

MICHAEL'S CARD COLLECTION	
Sport	**Number Collected**
Football	64
Soccer	28
Baseball	110
Basketball	35

Maintain Skills

26. Use the model to find $0.9 - 0.7$.

CRCT Test Prep

27. **M4N1.b.** What is seven thousand, five written in standard form? (p. 4)

    A. 75   C. 7,005
    B. 705   D. 7,500

28. **M4A1.c.** Which is the value of $(38 - \square) + 45$ if $\square = 20$? (p. 46)

    A. 27   C. 83
    B. 63   D. 103

Multiply and Divide Facts Through 10

M4N4.a. Know the division facts with understanding and fluency. *also* M4P2.
Concepts/Skill to Maintain Multiplication and division of whole numbers

▶ **Learn**

PUT IT IN REVERSE! Mrs. Frazier asked her students to use models to show that division is the inverse of multiplication. This is how her students showed that division is the inverse of multiplication.

Emma

$3 \times 5 = 15$

$15 \div 3 = 5$

First, I made 3 groups of 5 sticks to get 15 sticks. Then, I used 15 sticks and separated them into 3 groups to get 5 in each group.

Blake

0 1 2 3 4 5 6 7 8 9
$3 \times 3 = 9$

0 1 2 3 4 5 6 7 8 9
$9 \div 3 = 3$

I started at 0 and made jumps of 3 on a number line to land at 9. Then, starting at 9 I took jumps of 3 back to 0.

Carlos

$5 \times 4 = 20$

$20 \div 4 = 5$

I made 5 rows of 4 blocks to make 20 blocks. Then I divided the 20 blocks into 4 columns to get 5 in each column.

Latoya

→ To multiply, I looked across row 6 and down column 4 to find the product 24.
→ To divide, I found 24 by looking down column 4. Then I looked left to find the quotient.

$6 \times 4 = 24$,
so $24 \div 4 = 6$.

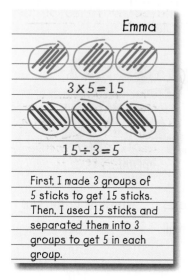

×	0	1	2	3	4	5	6	7	8	9
0	0	0	0	0	0	0	0	0	0	0
1	0	1	2	3	4	5	6	7	8	9
2	0	2	4	6	8	10	12	14	16	18
3	0	3	6	9	12	15	18	21	24	27
4	0	4	8	12	16	20	24	28	32	36
5	0	5	10	15	20	25	30	35	40	45
6	0	6	12	18	24	30	36	42	48	54

• Which model do you like the best? Explain.

• How could you use the inverse operation and the multiplication table to find $40 \div 8$?

MATH IDEA The product in a multiplication fact is the dividend in the related division fact.

More Ways to Multiply and Divide

There are other ways to help you learn the multiplication and division facts that you do not know.

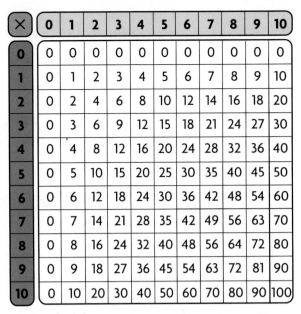

Think of the inverse operation.

What is $36 \div 9$?

Think: $4 \times 9 = 36$

So, $36 \div 9 = 4$.

Use the Commutative Property.

What is 8×5?

Think: $5 \times 8 = 40$

So, $8 \times 5 = 5 \times 8 = 40$.

Technology Link

More Practice: Harcourt Mega Math The Number Games, *Up, Up, and Array,* Levels B, C, F, and G; Fraction Action, *Number Line Mine,* Level D

Use a pattern.

What is 6×9?

Think: $6 \times 5 = 30$, so I can count on from 30 by 6 for the remaining 4 times.

Count: 30 . . . 36, 42, 48, 54.

So, $6 \times 9 = 54$.

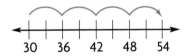

Use the *break apart* strategy.

What is 7×6?

Think: $6 = 2 + 4$

$7 \times 2 = 14$ and $7 \times 4 = 28$,
$7 \times 6 = 14 + 28$

So, $7 \times 6 = 42$.

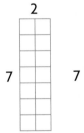

▶ Check

1. **Draw** a model that shows the inverse operation of 5×6. Then write the related number sentence.

Write a related multiplication or division number sentence.

2. $10 \div 2 = 5$

3. $4 \times 4 = 16$

4. $4 \times 3 = 12$

LESSON CONTINUES ▶

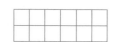 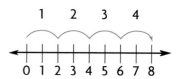

Write a related multiplication or division number sentence.

5. $2 \times 6 = 12$

6. $2 \times 3 = 6$

7. $4 \times 2 = 8$

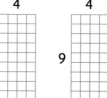

Use the arrays to show how to find 9×8.

8. What is 9×8?

$9 \times 4 = \blacksquare$

$9 \times 4 = \blacksquare$

$9 \times 8 = \blacksquare + \blacksquare$

So, $9 \times 8 = \blacksquare$.

Find the product or quotient. Show the method you used.

9. 5×9	**10.** 4×9	**11.** 4×6	**12.** 2×5
13. 9×9	**14.** 8×8	**15.** 10×7	**16.** 3×0
17. 9×7	**18.** 7×8	**19.** 8×9	**20.** 5×5
21. $48 \div 6$	**22.** $72 \div 8$	**23.** $48 \div 8$	**24.** $14 \div 2$
25. $70 \div 10$	**26.** $54 \div 6$	**27.** $63 \div 9$	**28.** $36 \div 4$

 **ALGEBRA** Find the missing factor.

29. $\blacksquare \times 6 = 60$　　　**30.** $7 \times \blacksquare = 49$　　　**31.** $\blacksquare \times 9 = 81$

For 32–35, look for patterns in the Facts of Nine table.

32. How does the pattern of the tens digits in the products relate to the pattern of the first factors?

33. How does each product relate to the second factor?

34. Explain how you can use the patterns you found to find 9×9 without the table.

35. **? What's the Error?** Gwyn used the *break apart* strategy to solve 8×9. Describe her error. Show a correct way to use the strategy.

$$8 \times 3 = 24 \quad \text{and} \quad 8 \times 3 = 24$$

$$24 + 24 = 48$$

Facts of Nine
$1 \times 9 = 9$
$2 \times 9 = 18$
$3 \times 9 = 27$
$4 \times 9 = 36$
$5 \times 9 = 45$
$6 \times 9 = 54$
$7 \times 9 = 63$
$8 \times 9 = 72$
$9 \times 9 = 81$

36. MULTISTEP Sandra shared some jacks equally with Maria and Tom. There were 2 jacks left. Maria got 11 jacks. How many jacks did Sandra have to start?

37. Vocabulary Power The word *inverse* means "opposite in effect." Describe how multiplication and division are inverse operations. Give an example.

Maintain Skills

38. What is the value of the digit 4 in 40,357?

39. $549 \div 9$

40. What is the length of the key to the nearest centimeter?

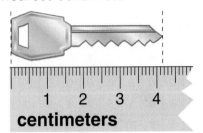

centimeters

41. Use the array to find 3×12.

CRCT Test Prep

42. **M4N2.a.** The Jimmy Carter Library and Museum in Atlanta has 15,269 square feet of exhibit space. What is 15,269 rounded to the nearest thousand? (p. 32)

A. 20,000 C. 15,300

B. 16,000 D. 15,000

43. **M4A1.b.** Alex had 5 dogs. One of the dogs had puppies. He gave 2 puppies away. Which expression BEST describes this? (p. 46)

A. $5 + \square - 2$ C. $\square - 5 - 2$

B. $5 - \square - 2$ D. $5 + \square + 2$

Problem Solving LiNKUP . . . to Art

The Romans often covered floors with small colored tiles made of material such as marble or stone. The picture shows part of a Roman floor. Works of art done in this style are known as *mosaics.*

You can use what you know about multiplying to find the total number of tiles you would need to make a design to cover part of your desk.

1. Draw a section of the design shown, or make your own design with pattern blocks.

2. Record the number of each of the different shapes you used in your design.

3. Write a multiplication sentence to find the total number of each shape of tile you would need if you made 8 designs like the one you drew.

HANDS ON

Multiplication Table Through 12

🔷 **M4N4.a.** Know the division facts with understanding and fluency. *also* **M4P2.a., M4P2.b., M4P2.c., M4P2.d., M4P3.a., M4P3.b., M4P3.c., M4P3.d., M4P5.b., M4P5.c.** **Concepts/Skill to Maintain** Multiplication and division of whole numbers

▶ **Explore**

Use strategies, properties, and patterns to learn new facts. Make your own multiplication table for the facts from 0 through 12.

Activity

THE ELEVENS

Complete the column for 11 to 10×11. Use the Distributive Property to find 11×11.

Think:

$$11 \times 11 = 11 \times (10 + 1)$$
$$= (11 \times 10) + (11 \times 1)$$
$$= 110 + 11$$
$$= 121$$

So, $11 \times 11 = 121$.

Complete the row for 11.

THE TWELVES

Complete the column for 12 to 10×12. Use the Distributive Property to find 12×12.

Think:

$$12 \times 12 = 12 \times (10 + 2)$$
$$= (12 \times 10) + (12 \times 2)$$
$$= 120 + 24$$
$$= 144$$

So, $12 \times 12 = 144$.

Complete the row for 12.

×	0	1	2	3	4	5	6	7	8	9	10	11	12
0	0	0	0	0	0	0	0	0	0	0	0	▪	▪
1	0	1	2	3	4	5	6	7	8	9	10	▪	▪
2	0	2	4	6	8	10	12	14	16	18	20	▪	▪
3	0	3	6	9	12	15	18	21	24	27	30	▪	▪
4	0	4	8	12	16	20	24	28	32	36	40	▪	▪
5	0	5	10	15	20	25	30	35	40	45	50	▪	▪
6	0	6	12	18	24	30	36	42	48	54	60	▪	▪
7	0	7	14	21	28	35	42	49	56	63	70	▪	▪
8	0	8	16	24	32	40	48	56	64	72	80	▪	▪
9	0	9	18	27	36	45	54	63	72	81	90	▪	▪
10	0	10	20	30	40	50	60	70	80	90	100	▪	▪
11	▪	▪	▪	▪	▪	▪	▪	▪	▪	▪	▪	▪	▪
12	▪	▪	▪	▪	▪	▪	▪	▪	▪	▪	▪	▪	▪

• Explain how you can use the Distributive Property to find 12×11.

I found the row for 8 and the column for 11. What's the product?

Try It

Use your multiplication table to find the product.

a. 8×11 **b.** 3×11 **c.** 4×12

Connect

A **multiple** is the product of a given number and another whole number. Look at the row or the column for 6 in the table on page 118. Find the multiples of 6 shown in the table.

So, 6, 12, 18, 24, 30, 36, 42, 48, 54, 60, 66, and 72 are all multiples of 6.

Technology Link

More Practice: Harcourt Mega Math, The Number Games, *Up, Up, and Array,* Level D

• What are the multiples of 11 shown in the table?

• What pattern do you see in the multiples for 11?

Practice and Problem Solving

Use the multiplication table to find the product or quotient.

1. 1×12
2. 2×10
3. 3×11
4. 4×12
5. 5×9
6. 6×10
7. 7×11
8. 8×12
9. $120 \div 12$
10. $88 \div 11$
11. $90 \div 10$
12. $144 \div 12$
13. $110 \div 11$
14. $121 \div 11$
15. $100 \div 10$
16. $132 \div 11$

 **ALGEBRA** **Find the value of the variable.**

17. $\triangle \times 12 = 120$
18. $11 \times \bigstar = 121$
19. $100 \div \triangle = 10$
20. $\square \div 11 = 7$

21. **REASONING** The first six multiples of 12 are 12, 24, 36, 48, 60, and 72. What are the next six multiples?

22. **MULTISTEP** Rosa collected 3 dozen eggs, and Peter collected 7 dozen. How many eggs did they collect altogether?

23. **FAST FACT • MUSIC** A piano keyboard has 52 white keys and some black keys. If there are 88 keys in all, how many are black keys?

24. **? What's the Question?** The answer is that one factor is 11 and the product is 132.

Maintain Skills

25. Which is longer, 15 mm or 15 cm?

26. Find the area of the rectangle.

27. Alicia has 68 cans. If she puts 8 cans in each of 8 boxes, how many cans will be left over?

CRCT Test Prep

28. **M4A1.a.** Find a rule. Use the rule to find the missing number in the table. (p. 52)

In	6	10	14	18	22
Out	4	8	12	16	□

A. 26
B. 22
C. 20
D. 18

Problem Solving Skill
Choose the Operation

 **M4P1.c.** Apply and adapt a variety of appropriate strategies to solve problems. *also*
M4N4.a., M4N7.a., M4P1.a., M4P1.b., M4P1.d., M4P3.a., M4P3.b., M4P3.c., M4P3.d.
Concepts/Skill to Maintain Multiplication and division of whole numbers

UNDERSTAND ⟩ **PLAN** ⟩ **SOLVE** ⟩ **CHECK**

Quick Review

Find the product.

1. $3 \times (5 \times 2)$

2. $(4 \times 3) \times 6$

3. $(2 \times 6) \times 3$

4. $2 \times 5 \times 6$

5. $8 \times 2 \times 3$

OPERATION PRECIPITATION Study the problems.
Use the chart to help you choose the operation
needed to solve each problem.

Add	Join groups of different sizes
Subtract	Take away or compare groups
Multiply	Join equal-size groups
Divide	Separate into equal-size groups, or find how many in each group

A. What if Wilmington gets the same amount of rainfall for the next 5 months as in September? What would be the total rainfall for these 5 months?

B. About how much rain fell each week in May?

C. How much more rain fell in May through July than in August and September?

D. What is the total amount of rainfall for Wilmington from April through September?

• Solve Problems A–D. Tell the operation you used.

• What two different operations could you use to solve Problem A? to solve Problem B?

Talk About It

• What words in the box at the top of the page help you decide which operation to use for each of Problems A–D?

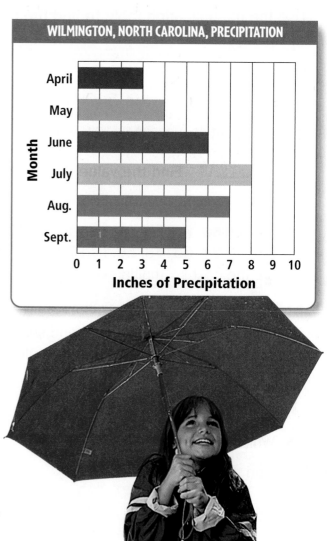

WILMINGTON, NORTH CAROLINA, PRECIPITATION

Month: April, May, June, July, Aug., Sept.
Inches of Precipitation: 0 1 2 3 4 5 6 7 8 9 10

Solve. Name the operation or operations you used.

1. During the past 9 weeks, the school chorus practiced for a total of 36 hours. If they practiced for the same number of hours each week, for how many hours did they practice each week?

2. **MULTISTEP** The cafeteria served 124 school lunches. There was a total of 11 pizzas cut into 12 slices each. If each student received 1 slice, how many slices were left?

3. Mrs. Ling ordered some pizzas cut into 8 slices each. She ordered a total of 96 slices. How many pizzas did she order?

4. Mr. Davis cut a sheet cake into 6 rows of 8 pieces. How many pieces of cake are there in all?

Choose the letter of the correct answer.

Before the concert, Michele sold 12 large umbrellas. Each umbrella was shared by 4 people. How many people used the umbrellas?

5. Which expression could you use to solve the problem?

   A $12 \div 4$ **C** 12×4

   B $12 - 4$ **D** $12 + 4$

6. How many people used the umbrellas?

   F 4   **G** 8   **H** 16   **J** 48

Mixed Applications

7. **MULTISTEP** Ben buys 2 board games and 4 books. How much change does he get from $5.00

8. **MULTISTEP** Tyler bought 3 tapes and 2 books. How much did he spend at the sale?

9. ✎ Write a problem using the information in the table.

10. **MULTISTEP** Caro bought 2 tapes, a book, and a board game. Chad bought 4 tapes. How much more did Chad spend than Caro?

Item	Price
Board Games	$0.50
Books	$0.25
Tapes	$0.75

Extra Practice

Set A (pp. 108–111)

Use mental math to find the product.

1. $4 \times 3 \times 3$ **2.** 12×1 **3.** 3×18 **4.** $4 \times 8 \times 2$

5. $9 \times 9 \times 0$ **6.** $2 \times 6 \times 2$ **7.** 9×2 **8.** 7×13

9. Which multiplication property could you use to find $5 \times (2 \times 7)$ mentally? Explain and write the product.

Set B (pp. 112–113)

Find the value of the variable. Write a related number sentence.

1. $15 \div 3 = \triangle$ **2.** $7 \times 4 = \star$ **3.** $4 \times 5 = \triangle$ **4.** $27 \div 9 = \square$

5. $24 \div 3 = \star$ **6.** $2 \times 6 = \triangle$ **7.** $8 \times 4 = \star$ **8.** $25 \div 5 = \square$

Write the fact family for each set of numbers.

9. 3, 4, 12 **10.** 4, 6, 24 **11.** 2, 9, 18 **12.** 3, 7, 21

13. Every week for 6 weeks Tony collected 4 plastic bottles for recycling. How many plastic bottles did he collect in all?

Set C (pp. 114–117)

Find the product or quotient.

1. 7×3 **2.** 8×4 **3.** 5×6 **4.** 4×4

5. $5 \div 5$ **6.** $36 \div 4$ **7.** $27 \div 3$ **8.** $12 \div 4$

9. 9×2 **10.** 5×4 **11.** 7×5 **12.** 5×8

13. $20 \div 5$ **14.** $16 \div 8$ **15.** $24 \div 4$ **16.** $45 \div 9$

17. 7×4 **18.** 8×9 **19.** 6×6 **20.** 9×4

21. $56 \div 7$ **22.** $36 \div 6$ **23.** $27 \div 9$ **24.** $60 \div 10$

25. 9×10 **26.** 6×9 **27.** 7×7 **28.** 7×8

29. $54 \div 6$ **30.** $48 \div 8$ **31.** $63 \div 9$ **32.** $64 \div 8$

33. For 7×6, draw one array to show the expression. Next, use the break-apart strategy, and draw two arrays that could be used to solve the problem.

Review/Test

✓ CHECK VOCABULARY AND CONCEPTS

Choose the best term from the box.

Vocabulary

inverse
fact family
Associative Property
product
Commutative Property

1. The ? states that when the grouping of factors is changed, the product remains the same. (p. 108)

2. Multiplication and division by the same number are opposite, or ?, operations. One operation undoes the other. (p. 112)

3. A set of related multiplication and division sentences using the same numbers is a ?. (p. 112)

✓ CHECK SKILLS

Use mental math to find the product.

4. 4×16
5. $4 \times 9 \times 2$
6. $7 \times 7 \times 0$

Find the value of the variable. Write a related number sentence. (pp. 112–113)

7. $18 \div 3 = \triangle$
8. $6 \times 7 = \square$
9. $\star \div 4 = 5$
10. $9 \times \triangle = 63$

Write a related division number sentence. (pp. 114–117)

11. $3 \times 5 = 15$

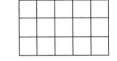

12. $3 \times 3 = 9$

13. $4 \times 2 = 8$

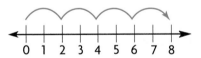

Find the product or quotient. (pp. 114–117, 118–119)

14. 4×7
15. $18 \div 3$
16. $56 \div 8$
17. 9×8
18. 12×5

19. $144 \div 12$
20. 8×11
21. 10×9
22. $48 \div 6$
23. $121 \div 11$

✓ CHECK PROBLEM SOLVING

Solve. Write the operation or operations you used. (pp. 120–121)

24. For a class field trip, 42 students went to a museum. If the museum takes groups of 7 students, how many groups were there?

25. Jack wants 6 packs of cards. If a store sells 1 pack of cards for $3 and a set of 6 packs of cards for $15, how much money will Jack save if he buys the set?

Chapter CRCT Test Prep

NUMBERS AND OPERATIONS

1. **M4N7.c.** Which property would you use to find the missing number?

$$(\square \times 2) \times 3 = 6 \times (2 \times 3)$$

A. associative property

B. commutative property

C. identity property

D. zero property

2. **M4N7.a.** Julie bought 3 types of postcards at the Callaway Gardens gift shop. She bought the same number of each type. She bought a dozen postcards in all. Which expression could be used to find how many of each postcard Julie bought?

A. 12×3

B. $12 + 3$

C. $12 - 3$

D. $12 \div 3$

3. **M4N4.a.** Find the quotient.

$$72 \div 8$$

A. 8

B. 9

C. 64

D. 80

ALGEBRA

4. **M4A1.c.** What is the missing factor?

$$6 \times \square = 0$$

A. 0

B. 1

C. 6

D. 60

5. **M4A1.c.** What is the missing factor?

$$\square \times 1 = 9$$

A. 0

B. 1

C. 9

D. 10

6. **M4A1.c.** What is the missing factor?

$$(7 \times 9) \times 5 = \square \times (9 \times 5)$$

A. 5

B. 7

C. 9

D. 63

7. **M4A1.c.** What is the missing factor?

$$8 \times 4 = \square \times 8$$

A. 48

B. 32

C. 12

D. 4

Cumulative CRCT Test Prep

DATA ANALYSIS

8. **M4D1.c.** There are 11 roller coasters at Wild Adventures, 1 roller coaster at Funsville, and 12 roller coasters at Six Flags Over Georgia. Which of the following would be the BEST to display this data?

A. line graph

B. coordinate system

C. pictograph

D. double-bar graph

Use the bar graph below to answer question 9.

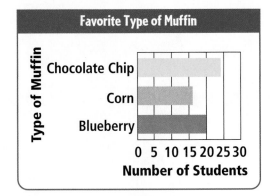

9. **M4D1.c.** How would the bars of the graph change if the interval were 10?

A. The bars would be shorter.

B. The bars would be wider.

C. The bars would be longer.

D. The bars would be narrower.

GEOMETRY

10. **M4G3.c.** What object is located at the ordered pair (7,5)?

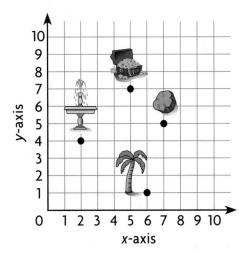

A. fountain

B. tree

C. rock

D. treasure chest

11. **M4G3.b.** What is the ordered pair at point X?

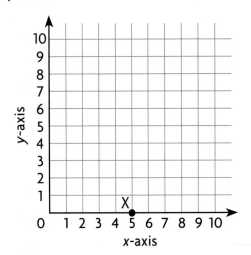

A. (6,0)

B. (5,0)

C. (0,6)

D. (0,5)

Algebra: Use Multiplication and Division Facts

≡FAST FACT

SOCIAL STUDIES Cookie jars came into common use in the United States during the Great Depression. Today, these jars are popular collectibles. There is even a Cookie Jar Museum in Lemont, IL, where over 2,000 jars are displayed!

INVESTIGATION The bar graph shows the number of cookies in each of four cookie jars. Suppose you had a cookie jar with 36 cookies. In how many different ways could you share them with your friends if each friend were to get a whole cookie?

Using Data

COOKIES GALORE!

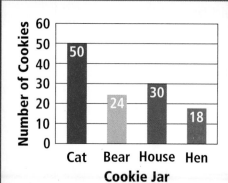

Bar graph — Number of Cookies vs. Cookie Jar:
- Cat: 50
- Bear: 24
- House: 30
- Hen: 18

CHECK WHAT YOU KNOW

Use this page to help you review and remember
important skills needed for Chapter 6.

MULTIPLICATION AND DIVISION FACTS

Find the product or quotient.

1. 6×10 **2.** 4×12 **3.** 5×6 **4.** 3×9

5. 8×2 **6.** 7×8 **7.** 9×9 **8.** 5×11

9. $49 \div 7$ **10.** $63 \div 7$ **11.** $45 \div 5$ **12.** $54 \div 6$

FIND A RULE

Write a rule for each table. Copy and complete each table.

13.

Bags	2	3	4	5	6
Apples	12	18	▣	▣	▣

14.

Octopus	2	3	4	5	6
Arms	16	24	▣	▣	▣

15.

Tricycles	3	4	5	6	7	8
Wheels	9	12	15	▣	▣	▣

16.

Dimes	2	3	4	5	6	7
Nickels	4	6	8	▣	▣	▣

17.

Birds	5	6	7	8	9
Wings	10	12	▣	▣	▣

18.

Dogs	4	5	6	7	8
Paws	16	20	▣	▣	▣

VOCABULARY POWER

REVIEW

expression [ik•spre′shen] *noun*

An expression is a way of communicating
something. An expression can use words
or actions. Explain how an expression is
related to a mathematical expression.

PREVIEW

order of operations

www.harcourtschool.com/mathglossary

Expressions

M4N7.b. Compute using the order of operations, including parentheses.
also **M4A1, M4N4.a., M4P3.a., M4P3.b., M4P3.c., M4P3.d., M4P4.c.**

▶ **Learn**

PLENTY OF PAGES Tyler collects comic books. He displays his collection in 3 binders, with 10 comic books in each. On a trip to the store, Tyler bought 2 new comic books. How many comic books does he have in his collection now?

You can write an expression to find the number of comic books in Tyler's collection.

Think: $\left(\begin{array}{c} \text{3 binders} \times \text{10 comic books} \\ \text{in each binder} \end{array}\right) + \begin{array}{c} \text{2 new comic} \\ \text{books} \end{array}$

$\downarrow \qquad\qquad \downarrow \qquad\qquad \downarrow$

$(3 \qquad \times \qquad 10) \qquad + \qquad 2$

Find the value of $(3 \times 10) + 2$.

$(3 \times 10) + 2$ Do what is in parentheses first.
$\downarrow$ Multiply 3 and 10.
$30 \quad + 2$ Then add 30 and 2.
$\downarrow$
32

So, Tyler has 32 comic books in his collection.

Quick Review

1. $12 - (4 + 1)$
2. $17 - (5 - 2)$
3. $35 - (3 - 1)$
4. $(17 - 7) + 10$
5. $(50 - 20) + 5$

Remember

An *expression* is part of a number sentence that has numbers and operation signs but does not have an equal sign.

Examples Write an expression. Then find the value of the expression.

A Grace had $50. She bought 6 tickets at $4 each. How much money does she have left?

$50 minus (6 tickets at $4 each)
$\downarrow \qquad\qquad \downarrow$
$50 \quad - \qquad (6 \times 4)$

$50 - (6 \times 4)$ Find the value.
$\downarrow$
$50 - \quad 24$
$\downarrow$
26

So, Grace has $26 left.

B John had 15 rocks in his collection. He divided his rocks into 3 boxes. How many rocks are in each box?

15 rocks divided into 3 boxes
$\downarrow \qquad\qquad \downarrow$
$15 \qquad \div \qquad 3$

$15 \div 3$ Find the value.
$\downarrow$
5

So, there are 5 rocks in each box.

Technology Link

More Practice: Harcourt
Mega Math Ice Station
Exploration, *Arctic
Algebra*, Level H

1. **Explain** where you would place the parentheses so that $8 \times 6 - 3$ has a value of 24.

Find the value of the expression.

2. $(4 \times 6) - 2$ 3. $24 \div 3$ 4. $(54 \div 9) - 1$ 5. $(8 \times 9) + 7$

Write an expression to match the words.

6. Eric divided 45 stickers equally among 9 pages.

7. Lauren had $8 and then worked 4 hours for $5 each hour.

▷ **Practice and Problem Solving** Extra Practice, page 138, Set A

Find the value of the expression.

8. $(26 - 6) \div 2$ 9. $46 + (15 \div 3)$ 10. $8 \times (7 + 2)$ 11. $(3 \times 6) + 12$

12. $35 \div 5 \times 9$ 13. $(14 - 2) \times 5$ 14. $19 + 21 - 37$ 15. $(2 \times 9) + 2$

Write the words to match the expression.

16. $27 \div 3$ 17. $9 \times (4 - 1)$ 18. 8×7 19. $(6 \div 2) \times 5$

For 20–21, write an expression to match the words. Then find the value of the expression.

20. **MULTISTEP** Lily had 15 postcards. She gave away 8 and then bought 2 more. How many cards does she have now?

21. **MULTISTEP** There are 6 rows with 5 desks in each row and 2 desks not in rows. How many desks are there in all?

22. ≡**FAST FACT** • **SOCIAL STUDIES** The Library of Congress has the largest comic book collection in the United States, containing about 100,000 pieces. It is growing by about 200 issues each month. About how many more issues will the library have in 3 months?

Maintain Skills

23. What is the length of the screw to the nearest $\frac{1}{4}$ inch?

24. $28 \div 7$ 25. 9×9

CRCT Test Prep

26. **M4N1.b.** Which is the standard form for $300,000 + 4,000 + 700 + 20 + 1$? (p. 4)

A. 34,721
B. 304,721
C. 340,721
D. 347,210

 HANDS ON

Order of Operations

M4N7.b. Compute using the order of operations, including parentheses. *also* **M4N4.a., M4P3.a., M4P3.b., M4P3.c., M4P3.d., M4P4.a., M4P4.b.**

▶ **Explore**

Quick Review

1. $81 \div 9$ 2. 8×9
3. $65 + 22$ 4. $98 - 12$
5. $3 + (7 - 4)$

VOCABULARY
order of operations

MATERIALS calculator

Miguel and Jill are looking at Miguel's cookie jar collection. He has 20 jars and wants to put 8 jars on each of 2 shelves. How many jars will not be on shelves?

$$20 - 8 \times 2$$

Activity 1

• Try solving the problem by performing the operations in order from left to right. What do you get?

• Try solving the problem by subtracting first and then multiplying. What do you get?

• Try solving the problem by multiplying first and then subtracting. What do you get?

When solving problems with more than one operation, you need to know what operation to do first. A special set of rules, called the **order of operations**, can be used to solve expressions with more than one operation.

First, perform any operations in parentheses.
Next, multiply and divide from left to right.
Then, add and subtract from left to right.

 Technology Link

More Practice: Harcourt Mega Math Ice Station Exploration, *Arctic Algebra*, Level Q

STEP 1

$20 - 8 \times 2$
$\downarrow$
$20 - 16$

There are no parentheses, so multiply from left to right.

STEP 2

$20 - 16$
$\downarrow$
4

Then subtract.

So, 4 cookie jars will not be on shelves.

Try It

Use the order of operations to find the value of each expression.

a. $(9 \times 3) + 8$ **c.** $(16 + 4) \div 2$

b. $1 + 6 \times 7$ **d.** $54 \div 9 - 3$

For $(9 \times 3) + 8$, first I perform the operation in the parentheses. What should I do next?

Connect

You can use a calculator that follows the order of operations to help you solve problems. Not all calculators follow the order of operations.

Example Evaluate 5 + 6 × 3 with a calculator.

Follows Order of Operations

$$\boxed{5} \quad \boxed{+} \quad \boxed{6} \quad \boxed{\times} \quad \boxed{3} \quad \boxed{\text{Enter} =}$$

$$23$$

Does Not Follow Order of Operations

$$\boxed{5} \quad \boxed{+} \quad \boxed{6} \quad \boxed{\times} \quad \boxed{3} \quad \boxed{=}$$

$$33$$

- Use a calculator to find the value of 8 + 32 ÷ 4 + 2. Then use paper and pencil and the order of operations to find the value.

- Does your calculator follow the order of operations? Explain.

Practice and Problem Solving

Write *correct* if the operations are listed in the correct order. If not, write the correct order of operations.

1. (9 + 3) × 4 Multiply, add

2. 2 × (3 + 4) Add, multiply

3. 27 − (14 ÷ 2) Subtract, divide

4. (23 − 11) ÷ 4 + 2 Divide, subtract, add

Follow the order of operations to find the value of each expression.

5. 95 − 8 × 2

6. 32 + 5 × 7

7. 63 ÷ 9 + 45

8. (30 − 6) ÷ 3

9. 81 + (54 ÷ 6)

10. (28 − 16) × 4

11. 13 + (36 ÷ 4)

12. 5 × (23 − 18) + 7

13. (78 − 16) + 12 ÷ 3

14. MULTISTEP A calculator displays 91 as the value of 9 + 4 × 7. Does the calculator follow the order of operations? Explain.

15. ✏️ **Write About It** Explain why you need to use the order of operations when finding the value of an expression with more than one operation.

Maintain Skills

16. What is the value of the digit 5 in 45,021?

17. What is the value of the digit 2 in 78,265?

CRCT Test Prep

18. M4N4.a. There are 72 chairs in rows in a room. Each row has 8 chairs. How many rows of chairs are there? (p. 114)

A. 7
B. 8
C. 9
D. 12

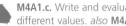

Expressions with Variables

LESSON
3

M4A1.c. Write and evaluate mathematical expressions using symbols and different values. *also* **M4A1.b., M4N4.a., M4N7.b., M4P2.a., M4P2.b., M4P2.c., M4P2.d., M4P3.**

Quick Review

Evaluate for △ = 13.

1. 6 + △   2. 22 − △

3. △ − 7   4. △ + 17

5. 43 − △

▶ Learn

LET IT SNOW Carly bought a snowdome in each state she visited on vacation. She visited Michigan, Indiana, and Ohio. Each snowdome cost the same amount in all three states. What expression can you write to find the amount she spent?

Remember

A *variable* can stand for any number.

You can use a variable to represent the price of each snowdome.

3 snowdomes × price of each snowdome
↓   ↓
3   ×   □

The variable □ stands for the price of each snowdome.

Suppose Carly paid $4 for each snowdome. To find the value of the expression, replace □ with the price of each snowdome.

3 × □
↓
3 × 4   Replace □ with 4 since she paid
↓ $4 for each snowdome.
12

So, Carly spent $12 for 3 snowdomes.

Examples On vacation, Alex bought some $3 magnets. His sister, Mia, spent $8 on some keychains.

A Suppose Alex bought 5 magnets. Use the expression ★ × 3 to find the amount he spent.

★ × 3   Replace ★ with 5.
↓
5 × 3   Evaluate the expression.
↓
15

So, Alex spent $15 for 5 magnets.

B Suppose Mia bought 4 keychains. Use the expression 8 ÷ □ to find the amount she spent on each keychain.

8 ÷ □   Replace □ with 4.
↓
8 ÷ 4   Evaluate the expression.
↓
2

So, Mia spent $2 on each keychain.

132

1. **Explain** how to write an expression that shows 5 shelves with the same number of books on each shelf.

Find the value of the expression.

2. $4 \times \square$ if $\square = 7$ 3. $5 \times \triangle$ if $\triangle = 7$ 4. $16 \div \square$ if $\square = 4$ 5. $54 \div \star$ if $\star = 6$

► **Practice and Problem Solving**   Extra Practice, page 138, Set B

Find the value of the expression.

6. $9 \times \triangle$ if $\triangle = 7$ 7. $9 \times \square$ if $\square = 9$ 8. $56 \div \star$ if $\star = 8$ 9. $96 \div \triangle$ if $\triangle = 12$

Write an expression that matches the words.

10. 7 times a number of pages, $\triangle$, in an album

11. 4 times the number of magnets, $\square$, on a refrigerator

12. 36 keys divided by a number of keychains, $\star$

13. a number of postcards, $\triangle$, times 8 stacks

Match the expression with the words.

14. $(36 \div \star) - 4$ 15. $48 \div \star$ 16. $25 + (\star \times 3)$ 17. $6 \times \star$

  a. forty-eight divided by a number, $\star$

  b. twenty-five plus the product of $\star$ times three

  c. six times a number, $\star$

  d. the quotient of thirty-six divided by $\star$ minus four

18. **? What's the Error?** Julio claims that $5 \times \star$ is 10 if $\star = 5$. Describe his error. Write the correct answer.

19. **Vocabulary Power** A *variable* is a symbol whose value can change. Explain how the value of a variable affects the value of an expression.

20. **MULTISTEP** Erin has 5 quarters in each of 4 stacks. Tyra has 8 quarters in each of 3 stacks. How much more money does Tyra have than Erin?

Maintain Skills

21. Write the related division sentence shown by the repeated subtraction.

$$\begin{array}{cccc} 12 & 9 & 6 & 3 \\ -3 & -3 & -3 & -3 \\ \hline 9 & 6 & 3 & 0 \end{array}$$

CRCT Test Prep

22. **M4D1.a.** In a pictograph, suppose 📖 = 10 books. Which of the following shows 25 books? (p. 72)

  A. 📖📖📖
  B. 📖📖
  C. 📖📖📖
  D. 📖📖📖📖

LESSON

4

Problem Solving Strategy
Work Backwards

M4P1.c. Apply and adapt a variety of appropriate strategies to solve problems. *also*
M4A1.b., M4A1.c., M4N4.a., M4N7.b., M4P1.a., M4P1.b., M4P1.d., M4P3.a., M4P3.b.,
M4P3.c., M4P3.d.

PROBLEM Tony had some dimes in his bank. He added
7 nickels and then had a total of 75¢. How much money
did Tony have in dimes?

Quick Review

1. $3 \times \bigstar = 27$
2. $\bigstar \div 3 = 5$
3. $36 \div \bigstar = 9$
4. $5 \times \bigstar = 30$
5. $5 + \bigstar = 9 \times 8$

UNDERSTAND

- What are you asked to find?
- What information will you use?

PLAN

- What strategy can you use to solve the problem?

  You can write an expression with a variable.
  Then *work backwards* to solve the problem.

SOLVE

- How can you solve the problem?

  Write an expression. Let $\bigstar$ represent the amount
  of money in dimes.

$$\bigstar + (7 \times 5)$$

  amount in dimes ⤴   ⤴ amount in nickels

  What number can you use to replace $\bigstar$ to get 75¢?

  To find the value of $\bigstar$, work backwards.

Total in bank	Amount in nickels	Amount in dimes, $\bigstar$
75¢	− 35¢	= 40¢

  So, the variable, $\bigstar$, has a value of 40.
  Tony had 40¢ in dimes.

CHECK

- What other strategies could you use to solve the
  problem? Explain.

Strategies

Act It Out or Use Objects
Make a Picture or Diagram
Guess and Check
Use or Look for a Pattern
Use Logical Reasoning
Make an Organized List
Use or Make a Table
▶ **Work Backwards**

Problem Solving

Work backwards to solve.

1. **What if** Tony had a total of 85¢ after adding 7 nickels? How much would Tony have had in dimes?

2. Sid had 5 trading cards. Then his mother gave him some packages with 8 cards in each package. Sid now has 37 cards. How many packages did his mother give him?

Joey and Nicole are playing a board game. In the first three turns, Joey moves 6 spaces forward, 3 back, and 4 forward. Nicole moves 5 spaces forward, 1 back, and 5 forward.

3. Who is ahead in the game?
   A Joey
   B Nicole
   C Lucy
   D They are on the same space.

4. How many spaces apart are Joey and Nicole's playing pieces?
   F 2 spaces
   G 3 spaces
   H 4 spaces
   J 5 spaces

LOSE 1 TURN   GO AHEAD 2   TAKE EXTRA TURN

Mixed Strategy Practice

5. The Snack Bar at the local skating rink uses 8 lemons for every 2 quarts of lemonade. How many lemons are used to make 8 quarts of lemonade?

6. Ty had some money in his coin bank. He put 3 dimes and 7 pennies in the bank and now has $1.17. How much money was in the bank to begin with?

7. On Sunday, the Snack Bar sold 341 drinks. On Monday, 85 drinks were sold in the morning and 163 in the afternoon. How many more drinks were sold on Sunday than on Monday?

8. Taylor had 127 baseball cards. He gave 18 cards to Felisha. Felisha then gave Taylor some cards. Taylor then had a total of 114 cards. How many cards did Felisha give Taylor?

9. Sally bought 9 packages of erasers. There were 3 erasers in each pack. She has 6 erasers left. How many packages of erasers did Sally use?

10. ✎ **Write a problem** involving coins that can be solved using the strategy *work backwards*. Then solve the problem.

Patterns: Find a Rule

M4A1.a. Understand and apply patterns and rules to describe relation-ships and solve problems. *also* **M4A1.b., M4A1.c., M4N4.a., M4P2.c., M4P2.d., M4P3.a., M4P3.b., M4P3.c., M4P3.d., M4P5.b., M4P5.c.**

Quick Review

1. 12 ÷ 3   **2.** 9 ÷ 3

3. 14 ÷ 7   **4.** 16 ÷ 4

5. 27 ÷ 9

▶ Learn

INPUT/OUTPUT The Math Factory sorts numbers into boxes. Use the input/output table to find what number comes out when 45 is put into the machine.

INPUT	OUTPUT
25	5
30	6
35	7
40	8
45	■

HINT: Look for a pattern to help you find a rule.

Pattern: Each output is the input divided by 5.

Rule: Divide by 5.
← *Input:* 45   *Output:* 45 ÷ 5 = 9

So, when you put in 45, the Math Factory puts out 9.

Examples

Ⓐ Find a rule.

Rule: Multiply by 6.

INPUT	3	4	5	6
OUTPUT	18	24	30	36

Test your rule on each pair of numbers in the table.

Input: 3   *Output:* 3 × 6 = 18

Input: 4   *Output:* 4 × 6 = 24

Input: 5   *Output:* 5 × 6 = 30

Input: 6   *Output:* 6 × 6 = 36

Ⓑ Find a rule.
Use the rule to find the next two numbers in the pattern.

INPUT	72	63	54	45	36	27
OUTPUT	8	7	6	5	■	■

Rule: Divide by 9.

Input: 36 *Output:* 36 ÷ 9 = 4

Input: 27 *Output:* 27 ÷ 9 = 3

The next two numbers in the pattern are 4 and 3.

1. **Explain** why it is important to test a rule with all the number pairs in the table.

Technology Link

More Practice: Harcourt Mega Math Ice Station Exploration, *Arctic Algebra*, Level K

Find a rule.

2.

INPUT	21	28	35	42
OUTPUT	3	4	5	6

3.

INPUT	8	9	10	11
OUTPUT	40	45	50	55

▶ **Practice and Problem Solving** Extra Practice, page 138, Set C

Find a rule. Use the rule to find the missing numbers.

4.

INPUT	12	11	9	7	■	■	■
OUTPUT	24	22	18	14	12	8	4

5.

INPUT	16	32	48	64	80	96
OUTPUT	2	4	6	8	■	■

6.

INPUT	■	■	6	8	10	12
OUTPUT	24	48	72	96	120	144

7.

INPUT	6	12	18	24	30	36
OUTPUT	■	■	6	8	10	12

Use the rule to make an input/output table.

8. Divide by 11.   9. Multiply by 4.   10. Divide by 10.   11. Multiply by 8.

12. Multiply by 7.   13. Divide by 6.   14. Multiply by 3.   15. Divide by 12.

16. **MULTISTEP** The first three inputs in the Number Cruncher are 48, 44, and 40. The first three outputs are 12, 11, and 10. Find a rule. Then extend the pattern to find the next two output numbers.

17. There are 18 boxes. There are twice as many large boxes as small boxes. How many large boxes are there? How many small boxes are there?

Maintain Skills

18. There are 59 students going on a field trip to the Blue and Gray Museum. Each van can hold 6 students. How many vans are needed for the field trip?

19. What is the value of the digit 6 in the number 2,684?

CRCT Test Prep

20. **M4N2.a.** Which number does NOT round to 18,700? (p. 32)
   A. 18,660
   B. 18,696
   C. 18,723
   D. 18,754

Extra Practice

Set A (pp. 128–129)

Find the value of the expression.

1. $4 \times 5 + 2$ **2.** $100 - (8 \times 5)$ **3.** $56 \div 7 + 20$ **4.** $13 + (5 \times 6)$

5. $(12 + 8) \div 4$ **6.** $(27 \div 3) \times 7$ **7.** $85 - (3 \times 7)$ **8.** $50 + (72 \div 9)$

Write an expression to match the words.

9. There were 3 shelves with 7 footballs each. Lin took 4 footballs out to the field.

10. The 5 cases of puppy food each contain 10 bags. Kate placed 6 extra bags next to the cases.

11. Tom had $20. He bought 2 movie tickets for $6 each.

12. There are 4 tomato plants, and each has 8 tomatoes. Another tomato plant has 7 tomatoes.

Set B (pp. 132–133)

Find the value of the expression.

1. $12 \times \square$ if $\square = 3$ **2.** $36 \div \triangle$ if $\triangle = 9$ **3.** $8 \times \star$ if $\star = 7$ **4.** $24 \div \triangle$ if $\triangle = 4$

5. $72 \div \star$ if $\star = 9$ **6.** $9 \times \square$ if $\square = 9$ **7.** $54 \div \triangle$ if $\triangle = 6$ **8.** $11 \times \star$ if $\star = 5$

9. $6 \times \triangle$ if $\triangle = 8$ **10.** $18 \div \star$ if $\star = 2$ **11.** $5 \times \square$ if $\square = 8$ **12.** $60 \div \triangle$ if $\triangle = 12$

Write an expression that matches the words.

13. 6 times the number of students, $\triangle$, on a team

14. 45 apples divided by the number of baskets, $\square$

Set C (pp. 136–137)

Find a rule. Use the rule to find the missing number.

1.

INPUT	OUTPUT
18	9
14	7
10	5
6	▇

2.

INPUT	OUTPUT
2	6
4	12
6	18
8	▇

3.

INPUT	OUTPUT
▇	54
8	72
10	90
12	108

4.

INPUT	OUTPUT
33	▇
27	9
24	8
21	7

Use the rule to make an input/output table.

5. Multiply by 5. **6.** Divide by 3. **7.** Multiply by 7. **8.** Divide by 6.

9. Multiply by 8. **10.** Divide by 4. **11.** Multiply by 2. **12.** Divide by 9.

Review/Test

✅ CHECK CONCEPTS

1. Explain which operation to do first to find the value of $2 + (3 \times 4)$. How do you know? (pp. 130–131)

2. Write an expression you could use to find the number of quarters that have the same value as any number of dollars. (pp. 132–133)

✅ CHECK SKILLS

Find the value of the expression. (pp. 128–129, 130–131)

3. $(18 \div 3) + 2$ **4.** $6 \times 7 - 5$ **5.** $63 \div 7 - 9$ **6.** $25 + (4 \times 6)$

7. $(32 - 8) \div 8$ **8.** $7 - (72 \div 12)$ **9.** $45 - (7 \times 6)$ **10.** $(8 \times 9) + 21$

Write the words to match the expression. (pp. 128–129)

11. 9×3 **12.** $7 \times (5 + 1)$ **13.** $48 \div 6$ **14.** $(8 \div 4) \times 2$

Find the value of the expression. (pp. 132–133)

15. $8 \times \square$ if $\square = 5$ **16.** $60 \div \star$ if $\star = 12$ **17.** $7 \times \triangle$ if $\triangle = 3$ **18.** $36 \div \square$ if $\square = 4$

Find a rule. Use the rule to find the missing number. (pp. 136–137)

19.

INPUT	OUTPUT
4	28
5	35
8	56
■	63

20.

INPUT	OUTPUT
72	9
56	7
40	5
48	■

21.

INPUT	OUTPUT
4	■
5	55
7	77
9	99

22.

INPUT	OUTPUT
144	12
132	11
120	10
■	9

✅ CHECK PROBLEM SOLVING

Work backwards to solve. (pp. 134–135)

23. Tommy had 3 nickels. Angela gave him some quarters. Now he has 90¢. How much money does Tommy have in quarters?

24. Jack had some dimes. He spent 4 dimes on candy and had 30¢ left over. How many dimes did Jack have before buying the candy?

25. Courtney bought 15 packs of balloons to share with her friends. There were 5 balloons in each pack. She has 10 balloons left. How many packs of balloons did Courtney give away?

Chapter CRCT Test Prep

NUMBERS AND OPERATIONS

1. **M4N7.b.** What is the value of the expression?

$$(17 - 8) \times 2$$

A. 1

B. 7

C. 11

D. 18

2. **M4N7.b.** What is the value of the expression?

$$56 \div 7 \times 4$$

A. 2

B. 4

C. 12

D. 32

3. **M4N7.b.** Which of the following does NOT have a value of 8?

A. $40 \div 4 + 1$

B. $4 + 32 \div 8$

C. $28 \div 7 \times 2$

D. $12 \times 4 \div 6$

4. **M4N7.b.** Which of the following has a value of 21?

A. $(6 + 5) \times 3$

B. $6 + 5 \times 3$

C. $6 \times 3 + 5$

D. $6 \times (3 + 5)$

ALGEBRA

5. **M4A1.b.** Which expression matches the words below?

six times the number of books, $\triangle$, on a bookshelf

A. $6 + \triangle$

B. $\triangle - 6$

C. $6 \times \triangle$

D. $6 \div \triangle$

6. **M4A1.b.** Lauren volunteered at the Museum of Arts and Sciences in Macon for 3 hours at a time. Let $\square$ represent the number of times Lauren volunteered. Which expression shows how many times Lauren volunteered?

A. $3 + \square$

B. $3 \times \square$

C. $3 - \square$

D. $3 \div \square$

Use the table below to answer question 7.

In	9	10	11	12
Out	36	40	44	

7. **M4A1.a.** What is the missing number in the table?

A. 39

B. 45

C. 46

D. 48

Cumulative CRCT Test Prep

DATA ANALYSIS

Use the line graph to answer question 8.

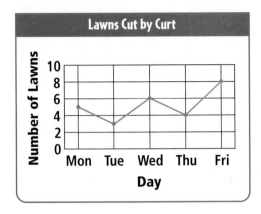

Lawns Cut by Curt

8. **M4D1.b.** What is the middle number of lawns that Curt cut this week?

A. 3

B. 4

C. 5

D. 6

Use the bar graph to answer question 9.

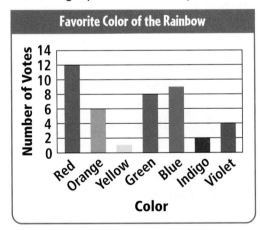

Favorite Color of the Rainbow

9. **M4D1.a.** Which color got 3 fewer votes than blue?

A. red

B. orange

C. indigo

D. violet

GEOMETRY

Use the coordinate grid below to answer question 10.

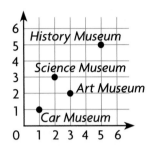

10. **M4G3.b.** What is the ordered pair for the Science Museum?

A. (1,1)

B. (2,3)

C. (3,2)

D. (5,5)

11. **M4G3.a.** Ariana graphed the points (1,3), (1,7), and (6,7) on a coordinate grid. What point should she plot next if she wants the points to form a rectangle?

A. (7,6)

B. (7,1)

C. (6,3)

D. (3,1)

12. **M4G3.b.** Yuko located a point on a coordinate grid only by moving up 3. What is the ordered pair for this point?

A. (0,3)

B. (3,0)

C. (3,3)

D. (0,0)

GPS/CRCT Vocabulary

ELA4R3 The student understands and acquires vocabulary and uses it correctly in reading and writing.

VOCABULARY
- **product**
- **inverse operation**
- **fact family**
- **order of operations**
- **Identity Property**
- **Zero Property**
- **Associative Property**
- **Commutative Property**
- **Distributive Property**

TIC-TAC-WORD

MATERIALS *For each pair* Definition Cards, construction paper, markers

- Make a large tic-tac-toe board on construction paper. Write the vocabulary terms on your board.

- Decide who is Player X and who is Player O. Take turns picking a definition card and reading the definition. Then mark an X or O on the word that matches the definition.

- Continue playing until one player fills a row, column, or diagonal with Xs or Os.

- Make a new tic-tac-toe board, and play the game again.

product	inverse operation	fact family
order of operations	Identity Property	Zero Property
Associative Property	Commutative Property	Distributive Property

MATH WORD WORK

MATERIALS *For each group of 4* Vocabulary Cards, 45 index cards

- Make letter cards using the 18 letters shown below. Make 3 cards for each letter. Mix up the cards, and spread them out face-up. Mix up the vocabulary cards, and place them face-down in a pile.

- Play in teams of 2 students. Team 1 draws a vocabulary card and places it face-up. Team 2 finds the letters to correctly spell the vocabulary word. Then Team 1 tells the definition.

- Teams take turns until all vocabulary words have been correctly spelled and defined.

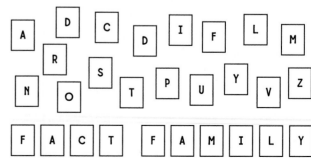

USE A CODE

- Choose five vocabulary terms from the list on page 142. Write a blank line for each letter in the word.

- Use the code shown at the right to spell each word in numbers. Write the number for each letter under the blank.

- Trade papers with a classmate, and decode each other's words. Write the definition or an example of each word after you have decoded it.

- After you both have finished, check each other's work.

CODE

A	B	C	D	E	F	G	H	I	J	K	L	M
21	12	17	24	15	22	18	14	19	10	26	2	13

N	O	P	Q	R	S	T	U	V	W	X	Y	Z
8	5	23	3	7	9	25	1	6	16	4	20	11

$$\underset{23}{P} \quad \underset{7}{R} \quad \underset{5}{O} \quad \underset{24}{D} \quad \underset{1}{U} \quad \underset{17}{C} \quad \underset{25}{T}$$

$$5 \times 6 = 30$$

PROPERTY FLASH CARDS

MATERIALS *For each pair* 5 index cards, Vocabulary Cards

- Select the vocabulary cards with the names of the 5 properties. On index cards, write an example of each of the properties.

- Hold up a property card. Your partner matches it with an example card and explains the property.

- Take turns until all cards are used.

Georgia Tasks

M4N7.d. Use mental math and estimation strategies to compute.
also **M4P2.a., M4P2.b., M4P2.d., M5P5.b., M5P5.c.**

S4L2. Students will identify factors that affect the survival or extinction of organisms such as adaptation, variation of behaviors (hibernation) and external features (camouflage and protection).

Task A

ZOO ATLANTA

Zoo Atlanta is one of the oldest zoos in the United States. It works to help endangered species and to educate people about how important it is to preserve the habitats of the endangered species.

▲ **The giant pandas Lun-Lun and Yang-Yang live at Zoo Atlanta. The giant panda is an endangered species.**

a. The Monroes are planning a day trip to visit the zoo. There are 6 Monroes on the trip. What is the cost for 2 adults, 1 senior citizen, and 3 children to visit the zoo?

b. The Monroes plan to eat lunch and dinner while on the trip. If they estimate that each meal will cost $8 per person, about how much will they spend on food?

c. Gas for the trip costs about $30. Estimate the total cost of the trip to Zoo Atlanta for gas, food, admission, and a souvenir for each person. You can make up your own price for the souvenir. Explain how you got your estimate of the total cost.

Admission Rates for Zoo Atlanta	
Ticket	**Cost**
Adult (12–54)	$17
Senior Citizen (55+)	$13
Children (3–11)	$12

Task B

WORK IT OUT

Nicole and Amy earn spending money by walking dogs and mowing lawns.

a. Nicole earns $2 for each dog she walks. Write an expression to find the number of dollars she will earn for walking any number of dogs. (Use □ to represent the number of dogs.) Then use the expression you wrote to find how much Nicole will earn if she walks 4 dogs.

b. Amy earns $6 for mowing 1 lawn, $12 for mowing 2 lawns, and $18 for mowing 3 lawns. Make a table to find how much she will earn for mowing 5 lawns.

Maintain/Preview

Maintain

Write the missing number. Then find the product. (pp. 108–111)

1. $6 \times 7 = 7 \times \square$ **2.** $6 \times 13 = (6 \times 10) + (6 \times \square)$ **3.** $4 \times (\square \times 9) = (4 \times 2) \times 9$

Use mental math to find the product. (pp. 108–111)

4. $5 \times 7 \times 0$ **5.** $8 \times 3 \times 2$ **6.** 7×15 **7.** 1×12

Follow the order of operations to find the value of the expression. (pp. 130–131)

8. $40 \div 5 + 5$ **9.** $7 + 8 \times 3$ **10.** $(34 - 24) \times 6$ **11.** $64 \div 8 - 7$

Find the value of the expression. (pp. 132–133)

12. $54 \div \triangle$ if $\triangle = 6$ **13.** $12 \times \square$ if $\square = 6$ **14.** $18 \div \bigstar$ if $\bigstar = 9$ **15.** $5 \times \triangle$ if $\triangle = 7$

16. Ben baked 2 dozen muffins. He ate 4 muffins. Write an expression that shows how many muffins Ben has now. (pp. 128–129)

17. Scarlett had $20. She bought 6 pounds of unshelled pecans for $3 per pound. Write an expression to show how much money has now. (pp. 128–129)

Preview

Write a multiplication sentence for the model. (Chapter 7)

1.

2.

3.

Find the product. (Chapter 7)

4.   3
   ×6

5.   7
   ×4

6.   8
   ×8

7.   9
   ×4

8.   7
   ×6

9.   2
   ×8

10.   5
   ×2

11.   10
   ×9

12.   6
   ×6

13.   8
   ×6

Multiply by 1-Digit Numbers

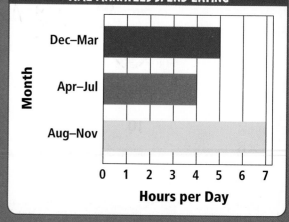

≡FAST FACT • SCIENCE An average adult manatee can eat up to 108 pounds of vegetation daily.

INVESTIGATION About how many hours would an adult manatee spend eating during one week in the month of October? Explain how you found your answer.

Using Data
TIME MANATEES SPEND EATING

Bar graph — Month vs. Hours per Day:
- Dec–Mar: 5
- Apr–Jul: 4
- Aug–Nov: 7

Hours per Day (0 1 2 3 4 5 6 7)

CHECK WHAT YOU KNOW

Use this page to help you review and remember important skills needed for Chapter 7.

✓ MODEL MULTIPLICATION

Write a multiplication sentence for the model.

1.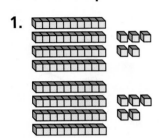

2.

3.

4.

5.

6.

✓ MULTIPLICATION FACTS

Find each product.

7. $\begin{array}{r} 5 \\ \times 6 \\ \hline \end{array}$

8. $\begin{array}{r} 8 \\ \times 3 \\ \hline \end{array}$

9. $\begin{array}{r} 9 \\ \times 5 \\ \hline \end{array}$

10. $\begin{array}{r} 9 \\ \times 8 \\ \hline \end{array}$

11. $\begin{array}{r} 9 \\ \times 7 \\ \hline \end{array}$

12. $\begin{array}{r} 2 \\ \times 6 \\ \hline \end{array}$

13. $\begin{array}{r} 7 \\ \times 4 \\ \hline \end{array}$

14. $\begin{array}{r} 3 \\ \times 5 \\ \hline \end{array}$

VOCABULARY POWER

REVIEW

multiplication [mul•tə•plə•kā′shən] *noun*

Multiplication and *multivitamin* begin with *multi*. Think of words that begin with *multi*, and look at their definitions. What do these words have in common?

PREVIEW

compatible numbers

 www.harcourtschool.com/mathglossary
ON-LINE

Algebra: Mental Math: Multiplication Patterns

M4N7.d. Use mental math and estimation strategies to compute. *also* **M4A1.a., M4N3, M4P1.a., M4P1.b., M4P1.c., M4P1.d., M4P2.d., M4P3.a., M4P3.b., M4P3.c., M4P3.d.**

▷ Learn

FOUND MONEY Kim is saving for a trip to see the manatees. She is wrapping pennies to take to the bank and has wrapped 7 rolls. Each roll has 50 pennies. How many pennies has she wrapped?

Example

Multiply.	$\begin{array}{r}50 \\ \times\ 7 \\ \hline 350\end{array}$	**Think:**	$7 \times 5 = 35$
			$7 \times 5 \text{ tens} = 35 \text{ tens}$
			$7 \times 50 = 350$

So, Kim has wrapped 350 pennies.

Use mental math to multiply greater numbers when you know basic facts and patterns.

More Examples

A
$7 \times 2 = 14$
$7 \times 20 = 140$
$7 \times 200 = 1{,}400$
$7 \times 2{,}000 = 14{,}000$

B
$5 \times 8 = 40$
$5 \times 80 = 400$
$5 \times 800 = 4{,}000$
$5 \times 8{,}000 = 40{,}000$

MATH IDEA With whole numbers, as the number of zeros in a factor increases, the number of zeros in the product increases.

▷ Check

1. Explain how to use a basic fact and a pattern to find $7 \times 5{,}000$.

Use mental math to complete.

2. $3 \times 2 = 6$
$3 \times 20 = 60$
$3 \times 200 = \blacksquare$
$3 \times 2{,}000 = \blacksquare$

3. $4 \times 4 = 16$
$4 \times 40 = \blacksquare$
$4 \times 400 = \blacksquare$
$4 \times 4{,}000 = \blacksquare$

4. $2 \times 6 = \blacksquare$
$2 \times 60 = \blacksquare$
$2 \times 600 = \blacksquare$
$2 \times 6{,}000 = \blacksquare$

5. $5 \times 2 = \blacksquare$
$5 \times 20 = \blacksquare$
$5 \times 200 = \blacksquare$
$5 \times 2{,}000 = \blacksquare$

Use mental math to complete.

6. $8 \times 6 = \blacksquare$
$8 \times 60 = \blacksquare$
$8 \times 600 = \blacksquare$
$8 \times 6,000 = \blacksquare$

7. $4 \times 3 = \blacksquare$
$4 \times 30 = \blacksquare$
$4 \times 300 = \blacksquare$
$4 \times 3,000 = \blacksquare$

8. $6 \times 5 = \blacksquare$
$6 \times 50 = \blacksquare$
$6 \times 500 = \blacksquare$
$6 \times 5,000 = \blacksquare$

9. $5 \times 4 = \blacksquare$
$5 \times 40 = \blacksquare$
$5 \times 400 = \blacksquare$
$5 \times 4,000 = \blacksquare$

Use mental math. Write the basic fact and use a pattern to find the product.

10. 6×400

11. $7 \times 4,000$

12. 3×600

13. 5×600

14. $7 \times 60,000$

15. 6×90

16. $3 \times 7,000$

17. $3 \times 30,000$

ALGEBRA Find the value of $\triangle$ or $\square$.

18. $5 \times 40,000 = \triangle$

19. $\square = 2 \times 3,000$

20. $6 \times \triangle = 4,200$

21. $8 \times 6,000 = \square$

22. $\triangle = 7 \times 5,000$

23. $3 \times \square = 2,700$

24. $5 \times \square = 25,000$

25. $8 \times \square = 72,000$

USE DATA Copy and complete each table.

26. 1 roll = 40 nickels

Number of Rolls	1	2	3	4	5	6
Number of Nickels	40	80	$\blacksquare$	$\blacksquare$	$\blacksquare$	$\blacksquare$

27. 1 roll = 50 dimes

Number of Rolls	1	2	3	4	5	6
Number of Dimes	50	100	$\blacksquare$	$\blacksquare$	$\blacksquare$	$\blacksquare$

28. MULTISTEP Micah and his family have been saving for the manatee trip for two years. They have three $100 bills, six $20 bills, and five $10 bills. How much money have they saved?

29. **What's the Error?** Renee has 20 rolls of pennies. Each roll has 50 pennies. Renee calculates that she has 100 pennies. Describe her error. Write the correct answer.

30. **Write About It** What is $80,000 \times 7$? Explain how you found the answer.

Maintain Skills

31. What is the length of the piece of yarn to the nearest centimeter?

32. What is the value of the digit 8 in 50,782?

CRCT Test Prep

33. **M4A1.b.** Which expression matches the words? (p. 132)

6 times a number, $\square$, of books

A. $6 \times \square$

B. $\square \div 6$

C. $6 + \square$

D. $\square - 6$

Estimate Products

M4N7.d. Use mental math and estimation strategies to compute. *also* M4N3, M4P3.a., M4P3.b., M4P3.c., M4P3.d., M4P4.c.

VOCABULARY

compatible numbers

▶ Learn

BIG SQUEEZE The Farmers Market ordered 249 quarts of orange juice and sold it by the cup. There are 4 cups in a quart. About how many cups of juice were sold?

You can estimate 4×249.

One Way Use rounding.

STEP 1

Round the greater factor to the nearest hundred.

$4 \times 249 \rightarrow 4 \times 200$

STEP 2

Use basic facts and patterns.

$4 \times 2 = 8$
$4 \times 20 = 80$
$4 \times 200 = 800$

Another Way Use compatible numbers.
Compatible numbers are numbers that are easy to compute mentally.

STEP 1

4×249 **Think:** 4×25 is
$\downarrow$ easy to compute
4×250 mentally.

STEP 2

Multiply.

If $4 \times 25 = 100$
Then $4 \times 250 = 1,000$

So, both 800 cups and 1,000 cups are reasonable estimates of the amount of orange juice sold.

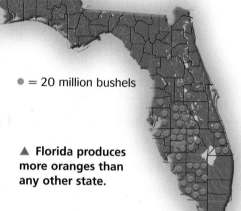

FLORIDA ORANGE PRODUCTION

● = 20 million bushels

▲ Florida produces more oranges than any other state.

More Examples Estimate the products.

A
$$\begin{array}{r} 63 \rightarrow 60 \\ \times\ 7 \quad \times\ 7 \\ \hline 420 \end{array}$$

B
$$\begin{array}{r} 479 \rightarrow 500 \\ \times\ 3 \quad \times\ 3 \\ \hline 1,500 \end{array}$$

C
$$\begin{array}{r} \$5.82 \rightarrow \$6 \\ \times\ 6 \quad \times\ 6 \\ \hline \$36 \end{array}$$

▶ Check

1. Explain how you can tell whether the estimated products in Examples B and C are greater than or less than the exact products.

Estimate the product. Choose the method.

2. 6×23 **3.** 9×507 **4.** 3×962 **5.** $4 \times \$5.76$

Estimate the product. Choose the method.

6. 187
   × 4

7. 87
   × 6

8. 764
   × 5

9. 679
   × 4

10. $1.18
    × 6

11. 247
    × 8

12. 389
    × 7

13. $6.24
    × 7

14. 8 × 26

15. 5 × $6.51

16. 4 × 749

17. 9 × 178

18. 3 × $9.85

19. 4 × 341

20. 7 × $8.12

21. 2 × 678

ALGEBRA Choose two factors from the box for each estimated product □ × △.

| 4 | 7 | 392 |
| 6 | 123 | 989 |

22. 1,600

23. 600

24. 7,000

25. 2,400

USE DATA For 26–27, use the graph.

26. In 1980, was $8 enough to buy 3 gallons of juice? Explain your thinking.

27. **MULTISTEP** Six gallons of orange juice cost about $12 in 1978. How much more did the same amount of juice cost in 2000?

28. **FAST FACT • SCIENCE** Each Florida orange tree produces about 5 bushels of oranges each year. A bushel of oranges weighs about 56 pounds. About how many pounds of oranges will 2 orange trees produce in a year?

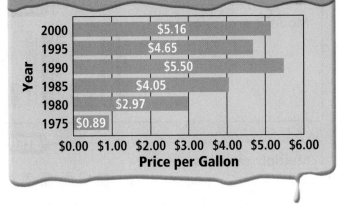

FRESH-SQUEEZED ORANGE JUICE

2000 $5.16
1995 $4.65
1990 $5.50
1985 $4.05
1980 $2.97
1975 $0.89

$0.00 $1.00 $2.00 $3.00 $4.00 $5.00 $6.00
Price per Gallon
Year

Maintain Skills

29. What is the product of 60 and 20?

30. Will is putting 125 books into boxes. He can put 8 books in each box. How many boxes does he need so that no books will be left over?

CRCT Test Prep

31. **M4A1.a.** Find a rule. Then use the rule to find the missing numbers. (p. 52)

In	19	47	28	52	36
Out	10	38	19		

A. 10, 1

B. 61, 45

C. 43, 27

D. 47, 28

Multiply 2-Digit Numbers

M4N3. Students will solve problems involving multiplication of
2-3 digit numbers by 1-2 digit numbers. *also* **M4P5, M4P5.b., M4P5.c.**

▶ **Learn**

VERY BERRY At last year's Strawberry Festival,
24 people entered the strawberry shortcake-eating
contest. This year, three times as many people entered.
How many people entered the contest this year?

Find 3×24.
Estimate. $3 \times 25 = 75$

HANDS ON

Activity

MATERIALS: base-ten blocks

Make a model, and use regrouping
to find the product.

STEP 1

Model 3 groups of 24.

$$\begin{array}{r} 24 \\ \times\ 3 \\ \hline \end{array}$$

STEP 2

Multiply the ones.

3×4 ones $= 12$ ones

Regroup the ones.

$$\begin{array}{r} {\scriptstyle 1} \\ 24 \\ \times\ 3 \\ \hline 2 \end{array}$$

Regroup
12 ones
as 1 ten
2 ones.

STEP 3

Multiply the tens.

3×2 tens $= 6$ tens

Add the regrouped ten.

$$\begin{array}{r} {\scriptstyle 1} \\ 24 \\ \times\ 3 \\ \hline 72 \end{array}$$

So, 72 people entered the contest.
Since 72 is close to the estimate of 75, it is reasonable.

• Make a model, and use regrouping to find the product 4×35.

Two Ways to Multiply

You can pick your own strawberries at the festival. If there are 16 pints of strawberries in a box, how many pints are in 5 boxes?

Find 5×16.

Technology Link

More Practice: Harcourt Mega Math The Number Games, *Up, Up, and Array,* Level J

One Way Use partial products.

STEP 1

Multiply the ones.

$$\begin{array}{r} 16 \\ \times\ 5 \\ \hline 30 \end{array} \longleftarrow 5 \times 6$$

STEP 2

Multiply the tens.

$$\begin{array}{r} 16 \\ \times\ 5 \\ \hline 30 \\ \underline{50} \end{array} \longleftarrow 5 \times 10$$

STEP 3

Add the products.

$$\begin{array}{r} 16 \\ \times\ 5 \\ \hline 30 \\ +50 \\ \hline 80 \end{array}$$

Another Way Use regrouping.

STEP 1

Multiply the ones.

$$\begin{array}{r} \overset{3}{1}6 \\ \times\ 5 \\ \hline 0 \end{array}$$

STEP 2

Multiply the tens.

$$\begin{array}{r} \overset{3}{1}6 \\ \times\ 5 \\ \hline 80 \end{array}$$

So, there are 80 pints of strawberries in 5 boxes.

More Examples

Partial Products

Ⓐ
$$\begin{array}{r} 42 \\ \times\ 7 \\ \hline 14 \\ +280 \\ \hline 294 \end{array}$$

Ⓑ
$$\begin{array}{r} 89 \\ \times\ 3 \\ \hline 27 \\ +240 \\ \hline 267 \end{array}$$

Regrouping

Ⓒ
$$\begin{array}{r} \overset{1}{2}3 \\ \times\ 5 \\ \hline 115 \end{array}$$

Ⓓ
$$\begin{array}{r} \overset{4}{5}8 \\ \times\ 6 \\ \hline 348 \end{array}$$

 Check

1. Explain how to find 4×58 by using either regrouping or the partial products method.

Find the product. Estimate to check.

2. 3×43 **3.** 6×51 **4.** 4×24 **5.** 5×38 **6.** 7×16

LESSON CONTINUES ▶

Find the product. Estimate to check.

7. 46 × 2	**8.** 57 × 4	**9.** 39 × 7	**10.** 82 × 4	**11.** 27 × 3
12. 62 × 4	**13.** 48 × 5	**14.** 59 × 3	**15.** 36 × 6	**16.** 74 × 8
17. 93 × 3	**18.** 35 × 7	**19.** 67 × 4	**20.** 81 × 5	**21.** 49 × 6

22. 6×43 **23.** 9×62 **24.** 5×84 **25.** 7×49 **26.** 4×73

ALGEBRA **Find the missing factor.**

27. $5 \times \blacksquare = 230$ **28.** $4 \times \blacksquare = 304$ **29.** $\blacksquare \times 37 = 222$

Compare. Write <, >, or = for each ●.

30. $8 \times 37 \ \bullet \ 5 \times 79$ **31.** $6 \times 27 \ \bullet \ 3 \times 54$ **32.** $9 \times 58 \ \bullet \ 5 \times 98$

USE DATA For 33–35 and 37–38, use the chart.

33. MULTISTEP A large bowl holds 8 cups of fresh strawberries. How many calories are in the bowl of fresh strawberries? (HINT: 1 pint = 2 cups)

34. MULTISTEP Chef Marie tops her strawberry pie with 20 whole strawberries. She made 10 pies for the Strawberry Festival. About how many seeds are on top of Chef Marie's pies?

35. There are 26 students in Cindy's fourth-grade class. About how many pounds of berries did Cindy's class eat during the last year?

36. **What's the Error?** Cory says that $7 \times 52 = 354$. Describe Cory's error, and find the correct product.

37. Write a problem that uses one of the Berry Facts and involves multiplying a 2-digit number by a 1-digit number.

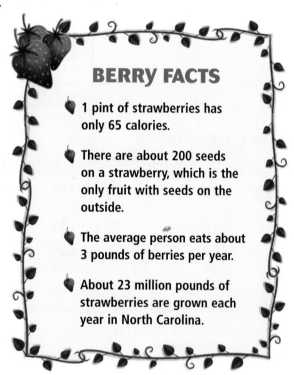

BERRY FACTS

- 1 pint of strawberries has only 65 calories.

- There are about 200 seeds on a strawberry, which is the only fruit with seeds on the outside.

- The average person eats about 3 pounds of berries per year.

- About 23 million pounds of strawberries are grown each year in North Carolina.

38. **What's the Question?** Olivia ate 1 pint of strawberries. Gabe and Matt shared 2 pints of strawberries. The answer is 195 calories.

39. Mrs. Kuwana bought 15 packages with 8 buns in each package for a neighborhood party. How many packages of 10 hot dogs each will she need for all of the hot dogs to have a bun and no buns left over?

40. Vocabulary Power The prefix *re-* when added to a root word can mean "again," as in *rerun*—"to run again." How does this information help you understand what *regroup* means?

Maintain Skills

41. Nicole received a box of chocolates. The box has 3 rows with 8 pieces of chocolate in each row. How many pieces of chocolate are in the box?

42. Estimate the length of your pencil. Then measure the length of your pencil to the nearest inch.

CRCT Test Prep

43. **M4A1.c.** What is the value of the expression if □ = 23? (p. 46)

$$(17 + \square) - 19$$

A. 19
B. 21
C. 23
D. 59

Problem Solving LINKUP . . . to Reading

ANALOGIES

An analogy shows a relationship between words or ideas.

Arm is to body as branch is to tree.

Product is to × as sum is to +.

▲ is to 3 as ■ is to 4.

Complete each analogy.

1. 2 × 14 is to ▦▦ as 3 × 21 is to __?__ .

2. Factor is to multiplication as addend is to __?__ .

3. 14 ones is to 1 ten 4 ones as 14 tens is to __?__ .

4. Add is to subtract as multiply is to __?__ .

5. 2 × 38 is to (2 × 30) + (2 × 8) as 3 × 45 is to __?__ .

TIP Find the relationship between the first pair. Then show the same relationship between the second pair.

4 Multiply 3-Digit Numbers

M4N3. Students will solve problems involving multiplication of 2-3 digit numbers by 1-2 digit numbers. *also* **M4N3, M4P2, M4P5.b., M4P5.c.**

1. 4×800 **2.** 600×7

3. $3{,}000 \times 5$ **4.** $9 \times 8{,}000$

5. $6 \times 1{,}200$

▶ Learn

ON THE GO Kurt and his family are traveling from Albany, Georgia, to Atlanta, Georgia, on vacation. They will drive 156 miles to get to Atlanta and will drive home on the same route. How many miles will they drive in all?

Find 2×156. Estimate. $2 \times 150 = 300$

Example 1

STEP 1

Multiply the ones.

2×6 ones $= 12$ ones

Regroup the ones.

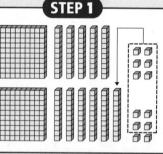

$$\begin{array}{r} \overset{1}{156} \\ \times\ \ 2 \\ \hline 2 \end{array}$$

Regroup the 12 ones as 1 ten 2 ones.

STEP 2

Multiply the tens.

2×5 tens $= 10$ tens

Add the regrouped ten.

Regroup the tens.

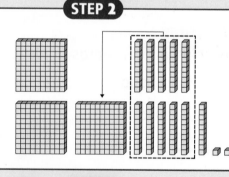

$$\begin{array}{r} \overset{11}{156} \\ \times\ \ 2 \\ \hline 12 \end{array}$$

Regroup the 11 tens as 1 hundred 1 ten.

STEP 3

Multiply the hundreds.

2×1 hundred $= 2$ hundreds

Add the regrouped hundred.

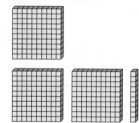

$$\begin{array}{r} \overset{11}{156} \\ \times\ \ 2 \\ \hline 312 \end{array}$$

So, they will travel 312 miles in all. Since 312 is close to the estimate of 300, it is reasonable.

Multiply with Zeros

While on vacation, Kurt enjoyed riding a roller coaster at a theme park. The roller coaster can carry 906 riders every hour. How many people can ride the roller coaster in 3 hours?

Find 3 × 906.
Estimate. 3 × 900 = 2,700

Example 2

STEP 1

Multiply the ones.
Regroup the ones.

$$\begin{array}{r} \overset{1}{906} \\ \times\ \ 3 \\ \hline 8 \end{array}$$

Regroup 18 ones as 1 ten 8 ones.

STEP 2

Multiply the tens.
Add the regrouped ten.

$$\begin{array}{r} \overset{1}{906} \\ \times\ \ 3 \\ \hline 18 \end{array}$$

STEP 3

Multiply the hundreds.

$$\begin{array}{r} \overset{1}{906} \\ \times\ \ \ \ 3 \\ \hline 2{,}718 \end{array}$$

So, 2,718 people can ride the roller coaster in 3 hours.
Since 2,718 is close to the estimate of 2,700, it is reasonable.

More Examples

Ⓐ

$$\begin{array}{r} \overset{11}{234} \\ \times\ \ 3 \\ \hline 702 \end{array}$$

Ⓑ

$$\begin{array}{r} \overset{31}{852} \\ \times\ \ 6 \\ \hline 5{,}112 \end{array}$$

Ⓒ

$$\begin{array}{r} \$7.09 \\ \times\ \ \ 5 \end{array} \qquad \begin{array}{r} \overset{4}{\$709} \\ \times\ \ \ \ 5 \\ \hline \$35.45 \end{array}$$

Multiply amounts of money the same way you multiply whole numbers. Write the product in dollars and cents.

▶ **Check**

Technology Link
More Practice: Harcourt Mega Math The Number Games, *Up, Up, and Array,* Level J

1. **Explain** how you record the 45 pennies when you multiply 9 by 5 in Example C.

Find the product. Estimate to check.

2. $\begin{array}{r} 136 \\ \times\ \ 5 \\ \hline \end{array}$

3. $\begin{array}{r} 254 \\ \times\ \ 2 \\ \hline \end{array}$

4. $\begin{array}{r} 321 \\ \times\ \ 3 \\ \hline \end{array}$

5. $\begin{array}{r} 125 \\ \times\ \ 9 \\ \hline \end{array}$

6. $\begin{array}{r} 307 \\ \times\ \ 8 \\ \hline \end{array}$

7. $\begin{array}{r} 980 \\ \times\ \ 3 \\ \hline \end{array}$

8. $\begin{array}{r} 602 \\ \times\ \ 4 \\ \hline \end{array}$

9. $\begin{array}{r} \$2.08 \\ \times\ \ \ \ 9 \\ \hline \end{array}$

10. 3 × 437

11. 5 × 505

12. 7 × 173

13. 6 × $7.04

LESSON CONTINUES ▶

Find the product. Estimate to check.

14. 241
    × 2

15. 632
    × 4

16. 318
    × 3

17. 653
    × 5

18. 702
    × 3

19. 450
    × 9

20. 805
    × 4

21. $6.03
    × 7

22. 2 × 825

23. 7 × 402

24. 4 × 973

25. 8 × 531

26. 3 × 403

27. 8 × $9.09

28. 5 × $2.08

29. 6 × $3.70

Multiply. Then add to find the product.

30. 3 × 472
    (3 × 400) + (3 × 70) + (3 × 2)

31. 3 × 509
    (3 × 500) + (3 × 9)

Compare. Write <, >, or = for each ●.

32. 4 × 326 ● 3 × 467

33. 8 × 199 ● 5 × 321

34. 2 × 750 ● 3 × 500

35. 5 × 272 ● 6 × 231

36. 7 × 408 ● 6 × 476

37. 4 × 809 ● 8 × 405

Use Data For 38–40, use the graph.

38. **MULTISTEP** During which months is the average temperature greater than 65°?

39. Name the month in which the average temperature is about 10°F less than the average temperature in May.

40. Which month has about the same average temperature as February?

41. ☀ **? What's the Question?** Jamal, Tim, and Lisa each brought 4 rolls of film on their vacation. They can take 36 pictures with each roll. The answer is 432 pictures.

42. **MULTISTEP** The theme park tickets for Tom and his 2 sisters cost $27 each. His parents' tickets cost $36 each. How much did the family's tickets cost?

43. **REASONING** Can two different multiplication problems have the same estimated product? Explain.

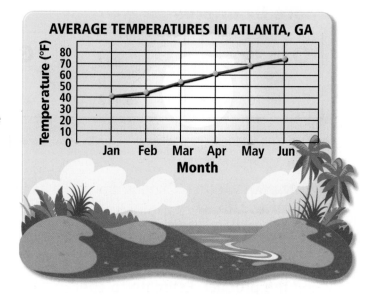

AVERAGE TEMPERATURES IN ATLANTA, GA

44. **? What's the Error?** Jeff made an error in his multiplication. Describe his error, and explain how to find the correct answer.

Jeff
```
      2
    206
  x   4
    884
```

45. Find the missing numbers on Keisha's paper. Explain your thinking.

Keisha
```
    623
  x   ■
  4,9■4
```

Maintain Skills

46. 32 × 3   **47.** 18 ÷ 2

Write the value of the blue digit.

48. 3,470   **49.** 73.5

Find the perimeter.

50.
6 ft
6 ft ☐ 6 ft
6 ft

51.
8 in.
5 in. ☐ 5 in.
8 in.

CRCT Test Prep

52. **M4G3.b.** Which ordered pair describes the location of the tree? (p. 82)

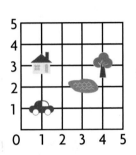

A. (1,1) B. (4,3) C. (1,3) D. (3,2)

Problem Solving   Thinker's Corner 💡

VISUAL THINKING Chris is drawing a picture to help him find the product 3 × 146.

He drew 146 by using a large square for a hundred, bars for tens, and small squares for ones.

1. Copy and complete Chris's drawing to show 3 × 146. What is the product?

2. What if you showed 3 × 246? How would your picture change?

Make drawings to find the products.

3. 3 × 423   **4.** 341 × 5   **5.** 4 × 209

Problem Solving Strategy
Make an Organized List

▶ **M4P1.c.** Apply and adapt a variety of appropriate strategies to solve problems.
also M4N3, M4P1.a., M4P1.b., M4P1.d., M4P2.d., M4P3.a., M4P3.b., M4P3.c.,
M4P3.d., M4P4.c.

PROBLEM Jeremy has 276 peaches to deliver to
8 small produce stands. Each stand must receive
between 30 and 35 peaches. If each stand receives
the same number of peaches, what is the greatest
number of peaches Jeremy can deliver to each stand?

UNDERSTAND

- What are you asked to find?
- What information will you use?

PLAN

- What strategy can you use to solve the problem?
  You can *make an organized list.* An organized list can
  show you all the possible solutions.

Georgia is known
as the "Peach State"
because of the
high-quality peaches
it grows. Since 1995,
the peach has been
the official state fruit.

SOLVE

- How can you use the strategy to find the answer?
  Make a list of all the possible numbers of peaches
  Jeremy can deliver to each stand.
  30 peaches per stand: $30 \times 8 = 240$
  31 peaches per stand: $31 \times 8 = 248$
  32 peaches per stand: $32 \times 8 = 256$
  33 peaches per stand: $33 \times 8 = 264$
  34 peaches per stand: $34 \times 8 = 272$
  35 peaches per stand: $35 \times 8 = 280$
  Since Jeremy has only 276 peaches, the greatest
  number he can deliver is 272.
  So, Jeremy can deliver 34 peaches to each stand.

CHECK

- What other strategy could you use?

Strategies

Act It Out or Use Objects
Make a Picture or Diagram
Guess and Check
Use or Look for a Pattern
Use Logical Reasoning
▶ Make an Organized List
Use or Make a Table
Work Backwards

Problem Solving

Make an organized list to solve.

1. **What if** Jeremy had 302 peaches and wanted to deliver between 35 and 40 peaches to each of the 8 produce stands? What is the greatest number of peaches he could deliver to each stand so that each received the same number?

2. Ryan does not want to pay more than $2.45 for three pounds of peaches. On any given day, peaches at Miller's Produce Stand cost between $0.79 and $0.82 per pound. What is the most Ryan will pay per pound for three pounds of peaches at Miller's Produce Stand?

Carrie bought 4 pounds of peaches at $0.85 per pound. She paid with a $5 bill. How much change did Carrie receive?

3. Which expression can you use to help you answer the question?

   A $5.00 − (4 × $0.85)
   B $5.00 + (4 × $0.85)
   C ($5.00 − $0.85) × 4
   D (4 × $0.85) − $5.00

4. What solution answers the question?

   F $6.40
   G $3.40
   H $1.60
   J $0.60

Mixed Strategy Practice

5. In August, peaches cost $0.89 per pound. In July, the price was $0.15 higher per pound than in August. In June, the price was $0.25 higher per pound than in July. How much did peaches cost in June?

6. Millie works between 34 and 38 hours each week. In one month, she worked the same number of hours each week. What is the greatest number of hours Millie worked each week if she did not work more than 142 hours in the 4-week period?

7. Mr. Beasley planted 8 peach trees last year and 7 more this year. Mr. Higgins has 12 peach trees. How many more trees must he plant to have as many as Mr. Beasley?

8. Sergio has some quarters and some nickels. He has twice as many nickels as quarters. If Sergio has $0.70, how many of each type of coin does he have?

9. Ben has three times as many marbles as Jon. Together they have between 18 and 25 marbles. How many marbles might Jon have?

10. The product of two numbers is 45. Their sum is 14. What are the numbers? What is their difference?

Extra Practice

Set A (pp. 148–149)

Use mental math to complete.

1. $3 \times 5 = \blacksquare$
$3 \times 50 = \blacksquare$
$3 \times 500 = \blacksquare$

2. $4 \times 8 = \blacksquare$
$4 \times 80 = \blacksquare$
$4 \times 800 = \blacksquare$

3. $2 \times 7 = \blacksquare$
$2 \times 70 = \blacksquare$
$2 \times 700 = \blacksquare$
$2 \times 7,000 = \blacksquare$

4. $5 \times 9 = \blacksquare$
$5 \times 90 = \blacksquare$
$5 \times 900 = \blacksquare$
$5 \times 9,000 = \blacksquare$

5. Ruiz has four $20 bills and three $5 bills. How much money does he have?

Set B (pp. 150–151)

Estimate the product. Choose the method.

1. 28×7 **2.** 219×8 **3.** 704×4 **4.** 237×4 **5.** 590×4 **6.** 814×6

7. About how many weeks are in 4 years?

8. About how many days are in 19 weeks?

9. About how many days are in 3 years?

Set C (pp. 152–155)

Find the product. Estimate to check.

1. 18×3 **2.** 27×5 **3.** 58×4 **4.** 83×7 **5.** 64×9 **6.** 47×6

7. Lucy earns $9 for each hour that she works. If Lucy works 55 hours in a month, how much would she earn that month?

Set D (pp. 156–159)

Find the product. Estimate to check.

1. 403×7 **2.** 783×2 **3.** 991×4 **4.** $\$8.61 \times 6$ **5.** $\$1.74 \times 5$ **6.** 668×6

7. $7 \times \$7.80$ **8.** $5 \times \$105$ **9.** $6 \times \$690$ **10.** 8×207

11. Mr. Jones bought 4 boxes of brushes for his students to use. Each box has 125 brushes. How many brushes did he buy?

Review/Test

✔ CHECK VOCABULARY AND CONCEPTS

Choose the best term from the box.

Vocabulary

compatible numbers
round
estimate

1. You can __?__ to find a number that is close to an exact amount. (p. 150)

2. Numbers that are easy to compute mentally are called __?__. (p. 150)

✔ CHECK SKILLS

Use mental math to complete. (pp. 148–149)

3. $5 \times 6 = \blacksquare$
$5 \times 60 = \blacksquare$
$5 \times 600 = \blacksquare$

4. $3 \times 7 = \blacksquare$
$3 \times 70 = \blacksquare$
$3 \times 700 = \blacksquare$

5. $4 \times 3 = \blacksquare$
$4 \times 30 = \blacksquare$
$4 \times 300 = \blacksquare$
$4 \times 3,000 = \blacksquare$

6. $2 \times 8 = \blacksquare$
$2 \times 80 = \blacksquare$
$2 \times 800 = \blacksquare$
$2 \times 8,000 = \blacksquare$

Estimate the product. Choose the method. (pp. 150–151)

7. 5×294

8. 5×66

9. 3×834

10. $6 \times \$5.36$

Find the product. Estimate to check. (pp. 152–155, 156–159)

11. $\begin{array}{r} 45 \\ \times\ 5 \\ \hline \end{array}$

12. $\begin{array}{r} 180 \\ \times\ 6 \\ \hline \end{array}$

13. $\begin{array}{r} 42 \\ \times\ 4 \\ \hline \end{array}$

14. $\begin{array}{r} 863 \\ \times\ 3 \\ \hline \end{array}$

15. $\begin{array}{r} \$8.21 \\ \times\ 4 \\ \hline \end{array}$

16. $\begin{array}{r} \$1.96 \\ \times\ 8 \\ \hline \end{array}$

17. $\begin{array}{r} \$7.50 \\ \times\ 3 \\ \hline \end{array}$

18. $\begin{array}{r} \$8.05 \\ \times\ 7 \\ \hline \end{array}$

✔ CHECK PROBLEM SOLVING

Solve. (pp. 160–161)

19. Peggy wants to spend no more than $5 for three bottles of apple juice. Different brands cost between $1.65 and $1.70 per bottle. What is the most Peggy will pay per bottle if she buys three bottles of the same brand?

20. Mr. Rodriguez bought 144 peaches. He will give each of his 5 brothers between 25 and 30 peaches. What is the greatest number of peaches he can give so that each brother gets the same number of peaches?

Chapter CRCT Test Prep

NUMBERS AND OPERATIONS

1. **M4N7.d.** Which pair of numbers has an estimated product of 2,400?

   A. 8 and 279

   B. 6 and 459

   C. 4 and 679

   D. 3 and 749

2. **M4N3.** Melissa uses 78 pecans in every pecan pie that she makes. How many pecans would she use in 9 pecan pies?

   A. 87

   B. 632

   C. 702

   D. 720

3. **M4N3.** Randy's family rented a cabin in the Blue Ridge Mountains. The cabin cost $160 per night. How much did it cost to stay in the cabin for 3 nights?

   A. $163

   B. $380

   C. $390

   D. $480

4. **M4N3.** What is the product 9 × 144?

   A. 16

   B. 153

   C. 966

   D. 1,296

ALGEBRA

5. **M4A1.a.** Use a pattern to find the product 7 × 300.

   A. 21,000

   B. 2,100

   C. 210

   D. 21

6. **M4A1.a.** Which of the following has a product of 20,000?

   A. 4 × 50

   B. 4 × 500

   C. 4 × 5,000

   D. 4 × 50,000

7. **M4A1.a.** Ashley is a bank teller. She has 8 fifty-dollar bills in her drawer. What is their value?

   A. $8.50

   B. $40.00

   C. $400.00

   D. $850.00

Use the table below to answer question 8.

Number of Packs	1	2	3	4	5
Number of Trading Cards	20	40	60		

8. **M4A1.a.** How many trading cards are in 5 packs?

   A. 100

   B. 80

   C. 25

   D. 24

🔺 Cumulative CRCT Test Prep

DATA ANALYSIS

Use the pictograph key below to answer question 9.

> **Key: Each** ❀ **= 4 flowers.**

9. **M4D1.a.** Fern used the key to make a pictograph of the flowers in her garden. How many symbols would be needed to show there are 8 dahlias in Fern's garden?

   A. 8

   B. 4

   C. 2

   D. 1

Use the bar graph below to answer question 10.

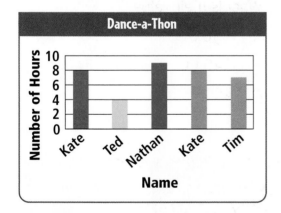

10. **M4D1.d.** The bar graph shows the number of hours that each person danced in a Dance-a-Thon. What is wrong with the bar graph?

   A. The bars are too narrow.

   B. Tim's data is duplicated.

   C. Kate's data is duplicated.

   D. Ted's data is missing.

NUMBERS AND OPERATIONS

11. **M4N2.a.** Jimmy drove 318 miles from his home in Dalton to Valdosta. What is 318 rounded to the nearest ten?

   A. 300

   B. 310

   C. 320

   D. 380

12. **M4N2.d.** On Monday afternoon, 883 children attended a children's concert. On Tuesday afternoon, 975 children attended the concert. Which is the BEST estimate for how many children attended both concerts?

   A. 1,700

   B. 1,800

   C. 1,900

   D. 2,000

13. **M4N7.a.** What operations are used to solve the following problem?

   The school store ordered 5 boxes of T-shirts. Each box contained 12 T-shirts. So far, 43 T-shirts have been sold. How many T-shirts are left in the school store?

   A. multiplication, then subtraction

   B. subtraction, then multiplication

   C. multiplication, then addition

   D. addition, then multiplication

Multiply by Tens

FAST FACT • **SOCIAL STUDIES** Whitewater rafting is a popular activity on the rivers of West Virginia, Tennessee, and North Carolina. More than 7,900 people raft down the Shenandoah River in West Virginia each year.

INVESTIGATION The table shows the minimum weights needed to raft safely. If there are 7 people in a raft who meet the minimum requirement, what is the least amount of weight a raft on each river will carry? Which rivers could you and six classmates raft on?

Using Data

MINIMUM RAFTING WEIGHT REQUIREMENTS (per person)

Shenandoah River, WV Class I–III	50 pounds
Upper Pigeon River, TN Class III–IV	70 pounds
Nantahala River, NC Class II–III	60 pounds

CHECK WHAT YOU KNOW

Use this page to help you review and remember important skills needed for Chapter 8.

MULTIPLY BY TENS, HUNDREDS, AND THOUSANDS

Multiply.

1. 3×900 **2.** 4×40 **3.** $2 \times 6,000$ **4.** 5×20

5. $8 \times 2,000$ **6.** 7×300 **7.** 9×50 **8.** $6 \times 1,000$

9.
$$\begin{array}{r} 10 \\ \times\ 9 \\ \hline \end{array}$$

10.
$$\begin{array}{r} 5,000 \\ \times\quad 3 \\ \hline \end{array}$$

11.
$$\begin{array}{r} 900 \\ \times\ 2 \\ \hline \end{array}$$

12.
$$\begin{array}{r} 600 \\ \times\ 5 \\ \hline \end{array}$$

MODEL MULTIPLICATION

Use the base-ten blocks to find the product.

13.
$$\begin{array}{r} 14 \\ \times\ 3 \\ \hline \end{array}$$
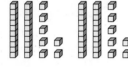

14.
$$\begin{array}{r} 25 \\ \times\ 2 \\ \hline \end{array}$$
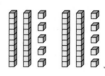

15.
$$\begin{array}{r} 27 \\ \times\ 2 \\ \hline \end{array}$$

16.
$$\begin{array}{r} 17 \\ \times\ 3 \\ \hline \end{array}$$

17.
$$\begin{array}{r} 12 \\ \times\ 5 \\ \hline \end{array}$$

VOCABULARY POWER

REVIEW

product [prä′dəkt] *noun*

A product is the result of putting things together. For example, a toy is a product from a toy factory. How is a product such as a toy like a product in multiplication? Explain.

  www.harcourtschool.com/mathglossary

Algebra: Mental Math: Multiplication Patterns

M4N7.d. Use mental math and estimation strategies to compute.
also **M4N3, M4P2.d., M4P3.a., M4P3.b., M4P3.c.**

▶ Learn

CROSS-COUNTRY Luis and his family drove from New York City to the Grand Canyon. They drove for a total of 50 hours at an average speed of 50 miles per hour. About how far did they drive?

Multiply. 50×50

Use a basic fact and a pattern.

Factors		Product	
5×5	=	25	**Think:** Use the basic fact $5 \times 5 = 25$.
5×50	=	250	Look for a pattern of zeros.
50×50	=	2,500	

↑ **1 zero**   ↑ **1 zero**   ↑ **2 zeros**

So, Luis and his family drove about 2,500 miles.

• What do you notice about the pattern of zeros in the factors and the products?

▲ The Grand Canyon is located in northern Arizona and surrounds 277 miles of the Colorado River.

Examples Use a basic fact and a pattern to find the product.

Ⓐ
$4 \times 1 = 4$
$4 \times 10 = 40$
$4 \times 100 = 400$
$4 \times 1,000 = 4,000$

Ⓑ
$7 \times 6 = 42$
$70 \times 60 = 4,200$
$70 \times 600 = 42,000$
$70 \times 6,000 = 420,000$

Ⓒ
$6 \times 5 = 30$
$60 \times 5 = 300$
$60 \times 50 = 3,000$
$600 \times 50 = 30,000$

MATH IDEA Basic facts and patterns can be used to help you find products when you multiply by multiples of 10, 100, or 1,000.

Technology Link

More Practice: Harcourt Mega Math The Number Games, *Up, Up, and Array,* Level I

▶ Check

1. Explain why the products in Example C have more zeros than the factors.

Use a basic fact and a pattern to find the products.

2. 9×10
9×100
$9 \times 1,000$

3. 6×60
60×60
600×60

4. 8×50
80×50
800×50

5. 30×9
300×90
$300 \times 9,000$

▶ Practice and Problem Solving   Extra Practice, page 178, Set A

Use a basic fact and a pattern to find the product.

6. 80×600

7. 700×500

8. 60×30

9. $300 \times 5,000$

10. 90
$\underline{\times \ 6}$

11. $8,000$
$\underline{\times \ \ \ 60}$

12. 40
$\underline{\times 30}$

13. 600
$\underline{\times \ 12}$

 **ALGEBRA** Find the value of □.

14. $\square \times 800 = 7,200$

15. $80 \times \square = 720,000$

16. $8,000 \times \square = 40,000$

17. $7,000 \times 10 = \square$

18. MULTISTEP On Tori's vacation, her dad drove about 60 miles per hour for 6 hours each day. About how far did he drive in 5 days?

19. Kim exercised 6 minutes one week, 9 minutes the second week, 12 minutes the third week, and 15 minutes the fourth week. If this pattern continues, how long will she exercise in the sixth week?

20. ? **What's the Error?** Describe Sheldon's error. Write the correct answer.

Tori's Summer Vacation

Grand Teton National Park, WY

Atlanta

Sheldon

$100,000 \times 10 = 1,100,000$

Maintain Skills

21. Use the model to find the sum $0.4 + 0.5$.

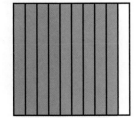

CRCT Test Prep

22. **M4D1.c.** Which type of graph would be the BEST to show how much a plant grew during an experiment? (p. 92)

A. bar graph
B. line graph
C. pictograph
D. double bar graph

The Distributive Property

HANDS ON

M4N7.c. Compute using the commutative, associative, and distributive properties. *also* M4N3, M4P3.a., M4P3.b., M4P3.c., M4P3.d., M4P4.a., M4P4.b., M4P5.

▶ **Explore**

Quick Review

Write each number in expanded form.

1. 62   **2.** 57

3. 23   **4.** 14

5. 77

MATERIALS grid paper, different-color markers

Cora and Mark are planting a flower garden. They want to plant 8 rows with 22 sunflowers in each row. How many sunflowers will they have in their garden?

You can use the Distributive Property to solve the problem. The Distributive Property states that multiplying a sum by a number is the same as multiplying each addend by the number and then adding the products.

Activity 1 Multiply. 8 × 22

You can make a model and use the Distributive Property to find the product.

STEP 1	STEP 2	STEP 3
Outline a rectangle that is 8 units wide and 22 units long. Think of the area as the product.	Break apart the rectangle by counting 20 units from the left and drawing a line.	Use the Distributive Property to show the sum of two products. Multiply what is in the parentheses first. Add the partial products.

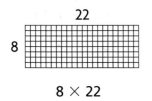

8 × 22

20   2

8

8 × (20 + 2)

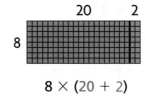

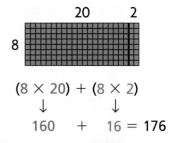

(8 × 20) + (8 × 2)
↓   ↓
160   +   16 = 176

So, they will have 176 sunflowers.

Try It

Make a model, and use the Distributive Property to find the product.

a. 6 × 18   **c.** 7 × 34

b. 5 × 27

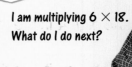

I am multiplying 6 × 18. What do I do next?

You can use the Distributive Property to multiply
by multiples of 10.

Activity 2 Multiply. 20 × 13

STEP 1

Show the model.
Break apart the model by counting
over 10 units from the left and
drawing a line.

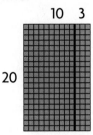

$$20 \times 13 = 20 \times (10 + 3)$$

STEP 2

Use the Distributive Property to show
the sum of two products. Multiply
what is in parentheses first. Add the
partial products.

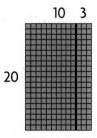

$$(20 \times 10) + (20 \times 3)$$
$$\downarrow \qquad\qquad \downarrow$$
$$200 \quad + \quad 60 = 260$$

So, 20 × 13 is 260.

▶ **Practice and Problem Solving**

Make a model, and use the Distributive Property to find the product.

1. 7 × 37   **2.** 20 × 15   **3.** 10 × 13   **4.** 30 × 22   **5.** 20 × 26

6. 50 × 34   **7.** 40 × 93   **8.** 60 × 48   **9.** 70 × 52   **10.** 40 × 16

11. **Write About It** Explain how to use the Distributive
Property to find 20 × 82.

12. MULTISTEP Kyle's Nursery planted 30 rows of trees with
35 trees in each row. This is 50 trees fewer than last year.
How many trees did the nursery plant last year?

Maintain Skills

13. In what place is the digit 4 in the
number 378.4?

14. What is the value of the digit 4 in the
number 95,402?

CRCT Test Prep

15. ◗ **M4N7.b.** Find the value. (p. 128)

$$(48 \div 8) - 2$$

A. 8   C. 4

B. 6   D. 2

Multiply by Tens

M4N3. Students will solve problems involving multiplication of 2-3 digit numbers by 1-2 digit numbers. *also* **M4P2.a., M4P2.c., M4P2.d., M4P3.a., M4P3.b., M4P3.c., M4P3.d.**

▷ **Learn**

ROUNDUP At the roundup, 30 ranchers each herded 52 cows. How many cows were herded in all?

Quick Review

1. 4×10 2. 4×100
3. $4 \times 1,000$ 4. 5×10
5. 5×100

Example Multiply. 30×52

STEP 1

Multiply by the ones. Place a zero in the ones place.

$$
\begin{array}{r}
52 \\
\times 30 \\
\hline
0
\end{array} \leftarrow \text{0 ones} \times 52
$$

STEP 2

Multiply by the tens.

$$
\begin{array}{r}
52 \\
\times 30 \\
\hline
1,560
\end{array} \leftarrow \text{3 tens} \times 52
$$

So, the ranchers herded 1,560 cows.

⚡ **MATH IDEA** When you multiply a whole number by a multiple of 10, the digit in the ones place of the product is always a zero.

▷ **Check**

1. **Tell** how many zeros are in the product of 18 and 20. How many zeros are in the product of 12 and 50? Explain how you can tell before you multiply.

Technology Link

More Practice:
Harcourt Mega Math
The Number Games,
Up, Up, and Array,
Level I

Find the product.

2. $\begin{array}{r} 12 \\ \times 10 \\ \hline \end{array}$	**3.** $\begin{array}{r} 18 \\ \times 30 \\ \hline \end{array}$	**4.** $\begin{array}{r} 28 \\ \times 20 \\ \hline \end{array}$	**5.** $\begin{array}{r} 32 \\ \times 40 \\ \hline \end{array}$	**6.** $\begin{array}{r} 47 \\ \times 30 \\ \hline \end{array}$
7. $\begin{array}{r} 46 \\ \times 40 \\ \hline \end{array}$	**8.** $\begin{array}{r} 91 \\ \times 20 \\ \hline \end{array}$	**9.** $\begin{array}{r} 55 \\ \times 60 \\ \hline \end{array}$	**10.** $\begin{array}{r} 72 \\ \times 30 \\ \hline \end{array}$	**11.** $\begin{array}{r} 33 \\ \times 30 \\ \hline \end{array}$

Find the product.

| **12.** 16
×10 | **13.** 19
×20 | **14.** 34
×40 | **15.** 27
×30 | **16.** 48
×50 |

17. 70×39 **18.** 52×80 **19.** 50×54 **20.** 69×70 **21.** 90×18

Find the missing digits.

22. ■0 × 40 = 400   **23.** 20 × ■0 = 600   **24.** ■7 × 40 = 680

25. 53 × ■0 = 3,180   **26.** 4■ × 50 = 2,250   **27.** 77 × 3■ = 2,■10

28. Ari's normal resting heart rate is 80 beats per minute. How many times would it beat if he rests for 25 minutes?

29. Anna Marie burns 14 calories per minute while running. How many calories will she burn if she runs for 30 minutes?

USE DATA For 30–32, use the bar graph.

30. How many shows does each wrangler do in 20 weeks?

31. How many shows does Carrie do in 50 weeks?

32. **MULTISTEP** In 30 weeks, how many more shows does Jake do than Floyd?

33. **Vocabulary Power** *Multiple* means "more than one." For example, you can make multiple copies of a story. Explain how multiple copies are like a multiple of a number like 10.

34. 📖 **Write a problem** that can be solved by multiplying by a multiple of 10 using data from the bar graph.

35. **ALGEBRA** Mr. Cano wrote the expression $\triangle \times 80 = 64{,}000$. Find the value of $\triangle$.

Maintain Skills

36. How can Julia show 7×4 as an addition problem?

37. $72 \div 6$

38. 50×3

39. Which is shorter, 5 ft or 5 yd?

CRCT Test Prep

40. ▶ **M4N3.** Pens come in boxes of 144 pens. How many pens are in 5 boxes? (p. 156)

A. 149

B. 500

C. 702

D. 720

Estimate Products

 M4N7.d. Use mental math and estimation strategies to compute.
also **M4N3, M4P2.d., M4P3.a., M4P3.b., M4P3.c., M4P3.d., M4P4, M4P4.c.**

▶ **Learn**

SPLISH SPLASH Lauren's class is going whitewater rafting. The trip costs $112 per student. If Lauren has 24 classmates, about how much will it cost the class to go rafting?

Example Estimate. 24 × $112

STEP 1

Round each factor.

$$\begin{array}{r} \$112 \\ \times\ 24 \end{array} \rightarrow \begin{array}{r} \$100 \\ \times\ 20 \end{array}$$

STEP 2

$$\text{Multiply.}\quad \begin{array}{r} \$100 \\ \times\ 20 \\ \hline \$2{,}000 \end{array}$$

So, it will cost about $2,000 for Lauren's class to go rafting.

• Will the actual cost be greater than or less than $2,000? Explain.

More Examples

Ⓐ $$\begin{array}{r} 73 \\ \times 42 \end{array} \rightarrow \begin{array}{r} 70 \\ \times 40 \\ \hline 2{,}800 \end{array}$$

Ⓑ $$\begin{array}{r} 254 \\ \times\ 65 \end{array} \rightarrow \begin{array}{r} 300 \\ \times\ 70 \\ \hline 21{,}000 \end{array}$$

Remember

To round a number:

• Find the place to which you want to round. Look at the digit to its right.
• If the digit is less than 5, the digit in the rounding place stays the same.
• If the digit is 5 or greater, the digit in the rounding place increases by 1.

▶ **Check**

1. Explain how you can estimate the product 52 × 168.

Round each factor. Estimate the product.

2. $$\begin{array}{r} 18 \\ \times 29 \end{array}$$

3. $$\begin{array}{r} 389 \\ \times\ 64 \end{array}$$

4. $$\begin{array}{r} \$45 \\ \times\ 12 \end{array}$$

5. $$\begin{array}{r} \$259 \\ \times\ 41 \end{array}$$

6. $$\begin{array}{r} 52 \\ \times 27 \end{array}$$

7. $$\begin{array}{r} 76 \\ \times 31 \end{array}$$

8. $$\begin{array}{r} 410 \\ \times\ 78 \end{array}$$

9. $$\begin{array}{r} 197 \\ \times\ 16 \end{array}$$

Round each factor. Estimate the product.

10. $19
    × 12

11. 278
    × 33

12. $548
    × 45

13. 38
    ×27

14. 32
    ×61

15. 419
    × 72

16. 78
    ×36

17. 64
    ×67

18. 219
    × 23

19. 634
    × 55

20. 13 × 85

21. 76 × 852

22. $49 × 24

23. 90 × 412

24. 18 × $319

Estimate to compare. Write <, >, or = for each ●.

25. 20 × 132 ● 3,000

26. 13,000 ● 26 × 645

27. 49 × 42 ● 1,800

USE DATA For 28–29, use the table.

28. The table shows the average number of apples in each size bag and the number of bags sold. Estimate the number of apples sold for each of the bag sizes.

29. **MULTISTEP** The fourth-grade students at Oak Elementary School are taking 8 large bags and 2 medium bags of apples to eat on their rafting trip. Estimate the total number of apples they are taking.

30. ≡**FAST FACT** • **SOCIAL STUDIES**
Each month, the average person in the United States uses about 46 pounds of paper. Estimate the amount of paper used by the average person in the United States in 1 year.

31. ✎ **Write About It** Explain how you would estimate the product 16 × 934.

Bags of Apples Sold

Bags	Average Number of Apples	Number of Bags Sold
Small	11	27
Medium	18	21
Large	26	12

Maintain Skills

For 32–33, estimate the product.

32. 4 × 65

33. 7 × 23

34. Which is longer, 1 yard or 1 foot?

35. Which is longer, 55 millimeters or 55 centimeters?

CRCT Test Prep

36. **M4N7.a.** A bag holds 20 balloons. What operation would you use to find the total number of balloons in 4 bags? (p. 120)

A. division
B. addition
C. subtraction
D. multiplication

Problem Solving Skill
Too Much/Too Little Information

M4N3. Students will solve problems involving multiplication of 2-3 digit numbers by 1-2 digit numbers. *also* **M4P1, M4P1.a., M4P1.b., M4P1.c., M4P1.d., M4P2.d., M4P3.a., M4P3.b., M4P3.c., M4P3.d.**

> UNDERSTAND > PLAN > SOLVE > CHECK >

LET'S GO CAMPING Sara's class is going on a camping trip to Cloudland Canyon State Park. The park has 16 cottages. Sara's class will rent 12 cottages at a cost of $95 each per night. There are 36 students going on the trip. About how much will the students have to pay in all to rent 12 cottages for one night?

- **Decide what the problem asks you to find.**
  The problem asks you to find about how much it will cost in all to rent 12 cottages for one night.

- **Decide what information you need to solve the problem.**
  You need to know the cost of one cottage and the number of cottages to be rented.

  cost of one cottage × number of cottages to be rented = total cost of cottages to be rented

- **Read the problem again carefully. Decide whether there is too much information or too little information in the problem.**
  There is too much information. You do not need to know the total number of cottages and the total number of students.

- **Solve the problem, if possible.**
  Round each factor: 95 × 12 is about 100 × 10.
  Multiply. 100 × 10 = 1,000

Quick Review

Write the missing number.
1. 3 × 12 = 12 × ☐
2. (2 × 3) × 5 = 2 × (☐ × 5)
3. 14 × 1 = ☐
4. ☐ × 8 = 0
5. ☐ × 9 = 9

Georgia

▲ Cloudland State Park is located in northwestern Georgia on the western edge of Lookout Mountain. Cottages are located on the canyon edge.

16 cottages *12 cottages to rent* *$95* *36 students*

So, the total cost to rent the 12 cottages will be about $1,000.

Talk About It

- **What if** the cost to rent a cottage were not given? Would you have too much or too little information to solve the problem? Explain.

Problem Solving Practice

Decide whether the problem has too much or too little information. Then solve the problem, if possible.

1. Sara took pictures from Lookout Mountain every day for the 5 days she was there. She made 2 copies of each picture she took. How many pictures does Sara have in all?

2. The trip back to the school from the park took 6 hours. The bus driver drove at a speed of 58 miles per hour. There were 36 students and 3 adults in the bus. About how far is the park from the school?

▲ Cloudland Canyon is on Lookout Mountain. The view is one of the most beautiful scenes in Georgia.

The students cooked hot dogs for supper one night. The adults cooked hamburgers. There were 12 packages of hot dogs with 8 hot dogs in a package and some packages of buns. Each of the 36 students ate 2 hot dogs.

3. Which question **cannot** be answered based on the information given?

   A How many hot dogs were left over?
   B How many students had buns with their hot dogs?
   C How many hot dogs were eaten by the students?
   D How many hot dogs did they have in all?

4. What information is **not** needed to find how many hot dog buns were left over?

   F the number of hot dog buns in a package
   G the number of students who had buns with their hot dogs
   H the cost of a package of hot dog buns
   J the number of packages of hot dog buns

Mixed Applications

USE DATA For 5–7, use the table.

5. Mt. McKinley is the highest point in North America. It is about 2,000 feet taller than twice the height of Mt. Isto. About how tall is Mt. McKinley?

6. So far, a mountain climber has climbed 795 feet from the base of Stone Mountain. How many feet must the climber still climb to reach the top of Stone Mountain?

7. ✎ **Write About It** Explain how to order the heights of the mountains from least to greatest. Then write the heights in that order.

SELECTED U.S. MOUNTAINS		
Mountain	**State**	**Height (in ft)**
Mt. Elbert	CO	14,433
Stone Mountain	GA	1,683
Mt. Isto	AK	9,060
Mt. Mitchell	NC	6,684

Extra Practice

Set A (pp. 168–169)

Use a basic fact and patterns to find the product.

1. 90×500 **2.** $40 \times 8,000$ **3.** 90×30 **4.** 700×200

5. $\begin{array}{r} 80 \\ \times 60 \\ \hline \end{array}$ **6.** $\begin{array}{r} 7,000 \\ \times \ 200 \\ \hline \end{array}$ **7.** $\begin{array}{r} 800 \\ \times \ 50 \\ \hline \end{array}$ **8.** $\begin{array}{r} 300 \\ \times \ 10 \\ \hline \end{array}$

Find the value of □.

9. $10,000 \times \square = 500,000$ **10.** $7,000 \times 7,000 = \square$ **11.** $\square \times 50 = 10,000$

12. $900 \times 12,000 = \square$ **13.** $\square \times 250,000 = 6,250,000$ **14.** $80 \times \square = 320,000$

Set B (pp. 172–173)

Find the product.

1. $\begin{array}{r} 11 \\ \times 20 \\ \hline \end{array}$ **2.** $\begin{array}{r} 45 \\ \times 30 \\ \hline \end{array}$ **3.** $\begin{array}{r} 18 \\ \times 40 \\ \hline \end{array}$ **4.** $\begin{array}{r} 25 \\ \times 30 \\ \hline \end{array}$ **5.** $\begin{array}{r} 62 \\ \times 50 \\ \hline \end{array}$

6. $\begin{array}{r} 43 \\ \times 20 \\ \hline \end{array}$ **7.** $\begin{array}{r} 32 \\ \times 60 \\ \hline \end{array}$ **8.** $\begin{array}{r} 17 \\ \times 50 \\ \hline \end{array}$ **9.** $\begin{array}{r} 65 \\ \times 30 \\ \hline \end{array}$ **10.** $\begin{array}{r} 84 \\ \times 40 \\ \hline \end{array}$

11. 73×40 **12.** 21×70 **13.** 19×20 **14.** 55×30 **15.** 47×80

16. 24×20 **17.** 64×40 **18.** 16×30 **19.** 12×80 **20.** 38×60

21. Erin swims 25 laps a day. How many laps does she swim in 30 days?

Set C (pp. 174–175)

Round each factor. Estimate the product.

1. $\begin{array}{r} 13 \\ \times 22 \\ \hline \end{array}$ **2.** $\begin{array}{r} 479 \\ \times \ 48 \\ \hline \end{array}$ **3.** $\begin{array}{r} \$73 \\ \times \ 18 \\ \hline \end{array}$ **4.** $\begin{array}{r} 529 \\ \times \ 11 \\ \hline \end{array}$ **5.** $\begin{array}{r} 91 \\ \times 27 \\ \hline \end{array}$

6. $\begin{array}{r} \$87 \\ \times 61 \\ \hline \end{array}$ **7.** $\begin{array}{r} 52 \\ \times 48 \\ \hline \end{array}$ **8.** $\begin{array}{r} 734 \\ \times \ 52 \\ \hline \end{array}$ **9.** $\begin{array}{r} \$618 \\ \times \ 37 \\ \hline \end{array}$ **10.** $\begin{array}{r} 129 \\ \times \ 23 \\ \hline \end{array}$

11. 32×79 **12.** 43×57 **13.** 89×531 **14.** 93×271 **15.** 32×197

16. 18×39 **17.** 58×129 **18.** 72×489 **19.** $21 \times \$625$ **20.** 42×385

Review/Test

✅ CHECK CONCEPTS

1. Explain how a basic fact and a pattern can help you find the product 60×400. (pp. 168–169)

2. Make a model, and use the Distributive Property to find the product 30×17. (pp. 170–171)

✅ CHECK SKILLS

Use a basic fact and a pattern to find the product. (pp. 168–169)

3. 20×900

4. 500×600

5. $9,000 \times 60$

6. 300×700

Find the product. (pp. 172–173)

7. 66×30

8. 44×60

9. 22×90

10. 75×80

11. 73×40

12. 36×30

13. 52×20

14. 64×50

15. 24×50

16. 86×20

17. 19×40

18. 93×70

Round each factor. Estimate the product. (pp. 174–175)

19. 222×48

20. 252×14

21. 931×56

22. 79×68

✅ CHECK PROBLEM SOLVING

For 23–25, decide whether the problem has too much or too little information. Then solve the problem, if possible. (pp. 176–177)

23. A choir has 98 members and needs to buy 30 new music stands and 20 sheets of music for each member. How many sheets do they need to buy?

24. The Toy Warehouse has 248 shelves. Each shelf has 16 boxes of toys. There are 12 toys in each box. About how many boxes are on the shelves?

25. Kevin is reading a series of books. There are 25 books in the series. How many total pages will Kevin have read when he has completed the series?

Chapter CRCT Test Prep

NUMBERS AND OPERATIONS

1. **M4N7.d.** Mr. Wong has 60 packages of drawing paper. Each package has 200 sheets of paper. How many sheets of paper are there?

   A.   120

   B.   260

   C. 12,000

   D. 120,000

2. **M4N7.d.** The table below shows the number of callers who pledged money to a public TV station.

Public TV Fund Drive	
Pledge Amount	**Number of Callers**
$10	29
$50	11
$100	9

   Which is the BEST estimate for how much money was pledged to the station in all?

   A. about $3,800

   B. about $2,800

   C. about $1,800

   D. about $1,000

3. **M4N3.** Audra travels 60 miles round trip from her house to work in Atlanta. Last month, she worked 22 days. How many miles did Audra travel to and from work last month?

   A. 1,500

   B. 1,320

   C. 1,220

   D. 1,200

NUMBERS AND OPERATIONS

4. **M4N7.c.** Which expression shows how to use the distributive property to multiply 30 × 54?

   A. (30 × 50) + (30 × 4)

   B. (30 + 50) × (30 + 4)

   C. (30 + 50) + (30 + 4)

   D. (30 × 50) × (30 × 4)

5. **M4N7.d.** There are about 114 students at each grade level in Washington Elementary School. The school ordered new math books for grades 3 through 5. About how many math books were ordered?

   A. about 200 books

   B. about 300 books

   C. about 400 books

   D. about 500 books

6. **M4N3.** One crate holds 25 peaches. On Monday, 20 crates were delivered to a fruit stand. On Tuesday, 10 more crates were delivered. How many peaches were delivered in all?

   A.   65

   B.   510

   C.   750

   D. 5,000

Cumulative CRCT Test Prep

DATA ANALYSIS

Use the bar graph below to answer question 7.

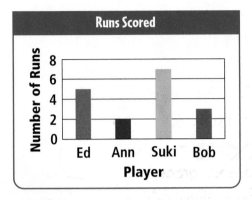

Runs Scored

Number of Runs — Player: Ed, Ann, Suki, Bob

7. **M4D1.a.** How many more runs did Suki score than Ann?

A. 7

B. 5

C. 3

D. 2

8. **M4D1.a.** Dee used the key below to make a pictograph to show the number of campers at Mistletoe State Park last weekend. There were 60 campers on Friday, 70 on Saturday, and 90 on Sunday.

Key: ▲ = 20 campers

How many symbols did Dee use to show the number of campers on Sunday?

A. $4\frac{1}{2}$

B. 4

C. $3\frac{1}{2}$

D. 3

ALGEBRA

9. **M4A1.b.** Which expression describes the situation?

a number of stickers shared equally among 9 students

A. □ × 9

B. 9 × □

C. 9 ÷ □

D. □ ÷ 9

10. **M4A1.c.** What is the value of the expression 15 × □ if □ = 5?

A. 90

B. 75

C. 60

D. 20

11. **M4A1.a.** What is the missing number in the table below?

In	Out
12	3
24	6
36	□
48	12

A. 7

B. 8

C. 9

D. 10

Multiply by 2-Digit Numbers

≡FAST FACT • SOCIAL STUDIES
The *Greetings from America* stamp set, introduced in early 2002, represents each of the 50 states. The postage rate to mail a letter then was 34 cents. Before 1863, postage rates were based on the number of sheets in a letter and the distance it was traveling. Beginning in 1863, rates became based on weight only.

INVESTIGATION Look at the graph. How much did 12 stamps cost in 1987? How many stamps could you buy for that amount of money in 2006?

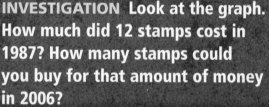

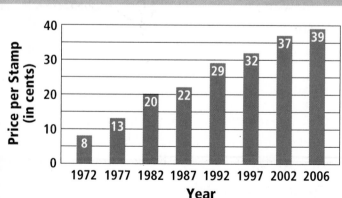

Using Data

UNITED STATES LETTER STAMP RATES

Price per Stamp (in cents)

40
30
20
10
0

Year	Price
1972	8
1977	13
1982	20
1987	22
1992	29
1997	32
2002	37
2006	39

Year

CHECK WHAT YOU KNOW

Use this page to help you review and remember important skills needed for Chapter 9.

✓ ESTIMATE PRODUCTS

Estimate the product.

1.	2.	3.	4.
12	14	21	18
× 9	× 6	× 8	× 5

5.	6.	7.	8.
272	350	649	212
× 3	× 7	× 4	× 7

9.	10.	11.	12.
322	817	444	145
× 9	× 2	× 3	× 2

13. 4 × 781   **14.** 5 × 550   **15.** 6 × 317   **16.** 4 × 385

✓ MULTIPLY BY 1-DIGIT NUMBERS

Find the product. Estimate to check.

17.	18.	19.	20.
12	43	39	61
× 6	× 4	× 3	× 5

21.	22.	23.	24.
35	25	125	163
× 7	× 5	× 2	× 3

25.	26.	27.	28.
350	100	49	101
× 3	× 5	× 7	× 9

VOCABULARY POWER

REVIEW	**PREVIEW**
money [mə′nē] *noun*	multistep problem

Money comes from the Latin *moneta*, meaning "mint" or "coinage." List three synonyms you can think of for *money*. Use each word in a sentence.

 www.harcourtschool.com/mathglossary

Multiply 2-Digit Numbers

 M4N3. Students will solve problems involving multiplication of 2-3 digit numbers by 1-2 digit numbers. *also* **M4P3, M4P4.a., M4P4.b.**

▶ **Learn**

TOTALLY TOMATOES Mr. Henson grows tomatoes. There are 35 plants on each tray. Mr. Henson has 88 trays. How many tomato plants does he have in all?

Example 1

Multiply.   35 × 88
                   ↓   ↓
Estimate.   40 × 90 = 3,600

You can use place value and regrouping to find 35 × 88.

STEP 1

Think of 35 as 3 tens 5 ones. Multiply by 5 ones.

```
  4
  88
 ×35
 440  ← 5 × 88
```

STEP 2

Multiply by 3 tens, or 30.

```
   2
   4
   88
  ×35
   440
  2640  ← 30 × 88
```

STEP 3

Add the products.

```
  2
  4
  88
 ×35
 440
+2 640
 3,080
```

So, there are 3,080 tomato plants. Since 3,080 is close to the estimate of 3,600, the answer is reasonable.

More Examples

A
```
  2
  7
  29
 ×38
 232  ← 8 × 29
+870  ← 30 × 29
1,102
```

B
```
   3
   1
  $55
 × 62
  110  ← 2 × 55
+3 300  ← 60 × 55
$3,410
```

• Explain how you know in which place to begin when you multiply by 2-digit numbers.

Find Products

The greenhouse has 45 bags of potting soil. Each bag has enough soil to pot 29 plants. How many plants can be potted?

Example 2

Multiply.   45 × 29
              ↓   ↓

Estimate.   50 × 30 = 1,500

One Way

Colleen used regrouping to find the product.

```
           Colleen

         3
         4
         29
        x45
        145  ← 5 x 29
      +1 160 ← 40 x 29
       1,305
```

Another Way

Brad used partial products.

```
           Brad

         29
        x45
         45  ← 5 x 9
        100  ← 5 x 20
        360  ← 40 x 9
       +800  ← 40 x 20
       1,305
```

So, there is enough soil to pot 1,305 plants. Since 1,305 is close to the estimate of 1,500, the answer is reasonable.

MATH IDEA You can find products using place value and regrouping, or you can use the partial-products method.

- Explain why the second partial-product is always greater than the first partial product when you multiply two 2-digit numbers.

Technology Link

More Practice: Harcourt Mega Math The Number Games, *Up, Up, and Array*, Level K; The Number Games, *Tiny's Think Tank*, Level F

Check

1. **Explain** how the partial-products method of finding products is different from the regrouping method.

Choose either method to find the product. Estimate to check.

2. 37 ×22	**3.** 54 ×31	**4.** 42 ×26	**5.** 78 ×41	**6.** $23 × 34
7. 67 ×14	**8.** 93 ×76	**9.** 82 ×47	**10.** 51 ×79	**11.** 38 ×64

LESSON CONTINUES ▶

Choose either method to find the product. Estimate to check.

12.   44
        ×35

13.   49
        ×26

14. $63
        × 42

15.   81
        ×22

16.   72
        ×59

17. $38
        × 29

18.   76
        ×45

19.   68
        ×79

20.   97
        ×65

21.   82
        ×35

Solve.

22. A peach tree is 17 feet tall. A redwood tree is 21 times as tall. What is the height of the redwood tree?

23. A nursery sold 36 pecan trees to a landscaper for $27 each. How much did the landscaper pay for the pecan trees?

MENTAL MATH   **Write the missing product.**

24. $20 \times 16 = 320$, so $20 \times 17 = $ ■.

25. $45 \times 28 = 1,260$, so $45 \times 29 = $ ■.

26. $13 \times 50 = 650$, so $13 \times 49 = $ ■.

27. $45 \times 17 = 765$, so $45 \times 16 = $ ■.

Copy and complete.

28.   45
           ×72
            10   ← ■ × ■
            80   ← ■ × ■
           350   ← ■ × ■
         +2 800 ← ■ × ■
          3,240

29.   23
           ×98
            24   ← ■ × ■
           160   ← ■ × ■
           270   ← ■ × ■
         +1 800 ← ■ × ■
          2,254

30. ⭐**ALGEBRA**   Find the missing numbers. Explain.

           35
          ×6■
           1■5
         +2 100
          2,275

31. ❓**What's the Error?** Describe Emilia's error. Write the correct answer.

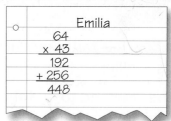

32. Vocabulary Power *Partial* means "relating to a part rather than a whole." How does this meaning relate to a partial product when multiplying 2-digit numbers?

33. REASONING Is 12×22 greater than or less than 200? Explain.

USE DATA For 34–35, use the graph.

34. Grace and her father belong to a garden club. How many more members were there in 2006 than in 2003?

35. **MULTISTEP** Each member pays $32 in dues each year. How much more in dues was collected in 2006 than in 2004?

36. Ellie rides her bike 22 miles each week for exercise. What is the total number of miles Ellie rides in a year?

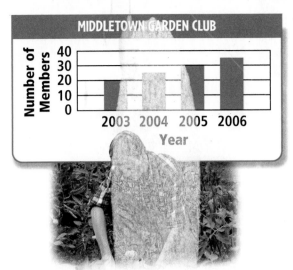

MIDDLETOWN GARDEN CLUB

Maintain Skills

37. What is the perimeter of the rectangle?

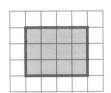

38. 41
    × 9

39. 70
    × 6

CRCT Test Prep

40. **M4N3.** Al has 14 rows of stamps. Each row has 9 stamps. How many stamps does Al have? (p. 152)
    A. 94   B. 126   C. 182   D. 443

41. **M4N4.a.** Mr. Konrad has 56 tulip bulbs. He plants them in 8 rows with the same number in each row. How many bulbs are in each row? (p. 114)
    A. 10   B. 9   C. 8   D. 7

Problem Solving LiNKUP ...to Science

NETWORKS A **network** is a system of parts that are connected. For example, computers in an office that are connected are part of a network.

This diagram shows a network of paths. Each path has a value.

For 1–2, follow these steps.

  a. Find a path from **Start** to **Finish**.
  b. Begin at Start with the number 2.
  c. As you move from letter to letter, multiply your results by the number along the path.

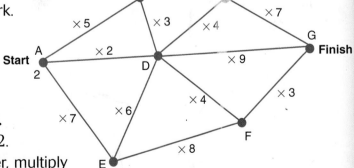

1. Name a path that has a product greater than 500.

2. Name a path that has a product less than 100.

Multiply 3-Digit Numbers

 M4N3. Students will solve problems involving multiplication of 2-3 digit numbers by 1-2 digit numbers. *also* **M4P3.c., M4P5.b., M4P5.c.**

Quick Review

1. 9×40 2. 10×30
3. 5×50 4. 7×20
5. 6×200

▶ Learn

WISH YOU WERE HERE Gulfside Gift Shop ordered 36 boxes of postcards to sell. There are 124 postcards in each box. How many postcards does the gift shop have to sell?

Example

Multiply. 36×124
     ↓   ↓
Estimate. $40 \times 120 = 4,800$

STEP 1	STEP 2	STEP 3
Multiply by the ones.	Multiply by the tens.	Add the products.
$$\begin{array}{r} {\scriptstyle 1\,2} \\ 124 \\ \times\ 36 \\ \hline 744 \end{array} \leftarrow 6 \times 124$$	$$\begin{array}{r} {\scriptstyle 1\ \overset{1}{2}} \\ 124 \\ \times\ 36 \\ \hline 744 \\ 3720 \end{array} \leftarrow 30 \times 124$$	$$\begin{array}{r} {\scriptstyle 1\ \overset{1}{2}} \\ 124 \\ \times\ 36 \\ \hline 744 \\ +3\,720 \\ \hline 4,464 \end{array}$$

So, Gulfside Gift Shop has 4,464 postcards to sell. Since 4,464 is close to the estimate of 4,800, the answer is reasonable.

More Examples

A
$$\begin{array}{r} {\scriptstyle 1} \\ 204 \\ \times\ 41 \\ \hline 204 \\ +8\,160 \\ \hline 8,364 \end{array}$$
$\leftarrow 1 \times 204$
$\leftarrow 40 \times 204$

B
$$\begin{array}{r} {\scriptstyle 5} \\ 109 \\ \times\ 60 \\ \hline 000 \\ +6\,540 \\ \hline 6,540 \end{array}$$
These zeros can be ← omitted.
$\leftarrow 60 \times 109$

C
$$\begin{array}{r} {\scriptstyle \overset{1}{3}\,1} \\ \$562 \\ \times\ 35 \\ \hline 2\,810 \\ +16\,860 \\ \hline \$19,670 \end{array}$$
$\leftarrow 5 \times 562$
$\leftarrow 30 \times 562$

▶ Check

1. **Explain** what happened to the regrouped digit, 5, in Example B when the 0 was multiplied by 60.

Find the product. Estimate to check.

2.   237
      × 21

3. $103
      × 29

4.   187
      × 35

5.   417
      × 72

6.   532
      × 20

Practice and Problem Solving

Extra Practice, page 196, Set B

Find the product. Estimate to check.

7.   888
      × 22

8. $794
      × 25

9.   204
      × 41

10.   437
       × 70

11. $837
       × 21

12. The Greens' car gets 22 miles per gallon. On a trip they used 102 gallons of gas. How many miles did they drive?

13. MULTISTEP Marla and Sasha are selling cookies. Each box has 15 cookies. Marla sells 173 boxes and Sasha sells 201 boxes. How many cookies did they sell in all?

 **ALGEBRA**   Find the value for □ or △ that makes the equation true.

14. $20 \times 543 = \square$

15. $30 \times 147 = \triangle$

16. $80 \times 209 = \triangle$

17. $\triangle \times 276 = 2{,}760$

18. $\triangle \times 900 = 54{,}000$

19. $\square \times 500 = 40{,}000$

USE DATA For 20–21, use the graph.

20. Medium fruit baskets sold for $16. What was the total value of sales in December for medium baskets?

21. MULTISTEP Small fruit baskets sold for $7. How much more did Fruit Galore make on sales of small fruit baskets in December than in November?

22. REASONING Find the missing digit in the number sentence $908 \times 3\blacksquare = 31{,}780$. Explain how you found your answer.

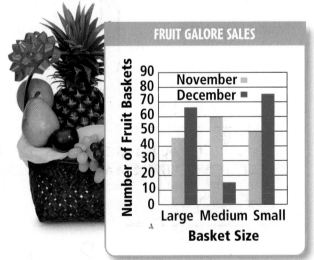

Maintain Skills

23. Keri bought a 32-ounce container of juice. She poured 6 ounces of juice into 5 cups. How many ounces of juice were left over?

24. What digit is in the tenths place of 1,429.5?

CRCT Test Prep

25. **M4N3.** Lenny delivers 132 newspapers every day. How many newspapers does he deliver in 7 days? (p. 156)

A. 139   C. 914

B. 714   D. 924

Chapter 9   **189**

Choose a Method

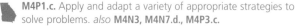

M4P1.c. Apply and adapt a variety of appropriate strategies to solve problems. *also* **M4N3, M4N7.d., M4P3.c.**

▶ **Learn**

FOREIGN EXCHANGE In the United States, the dollar is used. In Chile, the peso is used. The last time that Elena visited her grandparents in Chile, one dollar was equal to 643 pesos. If Elena spent 52 dollars on gifts, how many pesos did she spend?

Example

Multiply. 52×643
                     ↓   ↓
Estimate. $50 \times 600 = 30,000$

Then choose a method of computation that will be useful for the numbers given.

Use Paper and Pencil. Find the product. $52 \times 643 = $ ■

STEP 1	STEP 2	STEP 3
Multiply by the ones.	Multiply by the tens.	Add the products.
$\begin{array}{r} 643 \\ \times\ \ 52 \\ \hline 1,286 \end{array}$ ← 2×643	$\begin{array}{r} \overset{2\,1}{643} \\ \times\ \ 52 \\ \hline 1\ 286 \\ 32150 \end{array}$ ← 50×643	$\begin{array}{r} \overset{2\,1}{643} \\ \times\ \ 52 \\ \hline 1\ 286 \\ +32\ 150 \\ \hline 33,436 \end{array}$

So, Elena spent 33,436 pesos. Since 33,436 is close to the estimate of 30,000, the answer is reasonable.

More Examples

A **Use Mental Math**
$40 \times 525 = $ ■
Think: $40 \times 500\ \ \ = 20,000$
      and $40 \times 25 = 1,000$
So, $40 \times 525 = 21,000$.

B **Use a Calculator**
$24 \times \$701 = $ ■

 $\boxed{2}\ \boxed{4}\ \boxed{\times}\ \boxed{7}\ \boxed{0}\ \boxed{1}\ \boxed{=}$

Estimate to check: $\boxed{16'824.}$
$20 \times 700 = 14,000$
So, $24 \times \$701 = \$16,824$.

 MATH IDEA You can find a product by using paper and pencil, a calculator, or mental math. Look at the numbers in the problem before you choose a method.

1. **Explain** when you might choose mental math instead of paper and pencil.

Tell whether each problem can be solved by using mental math, paper and pencil, or a calculator. Then solve each problem using the method you chose.

2. A book of stamps contains 20 stamps. How many stamps are in 25 books of stamps?

3. Super Garden has 128 trays of various plants on sale. Each tray has 35 plants. How many plants are on sale?

4. Look back at Problems 2 and 3. Did you choose the best method? Could you solve the problems another way? Explain.

► **Practice and Problem Solving** (Extra Practice, page 196, Set C)

Tell whether each problem can be solved by using mental math, paper and pencil, or a calculator. Then solve each problem using the method you chose.

5. An office building has 449 offices. Each office has 38 or more workers. What is the least number of workers in the office building?

6. Elena has 10 pen pals around the world. She writes a letter to each one every month. How many letters does Elena write in 12 months?

7. Keiko works 5 days per week at the post office. Each day, she travels 24 miles to work and 24 miles back home. How many miles does Keiko travel to and from work each week?

8. There are 165 packages of drawing paper. Each package has 48 sheets of paper. How many sheets of drawing paper are there in all?

9. Look back at Problems 5–8. Did you choose the best method? Could you solve the problems another way? Explain.

10. **≡FAST FACT • HEALTH** The recommended serving of water for the average person is 8 glasses a day. How many glasses would that be in a week? in 30 days?

11. **REASONING** Find the product. Explain your method. 684
$\times\,306$

Maintain Skills

12. There are 28 students in Mrs. Green's class. She assigned them to groups of 4 to do a science project. How many groups are there?

CRCT Test Prep

13. **M4N7.b.** Find the value of the expression. (p. 130)

$$4 + 5 \times 8$$

A. 44   C. 62

B. 53   D. 72

Practice Multiplication Using Money

M4N3. Students will solve problems involving multiplication of 2-3 digit numbers by 1-2 digit numbers. *also* **M4P3.a., M4P3.b., M4P3.c., M4P3.d., M4P4.a., M4P4.b., M4P5.b., M4P5.c.**

▶ Learn

BIKE BONANZA Bill owns a bike shop. Last month at his bike sale, Bill sold 24 bike locks for $8.95 each. How much did he collect on the sale of these bike locks?

Example

Multiply. $24 \times \$8.95$

$\qquad\quad\ \downarrow \qquad \downarrow$

Estimate. $20 \times \$9 = \$180$

Multiply money the way you multiply whole numbers.

Technology Link

More Practice: Harcourt Mega Math The Number Games, *Buggy Bargains*, Level J

STEP 1	**STEP 2**	**STEP 3**	**STEP 4**
Multiply the ones.	Multiply the tens.	Add the products.	Write the answer in dollars and cents.
$\begin{array}{r} {}^{3\,2} \\ 895 \\ \times\ 24 \\ \hline 3580 \end{array}$ ←4 × 895	$\begin{array}{r} {}^{1\,1} \\ {}^{3\,2} \\ 895 \\ \times\ 24 \\ \hline 3580 \\ 17900 \end{array}$ ←20 × 895	$\begin{array}{r} {}^{1\,1} \\ {}^{3\,2} \\ 895 \\ \times\ 24 \\ \hline 3580 \\ +17900 \\ \hline 21480 \end{array}$	The product is $214.80.

So, Bill took in $214.80. Since $214.80 is close to the estimate of $180, the answer is reasonable.

More Examples

A
$\begin{array}{r} {}^{1}_{4} \\ \$406 \\ \times\ \ 27 \\ \hline 2\,842 \\ +8\,120 \\ \hline \$10,962 \end{array}$ ←7 × 406
←20 × 406

B
$\begin{array}{r} {}^{3}_{2} \\ \$5.09 \\ \times\ \ 43 \\ \hline 15\,27 \\ +203\,60 \\ \hline \$218.87 \end{array}$ ←3 × 509
←40 × 509
←Add decimal point and dollar sign.

▶ Check

1. **Explain** how you know where to put the decimal point in a money problem.

Find the product. Estimate to check.

2.	$892 × 37	3.	$637 × 51	4.	$5.68 × 21	5.	$215 × 24	6.	$8.03 × 39

Practice and Problem Solving   (Extra Practice, page 196, Set D)

Find the product. Estimate to check.

7.	$735 × 43	8.	$0.97 × 68	9.	$7.45 × 28	10.	$2.56 × 81	11.	$505 × 79

12. One bike light sells for $7.99. How much will 12 bike lights cost?

13. A bike store bought a box of 48 bicycle tubes. Each tube cost $6.49. How much did the tubes cost in all?

 **ALGEBRA**   **Find the number for ☐ or △ that makes the equation true.**

14. 45 × $236 = △   **15.** 36 × $287 = ☐   **16.** 93 × $47 = △   **17.** 24 × ☐ = $2,400

USE DATA For 18–21, use the table.

18. How much will Train Museum tickets cost for 25 students?

19. **MULTISTEP** How much more are two adult tickets than two student tickets?

20. **MULTISTEP** Bradley has $12. Can he buy a student ticket and a book that costs $4.50? Explain.

21. ✎ **Write a problem** about buying tickets for more than 1 adult and more than 1 student who visit the museum. Show the solution.

TRAIN MUSEUM	
Ticket	**Price**
Child (under 6)	$5.25
Student	$7.75
Adult	$9.75

Maintain Skills

22. Twenty-nine students are going on a field trip. Only 5 students can ride in each car. How many cars do they need?

23. What is the value of the digit 7 in the number 47,391?

CRCT Test Prep

24. **M4A1.a.** Find the missing numbers. (p. 136)

In	6	11	8		
Out	48	88	64	96	16

A. 13, 10   C. 12, 2
B. 5, 2   D. 9, 10

Problem Solving Skill
Multistep Problems

 M4P1.b. Solve problems that arise in mathematics and in other contexts. *also* M4N3, M4P1.a., M4P1.c., M4P1.d., M4P2.a., M4P2.b., M4P2.c., M4P3.a., M4P3.b., M4P3.c., M4P3.d.

Quick Review

1. 4×217 **2.** 2×340
3. 2×497 **4.** 3×526
5. 3×705

VOCABULARY

multistep problem

REACH YOUR GOAL The soccer players sold bottles of water to earn money for equipment. They charged $2.25 for each bottle of water. They sold 52 bottles on Saturday and 45 bottles on Sunday. How much money did they collect?

MATH IDEA Sometimes it takes more than one step to solve a problem. To solve **multistep problems**, decide *what* the steps are and *in what order* you should do them.

Example

To find how much money the soccer players collected, multiply the total number of bottles sold by $2.25.

STEP 1

Add to find the total number of bottles sold.

$52 \leftarrow$ bottles sold on Saturday
$\underline{+45} \leftarrow$ bottles sold on Sunday
97

The players sold 97 bottles of water.

STEP 2

Multiply to find the amount of money collected.

$\$2.25 \leftarrow$ price for each bottle
$\underline{\times \quad 97} \leftarrow$ total number of bottles
$\$218.25$

So, the players collected $218.25.

Talk About It

• Could you use the number sentence $(52 + 45) \times \$2.25 = \star$ to solve the problem? Explain.

• Would you get the same answer if you first multiplied $52 \times \$2.25$ and $45 \times \$2.25$ and then added the two products? Explain.

Problem Solving Practice

1. **MULTISTEP** What if the soccer players had charged $3.25 for each bottle of water they sold? How much more money would they have collected?

2. **MULTISTEP** The soccer coach bought 12 pairs of socks for $3.75 each and 6 soccer balls for $8.25 each. How much did he spend in all?

USE DATA For 3–4, use the table.

During soccer season, Darren's Snack Bar sells lunches. Darren kept this record of the number of items sold at last Saturday's game.

3. Which expression can you use to find the amount of money Darren took in from the sale of fruit salads and turkey sandwiches?
    A $2.59 + $5.87
    B ($2.59 × 33) + ($5.87 × 29)
    C ($2.59 × 33) − ($5.87 × 29)
    D ($2.59 + $5.87) × (33 + 29)

DARREN'S SNACK BAR - Specials		
Item	Price	Number Sold
Fruit Salad	$2.59	33
Turkey Sandwich	$5.87	29
Veggie Sandwich	$4.38	18
Chicken Soup	$1.39	15
Chocolate Pie	$1.21	12

4. **MULTISTEP** How much more money did Darren take in from the sale of fruit salads than from the sale of veggie sandwiches?
    F $4.37 more   H $6.63 more
    G $4.43 more   J $17.43 more

Mixed Applications

5. **MULTISTEP** Mrs. Ling had a bucket of crayons. She gave 14 crayons to each of 21 students. If 131 crayons were left in the bucket, how many crayons were there to start?

6. **MULTISTEP** Norman spent $15.00 on a pizza and 2 salads. The pizza cost twice as much as the 2 salads. What was the price of each item?

7. **MULTISTEP** Tommy and Helen were playing a game. First, Helen picked a number and added 4. Then she multiplied by 6. Finally, she subtracted 3. The result was 51. What number did Helen pick?

8. Harry, Eli, Macy, and Sandy are standing in line at the movies. Harry is just behind Eli. Macy is between Harry and Sandy. Who is first in line?

9. **MULTISTEP** Band members practice for 2 hours a day twice a week. For how many hours do they practice in 4 weeks?

10. Write a problem that requires more than two steps to solve. Show the solution.

Extra Practice

Set A (pp. 184–187)

Choose a method to find the product. Estimate to check.

1. 71 ×64	**2.** $29 × 23	**3.** 92 ×33	**4.** 89 ×16	**5.** 46 ×96

6. An orange tree grove has 43 rows of trees. Each row has 35 trees. How many trees are in the grove?

Set B (pp. 188–189)

Find the product. Estimate to check.

1. $226 × 65	**2.** 547 × 53	**3.** 924 × 38	**4.** 839 × 22	**5.** 409 × 28

6. A skyscraper has 102 floors. Each floor has 16 windows. How many windows does the skyscaper have?

Set C (pp. 190–191)

Tell whether each problem can be solved by using mental math, paper and pencil, or a calculator. Then solve each problem using the method you chose.

1. The Craft Store ordered 20 boxes of beads. Each box contains 600 beads. How many beads were ordered in all?

2. The town theater has 246 seats. Last year, the theater was sold out for all of its 45 shows. How many tickets were sold in all?

Set D (pp. 192–193)

Find the product. Estimate to check.

1. $19 × 66	**2.** $74 × 76	**3.** $805 × 45	**4.** $249 × 64	**5.** $3.95 × 25
6. $57 × 20	**7.** $809 × 50	**8.** $454 × 18	**9.** $7.68 × 90	**10.** $6.10 × 32

11. Lily bought 15 tickets to the movies. Each ticket cost $7.75. How much did she spend?

12. The swim team sold shirts for a fund-raiser. If the team members sold 68 shirts for $8.95 each, how much money did they raise?

Review/Test

✓ CHECK VOCABULARY AND CONCEPTS

Choose the best term from the box.

(p. 194)

1. A ? requires two or more steps to find the solution.

2. When multiplying by two-digit numbers, you add the ? to get the final product. (p. 185)

Vocabulary

multistep problem

estimate

partial products

ones

✓ CHECK SKILLS

Find the product. Estimate to check. (pp. 184–187, 188–189, 190–191, 192–193)

3.	4.	5.	6.
39 ×16	54 ×33	$143 × 62	472 × 73

7.	8.	9.	10.
92 ×58	$0.61 × 29	303 × 67	845 × 53

11.	12.	13.	14.
67 ×82	$297 × 34	709 × 36	$2.11 × 85

Tell whether each problem can be solved by using mental math, paper and pencil, or a calculator. Then solve each problem using the method you chose.

(pp. 190–191)

15. Ellen made a car payment of $325 each month for the last 12 months. How much did she make in car payments over the last year?

16. There are 25 seeds in a packet of sunflower seeds. How many seeds are in 40 packets?

17. Amanda bought 28 azalea shrubs to plant in her backyard. Each shrub cost $16. How much did Amanda pay for the azaleas?

18. Each of the 500 students in King Elementary School are given 5 textbooks. How many textbooks are given out altogether?

✓ CHECK PROBLEM SOLVING

Solve. (pp. 194–195)

19. Josh plays on a bowling team. There are 13 players. If 5 players scored an average of 145 each and 8 players scored an average of 134 each, what is the average total score of the team?

20. The deli ordered 25 boxes of napkins. Each box holds 275 napkins. How many more napkins would the store have gotten if there had been 29 boxes?

Chapter CRCT Test Prep

NUMBERS AND OPERATIONS

1. **M4N3.** The table below shows the cost of items at Pete's Pet Store.

Pete's Pet Store	
Item	Price
Bag of cat food	$5.59
Bag of dog food	$5.98
5-lb of bird seed	$6.45

The animal shelter bought 24 bags of dog food. How much did it pay for the dog food?

A. $134.16

B. $143.52

C. $153.52

D. $153.62

2. **M4N3.** The table below shows the number of students in each grade.

Martin Luther King, Jr., Elementary School	
Grade	Number of Students
1	84
2	108
3	97
4	121

The school sweatshirt costs $25. If all the fourth graders buy a school sweatshirt, how much will they pay altogether?

A. $484

B. $2,700

C. $3,025

D. $10,250

NUMBERS AND OPERATIONS

3. **M4N3.** Mack's car can travel 23 miles on one gallon of gas. During a trip, Mack filled up the gas tank with 20 gallons of gas 6 times. How many miles did Mack travel on his trip?

A. 2,760 miles

B. 2,670 miles

C. 1,430 miles

D. 466 miles

4. **M4N3.** Georgia's Antebellum Trail runs from Athens to Macon. Li hiked 13 kilometers per day for 12 days. On the last day, Li hiked 4 kilometers. How long is the trail?

A. 142 kilometers

B. 152 kilometers

C. 160 kilometers

D. 168 kilometers

5. **M4N3.** Carmen bought 21 rolls of film. Each roll holds 27 pictures. What is the GREATEST number of pictures she can take using all of the film?

A. 48

B. 81

C. 467

D. 567

Cumulative CRCT Test Prep

DATA ANALYSIS

6. **M4D1.a.** Which bar graph shows that 25 DVDs were rented on Day 1, 20 on Day 2, and 35 on Day 3?

A.
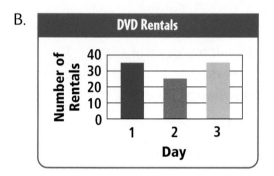

B.
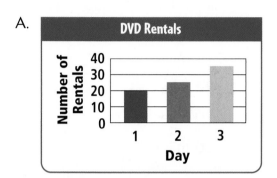

C.
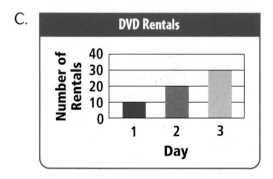

D.
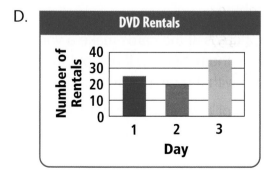

ALGEBRA

7. **M4A1.c.** What is the value of $5 + (\square - 6)$ if $\square = 9$?

A. 7

B. 8

C. 11

D. 20

8. **M4A1.b.** Which expression BEST represents the situation?

Carey collected 25 trading cards. Her brother had some trading cards and gave her all but 6 of them.

A. $25 + (\triangle - 6)$

B. $25 - (\triangle + 6)$

C. $\triangle + (6 - 25)$

D. $6 + (\triangle - 25)$

9. **M4A1.a.** What is the missing number?

In	Out
58	
46	39
34	27
22	15

A. 51

B. 49

C. 47

D. 41

GPS/CRCT Vocabulary

ELA4R3 The student understands and acquires vocabulary and uses it correctly in reading and writing.

FILL IN THE BLANKS

MATERIALS *For each student* 3 index cards

• Write the definition of each vocabulary term on an index card. Leave out two words from each definition, and make a blank for each word.

• Choose a partner, and trade index cards with your partner. Write the missing words in each definition.

• After you both have finished, compare your definitions. Discuss which definitions were the easiest to complete.

MATH WORD WORK

Distributive

problem

numbers

multistep

Property

compatible

MATERIALS *For each student* 6 index cards

• Write each word of each vocabulary term on an index card.

• Mix up the cards, and place them face-down on the table.

• Choose 2 cards. If the cards make a vocabulary term, place them face-up. If not, put them back face-down with the other cards.

• Keep track of how many turns it takes you to find all the vocabulary terms.

WORDS WITHIN WORDS

- Choose one of the vocabulary words.

- Make a list of as many three- and four-letter words as you can with the letters of your vocabulary term.

- Find a classmate who chose the same vocabulary term as you did, and compare your lists of words.

DISTRIBUTIVE PROPERTY

BUT
TOP
RIB
PROP
BIDS

SCRAMBLED UP

MATERIALS *For each group* 53 index cards, Definition Cards

- Write each letter of each vocabulary term on an index card.

- Mix up the letter cards, and place them on the desk.

- Choose a group member to be the timekeeper.

- Pick a definition card, and read it aloud. Use the letter cards to spell the vocabulary word correctly.

- Repeat the activity for all three vocabulary terms. Discuss which term was the quickest to be spelled.

Georgia Tasks

M4N3. Students will solve problems involving multiplication of 2–3 digit numbers by 1–2 digit numbers. *also* **M4P5.b., M4P5.c.**

S4L1.c. Predict how changes in the environment would affect a community (ecosystem) of organisms.

Task A

MACON, GA, CHERRY BLOSSOM CAPITAL OF THE WORLD

In 1949, William Fickling discovered the first Yoshino cherry tree in Macon. Today there are more than 285,000 Yoshino cherry trees in Macon, and Macon is known as the "Cherry Blossom Capital of the World."

▲ **Macon's Cherry Blossom Festival takes place each year in March.**

a. A town wants to plant 600 cherry trees. If the town is given 25 trees for free and purchases the rest for $15 each, what is the cost of the trees?

b. The town has 155 streets and a park. How many trees do you think should be planted on each street? How many of the 600 trees will be left over to plant in the park? Explain how you found your answer.

Task B

FISH STORY

Andy received an aquarium and $35.00 to buy gravel, plants, and fish for it for his birthday. He read these directions for setting up the aquarium.

Add between 7 and 10 pounds of gravel. Add 4 or 5 plants. Add your choice of fish.

Andy wants to have at least two of each type of fish.

a. Use estimation to find the cost of the gravel, plants, and the numbers and types of fish that Andy could buy so that the total cost is $35.00 or less.

b. What is the actual total cost of the items you chose?

Aquarium Supplies	
Item	**Price**
Gravel	$0.65 per pound
Plants	$3.25 each
Tetra fish	$1.79
Platy fish	$2.19
Molly fish	$2.99

Maintain/Preview

Maintain

Estimate the product. (pp. 150–151)

1. 8×51 **2.** 48×6 **3.** 3×837 **4.** 9×294

Multiply. (pp. 152–155, 156–159, 184–187, 188–189)

5. $\begin{array}{r} 27 \\ \times\ 6 \\ \hline \end{array}$ **6.** $\begin{array}{r} 38 \\ \times\ 4 \\ \hline \end{array}$ **7.** $\begin{array}{r} 57 \\ \times\ 9 \\ \hline \end{array}$ **8.** $\begin{array}{r} 46 \\ \times\ 8 \\ \hline \end{array}$

9. $\begin{array}{r} 531 \\ \times\ 4 \\ \hline \end{array}$ **10.** $\begin{array}{r} 328 \\ \times\ 5 \\ \hline \end{array}$ **11.** $\begin{array}{r} 721 \\ \times\ 9 \\ \hline \end{array}$ **12.** $\begin{array}{r} 522 \\ \times\ 7 \\ \hline \end{array}$

13. $\begin{array}{r} 29 \\ \times 41 \\ \hline \end{array}$ **14.** $\begin{array}{r} 36 \\ \times 82 \\ \hline \end{array}$ **15.** $\begin{array}{r} 246 \\ \times\ 25 \\ \hline \end{array}$ **16.** $\begin{array}{r} 452 \\ \times\ 31 \\ \hline \end{array}$

Use a model and the Distributive Property to find the product. (pp. 170–171)

17. 20×32 **18.** 50×54 **19.** 40×18 **20.** 80×13

21. Sami made 8 copies of each of 48 photos. How many copies did he make? (pp. 152–155)

22. Each of 12 newspaper carriers delivers 426 papers. How many newspapers do they deliver? (pp. 188–189)

Preview

Find the product. (Chapter 10)

1. 8×7 **2.** 9×3 **3.** 7×5 **4.** 6×7

5. 2×6 **6.** 5×4 **7.** 8×3 **8.** 9×5

Find the quotient. (Chapter 10)

9. $36 \div 4$ **10.** $28 \div 7$ **11.** $56 \div 8$ **12.** $45 \div 5$

13. $81 \div 9$ **14.** $72 \div 8$ **15.** $32 \div 4$ **16.** $10 \div 5$

17. $36 \div 6$ **18.** $49 \div 7$ **19.** $63 \div 9$ **20.** $40 \div 8$

21. Seth has 18 cupcakes. He places 2 cupcakes on each plate. How many plates does he need?

22. Rosa buys 21 tennis balls. There are 3 tennis balls in each can. How many cans does she buy?

CHAPTER 10

Divide by 1-Digit Numbers

≡FAST FACT • SOCIAL STUDIES Hawaiians often welcome visitors to their state with wreaths of flowers called leis (LAYZ). Leis are made from 200 different types of flowers found in Hawaii.

INVESTIGATION Look at the table. Which type of lei has the most flowers in each lei? Suppose you had only 35 carnations to put into 7 leis. How many flowers would be in each lei? Use a model to show how you found your answer.

Using Data
HAWAIIAN LEIS MADE AT ONE SHOP

Type of Lei	Number of Flowers Used	Number of Leis Made
Carnation	350	7
Orchid	400	5
Plumeria	480	6
Rosebud	420	6
Tuberose	320	8

CHECK WHAT YOU KNOW

Use this page to help you review and remember
important skills needed for Chapter 10.

✅ DIVISION FACTS

Write the division fact that each picture represents.

1.

2.

3.

4.

5.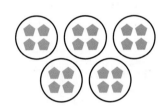

6.

✅ FIND THE QUOTIENT

Find the quotient.

7. 30 ÷ 5	**8.** 28 ÷ 7	**9.** 72 ÷ 9	**10.** 54 ÷ 6
11. 48 ÷ 8	**12.** 24 ÷ 3	**13.** 14 ÷ 2	**14.** 36 ÷ 9
15. 12 ÷ 4	**16.** 81 ÷ 9	**17.** 40 ÷ 8	**18.** 42 ÷ 6

VOCABULARY POWER

REVIEW

divide [di•vīd′] *verb*

Divide contains the root *vidua,* which
means "to separate." Explain what you
are separating when you divide in
mathematics.

PREVIEW

▶ quotient

www.harcourtschool.com/mathglossary

HANDS ON

Model Division

Concepts/Skill to Maintain Multiplication and division of whole numbers. *also* M4P3.a., M4P3.b., M4P3.c., M4P3.d., M4P5, M4P5.a., M4P5.b., M4P5.c.

▶ **Explore**

TAKE A LOOK! The Berkshire Museum has pictures of 48 extinct animals in 3 different rooms. Each room has the same number of pictures. How many pictures are in each room?

Activity 1

Divide 48 into 3 equal groups. Write $48 \div 3$ or $3)\overline{48}$.
Make a model to show how many are in each group.

STEP 1 Show 48 as 4 tens 8 ones. Draw circles to make 3 equal groups.

STEP 2 Place an equal number of tens into each group.

STEP 3 Regroup 1 ten 8 ones as 18 ones. Place an equal number of ones into each group.

So, there are 16 pictures in each room.

• How many groups did you make?

• How many are in each group?

Try It

Model. Tell how many are in each group.

a. $26 \div 2$ b. $42 \div 3$ c. $64 \div 4$

We have modeled 26. How many circles should we draw to show $26 \div 2$?

Activity 2

Here is a way to record division. Divide 57 by 2.

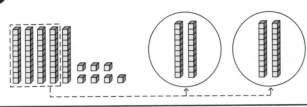

| STEP 1 | Show the model and 2 equal groups. | Record: |
| | | $2\overline{)57}$ |

| STEP 2 | Divide the tens. | $\begin{array}{r} 2 \\ 2\overline{)57} \\ -4 \\ \hline 1 \end{array}$ 2 tens in each group
4 tens used
1 ten left |

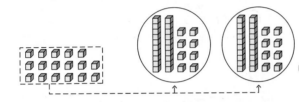

| STEP 3 | Regroup. Divide the ones. | $\begin{array}{r} 28\ r1 \\ 2\overline{)57} \\ -4 \\ \hline 17 \\ -16 \\ \hline 1 \end{array}$ 8 ones in each group
16 ones used
1 one left
So, $57 \div 2 = 28\ r1$. |

Read: 57 divided by 2 equals 28 remainder 1.

▶ **Practice and Problem Solving**

Make or draw a model. Record and solve.

1. $35 \div 2$ **2.** $45 \div 3$ **3.** $49 \div 4$ **4.** $47 \div 2$ **5.** $72 \div 6$

6. $7\overline{)88}$ **7.** $3\overline{)56}$ **8.** $6\overline{)78}$ **9.** $5\overline{)66}$ **10.** $4\overline{)72}$

11. **?** **What's the Error?** Emily made this model for $3\overline{)42}$. Describe her error. Draw a correct model.

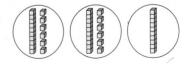

Maintain Skills

12. $\begin{array}{r} 36 \\ \times\ 9 \\ \hline \end{array}$ **13.** $\begin{array}{r} 92 \\ \times\ 7 \\ \hline \end{array}$

14. $9\overline{)81}$ **15.** $6\overline{)240}$

CRCT Test Prep

16. **M4N2.a.** Round 73,864 to the nearest ten. (p. 32)

A. 70,900   C. 73,860

B. 73,870   D. 73,000

Division Procedures

M4N4.c. Understand the relationship between dividend, divisor, quotient, and remainder. *also* **M4P4.a., M4P4.b.** **Concepts/Skill to Maintain** Multiplication and division of whole numbers

▶ **Learn**

TINY HATCHLINGS Volunteers are responsible for watching turtle nests on the beach. There are 96 nests. If there are 7 volunteers, how many nests does each volunteer watch? How many nests are left over? Find the quotient and the remainder.

The **quotient** is the number, not including the remainder, that results from dividing. To check your answer, you can compute: (divisor × quotient) + remainder = dividend.

Example Divide 96 by 7. Write $96 \div 7$ or $7\overline{)96}$.

STEP 1	**STEP 2**	**STEP 3**	**STEP 4**
Divide the 9 tens.	Bring down the 6 ones.	Divide the 26 ones.	Check.

STEP 1

Divide the 9 tens.

$$\begin{array}{r} 1 \\ 7\overline{)96} \\ -7 \\ \hline 2 \end{array}$$

Divide. $9 \div 7$
Multiply. 1×7
Subtract. $9 - 7$
Compare. $2 < 7$

The difference, 2, must be less than the divisor, 7.

STEP 2

Bring down the 6 ones.

$$\begin{array}{r} 1 \\ 7\overline{)96} \\ -7\downarrow \\ \hline 26 \end{array}$$

STEP 3

Divide the 26 ones.

$$\begin{array}{r} 13 \text{ r5} \\ 7\overline{)96} \\ -7\downarrow \\ \hline 26 \\ -21 \\ \hline 5 \end{array}$$

Divide. $26 \div 7$
Multiply. 3×7
Subtract. $26 - 21$
Compare. $5 < 7$

Write the remainder next to the quotient.

STEP 4

Check.

$$\begin{array}{r} 13 \quad \text{quotient} \\ \times\ 7 \quad \text{divisor} \\ \hline 91 \\ +\ 5 \quad \text{remainder} \\ \hline 96 \quad \text{dividend} \end{array}$$

So, each volunteer watches 13 nests. There are 5 nests left over to assign to a new volunteer.

MATH IDEA The order of division is as follows: divide, multiply, subtract, and compare. This order is repeated until the division is complete.

Technology Link

More Practice: Harcourt Mega Math The Number Games, *Up, Up, and Array,* Level O

Another Way to Divide

You can break apart a dividend into a sum. The first addend is the divisor times a multiple of 10. Then use multiples of the divisor to find the other addends.

Example Use the break-apart method to divide 96 by 7.

STEP 1

Break apart the dividend into a multiple of the divisor plus the remaining addend.

$$7\overline{)96} = 7\overline{)70 + 26}$$

Think: 70 is 10 times the divisor, 7.
96 − 70 = 26

STEP 2

Break apart the remaining addend into a multiple of the divisor plus another addend.

$$7\overline{)96} = 7\overline{)70 + 21 + 5}$$

Think: 21 is 3 times the divisor, 7.
26 − 21 = 5

STEP 3

Divide each addend of the dividend by 7.

$$7\overline{)96} = 7\overline{)\overset{10 + 3}{70 + 21 + 5}}$$

Think: 70 ÷ 7 = 10, 21 ÷ 7 = 3.
The remainder is 5.

STEP 4

Write the quotient and the remainder.

$$7\overline{)96}^{\ 13\ r5}$$

• Explain how you would break apart 96 if you wanted to divide 96 by 5.

► Check

1. **Explain** why you can use multiplication to check a division problem.

Divide and check.

2. $4\overline{)58}$ 3. $3\overline{)65}$ 4. $5\overline{)84}$ 5. $5\overline{)79}$ 6. $7\overline{)99}$

7. $39 \div 2$ 8. $84 \div 6$ 9. $62 \div 4$ 10. $95 \div 8$ 11. $55 \div 3$

LESSON CONTINUES ►

Use multiplication to check each answer.

12. 78 ÷ 6 = 13   **13.** 93 ÷ 7 = 13 r2   **14.** 52 ÷ 3 = 17 r1   **15.** 64 ÷ 5 = 12 r4

16. Compare each remainder in Exercises 2–5 on page 209 with the divisor. Why is the remainder always less than the divisor?

Practice and Problem Solving   Extra Practice, page 224, Set A

Divide and check.

17. 4)84̅   **18.** 4)51̅   **19.** 7)52̅   **20.** 2)46̅

21. 3)89̅   **22.** 5)67̅   **23.** 8)90̅   **24.** 3)76̅

25. 93 ÷ 8   **26.** 73 ÷ 4   **27.** 94 ÷ 3   **28.** 87 ÷ 5

Use multiplication to check each answer.

29. 57 ÷ 4 = 14 r1   **30.** 85 ÷ 7 = 12 r1   **31.** 39 ÷ 3 = 13   **32.** 82 ÷ 7 = 11 r5

Complete.

33. (6 × 12) + 3 = 75, so 75 ÷ 6 = 12 r■   **34.** (3 × 25) + 2 = 77, so ■ ÷ 3 = 25 r2

35. (6 × 14) + 3 = 87, so 87 ÷ 6 = ■ r3   **36.** (5 × 13) + 0 = 65, so 65 ÷ ■ = 13

USE DATA For 37–41, use the graph.

37. **REASONING** Ms. Juanita put the Thursday and Friday volunteers into equal groups for training classes. Each class had 8 members. How many classes did Ms. Juanita need? Explain.

38. **MULTISTEP** The Monday and Tuesday volunteers meet for lunch. Each table seats 4 people. How many tables are needed for the volunteers?

39. The Surfside Restaurant gave each Friday volunteer a free lunch. The value of each lunch was $7. What was the total value of the lunches given to the Friday volunteers?

40. **? What's the Question?** The answer is 25 volunteers.

41. Write a problem that requires division, using the data in the graph.

210

42. Jeremy has 37 pictures of his classmates. He wants to arrange them into groups of 6. How many groups can he make? How many pictures will be left over?

43. Vocabulary Power *Remain* means "to be a part not taken or used up." How does this information help you understand what a remainder is?

Maintain Skills

For 44–45, estimate the product.

44. 7×52 **45.** 6×79

46. What is the value of the digit 2 in 26,097?

47. Find the length of the crayon to the nearest $\frac{1}{2}$ inch.

48. If 4 boxes have 60 books, how many books are in each box?

49. Which is longer, a piece of ribbon that is 5 feet long or a piece of ribbon that is 5 yards long?

CRCT Test Prep

Use the bar graph below to answer question 50.

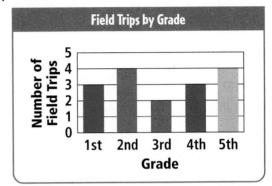

50. **M4D1.a.** The principal at Meade School is planning 2 times as many field trips next year. How many field trips are being planned? (p. 12)

A. 17   C. 30

B. 20   D. 32

Problem Solving Thinker's Corner

REASONING Miranda has a collection of jungle cats and sea animals. She has 13 jungle cats and 11 sea animals. She wants to display them on some shelves.

• Each shelf will have the same number of items.

• No shelf can have all jungle cats or all sea animals.

Decide how many shelves Miranda needs. Use models or draw a diagram to help you.

1. How many shelves will Miranda need?

2. How many jungle cats and sea animals will be on each shelf?

3. Draw a diagram to show your answer.

Algebra: Mental Math: Division Patterns

M4N7.d. Use mental math and estimation strategies to compute.
also **M4N7.a., M4P1.c., M4P2.a., M4P3.a., M4P3.b., M4P3.c., M4P3.d.**
Concepts/Skill to Maintain Multiplication and division of whole numbers

▶ Learn

EXTREME FUN Best Sports Shop orders 1,800 skateboards for 3 of its stores to share equally. How many skateboards will each store get?

Example

Find $1,800 \div 3$.

Use basic facts and patterns to find quotients mentally.

dividend		divisor		quotient
18	÷	3	=	6
180	÷	3	=	60
1,800	÷	3	=	600
↑↑ two zeros				two zeros ↑↑

So, each store will get 600 skateboards.

MATH IDEA If the divisor remains the same, as the number of zeros in the dividend increases, the number of zeros in the quotient also increases.

More Examples

Ⓐ $40 \div 8 = 5$ Think: $5 \times 8 = 40$
$400 \div 8 = 50$
$4,000 \div 8 = 500$

Ⓑ $70 \div 10 = 7$ Think: $7 \times 10 = 70$
$700 \div 10 = 70$
$7,000 \div 10 = 700$

• In Example A, why is there one more zero in the dividend than in the quotient?

▶ Check

1. Tell how many zeros are in the quotient $72,000 \div 9$ and in the quotient $40,000 \div 8$.

Use a basic division fact and patterns to write each quotient.

2. a. $560 \div 7$ **3. a.** $540 \div 6$ **4. a.** $200 \div 5$ **5. a.** $8,000 \div 8$
   b. $5,600 \div 7$ **b.** $5,400 \div 6$ **b.** $2,000 \div 5$ **b.** $80,000 \div 8$

Practice and Problem Solving   Extra Practice, page 224, Set B

Use a basic division fact and patterns to write each quotient.

6. a. $270 \div 3$ **7. a.** $630 \div 9$ **8. a.** $300 \div 5$ **9. a.** $4,000 \div 10$
   b. $2,700 \div 3$ **b.** $6,300 \div 9$ **b.** $3,000 \div 5$ **b.** $40,000 \div 10$

Divide mentally. Write the basic division fact and the quotient.

10. $450 \div 9$ **11.** $210 \div 7$ **12.** $160 \div 8$ **13.** $180 \div 9$

14. $2,800 \div 4$ **15.** $3,600 \div 9$ **16.** $15,000 \div 3$ **17.** $48,000 \div 6$

ALGEBRA   **Write the value of □.**

18. $420 \div 7 = \square$ **19.** $\square \div 9 = 30$ **20.** $350 \div \square = 50$

21. $4,800 \div 8 = \square$ **22.** $24,000 \div \square = 8,000$ **23.** $72,000 \div 9 = \square$

USE DATA For 24–27, use the pictograph.

24. Each can of tennis balls holds 3 balls. How many cans of tennis balls does the shop have?

25. If golf balls are sold in packages of 4 and each can of tennis balls holds 3 balls, how many more cans of tennis balls does the store have than packages of golf balls?

26. ✍ Write a problem about the data in the pictograph that can be solved by using a basic division fact and patterns.

27. What if the shop received a new shipment of 2,000 balls, made up of an equal number of each type of ball? How many of each type of ball would be in the shop?

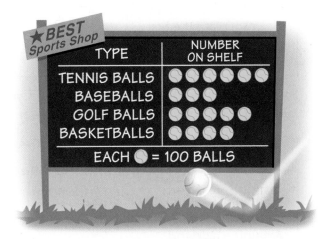

Maintain Skills

28. What is the value of the digit 8 in 34,824?

29. Which is longer, 60 m or 60 km?

30. 56×8 **31.** 307×9

CRCT Test Prep

32. **M4N7.b.** Find the value of the expression. (p. 130)

$$56 - 4 \times 9$$

A. 20   C. 92
B. 61   D. 468

Divide 3-Digit Numbers

M4N4.a. Know the division facts with understanding and fluency.
also M4P2.a., M4P2.b., M4P2.c., M4P2.d., M4P3.a., M4P3.b., M4P3.c., M4P3.d.
Concepts/Skill to Maintain Multiplication and division of whole numbers

▶ **Learn**

ISLAND ADVENTURE The Aloha Tour Company divided 178 flyers for guided tours equally among 3 resorts. How many flyers did each resort get?

Quick Review

1. $21 \div 3$
2. 4×2
3. 5×3
4. $35 \div 5$
5. $7 \overline{)44}$

One Way Divide 178 by 3. Write $3\overline{)178}$.

STEP 1

Estimate to place the first digit in the quotient.

Think: $\dfrac{50}{3\overline{)150}}$ or $\dfrac{60}{3\overline{)180}}$

■ $3\overline{)178}$ The quotient will be between 5 tens and 6 tens. So, place the first digit in the tens place.

STEP 2

Divide the 17 tens.

$$\begin{array}{r} 5 \\ 3\overline{)178} \\ -15 \\ \hline 2 \end{array}$$ Divide.
Multiply.
Subtract.
Compare.

STEP 3

Bring down the 8 ones. Divide the 28 ones.

$$\begin{array}{r} 59\ r1 \\ 3\overline{)178} \\ -15\downarrow \\ \hline 28 \\ -27 \\ \hline 1 \end{array}$$ Divide.
Multiply.
Subtract.
Compare.

STEP 4

To check, multiply the quotient by the divisor. Then add the remainder.

$$\begin{array}{r} 2 \\ 59 \\ \times\ 3 \\ \hline 177 \\ +\ 1 \\ \hline 178 \end{array}$$
quotient
divisor

remainder
dividend

So, each resort will get 59 flyers, with 1 flyer left over.
Since 59 is between 50 and 60, the answer is reasonable.

Another Way Use the break-apart method to divide 178 by 3.

STEP 1

Break apart the dividend into a multiple of the divisor plus the remaining addend.

$3\overline{)178} = 3\overline{)150 + 28}$ **Think:** $3 \times 50 = 150$, $3 \times 60 = 180$, $150 < 178$, $178 - 150 = 28$

STEP 2

Break apart the remaining addend into a multiple of the divisor plus another addend.

$3\overline{)178} = 3\overline{)150 + 27 + 1}$ **Think:** 27 is 9 times the divisor, 3. $28 - 27 = 1$

STEP 3

Divide each addend by 3.

$3\overline{)178} = 3\overline{\underset{150 + 27 + 1}{\overline{50 + 9}}}$ **Think:** $150 \div 3 = 50$, $27 \div 3 = 9$. The remainder is 1.

STEP 4

Write the quotient.

$\begin{array}{r} 59\ r1 \\ 3\overline{)178} \end{array}$

Hawaii's Kapoloa Falls drop 1,400 feet to the Pololu Valley floor. ▼

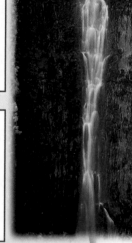

• Explain how to divide 680 by 3 using the break-apart method.

1. **Explain** how to find the first digit in the quotient of 324 ÷ 7.

Divide and check.

2. $4\overline{)187}$ 3. $2\overline{)453}$ 4. $5\overline{)592}$ 5. $7\overline{)241}$ 6. $6\overline{)687}$

▶ **Practice and Problem Solving** (Extra Practice, page 224, Set C)

Divide and check.

7. $6\overline{)178}$ 8. $4\overline{)472}$ 9. $7\overline{)241}$ 10. $9\overline{)709}$ 11. $3\overline{)470}$

12. $5\overline{)337}$ 13. $2\overline{)\$3.72}$ 14. $8\overline{)697}$ 15. $4\overline{)\$4.68}$ 16. $6\overline{)749}$

17. $186 \div 3$ 18. $247 \div 8$ 19. $546 \div 5$ 20. $\$3.02 \div 2$ 21. $614 \div 6$

 **ALGEBRA** Find the value of 448 ÷ ★ for each value of ★.

22. ★ = 2 23. ★ = 3 24. ★ = 4 25. ★ = 5 26. ★ = 6

27. **Mental Math** Which is greater, 345 ÷ 2 or 345 ÷ 3?

28. Which is greater, $2\overline{)452}$ or $4\overline{)452}$? How much greater?

USE DATA For 29–31, use this information. The Island Tours Theater seats 45 people. There are 210 people on a tour.

29. **MULTISTEP** Each tourist's ticket to the play costs $8. The tour guide gives the cashier at the window $1,800. How much change does the guide receive?

30. If the play is performed 5 times, will all the people on the tour be able to see it? Explain.

31. ✎ Write a problem about Island Tours that requires dividing three-digit numbers.

Maintain Skills

32. 7×54 33. 4×81
34. $3\overline{)63}$ 35. $6\overline{)78}$

CRCT Test Prep

36. ⟨ M4A1.c. ⟩ Find the value of 48 ÷ △ if △ = 6. (p. 132)
   A. 8 C. 42
   B. 12 D. 54

Zeros in Division

M4N4.a. Know the division facts with understanding and fluency.
also **M4P3.a., M4P3.b., M4P3.c., M4P3.d.**
Concepts/Skill to Maintain Multiplication and division of whole numbers

▶ **Learn**

POSTAGE DUE The post office sold 432 stamps in 4 hours. If the same number of stamps was sold each hour, how many stamps were sold each hour?

Example Divide 432 by 4. Write 4)432.

STEP 1

Estimate to place the first digit in the quotient.

Think:

$$\frac{100}{4)400} \quad or \quad \frac{200}{4)800}$$

■ So, place the
4)432 first digit in the hundreds place.

STEP 2

Divide the 4 hundreds.

$$\begin{array}{r} 1 \\ 4)\overline{432} \\ -4 \\ \hline 0 \end{array}$$

STEP 3

Bring down the 3 tens. Divide the 3 tens.

$$\begin{array}{r} 10 \\ 4)\overline{432} \\ -4\downarrow \\ \hline 03 \\ -\ 0 \\ \hline 3 \end{array}$$
4 > 3, so write a 0 in the quotient.

STEP 4

Bring down the 2 ones. Divide the 32 ones.

$$\begin{array}{r} 108 \\ 4)\overline{432} \\ -4 \\ \hline 03 \\ -\ 0 \\ \hline 32 \\ -32 \\ \hline 0 \end{array}$$

So, the post office sold 108 stamps each hour.

More Examples

A
$$\begin{array}{r} 101\ r1 \\ 5)\overline{506} \\ -5 \\ \hline 00 \\ -\ 0 \\ \hline 06 \\ -\ 5 \\ \hline 1 \end{array}$$

B
$$\begin{array}{r} 130 \\ 6)\overline{780} \\ -6 \\ \hline 18 \\ -18 \\ \hline 00 \\ -\ 0 \\ \hline 0 \end{array}$$

C
$$\begin{array}{r} 104\ r6 \\ 7)\overline{734} \\ -7 \\ \hline 03 \\ -\ 0 \\ \hline 34 \\ -28 \\ \hline 6 \end{array}$$

• Explain what would happen in Example A if you did not write a zero in the tens place of the quotient.

• Explain how you can check the answer in Example C.

Correcting Quotients

The fourth graders collected stamps. They put 4 stamps on each page of an album. The students in Lee Ann's class collected 240 stamps. How many pages did they need?

Look at Lee Ann's paper. Lee Ann divided 240 by 4.

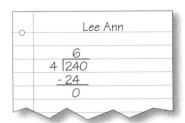

```
            Lee Ann
            6
       4 )240
         - 24
            0
```

- Describe her error. Write the division correctly.

The students in Craig's class collected 412 stamps. How many pages did they need?

Look at Craig's paper. Craig divided 412 by 4.

```
            Craig
           13
      4 )412
        - 4
          12
        - 12
           0
```

- Describe his error. Write the division correctly.

MATH IDEA Estimate to decide how many digits should be in the quotient so you do not forget to include zeros.

Technology Link

More Practice: Harcourt Mega Math The Number Games, *Up, Up, and Array*, Level P

Check

1. **Explain** how an estimate could help you remember to write a zero in a quotient.

2. **Explain** how you know whether a quotient is reasonable.

Write the number of digits in each quotient.

3. 4)406   4. 7)610   5. 5)309   6. 4)804   7. 5)650

Divide and check.

8. 5)800   9. 9)308   10. 3)609   11. 3)305   12. 5)407

LESSON CONTINUES ▶

Write the number of digits in each quotient.

13. 8)818   **14.** 6)510   **15.** 3)207   **16.** 4)600   **17.** 5)405

Divide and check.

18. 6)40   **19.** 8)60   **20.** 5)70   **21.** 7)80   **22.** 9)97

23. 5)405   **24.** 4)240   **25.** 6)243   **26.** 7)636   **27.** 8)706

28. 7)308   **29.** 6)230   **30.** 4)580   **31.** 5)306   **32.** 4)803

33. $402 \div 7$ **34.** $362 \div 9$ **35.** $760 \div 3$ **36.** $860 \div 8$ **37.** $603 \div 6$

38. $361 \div 3$ **39.** $247 \div 8$ **40.** $654 \div 5$ **41.** $421 \div 2$ **42.** $642 \div 6$

 **ALGEBRA**   Write $+$, $-$, $\times$, or $\div$ for each ●.

43. $(35 ● 5) ● 5 = 2$ **44.** $(9 ● 8) ● 4 = 18$ **45.** $(36 ● 4) ● 3 = 27$

USE DATA For 46–49, use the table.

46. **MULTISTEP** Juan ordered three toys. A board game weighs 4 pounds. A scooter weighs 8 pounds, and a train set weighs 21 pounds. How much did Juan pay to have the toys shipped in one shipment?

Toy Company Shipping Costs	
Weight	**Cost per lb**
0–9.99 lb	$0.80
10–19.99 lb	$0.75
20–34.99 lb	$0.70

47. **REASONING** Madeleine paid $9.00 in shipping for 4 stuffed animals that weigh 3 pounds each. Did her order weigh 0–9.99 pounds or 10–19.99 pounds?

48. **MULTISTEP** Alex has $4.50. Does he have enough money to pay for shipping on a 5-pound globe? How much will the shipping cost?

49. **? What's the Question?** Lucy has $13.00. A toy camera weighs 2 pounds, a doll weighs 3 pounds, and an art kit weighs 3 pounds. She has $6.60 left.

50. **Write About It** Explain how you can decide how many digits will be in a quotient.

51. **FAST FACT • SOCIAL STUDIES** A postal carrier delivers mail to about 500 addresses each day. If a carrier delivers mail for 4 hours, to about how many addresses does the carrier deliver each hour?

52. **? What's the Error?** Describe the error, and then show the correct way to divide.

$$\begin{array}{r} 5 \ \text{r2} \\ 9{\overline{)47}} \\ -45 \\ \hline 2 \end{array}$$

53. Yoko takes the train to the city and back 4 times each month. She travels a total of 376 miles. How far away is the city?

54. What is the value of eight $10 bills, six $1 bills, 17 dimes, and 9 pennies?

Maintain Skills

55. Which is the best estimate for the length of a toothbrush, 7 in. or 7 ft?

56. Find the number of square units in the area of the rectangle.

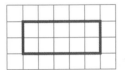

57. Find the length of the ribbon to the nearest $\frac{1}{4}$ inch.

CRCT Test Prep

58. **M4G3.b.** What is the ordered pair for point A in this coordinate system? (p. 82)

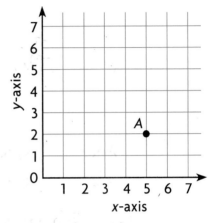

A. (2,5) C. (4,3)

B. (3,4) D. (5,2)

Problem Solving   LiNKUP ... to Social Studies

On April 3, 1860, the Pony Express began carrying mail between Missouri and California. The riders traveled about 150 miles each day—almost twice as far as a day's travel by stagecoach.

USE DATA For 1–4, use the information above.

1. It took the Pony Express riders about 11 days to travel from St. Joseph, Missouri, to Sacramento, California. About how many miles did they travel?

2. It took a Pony Express rider about 4 hours to travel from Sacramento to Placerville, a distance of 45 miles. About how many miles did the rider travel each hour?

3. One of the longest nonstop rides was made by Buffalo Bill. He rode for about 22 hours at about 15 miles per hour. He used 21 different horses. About how many miles did he ride?

4. **CHALLENGE** The Pony Express carried a total of 34,753 pieces of mail in 308 trips of 2,000 miles each. How many miles did the Pony Express riders travel?

Problem Solving Skill
Interpret the Remainder

M4N4.a. Know the division facts with understanding and fluency. *also* **M4N4.c.,**
M4P1.a., M4P1.b., M4P1.c., M4P1.d., M4P3.a., M4P3.b., M4P3.c., M4P3.d.
Concepts/Skill to Maintain Multiplication and division of whole numbers

UNDERSTAND ❯ PLAN ❯ SOLVE ❯ CHECK

WHAT'S LEFT? Portia and Preston are planning for the school carnival.

When you solve a division problem that has a remainder, the way you interpret the remainder depends on the situation in the problem.

Examples

Ⓐ Drop the remainder, and increase the quotient by 1.

They need 250 cans of soda for the food booth. A carton holds 6 cans of soda. How many cartons of soda will they need to buy?

$$\begin{array}{r} 41\ r4 \\ 6)\overline{250} \\ -24 \\ \hline 10 \\ -6 \\ \hline 4 \end{array}$$

Since 41 cartons hold less than 250 cans, increase the quotient by 1.

So, they need to buy 42 cartons of soda.

Ⓑ Drop the remainder.

They have a 250-foot roll of paper to make posters for the carnival. They will cut the roll into 3-foot posters. How many posters will they have?

$$\begin{array}{r} 83\ r1 \\ 3)\overline{250} \\ -24 \\ \hline 10 \\ -9 \\ \hline 1 \end{array}$$

Drop the remainder. The remainder is not enough for another 3-foot poster.

So, they will have a total of 83 posters.

Ⓒ Use the remainder as the answer.

Portia made 126 cookies to sell. She divided the cookies into packages of 4 and gave the leftover cookies to her brother. How many cookies did she give to her brother?

$$\begin{array}{r} 31\ r2 \\ 4)\overline{126} \\ -12 \\ \hline 06 \\ -4 \\ \hline 2 \end{array}$$

Use the remainder as the answer.

So, she gave her brother 2 cookies.

Talk About It

• Why isn't 41 cartons of soda the correct answer to the first question?

• Why is the remainder dropped to answer the second question?

Problem Solving Practice

Solve. Then write _a, b,_ or _c_ to tell how you interpreted the remainder.

a. increase the quotient by 1

b. drop the remainder

c. use the remainder as the answer

1. An 85-inch piece of wire must be cut into 9-inch lengths. How many 9-inch lengths will there be?

2. Dave must pack 55 bottles of juice. Boxes for the bottles hold 8 bottles. How many boxes are needed?

3. Lena has a 50-foot roll of ribbon. She cuts the ribbon into 9-foot pieces to make bows. How many 9-foot pieces does she have?

4. Dora needs to buy pages for her photo album. Each page holds 6 photos. How many pages will she need for 94 photos?

5. Jan's Pillow Factory stuffs each pillow with 3 pounds of duck feathers. Jan has 67 pounds of feathers. How many pounds of feathers will be left over?

6. The Pool Supply Shop had 179 outdoor games. It shipped the same number of games to each of 8 stores. How many outdoor games were left over at the shop?

Mixed Applications

USE DATA For 7–9, use the bar graph.

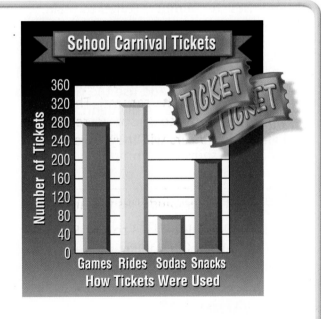

7. MULTISTEP If 900 tickets were sold at the carnival, how many tickets did not get used?

A 20   **B** 40   **C** 120   **D** 140

8. If each ticket cost 50¢, what was the total spent on snacks?

F $50   **G** $80   **H** $100   **J** $120

9. MULTISTEP Games and snacks each cost 2 tickets. Sodas were 1 ticket each, and each ride cost 4 tickets. What was the most popular choice?

10. Nick bought two magazines for $18.50. The difference in the cost of the magazines was $2.50. How much did each magazine cost?

11. ✎ Write a problem in which the solution requires that you increase the quotient by 1.

Division Relationships

 M4N4.c. Understand the relationship between dividend, divisor, quotient, and remainder. *also* M4P2.a., M4P2.b., M4P2.c., M4P2.d., M4P3.a., M4P3.b., M4P3.c., M4P3.d.

▶ **Explore**

As you do the Activity, think about how the divisor, dividend, quotient, and remainder in each problem are related.

Activity

Number of players: 2 or more

Rules

- Roll one number cube to determine the order of play. The player with the greatest number goes first.

- The first player rolls 3 number cubes and uses the numbers rolled to make a division problem with a 1-digit divisor and a 2-digit dividend.

- The rest of the players go in order to roll one number cube and use the number rolled as a divisor for the same dividend.

- Each player finds the quotient and remainder of the problem they made and shows the computation. The remainder becomes the number of points each player wins.

- Discuss who won the round and why.

- Play 4 more rounds. The player with the most points at the end of 5 rounds wins the game.

How many points will I get for 31 ÷ 4?

Talk About It

- Is it possible for a player to not get any points? Explain.

- What is the greatest number of points possible if the divisor is 3? Explain.

- What happens to the quotient if the dividend remains the same and a lesser divisor is used?

- What happens to the quotient if the dividend remains the same and a greater divisor is used?

▶ Connect

When either the dividend or the divisor changes in a division problem, the quotient and the remainder change.

Examples

Ⓐ Divisor changes.

$$5\overline{)24} = 4\text{ r}4 \qquad 6\overline{)24} = 4 \qquad 7\overline{)24} = 3\text{ r}3 \qquad 8\overline{)24} = 3$$

Ⓑ Dividend changes.

$$6\overline{)25} = 4\text{ r}1 \qquad 6\overline{)26} = 4\text{ r}2 \qquad 6\overline{)27} = 4\text{ r}3 \qquad 6\overline{)28} = 4\text{ r}4$$

- In Example A, what did you notice about the quotient?
- In Example B, what did you notice about the remainder?

▶ Practice and Problem Solving

Use the pattern to choose the problem in each set that will have the greatest remainder.

1. $8\overline{)39}$, $8\overline{)37}$, $8\overline{)35}$ **2.** $4\overline{)17}$, $4\overline{)18}$, $4\overline{)20}$ **3.** $5\overline{)62}$, $5\overline{)63}$, $5\overline{)64}$

Use the pattern to choose the problem in each set that will have the greatest quotient.

4. $5\overline{)72}$, $6\overline{)72}$, $7\overline{)72}$ **5.** $4\overline{)85}$, $4\overline{)92}$, $4\overline{)108}$ **6.** $8\overline{)124}$, $8\overline{)114}$, $8\overline{)120}$

Continue the pattern to find the missing quotient.

7. $4\overline{)68} = 17$, $4\overline{)72} = 18$, $4\overline{)76}$ **8.** $9\overline{)108} = 12$, $9\overline{)117} = 13$, $9\overline{)135}$ **9.** $7\overline{)315} = 45$, $7\overline{)322} = 46$, $7\overline{)336}$

10. **ALGEBRA** If $46 \div 9 = 5\text{ r}1$, what is the dividend in the number sentence $\blacksquare \div 9 = 5\text{ r}3$?

11. Can $157 \div 6$ have a remainder of 8? Why or why not?

12. 📖 **Write About It** If you know that $170 \div 5 = 34$, explain how you can use a pattern to find the remainder of $174 \div 5$ without dividing.

Maintain Skills

13. 7×3 **14.** $93 \div 3$

15. 40×6 **16.** $70 \div 5$

17. What is the perimeter of the square?

8 in.

8 in. ☐ 8 in.

8 in.

CRCT Test Prep

18. **M4N7.d.** Lincoln Elementary School ordered 1,200 notebooks to share equally among the six grade levels. How many notebooks will each grade level receive? (p. 212)

A. 2 C. 200

B. 20 D. 2,000

Extra Practice

Set A (pp. 208–211)

Divide and check.

1. $5\overline{)84}$ 2. $6\overline{)68}$ 3. $2\overline{)47}$ 4. $4\overline{)75}$ 5. $3\overline{)31}$

6. $95 \div 3$ 7. $69 \div 4$ 8. $77 \div 6$ 9. $58 \div 5$ 10. $76 \div 9$

Use multiplication to check each answer.

11. $73 \div 9 = 8$ r1   12. $64 \div 5 = 12$ r4   13. $99 \div 6 = 16$ r3   14. $87 \div 7 = 12$ r3

15. Patty brought 30 cookies to a party. Each of 7 children took the same number of cookies. How many cookies were left over?

Set B (pp. 212–213)

Use a basic division fact and patterns to write each quotient.

1. $480 \div 6$ 2. $210 \div 7$ 3. $320 \div 4$ 4. $360 \div 6$
   $4,800 \div 6$ $2,100 \div 7$ $3,200 \div 4$ $3,600 \div 6$

Write the value of □.

5. $36,000 \div 6 = \square$ 6. $\square \div 6 = 200$ 7. $2,800 \div \square = 40$ 8. $2,400 \div 8 = \square$

9. $4,200 \div 7 = \square$ 10. $\square \div 3 = 900$ 11. $560 \div 8 = \square$ 12. $\square \div 7 = 900$

13. The toy factory made 5,400 stuffed bears. If 6 bears fit in a box, how many boxes are needed to ship the bears?

Set C (pp. 214–215)

Divide and check.

1. $4\overline{)672}$ 2. $9\overline{)121}$ 3. $2\overline{)496}$ 4. $5\overline{)453}$ 5. $3\overline{)587}$

6. There are 8 swimmers on a team. The swim club has 152 swimmers. How many teams does the swim club have?

Set D (pp. 216–219)

Divide and check.

1. $6\overline{)700}$ 2. $4\overline{)828}$ 3. $3\overline{)921}$ 4. $5\overline{)740}$ 5. $7\overline{)370}$

6. $570 \div 4$ 7. $722 \div 8$ 8. $310 \div 4$ 9. $890 \div 7$ 10. $820 \div 4$

Review/Test

✓ CHECK VOCABULARY AND CONCEPTS

Choose the best term from the box.

1. The _?_ is the number, not including the remainder, that results from dividing. (p. 208)

2. The order of division is _?_, multiply, subtract, and compare. (p. 208)

For 3–6, think of how to model 47 ÷ 3. (pp. 206–207)

3. How many equal groups are needed to model the divisor?

4. Draw the base-ten blocks needed to show the dividend.

5. How many are in each group?

6. How many are left over?

✓ CHECK SKILLS

Divide and check. (pp. 208–211, 214–215, 216–219)

7. $3\overline{)23}$ 8. $4\overline{)33}$ 9. $2\overline{)28}$ 10. $6\overline{)72}$

11. $9\overline{)71}$ 12. $5\overline{)85}$ 13. $4\overline{)65}$ 14. $5\overline{)69}$

15. $7\overline{)91}$ 16. $6\overline{)79}$ 17. $8\overline{)98}$ 18. $7\overline{)90}$

19. $809 \div 7$ 20. $299 \div 8$ 21. $124 \div 3$ 22. $234 \div 4$

23. $569 \div 5$ 24. $831 \div 7$ 25. $971 \div 8$ 26. $325 \div 3$

Divide mentally. Write the basic division fact and the quotient. (pp. 212–213)

27. $150 \div 5$ 28. $210 \div 3$ 29. $360 \div 6$ 30. $4,500 \div 9$ 31. $5,600 \div 8$

✓ CHECK PROBLEM SOLVING

Solve. (pp. 220–221)

32. Tyrone and Jimmy want to build a tree fort. They need 153 feet of lumber. If the lumber comes in 8-foot lengths, how many pieces of lumber do they need?

33. Ling has 231 photos. If she puts 8 photos on a page, how many pages will she need for her photo album?

Chapter CRCT Test Prep

NUMBERS AND OPERATIONS

1. **M4N4.c.** Which expression shows the relationship between the dividend, divisor, quotient, and remainder for $67 \div 5 = 13\ r2$?

   A. $(13 \times 5) + 2$

   B. $(13 \times 2) + 5$

   C. $(13 \times 5) - 2$

   D. $(5 \times 2) + 13$

2. **M4N4.a.** The 6 children in the Ripley family save all of their pennies in a jar. They divide the pennies equally every month. At the end of February, they have 252 pennies to share. How many pennies will each child receive?

   A. 4

   B. 42

   C. 420

   D. 422

3. **M4N4.a.** The Photo Gallery will display up to 156 different photos each day. Each photographer has 9 photos to display. How many photographers can show all of their work each day?

   A. 16

   B. 17

   C. 18

   D. 19

NUMBERS AND OPERATIONS

4. **M4N4.a.** The table below shows how many bags of fruit snacks there are in different-size packages.

Type of Package	Number of Bags
Large	8
Medium	6
Small	4

   Jefferson Elementary School needs 342 bags of fruit snacks for lunch. How many large packages does the school need to buy in order to have enough bags?

   A. 86

   B. 57

   C. 43

   D. 42

5. **M4N4.a.** Harlan works 8 hours per day. How many days did he work last year if he worked a total of 840 hours?

   A. 105

   B. 15

   C. 10 r5

   D. 10

6. **M4N7.d.** Use mental math to find the quotient $3,500 \div 5$.

   A. 7

   B. 70

   C. 700

   D. 7,000

Cumulative CRCT Test Prep

GEOMETRY

7. `M4G3.b.` Which ordered pair describes the location of Claudia's house?

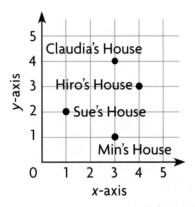

A. (3,4)

B. (4,3)

C. (3,3)

D. (4,4)

8. `M4G3.a.` Whose desk is located at point (1,2) in the coordinate system below?

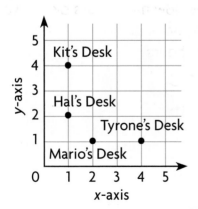

A. Hal's desk

B. Mario's desk

C. Tyrone's desk

D. Kit's desk

ALGEBRA

9. `M4A1.b.` Raj is driving 90 miles from Macon, Georgia, to Athens, Georgia. Let □ stand for the number of miles he has driven so far. Which expression stands for the number of miles Raj has left to drive?

A. 90 + □

B. 90 − □

C. 90 × □

D. 90 ÷ □

10. `M4A1.a.` The table shows how much Henry earns for the different number of hours he works in a day.

Money Henry Earns				
Hours	2	4	6	8
$ earned	$10	□	$30	$40

How much does Henry earn if he works for 4 hours?

A. $12

B. $15

C. $20

D. $25

11. `M4A1.c.` What is the value of 48 ÷ □ if □ = 6?

A. 5

B. 6

C. 7

D. 8

Divide by 2-Digit Numbers

≡**FAST FACT** •

SCIENCE Kites were used in ancient China to send messages and to spy on enemies. In modern times, kites have been used to gather weather data and for recreation.

INVESTIGATION For a kite to fly well, the tail needs to be seven times the length of the kite. The length of the kite from top to bottom is called the spine, which can be made of wood. Randy has 40 inches of wood to make kites. Look at the table. How long should each spine be? Which kites can Randy make?

Using Data

KITE TAILS		
Type of Kite	**Length of Tail**	**Length of Spine**
Diamond	175 in.	▪
Delta	133 in.	▪
Sled	252 in.	▪
Butterfly	105 in.	▪

Use this page to help you review and remember important skills needed for Chapter 11.

✓ DIVIDE BY 1-DIGIT NUMBERS

Divide.

1. $58 \div 4$

2. $73 \div 5$

3. $37 \div 7$

4. $93 \div 8$

5. $69 \div 9$

6. $43 \div 3$

7. $6\overline{)77}$

8. $7\overline{)46}$

9. $2\overline{)39}$

10. $5\overline{)52}$

11. $8\overline{)74}$

12. $4\overline{)66}$

13. $2\overline{)703}$

14. $3\overline{)588}$

15. $6\overline{)458}$

16. $9\overline{)635}$

17. $7\overline{)815}$

18. $4\overline{)121}$

✓ 2-DIGIT SUBTRACTION

Find the difference.

19. $\begin{array}{r} 92 \\ -24 \\ \hline \end{array}$

20. $\begin{array}{r} 79 \\ -44 \\ \hline \end{array}$

21. $\begin{array}{r} 66 \\ -29 \\ \hline \end{array}$

22. $\begin{array}{r} 53 \\ -37 \\ \hline \end{array}$

23. $\begin{array}{r} 45 \\ -18 \\ \hline \end{array}$

24. $87 - 56$

25. $38 - 25$

26. $71 - 52$

27. $99 - 73$

28. $64 - 35$

VOCABULARY POWER ✓

REVIEW

quotient [kwō′shənt] *noun*

Quotient contains the root word *quot,* meaning "how many." Think about what the quotient is in a division problem. Use this information to write a definition for *quotient.*

www.harcourtschool.com/mathglossary

Algebra: Mental Math: Division Patterns

 M4N4.d. Understand and explain the effect on the quotient of multiplying or dividing both the divisor and dividend by the same number (2050 ÷ 50 yields the same answer as 205 ÷ 5). *also* **M4N4.a., M4N4.b., M4P1.c., M4P2.a., M4P2.b., M4P4.a., M4P4.b.**

▶ Learn

REPORT DUE Marsha must write 160 spelling words. She wants to have an equal number of words on each page. If she writes 20 words on each page, how many pages does she need?

Example

Find 160 ÷ 20.

Use basic facts and patterns to find quotients mentally.

dividend	divisor	quotient
16	÷ 2	= 8
160	÷ 2	= 80
160	÷ 20	= 8
1,600	÷ 20	= 80

Think: 2 × 8 = 16

So, Marsha needs 8 pages to write her spelling words.

MATH IDEA If you multiply the dividend by 10, then multiply the quotient by 10. If you multiply both the dividend and divisor by 10, the quotient remains the same.

More Examples

A 63 ÷ 9 = 7   Think: 9 × 7 = 63
630 ÷ 9 = 70
630 ÷ 90 = 7
6,300 ÷ 90 = 70

B 40 ÷ 8 = 5   Think: 8 × 5 = 40
400 ÷ 8 = 50
400 ÷ 80 = 5
4,000 ÷ 80 = 50

• Which multiplication number sentences can you use to show whether the division number sentences in Example A are correct?

▶ Check

1. **Explain** the effect on the quotient when the dividend and the divisor are both multiplied by 10. Give an example.

Use mental math to divide.

2. $180 \div 9$ **3.** $420 \div 70$ **4.** $640 \div 8$ **5.** $720 \div 90$

6. $2,800 \div 70$ **7.** $3,000 \div 50$ **8.** $3,500 \div 50$ **9.** $140 \div 20$

Practice and Problem Solving   Extra Practice, page 244, Set A

Use mental math to divide.

10. $90 \div 9$ **11.** $150 \div 3$ **12.** $360 \div 6$ **13.** $490 \div 70$

14. $200 \div 50$ **15.** $2,400 \div 60$ **16.** $2,000 \div 40$ **17.** $1,600 \div 20$

18. REASONING Explain how you can write a division fact related to $180 \div 9$ with the same quotient. Then write the related fact.

 **ALGEBRA**   Find the value of $\square$.

19. $80 \div \square = 20$ **20.** $160 \div 4 = \square$ **21.** $\square \div 6 = 40$

22. $300 \div \square = 6$ **23.** $3,200 \div \square = 40$ **24.** $\square \div 50 = 80$

USE DATA For 25–27, use the table.

25. The *Daily Reader* will deliver the same number of newspapers to each of 60 classrooms. How many newspapers will each classroom receive?

26. MULTISTEP Each of 40 classrooms received 50 copies of the *School Reporter*. How many copies of the newspaper are left?

27. What if the *School News* printed another 300 copies and then delivered an equal number of papers to each of 30 classrooms? How many newspapers would each classroom receive?

SCHOOL NEWSPAPER PRODUCTION	
Newspaper	**Number**
Daily Reader	1,800
School Reporter	2,400
School News	900

Maintain Skills

For 28–29, write the value of the blue digit.

28. 67.8   **29.** 46,023

30. Mr. Adams wants to give 8 markers to each of his 27 students for their art projects. How many markers does he need?

CRCT Test Prep

31. M4N2.a Rounded to the nearest thousand, the number of people who went to a basketball game at the arena is 10,000. How many people could have gone to the game? (p. 32)

A. 9,498   C. 10,510

B. 9,670   D. 11,001

Model Division

M4N4.b. Solve problems involving division by a 2-digit number (including those that generate a remainder). *also* **M4N4.a., M4N4.c., M4P3.a., M4P3.b., M4P3.c., M4P3.d., M4P5, M4P5.a., M4P5.b., M4P5.c.**

Quick Review

1. $7\overline{)210}$ **2.** $9\overline{)45}$

3. $8\overline{)480}$ **4.** $4\overline{)160}$

5. $123 \div 5$

MATERIALS base-ten blocks

▶ **Explore**

TEA TIME Ann's Gift Shop has 65 teacups to put on display. Each rack holds 31 cups. How many racks will be filled with teacups? How many teacups will be left over?

Activity 1

Divide. $65 \div 31$

Make a model to divide with a two-digit divisor.

STEP 1	STEP 2	STEP 3
Show 65 as 6 tens 5 ones.	Make 1 group of 31.	Make 2 groups of 31. Count how many ones are left over.

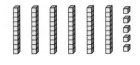 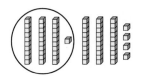

$$65 \div 31 = 2 \text{ r}3$$

So, 2 racks will be filled with teacups. There will be 3 teacups left over.

• **Explain** how you can check the quotient and remainder.

Try It

Use base-ten blocks to solve each division problem.

    a. $89 \div 22$

    b. $76 \div 14$

    c. $92 \div 18$

    d. $64 \div 12$

I have one group of 22. How many more groups of 22 can I make to show $89 \div 22$?

Activity 2 Here is a way to record division. Divide 65 by 21.

STEP 1 Write the problem 65 ÷ 21.

Model

Record
$21\overline{)65}$

STEP 2 Estimate. 65 ÷ 21

Think: 60 ÷ 20 = 3
Try 3 groups of 21.

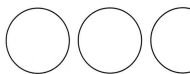

$\dfrac{3}{21\overline{)65}}$

STEP 3 Make 3 groups of 21.

Multiply. 3 × 21 = 63
Count how many ones are left over.
Subtract. 65 − 63 = 2
Compare. 2 < 21

$\begin{array}{r} 3\ r2 \\ 21\overline{)65} \\ -63 \\ \hline 2 \end{array}$

▶ **Practice and Problem Solving**

Make a model to divide.

1. $17\overline{)58}$ **2.** $18\overline{)77}$ **3.** $35\overline{)108}$ **4.** $41\overline{)129}$

Divide. You may use base-ten blocks.

5. 259 ÷ 51 **6.** 158 ÷ 25 **7.** 237 ÷ 35 **8.** 301 ÷ 29

9. MULTISTEP Mrs. Ching has 8 boxes of 6 cups. She can display 14 cups on each shelf. How many shelves does Mrs. Ching need for her teacups?

10. REASONING There were 6 groups, with 3 tens blocks and 1 ones block in each. What division number sentence can you write to tell the size of each group?

11. **? What's the Error?** Silvia made this model for 59 ÷ 14. Describe her error. Draw the correct model.

Maintain Skills

Find the product.

12. 4 × 2 **13.** 3 × 3

14. 8 × 5 **15.** 6 × 7

CRCT Test Prep

16. **M4N7.b.** (47 + 7) ÷ (3 × 3) (p. 128)

A. 9 C. 6
B. 8 D. 4

Divide by 2 Digits

M4N4.b. Solve problems involving division by a 2-digit number (including those that generate a remainder). *also* **M4N4.a., M4N4.c., M4P2.**

Quick Review

1. $3\overline{)96}$ 2. $5\overline{)144}$

3. $7\overline{)219}$ 4. $6\overline{)512}$

5. $9\overline{)136}$

▶ **Learn**

LUNAR PHASES It takes about 27 days for the moon to revolve around Earth. How many times does the moon revolve around Earth in 365 days?

One Way You can estimate to place the first digit in the quotient.

Divide. $365 \div 27$ or $27\overline{)365}$

STEP 1

Estimate.

Think:

$$\begin{array}{cc} 10 & 12 \\ 30\overline{)300} & \text{or } 30\overline{)360} \end{array}$$

■

$27\overline{)365}$ So, place the first digit in the tens place.

STEP 2

Divide 36 tens. Write a 1 in the tens place in the quotient.

$$\begin{array}{r} 1 \\ 27\overline{)365} \\ -27 \\ \hline 9 \end{array}$$ Multiply. 27×1
Subtract. $36 - 27$
Compare. $9 < 27$

STEP 3

Bring down the 5 ones. Divide the 95 ones.

$$\begin{array}{r} 13\ r14 \\ 27\overline{)365} \\ -27\downarrow \\ \hline 95 \\ -81 \\ \hline 14 \end{array}$$ Multiply. 27×3
Subtract. $95 - 81$
Compare. $14 < 27$

Write the remainder.

$365 \div 27 = 13\ r14$

So, the moon revolves around Earth a little more than 13 times in 365 days.

Another Way You can break apart the dividend into multiples of the divisor.

Divide. $462 \div 42$

STEP 1

List the multiples of the divisor. Then break apart the dividend into multiples of the divisor.

$462 = 420 + 42$

STEP 2

Divide each multiple by the divisor.

$$\begin{array}{r} 10 + 1 \\ 42\overline{)420 + 42} \\ 420 \quad 42 \end{array}$$

STEP 3

Add the quotients.

$$\begin{array}{r} 10 + 1 = 11 \\ 42\overline{)420 + 42} \\ 420 \quad 42 \end{array}$$

So, $462 \div 42 = 11$.

• How can you be sure the answer for $365 \div 27 = 13\ r14$ is correct?

• How can you use the number sentence $462 \div 42 = 11$ to find the quotient $473 \div 42$?

More Examples

A Divide. 68 ÷ 17
Estimate. 60 ÷ 20 = 3 or 80 ÷ 20 = 4

```
      4
17)68
  -68
    0
```

B Divide. 90 ÷ 36
Think. 90 = 72 + 18

```
        2  r18
36)72 + 18
   72
```

C Divide. 123 ÷ 24
Estimate. 120 ÷ 20 = 6 or 140 ÷ 20 = 7

```
       5 r3
24)123
  -120
     3
```

D Divide. 156 ÷ 40
Think. 156 = 120 + 36

```
         3  r36
40)120 + 36
  -120
```

E Divide. 840 ÷ 31
Estimate. 800 ÷ 20 = 40 or 800 ÷ 40 = 20

```
      27r3
31)840
  -62
   224
   217
     3
```

F Divide. 312 ÷ 13
Think. 312 = 260 + 52

```
      20 + 4 = 24
13)260 + 52
   260    52
```

⚡ **MATH IDEA** The remainder in division must always be less than the divisor. If the remainder is greater than the divisor, correct the quotient by increasing it.

Technology Link

More practice: Harcourt Mega Math The Number Games, *Up, Up, and Array*, Levels Q and R

▷ **Check**

1. **Explain** how an estimate is useful when you divide two-digit numbers.

Tell where to place the first digit. Then divide.

2. 32)195 **3.** 25)582 **4.** 12)28 **5.** 17)365

Complete by breaking apart the dividend into multiples of the divisor.

6. 329 ÷ 32
329 = 320 + ■
32)320 + ■

7. 48 ÷ 36
48 = ■ + 12
36)■ + 12

8. 170 ÷ 15
170 = 150 + ■ + 5
15)150 + ■ + 5

LESSON CONTINUES ▷

Tell where to place the first digit. Then divide.

9. $42\overline{)731}$ **10.** $81\overline{)325}$ **11.** $29\overline{)90}$ **12.** $25\overline{)549}$

Complete by breaking apart the dividend into multiples of the divisor.

13. $258 \div 24$
$258 = 240 + \blacksquare$
$24\overline{)240 + \blacksquare}$

14. $52 \div 12$
$52 = 48 + \blacksquare$
$12\overline{)48 + \blacksquare}$

15. $390 \div 35$
$390 = 350 + \blacksquare + 5$
$35\overline{)350 + \blacksquare + 5}$

Divide.

16. $13\overline{)246}$ **17.** $20\overline{)483}$ **18.** $12\overline{)148}$ **19.** $15\overline{)25}$

20. $11\overline{)201}$ **21.** $54\overline{)612}$ **22.** $21\overline{)825}$ **23.** $34\overline{)249}$

Complete.

24. $(17 \times 18) + 4 = 310$,
so $310 \div 17 = 18$ r$\blacksquare$.

25. $(36 \times 20) + 1 = 721$,
so $\blacksquare \div 36 = 20$ r1.

26. $(25 \times 31) + 5 = 780$,
so $780 \div 25 = \blacksquare$ r5.

27. $(14 \times 30) + 3 = 423$,
so $423 \div 14 = 30$ r$\blacksquare$.

28. $(40 \times 22) + 8 = 888$,
so $888 \div \blacksquare = 22$ r8.

29. $(52 \times 14) + 40 = 768$,
so $768 \div \blacksquare = 14$ r40.

USE DATA For 30–32, use the map.

30. MULTISTEP The Bensons and Reeds met in Savannah. The Bensons drove from Atlanta, and the Reeds drove from Rome. After a week's stay, they drove home. Who drove farther? How much farther?

31. If the average speed of travel were 60 miles an hour, about how long would it take to drive from Savannah to Atlanta? from Savannah to Rome?

32. **? What's the Question?** Felix and his family drove from Columbus to Savannah and back for a vacation. The answer is 536 miles.

33. ≡**FAST FACT** • **SCIENCE** The greatest distance from Earth to the moon is 251,927 miles, and the least distance is 225,745 miles. How much closer is the moon to Earth at its least distance?

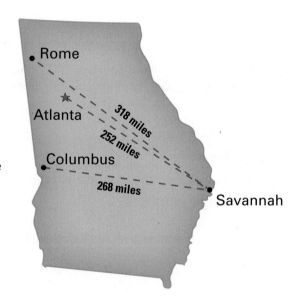

Rome

Atlanta
318 miles
252 miles
Columbus
268 miles
Savannah

34. 📓 **Write About It** The first digit in the quotient is not correct. Explain how the difference $65 - 42 = 23$ can help you correct the first digit.

$$\begin{array}{r} 2 \\ 21\overline{)652} \\ -42 \\ \hline 23 \end{array}$$

Maintain Skills

35.
$$\begin{array}{r} 46 \\ \times 9 \\ \hline \end{array}$$

36.
$$\begin{array}{r} 214 \\ \times 3 \\ \hline \end{array}$$

37. $98 \div 7$

38. $12 \times 5 \times 7$

39. Hank wants to tile part of his patio with tiles that are 1 foot long on each side. The diagram shows the part of the patio he wants to tile. How many tiles does Hank need?

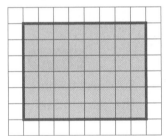

CRCT Test Prep

40. **M4N3.** Joshua travels 23 miles to work and 23 miles home 5 days a week. How many miles does he travel in 4 weeks? (p. 156)
A. 920 miles   C. 720 miles
B. 890 miles   D. 690 miles

41. **M4A1.b.** Keesha bought gifts for Ally, Derick, and Paula. Each gift was the same price. If ▨ stands for the price of each gift, which expression stands for the amount Keesha spent in all? (p. 128)
A. $3 + ▨$ C. $3 \div ▨$
B. $3 \times ▨$ D. $3 - ▨$

Problem Solving LINKUP ... to Science

The sun is the center of our solar system. All of the planets revolve, or travel around, the sun at different speeds.

USE DATA For 1–2, use the table.

1. Orbital velocity is the speed that a planet travels as it revolves around the sun. What is Mars' orbital velocity per second? (60 seconds = 1 minute)

2. Pluto has an orbital velocity of 10,548 miles per hour. How much faster is Jupiter's orbital velocity per hour than Pluto's? (60 minutes = 1 hour)

ORBITAL VELOCITY OF SELECTED PLANETS (to the nearest whole number)	
Planet	**Miles Per Minute**
Earth	1,110
Mars	900
Mercury	1,785
Jupiter	487

3. The number of Earth days it takes for a planet to orbit the sun once is called a sidereal revolution. Mercury's sidereal revolution is about 88 days. About how many times does Mercury revolve around the sun in 365 days?

Correcting Quotients

M4N4.b. Solve problems involving division by a 2-digit number (including those that generate a remainder). *also* M4A1.b., M4N4.a., M4P3.a., M4P3.b., M4P3.c., M4P3.d.

Quick Review

1. $20\overline{)800}$ 2. $80\overline{)720}$

3. $40\overline{)840}$ 4. $25\overline{)150}$

5. $50\overline{)350}$

▶ **Learn**

THE BAND MARCHES ON! There are 184 band members going to the Cherry Blossom Festival in Washington, D.C. School policy requires a chaperone for every 21 students. How many chaperones are needed?

Since a chaperone is needed for every 21 students, divide 184 by 21.

Example

Divide. $184 \div 21$ or $21\overline{)184}$

↓   ↓

Estimate. $180 \div 20 = 9$

STEP 1

Try the estimate, 9.
$21 \times 9 = 189$

$$\begin{array}{r} 9 \\ 21\overline{)184} \\ -189 \end{array}$$ Since 189 > 184, the estimate is too large.

STEP 2

Try 8.
$21 \times 8 = 168$

$$\begin{array}{r} 8 \\ 21\overline{)184} \\ -168 \end{array}$$

STEP 3

Subtract to find the remainder.

$$\begin{array}{r} 8 \ \text{r}16 \\ 21\overline{)184} \\ -168 \\ \hline 16 \end{array}$$ Compare. 16 < 21

There are 8 chaperones, each in charge of 21 students, and 1 more chaperone is needed for the 16 remaining students. So, 9 chaperones are needed.

More Examples

A Divide. $244 \div 27$
Estimate. $240 \div 30 = 8$

Try 8.

$$\begin{array}{r} 8 \\ 27\overline{)244} \\ -216 \\ \hline 28 \end{array}$$ Since 28 > 27, the estimate is too small.

Try 9.

$$\begin{array}{r} 9 \ \text{r}1 \\ 27\overline{)244} \\ -243 \\ \hline 1 \end{array}$$

B Divide. $319 \div 84$
Estimate. $320 \div 80 = 4$

Try 4.

$$\begin{array}{r} 4 \\ 84\overline{)319} \\ -336 \end{array}$$ Since 336 > 319, the estimate is too large.

Try 3.

$$\begin{array}{r} 3 \ \text{r}67 \\ 84\overline{)319} \\ -252 \\ \hline 67 \end{array}$$ 67 < 84

1. **Explain** how to correct a quotient.

Write *too small, too large,* or *just right* for each estimate.
Then divide.

2. $27\overline{)257}$ with estimate 8 **3.** $43\overline{)362}$ with estimate 9 **4.** $86\overline{)536}$ with estimate 6 **5.** $51\overline{)462}$ with estimate 9

▶ **Practice and Problem Solving**   (Extra Practice, page 244, Set C)

Write *too large, too small,* or *just right* for each estimate.
Then divide.

6. $18\overline{)108}$ with estimate 6 **7.** $35\overline{)215}$ with estimate 5 **8.** $85\overline{)798}$ with estimate 9 **9.** $85\overline{)367}$ with estimate 3

10. $22\overline{)221}$ with estimate 10 **11.** $45\overline{)369}$ with estimate 9 **12.** $36\overline{)853}$ with estimate 25 **13.** $79\overline{)487}$ with estimate 5

Divide.

14. $52\overline{)456}$ **15.** $82\overline{)736}$ **16.** $45\overline{)236}$ **17.** $62\overline{)336}$

18. $511 \div 42$ **19.** $754 \div 15$ **20.** $875 \div 23$ **21.** $488 \div 37$

For 22–24, use what you know about division to find
the mystery digits for each problem.

> **Mystery Digits**
> 0, 1, 2, 3, 4, 7

22. $28\overline{)364}$ with quotient ■■   **23.** ■■$\overline{)702}$ with quotient 26 **24.** $3■\overline{)1,700}$ with quotient $5■$

25. **MULTISTEP** Paul had 10 school books, 45 fiction books, 35 nonfiction books, and 78 science fiction books. He gave away 10 fiction books and 15 science fiction books. How many books does he have left?

26. **?** **What's the Error?** First Susan estimated $322 \div 42$ as 8. Then she corrected the quotient by writing 9. Describe her error, and tell what she should have written.

27. **Vocabulary Power** *Estimate* used as a verb means "to give an approximate value." *Estimate* can also be used as a noun. What is the difference when it is used as a noun?

Maintain Skills

Write the value of the blue digit.

28. 371,249   **29.** 961,307

Show another way to group the factors. Then find the product.

30. $2 \times (3 \times 4)$ **31.** $4 \times (5 \times 2)$

CRCT Test Prep

32. **M4N4.b.** A group of 52 boys, 67 girls, and 4 teachers is taking a bus trip. If each bus holds 48 people, how many buses will be needed? (p. 234)

A. 2   B. 3   C. 4   D. 5

Zeros in Quotients

M4N4.b. Solve problems involving division by a 2-digit number (including those that generate a remainder). *also* **M4P2.a., M4P2.b., M4P2.c., M4P3.a., M4P3.b., M4P3.c., M4P3.d.**

Quick Review

1. $4\overline{)28}$ 2. $4\overline{)36}$

3. $7\overline{)63}$ 4. $2\overline{)22}$

5. $5\overline{)41}$

Learn

CARD MANIA A trading card collector sold 720 baseball trading cards to 24 customers. Each customer bought the same number of cards. How many trading cards did each customer buy?

Example Divide 720 by 24.

STEP 1	**STEP 2**	**STEP 3**
Estimate to place the first digit in the quotient.	Divide 72 tens. Write a 3 in the tens place in the quotient.	Bring down the 0 in the ones. Divide 0 by 24.

STEP 1

Think:
$$\frac{30}{20\overline{)600}} \text{ or } \frac{40}{20\overline{)800}}$$

■

$24\overline{)720}$ So, place the first digit in the tens place.

STEP 2

$$\begin{array}{r} 3 \\ 24\overline{)720} \\ -72 \\ \hline 0 \end{array}$$ Multiply. 24×3
Subtract. $72 - 72$
Compare. $0 < 24$

STEP 3

$$\begin{array}{r} 30 \\ 24\overline{)720} \\ -72 \\ \hline 00 \\ -0 \\ \hline 0 \end{array}$$ Write 0 in the quotient.

So, each customer bought 30 trading cards.

More Examples

A
$$\begin{array}{r} 20 \text{ r6} \\ 12\overline{)246} \\ -24\downarrow \\ \hline 06 \\ -0 \\ \hline 6 \end{array}$$

B
$$\begin{array}{r} 40 \text{ r8} \\ 15\overline{)608} \\ -60\downarrow \\ \hline 08 \\ -0 \\ \hline 8 \end{array}$$

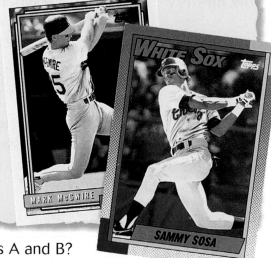

MARK McGWIRE

WHITE SOX

SAMMY SOSA

• Why do you need a zero in the quotient in Examples A and B?

Check

1. **Explain** how an estimate could help you remember to write a zero in a quotient.

Divide.

2. $11\overline{)220}$ 3. $14\overline{)980}$ 4. $26\overline{)788}$ 5. $32\overline{)643}$

6. $29\overline{)876}$ 7. $19\overline{)551}$ 8. $13\overline{)104}$ 9. $23\overline{)692}$

Divide.

10. $16\overline{)320}$ **11.** $12\overline{)720}$ **12.** $27\overline{)810}$ **13.** $41\overline{)820}$

14. $35\overline{)805}$ **15.** $19\overline{)951}$ **16.** $16\overline{)144}$ **17.** $23\overline{)927}$

18. $330 \div 11$ **19.** $940 \div 47$ **20.** $999 \div 33$ **21.** $730 \div 18$

22. $457 \div 15$ **23.** $224 \div 56$ **24.** $832 \div 39$ **25.** $910 \div 30$

26. If $360 \div 12 = 30$, what will the remainder be for $368 \div 12$?

27. How many digits are in the quotient if you divide 750 by 25?

ALGEBRA Write $+$, $-$, $\times$, or $\div$ for each ●.

28. 396 ● $37 = 10 \text{ r}26$ **29.** 25 ● $13 = 325$ **30.** 125 ● $15 = 140$

USE DATA For 31–33, use the table.

31. Darryl has 31 sets of basketball cards. Each set has the same number of cards. What is the greatest number of cards that could be in each set?

32. **MULTISTEP** Darryl sold all of his basketball cards, 100 football cards, and 200 hockey cards. How many cards does he have left?

33. ✎ **Write a problem** that involves dividing by a 2-digit number.

| DARRYL'S TRADING CARD COLLECTION ||
Trading Cards	Total Number
Football	542
Basketball	625
Hockey	900

Maintain Skills

For 34–37, write the value of the blue digit.

34. 3,453.7   **35.** 24,098

36. 235.7   **37.** 15.6

38. Allan is 10 years old. During his last check-up, the doctor measured Allan's height. Is Allan 48 inches tall or 48 feet tall?

CRCT Test Prep

39. **M4N7.d.** There are 58 boxes of markers. Each box contains 28 markers. What is the BEST estimate for the total number of markers? (p. 174)

A.   90

B.   180

C.   900

D. 1,800

Problem Solving Skill
Choose the Operation

M4P1.c. Apply and adapt a variety of appropriate strategies to solve problems. *also* M4N4.a., M4N4.b., M4N7.a., M4P1.a., M4P1.b., M4P1.d., M4P2.a., M4P2.b., M4P2.c., M4P2.d., M4P3.b., M4P3.c., M4P4.c., M4P5.b., M4P5.c.

UNDERSTAND ❯ **PLAN** ❯ **SOLVE** ❯ **CHECK** ❯

MOVING PICTURES Mr. Regis teaches animation classes. Read problems A–D below. Use the table about the operations and Mr. Regis's notes to help you solve the problems.

Add	• Join groups of different sizes.
Subtract	• Take away or compare groups.
Multiply	• Join equal-size groups.
Divide	• Separate into equal-size groups.
	• Find how many in each group.

Ⓐ How many students are taking animation classes at the art school?

Ⓑ For Tuesday's class, there are 25 sheets of drawing paper for each student. How many sheets of paper are there in all?

Ⓒ How many more drawings did Maria's group make than Jerry's group?

Ⓓ For every second of animation, 12 drawings are needed. How long will Tran's animation last? Will there be any drawings left over? If so, how many?

Art School Sign-Up

Day	Students
Monday	95
Tuesday	123
Thursday	78
Saturday	107

Animation Drawings

Group	Drawings
Jerry	501
Maria	810
Greg	642
Tran	756

Talk About It

• How can you decide which operation or operations to use for each problem?

• Solve Problems A–D.

• What operation or operations did you use in each of Problems A–D?

Problem Solving Practice

Solve. Name the operation or operations you used.

1. Eric took 5 rolls of film with him on vacation. He can take 24 pictures with each roll of film. How many pictures can he take?

2. Eric took 18 pictures in Germany, 28 in France, 13 in Spain, and 11 in Portugal. How many pictures did he take?

Mary took 96 pictures last year. If each roll of film had 24 pictures, how many rolls of film did she use?

3. What operation would you use to solve the problem?
   - **A** multiplication
   - **B** division
   - **C** addition
   - **D** subtraction

4. How many rolls of film did she use?
   - **F** 5   **H** 3
   - **G** 4   **J** 2

Mixed Applications

USE DATA For 5–7, use the graph.

5. In 2008, Jon visited all the pottery, jewelry, and crafts booths. What was the total number of booths he visited?

6. **MULTISTEP** Mr. Marcel spent 10 minutes talking to each booth owner in 2007. How many minutes did Mr. Marcel spend talking to the booth owners?

7. **MULTISTEP** In which year were there more booths at the Carson City Art Festival? How many more?

8. **REASONING** There are 45 people at a meeting. Twice as many women as men are at the meeting. How many women are there? How many men?

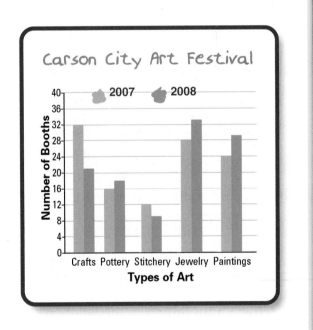

Extra Practice

Set A (pp. 230–231)

Use mental math to divide.

1. $120 \div 4$ **2.** $280 \div 7$ **3.** $450 \div 9$ **4.** $300 \div 6$

5. $800 \div 40$ **6.** $640 \div 80$ **7.** $560 \div 70$ **8.** $400 \div 50$

9. $1{,}600 \div 80$ **10.** $8{,}100 \div 90$ **11.** $2{,}400 \div 30$ **12.** $3{,}000 \div 50$

Set B (pp. 234–237)

Divide.

1. $12\overline{)645}$ **2.** $24\overline{)751}$ **3.** $18\overline{)212}$ **4.** $34\overline{)310}$

5. $15\overline{)927}$ **6.** $13\overline{)172}$ **7.** $26\overline{)565}$ **8.** $37\overline{)454}$

9. A pen manufacturer packed 718 pens. Each package holds 12 pens. How many packages is this? How many pens are left over?

10. The members of the bicycle club cycled 375 miles in 15 days. If they cycled the same number of miles each day, how many miles did they cycle each day?

Set C (pp. 238–239)

Write *too large, too small,* or *just right* for each estimate. Then divide.

1. $\overset{7}{78\overline{)612}}$ **2.** $\overset{8}{34\overline{)312}}$ **3.** $\overset{6}{26\overline{)156}}$ **4.** $\overset{9}{56\overline{)448}}$

Divide.

5. $49\overline{)872}$ **6.** $63\overline{)917}$ **7.** $14\overline{)275}$ **8.** $32\overline{)564}$

9. $25\overline{)743}$ **10.** $52\overline{)816}$ **11.** $17\overline{)194}$ **12.** $21\overline{)836}$

Set D (pp. 240–241)

Divide.

1. $17\overline{)680}$ **2.** $21\overline{)435}$ **3.** $30\overline{)924}$ **4.** $40\overline{)830}$

5. $56\overline{)589}$ **6.** $28\overline{)673}$ **7.** $45\overline{)928}$ **8.** $19\overline{)234}$

9. $42\overline{)307}$ **10.** $75\overline{)818}$ **11.** $23\overline{)924}$ **12.** $60\overline{)532}$

13. The 15 members of the Science Club sold 300 bags of popcorn at a fundraiser. Each member sold the same number of bags of popcorn. How many bags did each member sell?

14. Mr. Matthews has to drive 720 miles on a business trip. He estimates it will take him 12 hours. About how many miles per hour does Mr. Matthews expect to drive?

Review/Test

✓ CHECK VOCABULARY AND CONCEPTS

Choose the best term from the box.

Vocabulary

divisor
estimate
quotient
remainder
dividend

1. Multiply the quotient by the _?_ and add the _?_ to the product to check the quotient and remainder of a division problem. (p. 232)

2. You can _?_ to place the first digit in the quotient. (p. 234)

✓ CHECK SKILLS

Use mental math to divide. (pp. 230–231)

3. $390 \div 30$

4. $6,300 \div 70$

5. $400 \div 20$

6. $1,500 \div 50$

7. $420 \div 60$

8. $4,000 \div 80$

Divide. (pp. 230–231, 234–237, 238–239, 240–241)

9. $19\overline{)98}$

10. $25\overline{)237}$

11. $32\overline{)453}$

12. $43\overline{)518}$

13. $27\overline{)394}$

14. $34\overline{)619}$

15. $17\overline{)123}$

16. $56\overline{)767}$

17. $59\overline{)613}$

18. $35\overline{)725}$

19. $47\overline{)950}$

20. $13\overline{)650}$

**Write *too large, too small,* or *just right* for each estimate.
Then divide.** (pp. 238–239)

21. $48\overline{)288}^{\,5}$

22. $35\overline{)175}^{\,4}$

23. $37\overline{)260}^{\,7}$

24. $71\overline{)513}^{\,8}$

25. $52\overline{)468}^{\,8}$

26. $74\overline{)298}^{\,4}$

27. $69\overline{)281}^{\,5}$

28. $54\overline{)432}^{\,7}$

29. $42\overline{)337}^{\,9}$

30. $63\overline{)441}^{\,6}$

✓ CHECK PROBLEM SOLVING

Solve. Name the operation or operations you used. (pp. 242–243)

31. Jeremy keeps his stamps in an album. Each sheet in the album holds 18 stamps. How many sheets will he need for 234 new stamps?

32. Mr. Davis is writing a 450-page book. He has written 13 pages each day for 25 days. How many more pages does he need to write?

33. Jesse has 320 ceramic beads to sell. If he puts 8 beads in each packet, how many packets can he make?

Chapter CRCT Test Prep

NUMBERS AND OPERATIONS

1. **M4N4.b.** Jamal has 154 baseball cards. He is putting them in equal piles of 12. How many cards will be left over?

   A. 6

   B. 8

   C. 10

   D. 12

2. **M4N4.b.** Which statement is TRUE?

   A. When 372 is divided by 16, the remainder is 23.

   B. When 372 is divided by 23, there is no remainder.

   C. When 372 is divided by 4, the divisor is 4, the quotient is 23, and the remainder is 16.

   D. When 372 is divided by 16, the quotient is 23, and the remainder is 4.

3. **M4N4.b.** A group of 672 people went on a bus tour of Atlanta. Each bus held 32 people. How many buses were needed for the tour?

   A. 19

   B. 20

   C. 21

   D. 22

NUMBERS AND OPERATIONS

4. **M4N4.d.** Which quotient is the same as 2,800 ÷ 40?

   A. 28 ÷ 4

   B. 280 ÷ 40

   C. 280 ÷ 4

   D. 2,800 ÷ 4

5. **M4N4.c.** What does the □ stand for in the division problem?

   $$(37 \times 21) + 19 = 796,$$
   $$\text{so } 796 \div \square = 21 \text{ r19.}$$

   A. quotient

   B. divisor

   C. dividend

   D. remainder

6. **M4N4.d.** Which quotient is the same as 360 ÷ 40?

   A. 36 ÷ 4

   B. 360 ÷ 4

   C. 3,600 ÷ 4

   D. 3,600 ÷ 40

7. **M4N4.b.** Alana bought 500 beads to make necklaces. She used 48 beads in each necklace. How many necklaces did she make?

   A. 10

   B. 11

   C. 20

   D. 48

Cumulative CRCT Test Prep

DATA ANALYSIS

Use the pictograph below to answer question 8.

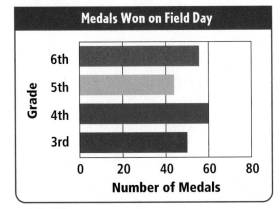

Number of Books Ordered by Fourth-Grade Classes at Book Fair	
Class	**Books Ordered**
Mr. Becker	📖 📖 📖 📖
Mrs. Green	
Ms. Fields	📖 📖 📖

Each 📖 = 10 Books

8. **M4D1.a.** How would you show that Mrs. Green's class ordered 35 books?

A. 📖 📖 📖 📖 📖

B. 📖 📖 📖 📖 📖

C. 📖 📖 📖 📖

D. 📖 📖 📖

Use the bar graph below to answer question 9.

Medals Won on Field Day

Grade: 6th, 5th, 4th, 3rd
Number of Medals: 0 20 40 60 80

9. **M4D1.c.** How would the lengths of the bars change if the intervals were 10?

A. The bars would be shorter.

B. The bars would be wider.

C. The bars would be longer.

D. The bars would be a different color.

ALGEBRA

10. **M4A1.b.** Julie put ☐ erasers into each of 15 bags. Which expression shows how many erasers Julie has in all?

A. 15 × ☐

B. 15 + ☐

C. 15 − ☐

D. 15 ÷ ☐

11. **M4A1.c.** What is the value of (☐ + 7) − △ if ☐ = 16 and △ = 8?

A. 15

B. 16

C. 23

D. 31

12. **M4A1.b.** Rachel feeds her dog △ cups of dry food each day. The dog food container holds 16 cups. Which expression shows how many days the container of food will last?

A. 16 + △

B. 16 − △

C. 16 × △

D. 16 ÷ △

GPS/CRCT Vocabulary

ELA4R3 The student understands and acquires new vocabulary and uses it correctly in reading and writing. *also* ELA4LSV1.f., ELA4LSV2.c.

VOCABULARY

divide	quotient
dividend	remainder
divisor	divisible

VOCABULARY CONCENTRATION

MATERIALS *For each pair* Vocabulary Cards, Definition Cards

• Work with a partner.

• Mix up the cards, and place them face-down.

• Take turns turning over two cards at a time. The player that matches a word with the correct definition removes the cards. If a word does not match the definition, turn both cards face-down, and continue playing.

• Play the game until all the words and definitions have been matched.

• The player with more matched cards wins the game.

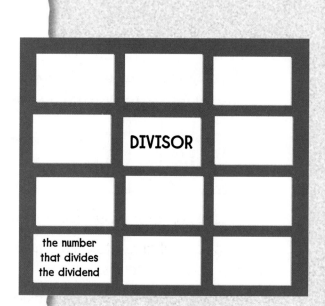

DIVISOR

the number that divides the dividend

MATH WORD WORK

R	A	M	E	S	N	R	D	E	S
E	D	I	V	I	D	E	N	D	R
M	Q	V	D	T	I	M	A	I	T
A	U	D	I	M	V	I	O	V	E
I	O	I	N	O	I	A	T	I	V
N	E	V	S	T	S	L	E	S	B
D	D	I	B	R	O	F	E	I	L
E	S	D	N	E	R	T	D	B	A
R	T	E	U	T	S	L	A	L	T
Q	U	O	T	I	E	N	T	E	V

• Use the vocabulary terms to make a word-search puzzle on a 10-by-10 grid.

• Write each vocabulary term on the grid. Place one letter in a square. Fill in the other squares with different letters.

• Trade puzzles with a partner. Circle all the vocabulary terms you find. The partner that finds all six terms first wins the game.

WORDS IN ACTION

MATERIALS *For each pair* 4 index cards, colored markers

- Work with a partner to make a set of division vocabulary cards for the words shown at the right. Write each term on an index card. Use a different colored marker for each word. Place the cards face-down on a table.

- Write a division problem like this one on a sheet of paper.

$$23 \div 7 = 3 \text{ r}2$$

- One partner turns over a vocabulary card, and the other tells which part of the division problem matches the vocabulary term.

- Continue playing until all the parts of the division problem have been identified. Write a new problem, trade roles with your partner, and play again.

DIVISION DICTIONARY

MATERIALS *For each group* construction paper, markers

- Work in a small group to create a dictionary of the vocabulary terms.

- Each group member chooses a different vocabulary term and makes a dictionary page for the term.

- For each term, include the phonetic respelling (which can be copied from the Glossary), the definition, a sentence using the word, a mathematical example, and a drawing or model.

- Put the completed pages in alphabetical order. Make a cover for your group's dictionary. Share it with another group.

divisible (də • vi′zə • bəl)

definition – capable of being divided so that the quotient is a whole number and the remainder is zero

sentences –
Many numbers are DIVISIBLE by 2.
A number is DIVISIBLE by 2 when I can divide it by 2 and have no remainder.
8 is DIVISIBLE by 2 because there is no remainder when I divide.

$$8 \div 2 = 4$$

Georgia Tasks

M4N4.b. Solve problems involving division by a 2-digit number (including those that generate a remainder). *also* **M4P5.b., M4P5.c.**

SS4H1a. locate where the American Indians settled with emphasis on Arctic (Inuit), Northwest (Kwakiutl), Plateau (Nez Perce), Southwest (Hopi), Plains (Pawnee), and Southeastern (Seminole).

Task A

THE CHIEFTAINS TRAIL

The Chieftains Trail in northwest Georgia highlights the history of Native Americans in the area. Suppose your family is planning a trip to sites near Rome, Cartersville, and Chatsworth. The chart shows the distances for the 3 parts of the trip.

a. If you drive 30 miles per hour, estimate how many hours each of the 3 parts of the trip will take.

b. You plan to leave from Rome at 8:00 A.M. You will spend 2 hours at sites around each city before returning to Rome. Can you do the entire trip in one day? If you can, about what time would you be back in Rome? Explain.

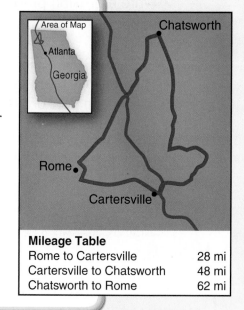

Mileage Table

Rome to Cartersville	28 mi
Cartersville to Chatsworth	48 mi
Chatsworth to Rome	62 mi

Task B

FACE PAINTING BOOTH

You are in charge of the face-painting booth at the school fair. You need to buy enough supplies, and you don't want many left over. Use the notes shown at the right to help you.

a. Estimate the number of students needed to work in the booth. Explain.

b. How many sheets of tattoos, boxes of paint kits, and packs of sponges should you buy? Explain why you think your answers are reasonable.

NOTES
- The fair will last 4 hours.
- 300 people visited the face-painting booth last year.
- A person can paint 6 faces an hour.
- 18 temporary tattoos on a sheet
- 12 paint kits in a box
- 8 sponges in a pack
- A sponge is used for 1 person only.

250 Unit 5 • Georgia Tasks

Maintain/Preview

Maintain

Divide and check. (pp. 208–211, 214–215, 216–219, 234–237, 240–241)

1. $6\overline{)92}$
2. $7\overline{)87}$
3. $3\overline{)52}$
4. $5\overline{)820}$

5. $7\overline{)163}$
6. $4\overline{)568}$
7. $9\overline{)274}$
8. $4\overline{)\$7.68}$

9. $23\overline{)75}$
10. $47\overline{)99}$
11. $14\overline{)621}$
12. $32\overline{)705}$

13. $12\overline{)490}$
14. $72\overline{)409}$
15. $36\overline{)731}$
16. $61\overline{)333}$

17. $75\overline{)675}$
18. $54\overline{)927}$
19. $47\overline{)138}$
20. $24\overline{)964}$

21. The garden shop plans to sell tomato plants in sets of 3. There are 80 tomato plants for sale. How many tomato plants cannot be sold in a set? (pp. 220–221)

22. The 18 members of the drama club sold 540 tickets for the show. If each member sold the same number of tickets, how many tickets did each member sell? (pp. 240–241)

Preview

Write the name of the figure. (Chapters 12 and 13)

1.

2.

3.

4.

5.

6.

Write a fraction for the shaded part. (Chapter 14)

7.

8.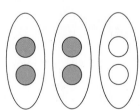

9.

10. A blueberry pie is cut into 6 equal pieces. What fraction of the pie is each piece?

11. A pizza has 8 equal slices. Trevor and Charlie eat 5 slices. What fraction of the pizza do they eat?

CHAPTER 12

Lines, Rays, and Angles

≡FAST FACT • SOCIAL STUDIES The Ambassador Bridge, between Detroit, Michigan, and Windsor, Ontario, Canada, is the busiest border crossing in North America. About 7,000 trucks cross it each day.

INVESTIGATION Tell what types of lines and angles you see in the photograph of the bridge. Explain how you would measure the angles.

Using Data

TYPES OF LINES AND ANGLES

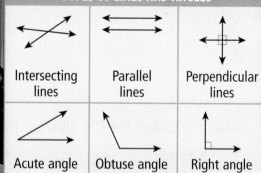

Intersecting lines	Parallel lines	Perpendicular lines
Acute angle	Obtuse angle	Right angle

Use this page to help you review and remember important skills needed for Chapter 12.

✅ IDENTIFY GEOMETRIC FIGURES

Write the name of each figure.

1. •——→

2. •

3. •———•

4. ↕

5. ↗ ↘

6. ↖

✅ IDENTIFY ANGLES

Tell whether each angle is a *right* angle, *greater than* a right angle, or *less than* a right angle.

7. ↗→

8. ↖↗

9. ↖↗

10.

11.

12.

VOCABULARY POWER

REVIEW

geometry [jē·ä′mə·trē] *noun*

Geometry comes from the Greek word for Earth, *Geos*, and from the Greek term, *metros,* "to measure." So, *geometry* means "to measure Earth." In your own words, tell what the study of geometry includes.

PREVIEW

point	right angle
line	acute angle
line segment	obtuse angle
ray	straight angle
plane	diagonal line
angle	rotation
vertex	intersecting lines
protractor	parallel
degree (°)	perpendicular

GO ON-LINE www.harcourtschool.com/mathglossary

Lines and Rays

M4G1. Students will define and identify the characteristics of geometric figures through examination and construction. *also* **M4P2.a., M4P2.c., M4P2.d., M4P3.a., M4P3.b., M4P3.d., M4P5.**

Learn

GEOMETRY EVERYWHERE! Everywhere you look, you can see points, lines, and rays in nature and in things people make. You can use the following geometric ideas and terms to describe the world around you.

VOCABULARY

point	ray
line	plane
line segment	

Term	Draw It	Read It	Write It
A **point** names an exact location in space.	• A	point A	point A
A **line** is a straight path of points that continues without end in both directions. It has no endpoints.	K L	line KL	$\overleftrightarrow{KL}$
A **line segment** is part of a line. It has two endpoints and all the points between them. It is the shortest distance between two points.	K L	line segment KL	$\overline{KL}$
A **ray** is part of a line. It has one endpoint and continues without end in one direction.	K L	ray KL	$\overrightarrow{KL}$
A **plane** is a flat surface of points that continues without end in all directions. A plane is named by at least three points in the plane.	A B C	plane ABC	plane ABC

• Find as many examples of these terms as you can in the photograph. Describe how the definitions of the terms match the figures.

1. **Give** some examples of line segments that you see in your classroom.

Name a geometric term that describes each.

2. side edge of a door   3. sharp tip of a pencil   4. laser beam

Practice and Problem Solving   Extra Practice, page 266, Set A

Name a geometric term that describes each.

5. flagpole   6. parking lot   7. tip of a tack

Draw and label an example of each.

8. line *BC*   9. line segment *PQ*   10. point *G*

11. plane *RST*   12. line *ST*   13. ray *XY*

Draw each line segment with the given length.

14. $\overline{BC}$, 3 cm   15. $\overline{AE}$, 2 in.   16. $\overline{JK}$, $3\frac{1}{2}$ in.   17. $\overline{RS}$, 6 cm

18. **REASONING** Which path is the shortest distance between point *C* and point *D*? Explain how you know.

a.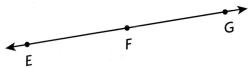

b.

C   D   C   D

19. Write all the names for the line below.

G

F

E

20. **MULTISTEP** For lunch each day, Mia buys a hot meal for $1.75 and milk for $0.50. What is the least number of $1 bills that her mother can give her so she will have enough lunch money for 5 days?

21. Name a geometric term that describes the floor of your classroom.

22. ✏ **Write About It** Explain the differences between a line, a ray, and a line segment.

Technology Link

More Practice: Harcourt Mega Math Ice Station Exploration, *Polar Planes*, Levels A and B

Maintain Skills

23. Phyllis bought 6 feet of ribbon. Myles bought 6 yards of ribbon. Who bought more ribbon?

24. 7×36 25. $87 \div 3$

CRCT Test Prep

26. **M4N1.a.** What is the value of the blue digit in 5,678,342? (p. 6)

A. 800   C. 80,000

B. 8,000   D. 800,000

Measure and Classify Angles

M4M2.a. Use tools, such as a protractor or angle ruler, and other methods, such as paper folding or drawing a diagonal in a square, to measure angles. *also* **M4P4.c.**

▶ Learn

FROM EVERY ANGLE Two rays with the same endpoint form an **angle**. The endpoint is called the **vertex**.

Quick Review

List the factors for each product.

1. 14   **2.** 25

3. 27   **4.** 12

5. 29

VOCABULARY

- **angle**
- **vertex**
- **protractor**
- **degree (°)**
- **right angle**
- **acute angle**
- **obtuse angle**
- **straight angle**
- **diagonal line**

Draw It	Read It	Write It
ray — A; B; C; vertex; ray	angle *ABC* angle *CBA* angle *B*	∠*ABC* ∠*CBA* ∠*B*
	NOTE: The vertex is always the middle letter or the single letter that names the angle.	

A **protractor** is a tool used to measure the size of an angle. The unit used for measuring angles is a **degree (°)**. The scale on a protractor is marked from 0° to 180°.

HANDS ON

Activity **MATERIALS:** protractor

Use a protractor to measure angle *ABC*.

STEP 1

Place the center of the protractor on the vertex of the angle.

Extend the ray.

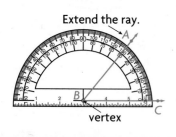

vertex

STEP 2

Line up the center point and the 0° mark on the protractor with one ray of the angle.

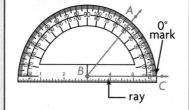

0° mark

ray

STEP 3

Read the measure of the angle where the other ray passes through the scale. Use the scale that makes sense for the angle size.

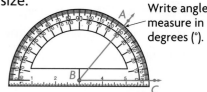

Write angle measure in degrees (°).

The measure of ∠*ABC* = 50°.

• Trace each angle. Then use a protractor to measure the angle.

a.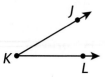

b.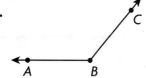

c.

Types of Angles

Activity MATERIALS: paper

Make an angle using a sheet of paper. Fold the paper twice to make an angle like this. The angle you made is called a right angle.

Use the right angle you made to find out which of the following are also right angles. Write *yes* or *no*.

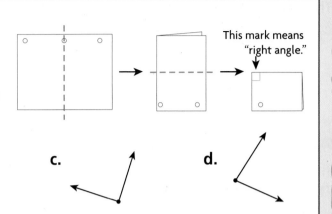

This mark means "right angle."

a.

b.

c.

d.

An angle can be classified according to the size of the opening between its rays.

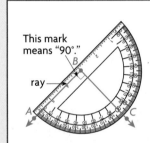

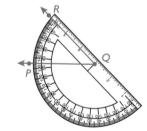

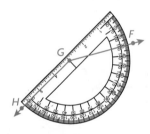

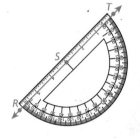

The measure of ∠B = 90°.

A **right angle** measures 90°. A right angle forms a square corner.

The measure of ∠Q = 45°.

An **acute angle** measures greater than 0° and less than 90°.

The measure of ∠G = 150°.

An **obtuse angle** measures greater than 90° and less than 180°.

The measure of ∠S = 180°.

A **straight angle** measures 180°. A straight angle forms a line.

- Find as many examples as you can of each type of angle in the painting *Three Musicians* by Pablo Picasso. You may trace the angle and use a protractor to measure it.

- Do you always need a protractor to determine whether an angle is acute, obtuse, right, or straight? Explain.

LESSON CONTINUES

Technology Link

More Practice: Harcourt
Mega Math Ice Station
Exploration, *Polar Planes*,
Level B

1. **Draw** a picture of an object that has a right angle, an acute angle, and a straight angle. Label each angle.

Trace each angle. Use a protractor to measure the angle. Then write *acute, obtuse, right,* **or** *straight.*

2.

3.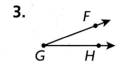

4.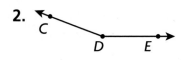

▶ **Practice and Problem Solving** Extra Practice, page 266, Set B

Trace each angle. Use a protractor to measure the angle. Then write *acute, obtuse, right,* **or** *straight.*

5.

6.

7.

Draw and label an example of each.

8. obtuse angle *RST*   **9.** acute angle *JKL*   **10.** right angle *E*

Classify each angle. Write *right, acute, obtuse,* **or** *straight.*

11.

12.

13.

Write the letter of the phrase that best describes each angle.

14.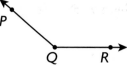
   a. less than 45°
   b. greater than 90°

15.
   a. less than 180°
   b. less than 90°

16.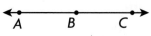
   a. less than 45°
   b. equal to 180°

17. Look at the figure below. Name the figure three different ways.

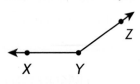

18. ❓ **What's the Error?** Wanda said that the letter *W* has two angles. What error did she make?

19. REASONING Use the corner of a sheet of paper to prove or disprove that the three angles in the letter *M* are right angles.

M

20. Give a time when the hands on a clock represent each type of angle: acute, obtuse, right, and straight.

21. MULTISTEP Suchada spent $15 at the gift shop. Later her father gave her $10 to buy lunch, but she spent only $7. At the end of the day, Suchada had $10. How much money did she have at the beginning of the day?

22. Vocabulary Power You use a *scale* to measure weight. Compare and contrast a scale for weight with a protractor scale. How are they alike? How are they different?

Maintain Skills

23. 98 ÷ 7

24. 400 ÷ 2

25. 8 × 16

26. 900 ÷ 3

27. Which is longer, 30 inches or 30 feet?

CRCT Test Prep

28. (M4N2.a.) What is 45,864 rounded to the nearest thousand? (p. 32)

A. 40,000   C. 46,000

B. 45,000   D. 750,000

Problem Solving ~ THINKER'S CORNER

COMPARING ANGLES To compare the measures of angles without using a protractor, you can make an angle using a square and its diagonal line. A **diagonal line** is a line segment joining nonadjacent vertices of a polygon.

Fold a square sheet of paper along its diagonal line. The diagonal line forms a 45° angle with two sides of the square.

This is a 45° angle.

This is a 45° angle.

Use your 45° angle to tell whether each of the following angles is greater than, less than, or equal to 45°.

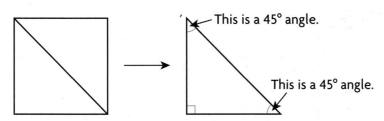

1.

2.

3.

4.

Rotations

M4M2.b. Understand the meaning and measure of a half rotation (180°) and a full rotation (360°). also **M4P3.a., M4P3.b., M4P3.d.**

▸ Explore

A **rotation** is a movement of a figure to a new position by rotating the figure around a point. Rotating ray *CD* around the circle makes angles of different sizes with ray *CE*. A full rotation around the circle is 360°.

Ray *CD* can be rotated clockwise, the direction clock hands move, or counterclockwise, the direction opposite from the way clock hands move.

clockwise   counterclockwise

Activity
Use rotations of geostrips to show different angles.

STEP 1

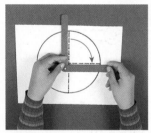

Open the geostrip to form a 90° angle.

This is a $\frac{1}{4}$, or quarter, rotation around a circle.

STEP 2

Now open the geostrip $\frac{1}{4}$ rotation more to make a 180° angle.

This is a $\frac{1}{2}$, or half, rotation around a circle.

STEP 3

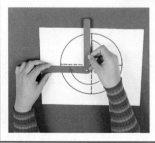

Open your geostrip another $\frac{1}{4}$ rotation to make a 270° angle.

This is a $\frac{3}{4}$, or three quarter, rotation around a circle.

STEP 4

Open your geostrip another $\frac{1}{4}$ rotation to make a 360° angle.

This is a full rotation around a circle.

Try It
Use rotations of a geostrip to form angles.
a. 90° counterclockwise   **b.** 270° counterclockwise

 **Connect**

Relate rotations and angles measured in degrees to the hands of a clock. Let the hands of a clock represent rays. There are 6° from one minute mark on a clock to the next.

15 minute marks
6° × 15 = 90°

30 minute marks
6° × 30 = 180°

45 minute marks
6° × 45 = 270°

Practice and Problem Solving

Tell whether the rays on the circle show a $\frac{1}{4}$, $\frac{1}{2}$, $\frac{3}{4}$, or full rotation.

1.

2.

3.

4.

Tell whether the figure has been rotated 90°, 180°, 270°, or 360°.

5.

6.

7.

8. How many 30° angles can be drawn in a circle without any overlapping? Explain.

9. **? What's the Question?** The minute hand on a clock moves from 12 to 4. The answer is 120°.

Maintain Skills

10. 6 × 143   11. 430 ÷ 2

12. What is the value of the digit 2 in 32,704?

13. Which digit is in the tenths place of 508.3?

CRCT Test Prep

14. **M4N7.c.** Which property can you use to find 5 × (20 + 3) = 5 × 23?
(p. 170)

A. Associative Property of Addition

B. Commutative Property of Multiplication

C. Zero Property

D. Distributive Property

4 Line Relationships

M4G1. Students will define and identify the characteristics of geometric figures through examination and construction. *also* **M4P2.a., M4P2.b., M4P2.c., M4P2.d., M4P3.a., M4P3.b., M4P3.c., M4P3.d., M4P4.c., M4P5.a., M4P5.b., M4P5.c.**

Quick Review

Use arrays to find all the factors of each product.

1. 18   **2.** 60

3. 32   **4.** 45

5. 22

▶ Learn

FOLLOW THE LINES Look at the term and definition for each line relationship. Find these same relationships on the road map.

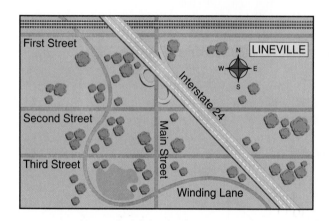

VOCABULARY
intersecting lines
▶ **parallel**
▶ **perpendicular**

Term and Definition	Draw It	Read It	Write It
Intersecting lines are lines that cross each other at exactly one point. They form four angles.	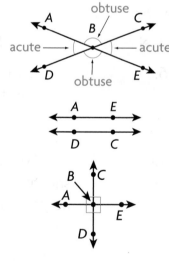	Line *AE* intersects line *DC* at point *B*.	$\overleftrightarrow{AE}$ intersects $\overleftrightarrow{DC}$ at point *B*.
Parallel lines are lines in the same plane that never intersect and are always the same distance apart.		Line *AE* is parallel to line *DC*.	$\overleftrightarrow{AE} \parallel \overleftrightarrow{DC}$
Perpendicular lines are lines that intersect to form four right angles.		Line *AE* is perpendicular to line *DC*.	$\overleftrightarrow{AE} \perp \overleftrightarrow{DC}$

• Which term identifies the relationship between Third Street and Second Street on the map?

Technology Link

More Practice: Harcourt Mega Math Ice Station Exploration, *Polar Planes*, Level C

▶ Check

1. **Name** two streets on the map that are perpendicular.
   Name two streets that are intersecting and not perpendicular.

Name any line relationships you see in each figure. Write
intersecting, parallel, **or** *perpendicular.*

2.

3.

4.

Practice and Problem Solving   Extra Practice, page 266, Set C

Name any line relationships you see in each figure. Write
intersecting, parallel, **or** *perpendicular.*

5.

6.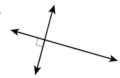

7.

For 8–14, use the drawing at the right.

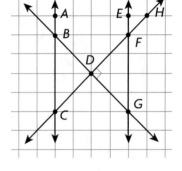

8. Name a right angle.

9. Name two parallel lines.

10. Name an acute angle.

11. Name an obtuse angle.

12. Name four line segments that include point G.

13. Name two intersecting lines.

14. Name two perpendicular lines.

Use grid paper to draw each line relationship.

15. perpendicular lines

16. parallel lines

17. intersecting lines

18. The product of two numbers is 45. Their sum is 18. What are the numbers?

19. **Write About It** Explain how you can tell the difference between intersecting lines and parallel lines.

20. **REASONING** Is this statement true or false? "Perpendicular lines are also intersecting lines." Explain your answer.

21. **? What's the Error?** Tricia said that all intersecting lines are perpendicular. Explain her error. Include a drawing with your explanation.

Maintain Skills

22. 42×6

23. $804 \div 5$

24. Which is longer, a chain that is 50 centimeters long or a chain that is 50 millimeters long?

CRCT Test Prep

25. **M4N1.a.** In what place is the 9 in 3,902,817? (p. 6)

A. thousands

C. hundred thousands

B. ten thousands

D. millions

Problem Solving Strategy
Make a Diagram

 M4P5.a. Create and use representations to organize, record, and communicate mathematical ideas. *also* **M4P1.a., M4P1.b., M4P1.c., M4P1.d., M4P3.a., M4P3.b., M4P3.c., M4P3.d., M4P5.**

PROBLEM Fairglen Elementary is planning an obstacle course for the school fair. The course will start on the south side of the playground. From the starting point, the course goes 7 units north to the slide. Then it goes 7 units east and 4 units south to the swing set. From the swing set, the course continues 4 units west, 2 units south, and 6 units west to the jungle gym. How long is the course when it crosses its own path?

UNDERSTAND

- What are you asked to find?
- What information will you use?

PLAN

- What strategy can you use to solve the problem?
  You can *make a diagram* to show a map of the obstacle course.

SOLVE

- How can you make a diagram?
  You can use grid paper. Label your grid *North*, *East*, *South*, and *West*. Follow the directions. Draw line segments to show the course. Label the distances and locations. Then add the units along the path until the path crosses itself.

  So, the obstacle course is 27 units long when it crosses its own path.

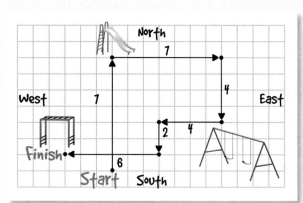

CHECK

- How can you check your answer?

Strategies

Act it Out or Use Objects
▶ **Make a Picture or Diagram**
Guess and Check
Use or Look for a Pattern
Use Logical Reasoning
Make an Organized List
Use or Make a Table
Work Backwards

Problem Solving

1. **What if** the obstacle course continued from the finish line 3 units north, 7 units east, and then 4 units north? How long would the course be when it crossed its own path a third time?

2. Suppose you were given these directions to a museum. On Main Street, go north for 28 miles. Turn right on Highway 33, and go east for 187 miles. How many miles would you travel to the museum?

≡**FAST FACT** • **SOCIAL STUDIES** About one third of the 1,500 labyrinths in the United States were built in the year 2000. Unlike mazes, labyrinths are walking paths with no dead ends. Study the path of the labyrinth drawing.

3. How many line segments can you find in the labyrinth from start to finish?

   A 10 line segments
   B 14 line segments
   C 15 line segments
   D 18 line segments

4. What type of angle is shown by the line segments in the labyrinth?

   F acute angle   **H** right angle
   G obtuse angle   **J** scalene angle

▲ The labyrinth at Forestheart Studios, Woodsboro, Maryland, is about 560 feet long.

Mixed Strategy Practice

5. If Carrie takes one guitar lesson a week, how much will it cost, including book rental, to take four lessons at the store?

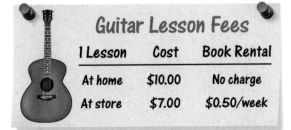

Guitar Lesson Fees		
I Lesson	Cost	Book Rental
At home	$10.00	No charge
At store	$7.00	$0.50/week

6. Mr. Ross designs mazes. He made 2 mazes during the first week, 3 during the second, and 5 during the third. If Mr. Ross continues this pattern, how many mazes will he make during the fourth week?

7. Zack is showing his brother 90° by using the hour and minute hands on a clock. Name some times Zack can use to show 90° on a clock.

Extra Practice

Set A (pp. 254–255)

Draw and label an example of each.

1. line segment *DC*
2. point *J*
3. ray *JK*
4. plane *RST*
5. line segment *AB*
6. line *GH*
7. Give some examples of lines that you see every day.
8. Name an object in your classroom that is like a line segment.

Set B (pp. 256–259)

**Trace each angle. Use a protractor to measure the angle.
Then write *acute, obtuse, right,* or *straight*.**

1.
2.
3.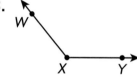

Draw and label an example of each.

4. obtuse angle *MNP*
5. acute angle *B*
6. straight angle *DEF*

7. The limbs of a tree form angles with the trunk of the tree. Classify angles *A* and *B* in this tree as *acute, obtuse,* or *right*.

8. Draw a rectangle with a diagonal line. What types of angles are formed by the diagonal line and the sides of the rectangle?

Set C (pp. 262–263)

**Name any line relationships you see in each figure.
Write *intersecting, parallel,* or *perpendicular*.**

1.
2.
3.

4. Give an example of parallel lines you see every day.

Review/Test

✓ CHECK VOCABULARY AND CONCEPTS

Choose the best term from the box.

1. The unit used to measure an angle is called a _?_. (p. 256)

2. The angle measure of a _?_ is 180°. (p. 260)

✓ CHECK SKILLS

Name the term that describes each. Write *point, plane, line, line segment,* or *ray.* (pp. 254–255)

3. A
•

4. K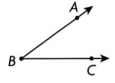

5. M   N

6.

Trace each angle. Use a protractor to measure the angle. Then write *acute, obtuse, right,* or *straight.* (pp. 256–259)

7.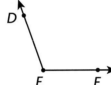

8. D
E   F

9. Z
X   Y

10.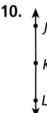
J
K
L

For 11–13, use the drawing at the right. (pp. 262–263)

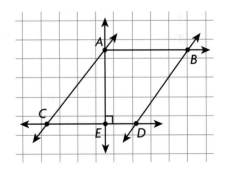

11. Name two parallel lines.

12. Name two intersecting lines.

13. Name two perpendicular lines.

✓ CHECK PROBLEM SOLVING

Solve. (pp. 264–265)

14. Kyle needs directions to Taylor's new house. Taylor drew a map for Kyle to use. Starting from Kyle's house, go 4 blocks south and then 2 blocks west. Turn left. Go 5 more blocks south. Taylor's house is the first house on the right. Make a diagram of Taylor's map.

15. From her apartment, Ellie walks 5 blocks north and 3 blocks west. Then she turns right and walks 1 more block to the library. How many blocks is the library from Ellie's apartment?

Chapter CRCT Test Prep

MEASUREMENT

1. **M4M2.a.** What is the measure of angle ABC?

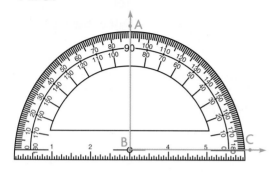

A. 180°

B. 90°

C. 80°

D. 45°

2. **M4M2.b.** Which figure shows a half rotation?

A.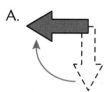

B.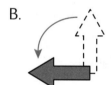

C.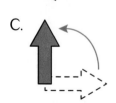

D.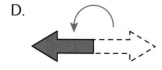

GEOMETRY

3. **M4G1.** Which figure shows segment $\overline{AB}$?

A.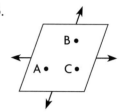

B.

C.

D.

4. **M4G1.b.** Which statement BEST describes the relationship in the figure below?

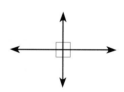

A. The lines are parallel and perpendicular.

B. The lines are intersecting and parallel.

C. The lines are perpendicular and intersecting.

D. The lines are parallel and form right angles.

Cumulative CRCT Test Prep

NUMBERS AND OPERATIONS

5. **M4N4.a.** Avalon, Georgia, has a population of 284 people and a land area of about 2 square miles. About how many people live in each square mile of Avalon?

A. about 568 people

B. about 282 people

C. about 142 people

D. about 14 people

6. **M4N7.c.** Which expression correctly shows how to use the Distributive Property to multiply 60×27?

A. $(60 \times 20) + (60 \times 7)$

B. $(60 + 20) \times (60 + 7)$

C. $(60 \times 20) \times (60 \times 7)$

D. $(60 + 20) + (60 + 7)$

7. **M4N3.** Sam's cell phone bill is $35 per month. How much per year does Sam pay for his cell phone?

A. $300

B. $350

C. $420

D. $450

DATA ANALYSIS

Use the bar graph below to answer question 8.

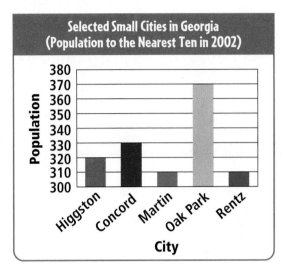

Selected Small Cities in Georgia (Population to the Nearest Ten in 2002)

8. **M4D1.b.** If the population data is ordered, what is the middle number?

A. 310

B. 320

C. 325

D. 330

9. **M4D1.c.** What type of graph would BEST display the population growth of the state of Georgia during the 1900s?

A. line graph

B. bar graph

C. double-bar graph

D. pictograph

Plane and Solid Figures

≡FAST FACT • SOCIAL STUDIES

Seaside, a planned community in Florida, was modeled after traditional neighborhoods of the 1920s and 1930s. Seaside covers 80 acres along the Gulf of Mexico. People who live there can easily walk or bike to the store or beach.

INVESTIGATION What types of plane figures can you see in the photo of Seaside? Explain how you would classify and sort the shapes.

Using Data

TYPES OF PLANE FIGURES

triangle	quadrilateral	pentagon
hexagon	octagon	circle

CHECK WHAT YOU KNOW

Use this page to help you review and remember important skills needed for Chapter 13.

✓ CLASSIFY ANGLES

Tell if each angle is *acute, right,* or *obtuse*.

1.

2.

3.

4.

✓ IDENTIFY PLANE FIGURES

Write the name of each figure.

5.

6.

7.

8.

✓ IDENTIFY SOLID FIGURES

Write the name of each solid figure.

9.

10.

11.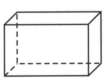

12.

VOCABULARY POWER

REVIEW

dimension [də•men'shən] *noun*

Dimension is from the Latin words *dis* and *meteri* which, when combined, mean "to measure out." The glossary definition of *dimension* is "a measure in one direction." Which dimensions of a prism do you think you would measure?

PREVIEW

regular polygon

quadrilateral

congruent

parallelogram

rhombus

trapezoid

Venn diagram

cube

rectangular prism

GO ON-LINE   www.harcourtschool.com/mathglossary

Polygons

M4G1. Students will define and identify the characteristics of geometric figures through examination and construction. *also* **M4P3.a., M4P3.b., M4P3.d.**

 Learn

SIDES AND ANGLES A polygon is a closed plane figure with straight sides. Polygons are named by the number of sides or number of angles they have. Here are some polygons.

triangle	quadrilateral	pentagon	hexagon	octagon
3 sides	4 sides	5 sides	6 sides	8 sides
3 angles	4 angles	5 angles	6 angles	8 angles

In a regular polygon, all the sides have equal length, and all the angles have equal measure.

VOCABULARY

polygon	pentagon
triangle	hexagon
quadrilateral	octagon
regular polygon	

Examples

These polygons are regular.

These polygons are not regular.

Activity

MATERIALS: dot paper, ruler

Draw a regular triangle.

STEP 1	STEP 2
Mark three points that are all the same distance apart.	Connect the three points to form a triangle.

Draw a triangle that is not regular.

STEP 1	STEP 2
Mark three points that are not the same distance apart.	Connect the three points to form a triangle.

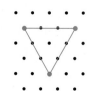

• How are the two triangles alike? How are they different?

Technology Link
More Practice: Harcourt
Mega Math Ice Station
Exploration, *Polar Planes,*
Level D

1. Explain how a polygon that is regular and a polygon that is not regular are different.

Name the polygon. Tell whether it appears to be *regular* or *not regular*.

2.

3.

4.

5.

Practice and Problem Solving (Extra Practice, page 288, Set A)

Name the polygon. Tell whether it appears to be *regular* or *not regular*.

6.

7.

8.

9.

Use dot paper to draw each polygon.

10. a pentagon that is not regular

11. a regular triangle

12. a quadrilateral that is not regular

13. a regular hexagon

14. A mosaic has 600 tiles. There are 80 more square tiles than triangular tiles. How many of each tile are there?

15. Draw two regular polygons that have the same shape but are different in size.

16. What types of polygons do you see in the lamp shade?

17. ✎ **Write About It** Explain how you can tell what type of polygon a figure is.

▲ Stained glass lamp by Tiffany Studios

Maintain Skills

18. Find the area of the rectangle in square units.

CRCT Test Prep

19. (M4G1.) What geometric term best describes the stripes in the U.S. Flag? (p. 262)

A. parallel lines
B. plane
C. point
D. triangle

Classify Triangles

M4G1.a. Examine and compare angles in order to classify and identify triangles by their angles. *also* **M4P1.c., M4P3.a., M4P3.b., M4P3.c., M4P3.d.**

▶ Learn

TAKE SIDES Triangles can be classified according to the lengths of their sides or the measures of their angles. The sides of a triangle are **congruent** if they have the same size and shape.

Classify by the lengths of their sides.	Classify by the measures of their angles.
A triangle with 3 congruent sides is an **equilateral triangle**. 2 cm / 2 cm / 2 cm	A triangle that has a right angle is a **right triangle**.
A triangle with 2 congruent sides is an **isosceles triangle**. 3 cm / 3 cm / 2 cm	A triangle that has 3 acute angles is an **acute triangle**.
A triangle with no congruent sides is a **scalene triangle**. 4 cm / 3 cm / 2 cm	A triangle that has 1 obtuse angle is an **obtuse triangle**.

• The equilateral triangle above is also an acute triangle. Is the scalene triangle above a right, an acute, or an obtuse triangle?

▶ Check

1. **Explain** the difference between a right, an acute, and an obtuse triangle.

Classify each triangle. Write *isosceles, scalene,* or *equilateral.* Then write *right, acute,* or *obtuse.*

2.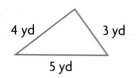
4 yd   3 yd
5 yd

3.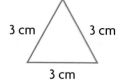
3 cm   3 cm
3 cm

4.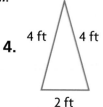
4 ft   4 ft
2 ft

Classify each triangle. Write *isosceles, scalene,* or *equilateral.*
Then write *right, acute,* or *obtuse.*

5.
7 ft
3 ft
9 ft

6.
5 yd   5 yd
5 yd

7.
9 cm
9 cm

8.
8 ft   6 ft
4 ft

9.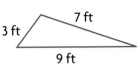

10.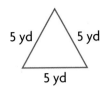

11.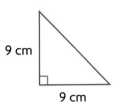

12.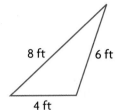

Classify each triangle by the lengths of its sides.
Write *isosceles, scalene,* or *equilateral.*

13. 12 ft, 12 ft, 12 ft   **14.** 9 cm, 7 cm, 4 cm   **15.** 13 mm, 13 mm, 8 mm

16. 6 in., 14 in., 14 in.   **17.** 43 mm, 43 mm, 43 mm   **18.** 29 yd, 28 yd, 6 yd

Measure the sides of each triangle using a centimeter
ruler. Write *isosceles, scalene,* or *equilateral.*

19.

20.

21.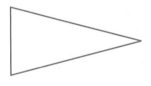

22. I have 3 sides and 3 angles. Only 2 of
my angles are acute. What types of
figure could I be?

23. Draw a triangle with 1 right angle and
2 congruent sides that each measure
3 units. Use square dot paper. Name
the triangle.

Maintain Skills

24. In June, Irma rode her bicycle
8 miles a day for 15 days. How far
did Irma ride her bicycle?

25. 7)362   **26.** 5)235

CRCT Test Prep

27. ⬤ **M4N4.a.** If 5 shelves hold 60 boxes,
how many shelves hold 144 boxes?
(p. 118)

A. 8   C. 13
B. 12   D. 14

Classify Quadrilaterals

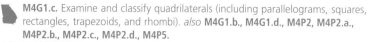 M4G1.c. Examine and classify quadrilaterals (including parallelograms, squares, rectangles, trapezoids, and rhombi). *also* **M4G1.b., M4G1.d., M4P2, M4P2.a., M4P2.b., M4P2.c., M4P2.d., M4P5.**

▶ **Learn**

CLASSIC LINES A figure with 4 sides and 4 angles is called a quadrilateral. There are many types of quadrilaterals. They can be classified by their features.

 Activity

MATERIALS: geoboard, rubber bands, dot paper

Copy each quadrilateral on a geoboard. Use dot paper to record your work.

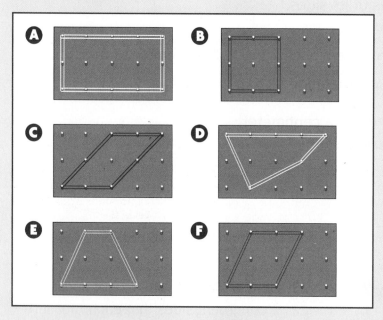

- Which have 2 pairs of parallel sides?
- Which have 4 right angles?
- Which have both pairs of opposite sides congruent?
- Which have only 1 pair of parallel sides?
- Which have no pairs of parallel sides?

Quick Review

Name any line relationship you see in each figure.

1. 2.

3. 4.

5.

VOCABULARY

▶ **parallelogram**

▶ **rhombus**

▶ **trapezoid**

▲ In 1930, Walter Dorwin Teague designed the No. 2A Beau Brownie camera with an Art Deco theme, using squares and rectangles. It originally cost $5.

Special Quadrilaterals

There are special types of quadrilaterals: **parallelogram**, square, rectangle, **rhombus**, and **trapezoid**. Each has different features, and some can be classified in more than one way. Use the diagram to help you identify each of these types of quadrilaterals.

The diagram shows that all rectangles are parallelograms and quadrilaterals.

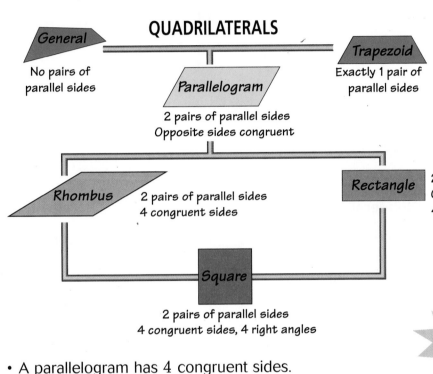

QUADRILATERALS

General — No pairs of parallel sides

Trapezoid — Exactly 1 pair of parallel sides

Parallelogram — 2 pairs of parallel sides — Opposite sides congruent

Rhombus — 2 pairs of parallel sides — 4 congruent sides

Rectangle — 2 pairs of parallel sides — Opposite sides congruent — 4 right angles

Square — 2 pairs of parallel sides — 4 congruent sides, 4 right angles

- A parallelogram has 4 congruent sides. What figures could it be?

Technology Link

More Practice: Harcourt Mega Math Ice Station Exploration, *Polar Planes*, Level G

Check

1. **Compare and contrast** a trapezoid and a parallelogram.

Classify each figure in as many ways as possible. Write *quadrilateral, parallelogram, rhombus, rectangle, square,* or *trapezoid.*

2.

3.

4.

Draw an example of each quadrilateral.

5. It has 4 congruent sides and no right angles.

6. Its opposite sides are parallel, and it has 4 right angles.

7. It is a trapezoid with 2 congruent sides.

LESSON CONTINUES

Classify each figure in as many ways as possible. Write
quadrilateral, parallelogram, rhombus, rectangle, square,
or *trapezoid.*

8.  9.   10.

11.  12.   13.

14.   15.   16.

Draw an example of each quadrilateral.

17. It has 2 pairs of parallel sides, and the opposite sides are congruent.

18. The 4 sides are congruent, and there are 4 right angles.

19. It has exactly 1 pair of parallel sides.

Choose the figure that does not belong. Explain.

20. a.  b.  c.   d.

21. a.   b. c.  d.

22. **REASONING** Is a square also a rhombus? Explain how you know.

23. I have 4 sides and 4 angles. At least one of my angles is acute. What figures could I be?

24. Draw a square that measures 2 inches on each side. What figures can you make if you draw a line that cuts the square in half?

25. **Write a problem** about a mystery quadrilateral. Give at least three clues that will help identify the quadrilateral.

26. At sunrise, the temperature was 72°F. At noon, it was 19° warmer. It cooled off 12° in the evening. What was the evening temperature?

27. Vocabulary Power The word *rectangle* comes from the words *rectus angulus*, meaning "right angle." How does the meaning relate to a rectangle?

Maintain Skills

28. 3×87 **29.** 62×5

Write the value of the blue digit.

30. 2,763.4   **31.** 15,708

32. What is the perimeter of the square?

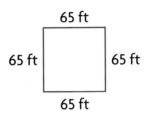
65 ft
65 ft   65 ft
65 ft

33. Lee has 136 books and 4 boxes. He wants to put an equal number of books in each box. How many books should Lee put in each box?

CRCT Test Prep

34. (**M4G1.a.**) Which term BEST classifies the triangle below? (p. 274)

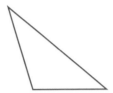

  A. isosceles   C. right
  B. obtuse   D. acute

35. (**M4M2.b.**) The minute hand on a clock made a half-rotation in a half-hour. What is the measure of the half-rotation? (p. 260)

  A. 30°   C. 180°
  B. 90°   D. 360°

Problem Solving LiNKUP ... to Reading

STRATEGY · CLASSIFY AND CATEGORIZE
When you *classify* information, you group similar information. When you *categorize*, you name the groups that you have classified.

The diagram on page 277 classifies and categorizes information about quadrilaterals.

For 1–6, use the diagram on page 277. Tell whether the statement is *true* or *false*. If the statement is false, explain why.

1. All rectangles are squares.

3. All squares are rectangles.

5. Some rhombuses are squares.

2. All rhombuses are parallelograms.

4. Some trapezoids are parallelograms.

6. No trapezoids have 2 pairs of parallel sides.

Problem Solving Strategy
Make a Diagram

M4P5. Students will represent mathematics in multiple ways. *also* **M4G1,**
M4P1.a., M4P2.a., M4P2.b., M4P2.c., M4P2.d., M4P3.a., M4P3.b., M4P3.c., M4P3.d.

> UNDERSTAND > PLAN > SOLVE > CHECK

VOCABULARY

Venn diagram

PROBLEM Mrs. Stein asked her students to sort these
figures into two groups according to how many congruent
sides each figure has. How can the figures be sorted?

A

B

C

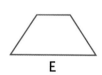
D

E

F

UNDERSTAND

- What are you asked to do?
- What information will you use?

PLAN

- What strategy can you use to solve the
problem?
Make a diagram to solve the problem.

SOLVE

- What type of diagram can you make?
Make a **Venn diagram** showing 2 separate
circles to sort the figures. Venn diagrams
show relationships among sets of things.

Label one circle *With 4 Congruent Sides*.
Put figures B and D in this circle. Label the
other circle *Without 4 Congruent Sides*. Put
figures A, C, E, and F in this circle.

Quadrilaterals
With 4 Congruent Sides

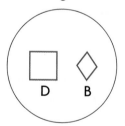

Without 4 Congruent Sides

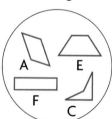

CHECK

- How do you know whether the answer is correct?

Strategies

Act it Out or Use Objects

▶ **Make a Picture or Diagram**

Guess and Check

Use or Look for a Pattern

Use Logical Reasoning

Make an Organized List

Use or Make a Table

Work Backwards

Use *make a diagram* to solve.

1. **What if** Mrs. Stein had asked the students to sort figures A–F into two groups, one with 2 pairs of parallel sides and one with fewer than 2 pairs of parallel sides? Make a diagram that shows those groupings.

2. Sort these numbers into a Venn diagram showing *Multiple of 2* and *Not Multiple of 2*: 2, 3, 4, 6, 8, 9, 10, 12.

Look at the Venn diagram. Section B shows what the figures have in common.

3. Which label best describes the polygons in Section A?
   A regular
   B not regular
   C quadrilaterals
   D not quadrilaterals

4. Which label best describes the polygons in Section B?
   F regular with an acute angle
   G not regular with an acute angle
   H regular with a right angle
   J not regular with a right angle

Mixed Strategy Practice

5. Make a Venn diagram to sort figures A–F on page 280 into these groups: *With Only Right Angles* and *With Other Types of Angles*.

6. ✎ **Write About It** Describe a rule for this pattern: 1, 2, 4, 8, 16, 32, 64.

7. Draw a trapezoid. What figure would you make if you extended the two nonparallel sides from the endpoints of the shorter side?

8. **REASONING** What is the length of one side of the smallest square that a 12-inch plate will fit into? Draw a picture to prove your answer.

9. Kris has 3 quarters. Zach has an equal amount of money in dimes and nickels. Zach has 9 coins. How many of each coin does Zach have?

10. A game has 24 squares. Each square is red or black. The number of red squares is twice the number of black squares. How many squares of each color are there?

Faces, Edges, and Vertices

M4G2.a. Compare and contrast a cube and a rectangular prism in terms of the number and shape of their faces, edges, and vertices. *also* **M4G2.b., M4P1.a., M4P4.c.**

▶ **Learn**

ANOTHER DIMENSION Polygons have only length and width, so they are **two-dimensional** figures.

Solid figures have length, width, and height, so they are **three-dimensional** figures.

Study these solid figures. A polygon that is a flat surface of a solid figure is a **face**. Look for polygons that are faces of each solid figure.

Quick Review

Tell the number of sides.

1. square   2. triangle

3. rectangle   4. pentagon

5. hexagon

VOCABULARY

two-dimensional	**triangular prism**
three-dimensional	**pentagonal prism**
face	**hexagonal prism**
cube	**edge**
rectangular prism	**vertex**

cube

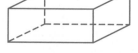

rectangular prism

triangular prism

pentagonal prism

hexagonal prism

▲ **Many buildings in New York City are rectangular prisms.**

• Name the plane figures found in the faces of each solid above.

Look carefully at the rectangular prism below. The top and bottom faces of the prism are parallel planes. The top face and front face are perpendicular planes.

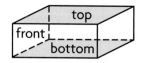

Some solid figures have curved surfaces and no faces.

cylinder

cone

sphere

☀ **Technology Link**

More Practice: Harcourt Mega Math Ice Station Exploration, *Frozen Solids*, Levels C, D, E, F, G, and L

Compare and Contrast Solid Figures

In the activity below, you will compare the faces, edges, and vertices of five solid figures.

Activity

Find the number of faces, edges, and vertices of the solid figures in the table below.

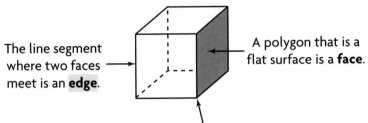

The line segment where two faces meet is an **edge**.

A polygon that is a flat surface is a **face**.

The point where three or more edges meet is a **vertex**. The plural of vertex is vertices.

Copy and complete the table.

FIGURE	NAME OF FIGURE	NUMBER OF FACES	NUMBER OF EDGES	NUMBER OF VERTICES
	Cube	6	12	8
	Rectangular prism	■	■	■
	Triangular prism	■	■	■
	Pentagonal prism	■	■	■
	Hexagonal prism	■	■	■

▲ David Smith's sculpture *Cubi XX* is made of a cylinder and rectangular prisms.

- Look at the table. Find a relationship between the number of faces and the number of edges of a rectangular prism.

- How are a cube and rectangular prism similar? How are they different?

LESSON CONTINUES ▶

1. **Name** two solid figures that have both parallel and perpendicular planes for their faces.

Name a solid figure that is described.

2. 9 edges　　　　**3.** 10 vertices　　　　**4.** more than 6 faces

▶ **Practice and Problem Solving**　Extra Practice, page 288, Set D

Name a solid figure that is described.

5. some triangular faces　　　　**6.** some or all rectangular faces

7. curved surfaces　　　　**8.** 8 vertices, 12 edges, 6 faces

Which solid figure do you see in each?

9. 　　**10.** 　　**11.** 　　**12.**

Write the names of the plane figures that are the faces of each solid figure.

13.

cube

14.

pentagonal prism

15.

hexagonal prism

16.

triangular prism

Copy the drawings. Circle each vertex, outline each edge in red, and shade one face in yellow.

17. 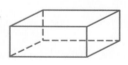　　**18.** 　　**19.** 　　**20.**

Write the names of the faces and the number of each type of face of the solid figure.

21. cube　　　　**22.** hexagonal prism　　　　**23.** triangular prism

24. ⭐ **What's the Question?** The answer is 2 triangular faces.

25. **REASONING** What plane figure is always found in a cube?

26. Explain how circles and spheres are alike. How are they different?

27. Explain how squares and cubes are alike. How are they different?

28. Look at the edges of the cube at the right. $\overline{AB}$ and $\overline{CD}$ are parallel line segments. $\overline{AC}$ and $\overline{AE}$ are perpendicular line segments. List two other pairs of parallel line segments and two other pairs of perpendicular line segments.

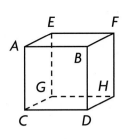

29. Laura has 1 dog and 2 cats. Laura hung 7 drawings of cats in her room. She hung 10 drawings of dogs. She has 8 more drawings to hang. How many drawings does Laura have in all?

30. MULTISTEP Brandon and Joe played a number game. Joe chose a number and subtracted 3. Then he added 7 and subtracted 5. The answer was 27. What number did Joe choose?

Maintain Skills

31. What digit is in the thousands place in the number 48,092?

32. 7×9

33. 8×8

CRCT Test Prep

34. **M4A1.c.** What is the value of $72 \div \square$ if $\square = 12$? (p. 132)

A. 6

C. 60

B. 16

D. 84

Problem Solving · THINKER'S CORNER

VISUAL THINKING Solid figures can look different when viewed from different directions. Here are some different ways of looking at the figure at the right.

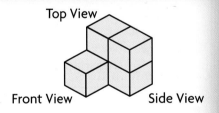

Top View · Front View · Side View

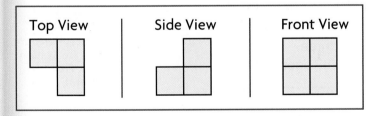

| Top View | Side View | Front View |

Write the letter of the figure that shows the correct view of the figure at the right.

1. top view

2. side view

3. front view

a.

b.

c.

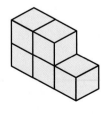

Patterns for Solid Figures

 M4G2.c. Construct/collect models for solid geometric figures (cubes, prisms, cylinders, etc.) *also* M4G2.a., M4P3.a., M4P3.b., M4P3.c., M4P3.d.

Quick Review

Tell the number of faces for each.

1. cube
2. pentagonal prism
3. triangular prism
4. rectangular prism
5. hexagonal prism

▶ Learn

SHAPE OF THINGS You can make a two-dimensional pattern of a three-dimensional figure. It can be folded to make a model of a solid figure.

 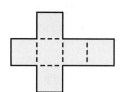 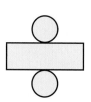

cube   pattern for cube   cylinder   pattern for cylinder

You can cut apart a three-dimensional figure to make a two-dimensional pattern.

HANDS ON

Activity **MATERIALS:** empty container, such as a cereal box; scissors and tape

STEP 1 Cut along some of the edges until the box is flat. Be sure that each face is connected to another face by at least one edge.

STEP 2 Trace the flat shape on a sheet of paper. This shape is a pattern of the box.

STEP 3 Cut out the pattern. Fold it into a three-dimensional box. Use tape to hold it together.

Technology Link

More Practice: Harcourt Mega Math Ice Station Exploration, *Frozen Solids,* Level H

• How is the pattern for a rectangular prism different from the pattern for a cube?

▶ Check

1. **Explain** how the pattern for a triangular prism is different from the pattern for a rectangular prism.

2. **Look** at the figure and the pattern at the right. Tell whether the figure can be made from the pattern.

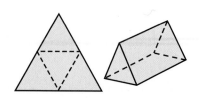

Write the letter of the figure that is made with each pattern.

3.

4.

5.

6.

a.

b.

c.

d.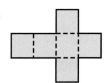

Draw a pattern that can be cut and folded to make a model of the solid figure shown.

7.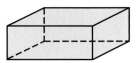

8.

9.

10.

Would the pattern make a cube? Write *yes* or *no*.

11.

12.

13.

14.

For 15–16, use the pattern.

15. Juanita drew the pattern at the right. What solid figure can she make?

16. Ernest folded Juanita's pattern into a model of a solid figure. How many faces, edges, and vertices did the model have?

17. **? What's the Error?** Nina says the pattern at the right can be folded to make a triangular prism. Explain Nina's error. Then draw a pattern for a triangular prism.

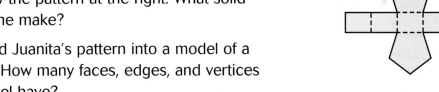

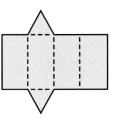

Maintain Skills

18. 11
     × 4

19. 12
     × 7

20. 60 ÷ 5

21. 99 ÷ 9

CRCT Test Prep

22. **M4G1.c.** Which quadrilateral has only one pair of parallel sides? (p. 276)

A. parallelogram   C. trapezoid
B. rhombus   D. rectangle

Extra Practice

Set A (pp. 272–273)

Name the polygon. Tell if it appears to be *regular* or *not regular*.

1.
2.
3.
4.

Set B (pp. 274–275)

Classify each triangle. Write *isosceles, scalene,* or *equilateral*. Then write *right, acute,* or *obtuse*.

1.
2.
3.
4.

Set C (pp. 276–279)

Classify each figure in as many ways as possible. Write *quadrilateral, parallelogram, rhombus, rectangle, square,* or *trapezoid*.

1.
2.
3.
4.

Set D (pp. 282–285)

Write the names of the plane figures that are the faces of each solid figure.

1.
hexagonal prism

2.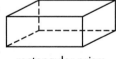
rectangular prism

3.
triangular prism

4.
cube

Set E (pp. 286–287)

Write the letter of the figure that is made with each pattern.

1.
2.
3.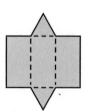
4.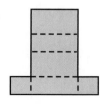

a.
b.
c.
d.

Review/Test

✓ CHECK VOCABULARY AND CONCEPTS

Choose the best term from the box.

1. A parallelogram with 4 equal sides is a ? or a ?. (p. 277)

2. A ? has 6 faces, 12 edges, and 8 vertices. (p. 282)

✓ CHECK SKILLS

Name the polygon. Tell if it appears to be *regular* or *not regular*. (pp. 272–273)

3.

4.

Classify each triangle by the lengths of its sides. Write *isosceles, scalene,* or *equilateral*. (pp. 274–275)

5. 17 ft, 22 ft, 16 ft   6. 5 cm, 5 cm, 5 cm   7. 11 mm, 11 mm, 8 mm

Classify each figure in as many ways as possible. Write *quadrilateral, parallelogram, rhombus, rectangle, square,* or *trapezoid*. (pp. 276–279)

8.

9.

10.

Write the letter of the figure that is made with each pattern. (pp. 286–287)

11.

12.

13.

a.

b.

c.

✓ CHECK PROBLEM SOLVING (pp. 280–281)

14. Sort these numbers into a Venn diagram showing *Multiple of 5* and *Not Multiple of 5*: 1, 5, 10, 12, 16, 20, and 24.

15. Make a Venn diagram to sort these figures into two groups: *With Only 2 Congruent Sides* and *With 4 Congruent Sides*.

J   K   L   M

Chapter CRCT Test Prep

GEOMETRY

1. **M4G1.a.** Classify the triangle according to the measures of its angles.

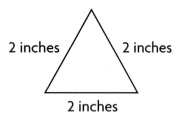

2 inches   2 inches

2 inches

   A. acute triangle

   B. right triangle

   C. equilateral triangle

   D. isosceles triangle

2. **M4G1.c.** Which figure can be classified as a parallelogram?

   A.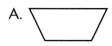

   B.

   C.

   D.

3. **M4G1.d.** Which statement is TRUE?

   A. A rectangle is also a trapezoid.

   B. A trapezoid is also a rhombus.

   C. A parallelogram is also a trapezoid.

   D. A rhombus is also a parallelogram.

GEOMETRY

4. **M4G2.a.** Which statement is TRUE?

   A. All cubes are rectangular prisms.

   B. All rectangular prisms are cubes.

   C. All rectangular prisms have 6 square faces.

   D. All cubes have 8 square faces.

5. **M4G2.a.** Which group of plane figures shows all of the faces of the solid figure below?

   A. ☐☐☐☐

   B. ☐☐☐☐☐☐

   C. ☐☐☐☐☐

   D. ☐☐☐☐☐☐

6. **M4G2.b.** Which pair of edges is parallel line segments?

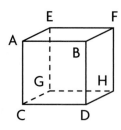

   A. $\overline{AE}$ and $\overline{EF}$

   B. $\overline{AB}$ and $\overline{EF}$

   C. $\overline{AE}$ and $\overline{AC}$

   D. $\overline{AC}$ and $\overline{EF}$

Cumulative CRCT Test Prep

ALGEBRA

7. **M4A1.a.** Find the rule for the number pattern in the following table.

Input	Output
13	19
26	32
39	45
52	58
65	71

A. Subtract 13.

B. Subtract 6.

C. Add 13.

D. Add 6.

8. **M4A1.c.** The expression $13 - \square$ represents the number of stripes on the Georgia state flag. If $\square = 10$, how many stripes are on the Georgia state flag?

A.   3

B.   10

C.   23

D. 130

9. **M4A1.c.** What is $\square \times 6$ if $\square = \$8$?

A. $6

B. $8

C. $14

D. $48

NUMBERS AND OPERATIONS

10. **M4N2.d.** In 1990, the population for Appling County, Georgia, was 15,744. By 2002, the population had increased by almost two thousand. About how many people lived in Appling County in 2002?

A. about 13,000

B. about 16,000

C. about 18,000

D. about 20,000

11. **M4N4.b.** Mohammed made the table below to show the number of sports cards in his collection.

Sports Card Collection	
Type of Card	**Number**
Baseball	73
Football	71
Basketball	90
Hockey	29

He wants to give away his baseball and football cards to 12 friends. He wants each friend to get an equal number of cards. How many cards will each friend get?

A. 144

B.   71

C.   14

D.   12

Understand Fractions

≡FAST FACT • SOCIAL STUDIES The piñata (pēn•yä'tə) has been used in many traditional Latin American celebrations since the early 1500s. Blindfolded children try to break open the piñata with a stick to get the treats inside.

INVESTIGATION

The table shows the contents of one piñata. Use manipulatives to represent what part of the piñata each treat is. What two treats make up $\frac{1}{2}$ of the treats? What two treats make up the other $\frac{1}{2}$?

Using Data

PIÑATA TREATS	
Treat	**Part of Piñata**
Chocolate Candy	$\frac{1}{6}$
Hard Candy	$\frac{2}{5}$
Toys	$\frac{1}{3}$
Play Jewelery	$\frac{1}{10}$

Use this page to help you review and remember important skills needed for Chapter 14.

✓ PARTS OF A WHOLE

Choose the word to name the equal parts in each whole.

> halves   thirds   fourths   sixths

1.  2. 3. 4.

Write a fraction for each shaded part.

5.   6.   7.   8.

✓ PARTS OF A GROUP

Write a fraction for the shaded part.

9.   10.  11. 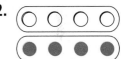 12.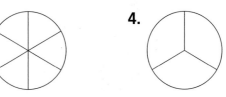

VOCABULARY POWER ✓

REVIEW

equivalent [i•kwiv′ə•lənt] *adjective*

The word *equivalent* comes from the Latin words *aequus,* meaning "equal," and *valere,* meaning "to be strong." What does the origin of the word *equivalent* tell you about two quantities that are equivalent?

PREVIEW

fraction	equivalent fractions
proper fraction	mixed number
numerator	mixed fraction
denominator	improper fraction

 GO ON-LINE   www.harcourtschool.com/mathglossary

Read and Write Fractions

M4N6. Students will further develop their understanding of the meaning of common fractions and use them in computations. *also* **M4P2.a., M4P2.b., M4P2.c., M4P2.d., M4P3.a., M4P3.b., M4P3.c.,M4P3.d.**

▷ Learn

BOW WOW BISCUITS Mario wants to cut the dog treats recipe in half. What fraction shows the amount of oats he needs?

A **fraction** is a number that can name a part of a whole. One whole can be divided into 2 equal parts. A fraction in which the numerator is less than the denominator is a **proper fraction**.

each part → 1 ← **numerator**
total equal parts → 2 ← **denominator**

Read: one half
one divided by two

Write: $\frac{1}{2}$

So, Mario needs $\frac{1}{2}$ cup of oats.

Mario baked 8 treats on one tray. He fed 2 treats to his puppy. What fraction of the treats was eaten?

A fraction can also name a part of a group.

number eaten → 2 ← **numerator**
number in the group → 8 ← **denominator**

Read: two eighths
two out of eight

Write: $\frac{2}{8}$

So, $\frac{2}{8}$ of the treats were eaten.

Quick Review

1. $20 \div 5 = \blacksquare + 1$

2. $4 \times \blacksquare = 10 \times 2$

3. $\blacksquare \div 6 = 7 - 4$

4. $\blacksquare \times 3 = 12 \div 2$

5. $30 - 2 = 4 \times \blacksquare$

VOCABULARY

fraction

▶ **proper fraction**

numerator

denominator

Dog Treats

2 cups flour
6 tablespoons oil
2 eggs, beaten
2 packages yeast
1 teaspoon salt
1 cup oats
1 cup bran
1 cup hot water

Mix ingredients. Spoon onto greased cookie sheet. Bake at 350° for 25 minutes.

▷ Check

1. **Explain** how to find what fraction of the treats was **not** eaten.

Write a fraction for the shaded part and for the unshaded part.

2.

3.

4. ☆ ☆ ☆ ☆
☆ ☆ ☆ ☆

5.

Write a fraction for the shaded part and for the unshaded part.

6.

7.

8.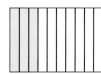

9.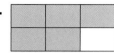

10.

11.

12.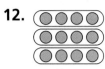

13.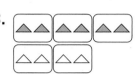

Draw a picture, and shade part of it to show the fraction.
Write a fraction for the unshaded part.

14. $\frac{3}{5}$ **15.** $\frac{1}{2}$ **16.** $\frac{4}{6}$ **17.** $\frac{6}{8}$ **18.** $\frac{1}{8}$ **19.** $\frac{3}{10}$

20. $\frac{2}{7}$ **21.** $\frac{4}{4}$ **22.** $\frac{2}{3}$ **23.** $\frac{10}{12}$ **24.** $\frac{6}{6}$ **25.** $\frac{1}{5}$

Write the fraction for each.

26. one out of nine   **27.** two divided by four   **28.** eight twentieths   **29.** one fourth

For 30–32, use the figure at the right.
Write a fraction for each part of the figure.

30. green   **31.** red   **32.** not yellow or red

33. MULTISTEP How much money can Mr. Drew save by buying 1 large box of dog biscuits for $0.96 rather than the same number of dog biscuits in 2 small boxes for $0.59 each?

Maintain Skills

34. $\begin{array}{r} 56 \\ \times\ 8 \\ \hline \end{array}$ **35.** $\begin{array}{r} 921 \\ \times\ 5 \\ \hline \end{array}$

36. Thomas bought 96 baseball cards. If there were 8 baseball cards in each pack, how many packs of baseball cards did he buy?

CRCT Test Prep

37. (M4G1.a.) What type of triangle is shown? (p. 274)

A. equilateral   C. acute
B. obtuse   D. right

Equivalent Fractions

M4N6.a. Understand representations of simple equivalent fractions.
also M4P3.a., M4P3.b., M4P3.c., M4P3.d., M4P4.a., M4P4.b., M4P4.c.,
M4P5, M4P5.b., M4P5.c.

 **Learn**

GO FOR THE GOLD U.S. short-track and speed skaters
won 8 medals in the 2002 Winter Olympics. Of these,
2 were gold medals. What fraction of the medals is this?

$\frac{2}{8}$ → gold medals
→ total medals

$\frac{1}{4}$ → gold medal group
→ all groups

So, $\frac{2}{8}$, or $\frac{1}{4}$, of the medals were gold. $\frac{2}{8}$ and $\frac{1}{4}$ are called
equivalent fractions because they name the same amount.

Quick Review

Find the missing number.

1. $\frac{0}{6}, \frac{1}{6}, \frac{2}{6}, \frac{\blacksquare}{6}$ 2. $\frac{3}{2}, \frac{2}{2}, \frac{\blacksquare}{2}, \frac{0}{2}$

3. $\frac{1}{4}, \frac{2}{4}, \frac{3}{4}, \frac{4}{\blacksquare}$ 4. $\frac{1}{5}, \frac{2}{5}, \frac{\blacksquare}{5}, \frac{4}{5}$

5. $\frac{4}{8}, \frac{5}{8}, \frac{\blacksquare}{\blacksquare}, \frac{7}{8}$

VOCABULARY

equivalent fractions

 Activity Find an equivalent fraction for $\frac{3}{4}$.
MATERIALS: fraction bars

One Way   Use fraction bars.

STEP 1

Line up fraction bars to show $\frac{3}{4}$.

STEP 2

Then line up other fraction bars of the
same type that show the same amount as $\frac{3}{4}$.

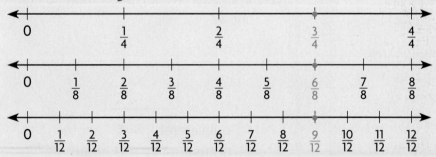

Another Way   Use number lines.

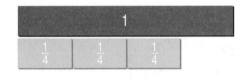

Fractions that line up
with $\frac{3}{4}$ are equivalent
to $\frac{3}{4}$.

So, $\frac{6}{8}$ and $\frac{9}{12}$ are equivalent to $\frac{3}{4}$.

296

1. **Explain** how you can find an equivalent fraction for $\frac{4}{12}$.

Write two equivalent fractions for each picture.

2.

3.

4.

▶ **Practice and Problem Solving** Extra Practice, page 304, Set B

Write two equivalent fractions for each picture.

5.

6.

7.

Use the number lines to write an equivalent fraction for each.

8. $\frac{2}{3}$

9. $\frac{6}{12}$

10. $\frac{4}{12}$

11. $\frac{6}{6}$

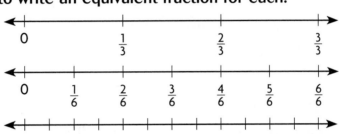

12. **MULTISTEP** James and his friends picked oranges in a grove. James picked 19 oranges, Sal picked 22, Tara picked 12, and Pam picked 11 oranges. If they share the oranges equally, how many oranges will each person get?

13. **FAST FACT** • **SOCIAL STUDIES**
The United States won a total of 34 medals in the 2002 Winter Olympics. Of these, 10 were gold medals. Write a fraction that shows how many of the medals were gold.

Maintain Skills

14. $160 \div 2$

15. $180 \div 3$

16. $295 \div 5$

17. $312 \div 6$

18. Which is longer, a piece of rope that is 3 m long, or a piece of rope that is 3 cm long?

CRCT Test Prep

19. **M4G1.c.** Which quadrilateral can have 4 congruent sides and no right angles? (p. 276)

A. trapezoid
B. parallelogram
C. rectangle
D. rhombus

Problem Solving Strategy
Make a Picture

M4P1.b. Solve problems that arise in mathematics and in other contexts. *also* **M4P1.a., M4P1.c., M4P1.d., M4P2.a., M4P2.b., M4P2.c., M4P2.d., M4P3.a., M4P3.b., M4P3.c., M4P3.d., M4P5.b., M4P5.c.**

PROBLEM Sammy, Henry, and Jeb are gopher tortoises. They are training for a 1-yard race. In the first week, who ran the same distance?

TORTOISE TRAINING	
Name	**Yards Run First Week**
Sammy	$\frac{1}{2}$
Henry	$\frac{3}{4}$
Jeb	$\frac{2}{4}$

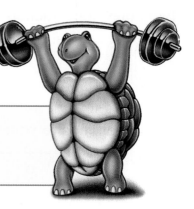

UNDERSTAND

- What are you asked to do?
- What information will you use?

PLAN

- What strategy can you use to solve the problem?
  Make a picture showing $\frac{1}{2}$, $\frac{3}{4}$, and $\frac{2}{4}$ by tracing around the fraction bars and using a different color to shade each fraction bar.

Sammy	$\frac{1}{2}$		
Henry	$\frac{1}{4}$	$\frac{1}{4}$	$\frac{1}{4}$
Jeb	$\frac{1}{4}$	$\frac{1}{4}$	

SOLVE

- How can you use the picture to solve the problem?
  The bars for $\frac{1}{2}$ and $\frac{2}{4}$ are the same length.

  So, Sammy and Jeb ran the same distance.

CHECK

- What other strategy can you use?

Strategies

Act it Out or Use Objects
▶ **Make a Picture or Diagram**
Guess and Check
Use or Look for a Pattern
Use Logical Reasoning
Make an Organized List
Use or Make a Table
Work Backwards

Problem Solving

Make a picture to solve.

1. **What if** Sammy ran $\frac{6}{8}$ yard the first week? Would he have run the same distance as Henry ran the first week? Explain.

A spinner has 12 equal sections. Two of the sections are blue, 3 sections are yellow, 2 sections are red, and 5 sections are green.

2. Which color covers $\frac{1}{4}$ of the spinner?
   A red   **C** green
   B blue   **D** yellow

3. If the red sections were changed to blue, what fraction of the spinner would be blue?
   F $\frac{2}{12}$ **G** $\frac{1}{8}$ **H** $\frac{1}{3}$ **J** $\frac{1}{4}$

Mixed Strategy Practice

4. Ty's tomato sauce has $\frac{3}{6}$ teaspoon basil, $\frac{1}{2}$ teaspoon oregano, and $\frac{1}{8}$ teaspoon pepper. For which seasonings does Ty use the same amounts?

5. **REASONING** Explain how you know which seasoning Ty used the least of in the tomato sauce.

6. Beatrice read 3 pages of her book on Monday, 6 pages on Tuesday, 12 pages on Wednesday, and 24 pages on Thursday. If this pattern continues, how many pages might she read on Friday?

7. Jon and his sister made cupcakes. They each ate 2 cupcakes. Jon took 12 cupcakes to school and left 8 cupcakes at home. What fraction of the cupcakes did Jon take to school?

USE DATA For 8–10, use the table.

8. Which assembly could be scheduled from 9:00 A.M. to 9:30 A.M.?

9. Which assembly will be the longest? Which will be the shortest?

10. How much longer will the longest assembly last than the shortest?

11. Cindy is making a square design with 16 tiles. The 4 corner tiles are red, and the rest of the outside border tiles are blue. She puts 4 green tiles in the middle. Show what Cindy's design will look like.

MORNING ASSEMBLY SCHEDULE	
Grade	**Length of Assembly**
Kindergarten and First Grade	30 minutes
Second Grade and Third Grade	40 minutes
Fourth Grade and Fifth Grade	60 minutes

Mixed Numbers

M4N6.c. Convert and use mixed numbers and improper fractions interchangeably. *also* **M4P4.a., M4P4.b., M4P5, M4P5.b., M4P5.c.**

▶ Learn

HOP TO IT Susan gave one and one-fourth cups of rabbit food to Whiskers, her pet rabbit.

A **mixed number**, or **mixed fraction**, is made up of a whole number and a fraction. Look at the picture that represents one and one-fourth cups of food.

Read: one and one fourth

Write: $1\frac{1}{4}$

Example 1 Write a mixed number for each picture.

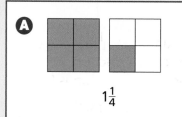

A $1\frac{1}{4}$

B $1\frac{4}{6}$, or $1\frac{2}{3}$

C $3\frac{1}{12}$

• Look at Example 1A. How many fourths does it take to make two wholes? How many fourths does it take to make $2\frac{1}{4}$?

You can locate mixed numbers on a number line.

Example 2 Locate a mixed number on a number line.

A Locate $2\frac{1}{4}$ on the number line.

Each mark between 2 and 3 represents $\frac{1}{4}$.

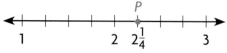

So, point *P* shows the location of $2\frac{1}{4}$.

B Locate $5\frac{1}{2}$ on the number line.

Each mark between 5 and 6 represents $\frac{1}{8}$. Since $\frac{4}{8} = \frac{1}{2}$, $5\frac{1}{2}$ will be at the fourth mark between 5 and 6.

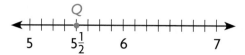

So, point *Q* shows the location of $5\frac{1}{2}$.

Rename Fractions and Mixed Numbers

Sometimes the numerator of a fraction is greater than the denominator. These fractions have a value greater than 1. They can be renamed as mixed numbers or whole numbers.

Example 3

A Rename $\frac{15}{4}$ as a mixed number.

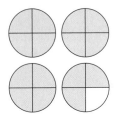

Think: How many fourths are shown?

Since $\frac{15}{4}$ means $15 \div 4$, you can use division to rename a fraction greater than 1 as a mixed number.

$$\text{denominator} \rightarrow 4\overline{)15}^{\ 3\ r3} \leftarrow \text{numerator}$$
$$\underline{-12}$$
$$3 \leftarrow \text{number of fourths left over}$$

Write the quotient as the whole-number part. Then write the remainder as the numerator and the divisor as the denominator.

So, $\frac{15}{4}$ renamed as a mixed number is $3\frac{3}{4}$.

B Rename $1\frac{3}{5}$ as a fraction.

Use fraction bars to rename the mixed number as a fraction.

Model $1\frac{3}{5}$, using fraction bars.

| 1 | $\frac{1}{5}$ | $\frac{1}{5}$ | $\frac{1}{5}$ |

Put $\frac{1}{5}$ bars under the 1 bar.

| 1 | $\frac{1}{5}$ | $\frac{1}{5}$ | $\frac{1}{5}$ |
| $\frac{1}{5}$ $\frac{1}{5}$ $\frac{1}{5}$ $\frac{1}{5}$ $\frac{1}{5}$ $\frac{1}{5}$ $\frac{1}{5}$ $\frac{1}{5}$ |

The total number of $\frac{1}{5}$ bars is the numerator of the fraction. The numerator of the fraction is 8.

So, $1\frac{3}{5}$ renamed as a fraction is $\frac{8}{5}$.

A fraction in which the numerator is greater than or equal to the denominator is called an **improper fraction**. So, $\frac{15}{4}$ and $\frac{8}{8}$ are examples of improper fractions.

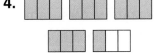

Technology Link

More Practice: Harcourt Mega Math The Number Games, Fraction Action, *Number Line Mine,* Level F

Check

1. **Explain** how you can tell that a fraction is greater than 1.

Write a mixed number for each picture.

2.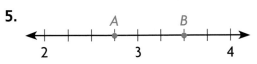

3.

4.

Write the mixed number represented by each letter.

5.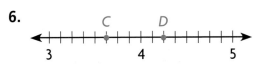

6.

Rename each fraction as a mixed number and each mixed number as a fraction. You can draw a picture.

7. $\frac{4}{3}$ **8.** $4\frac{3}{4}$ **9.** $\frac{13}{4}$ **10.** $9\frac{1}{6}$ **11.** $\frac{5}{2}$

> ## Practice and Problem Solving
> Extra Practice, page 304, Set C

Write a mixed number for each picture.

12. 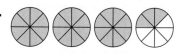 **13.** **14.**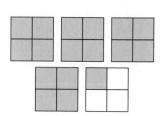

Write the mixed number represented by each letter.

15.

16.

Rename each fraction as a mixed number and each mixed number as a fraction. You can draw a picture.

17. $\frac{5}{2}$ **18.** $9\frac{1}{3}$ **19.** $\frac{10}{8}$ **20.** $5\frac{1}{4}$

21. $4\frac{5}{12}$ **22.** $\frac{21}{8}$ **23.** $7\frac{4}{7}$ **24.** $\frac{25}{9}$

For 25–29, use the figures at the right.

25. Write a fraction for the shaded part in the third figure.

26. How many whole figures are shaded in the picture?

27. What improper fraction and mixed number can you write for the picture?

28. How can you change the picture to show 3 wholes?

29. How can you change the picture to show $1\frac{4}{6}$?

30. **ESTIMATION** Mrs. James cut some grapefruit into quarters. She used 9 quarters to make juice. Is that closer to 2 or 3 whole grapefruit?

31. A cup holds 8 ounces of liquid. Mary used 24 ounces of milk to make waffles. How many cups of milk did she use?

32. MULTISTEP Mrs. Morgan bought a dishwasher for $340. She made a down payment of $100 and paid the rest in 4 equal payments. How much was each of the payments?

33. Vocabulary Power The word *mix* means "to combine or unite." How does this help you understand the term *mixed number*?

Maintain Skills

34. Melinda invited 8 friends to her party. She had 42 party favors. She gave the same number of favors to each friend. How many favors were left over?

35. Which is shorter, a chain that is 5 in. long or a chain that is 5 ft long?

CRCT Test Prep

36. **M4N4.b.** Santiago is putting his rock collection of 156 rocks into egg cartons. Each carton can hold 12 rocks. How many cartons does he need? (p. 232)

A. 12   C. 14
B. 13   D. 144

Problem Solving LiNKUP . . . . to Music

In music, one whole note is equivalent to two $\frac{1}{2}$ notes, four $\frac{1}{4}$ notes, or eight $\frac{1}{8}$ notes. The diagram shows how the notes are related.

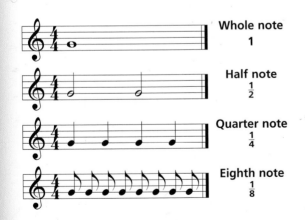

Whole note
1

Half note
$\frac{1}{2}$

Quarter note
$\frac{1}{4}$

Eighth note
$\frac{1}{8}$

Copy and complete.

1. __?__ $\frac{1}{4}$ notes equal two $\frac{1}{2}$ notes.

2. Two $\frac{1}{8}$ notes equal one __?__ note.

3. One whole note equals one $\frac{1}{2}$ note and __?__ $\frac{1}{4}$ note(s).

Extra Practice

Set A (pp. 294–295)

Write a fraction for the shaded part.

1.
2.
3.
4.

Draw a picture, and shade part of it to show the fraction. Write a fraction for the unshaded part.

5. $\frac{1}{3}$ 6. $\frac{8}{8}$ 7. $\frac{5}{12}$ 8. $\frac{3}{3}$ 9. $\frac{2}{6}$

Set B (pp. 296–297)

Write two equivalent fractions for each picture.

1.   2.   3.

Use the number lines to write an equivalent fraction for each.

4. $\frac{3}{4}$

5. $\frac{2}{2}$

6. $\frac{4}{8}$

7. $\frac{1}{4}$

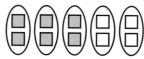

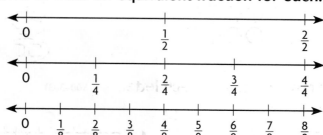

Set C (pp. 300–303)

Write a mixed number for each picture.

1.   2.   3.

Write the mixed number represented by each letter.

4. 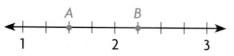   5.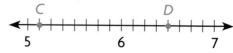

Rename each fraction as a mixed number and each mixed number as a fraction.

6. $\frac{7}{2}$ 7. $\frac{13}{8}$ 8. $\frac{11}{5}$ 9. $\frac{14}{6}$

10. $2\frac{3}{4}$ 11. $5\frac{1}{2}$ 12. $4\frac{11}{12}$ 13. $7\frac{6}{7}$

Review/Test

✓ CHECK VOCABULARY AND CONCEPTS

Choose the best term from the box.

Vocabulary

- equivalent fractions
- proper fraction
- mixed fraction

1. Different fractions that name the same amount are called __?__ . (p. 296)

2. A __?__ is made up of a whole number and a fraction. (p. 300)

✓ CHECK SKILLS

Write the fraction or mixed number for the shaded part. (pp. 294–295, 300–303)

3.

4.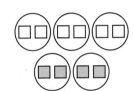

5.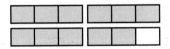

Write two equivalent fractions for each picture.

6.

7.

8.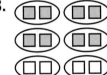

Write the mixed number represented by each letter. (pp. 300–303)

9.

10.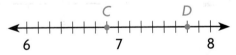

Rename each fraction as a mixed number and each mixed number as a fraction. (pp. 300–303)

11. $\frac{7}{2}$

12. $8\frac{1}{3}$

13. $\frac{16}{3}$

14. $1\frac{1}{12}$

15. $\frac{9}{5}$

16. $5\frac{3}{4}$

17. $\frac{12}{5}$

18. $3\frac{1}{6}$

✓ CHECK PROBLEM SOLVING

Make a picture to solve. (pp. 298–299)

19. Tom made $\frac{1}{3}$ of his free throws, Lil made $\frac{2}{6}$ of her free throws, and Maria made $\frac{4}{6}$ of hers. Which two people made the same part of their free throws?

20. Sue has a set of measuring cups. Three of the sizes are $\frac{1}{2}$, $\frac{3}{4}$, and $\frac{1}{4}$ cup. How many $\frac{1}{4}$-cup measures are equivalent to a $\frac{1}{2}$-cup measure?

Chapter CRCT Test Prep

NUMBERS AND OPERATIONS

1. **M4N6.c.** What is $\frac{11}{5}$ renamed as a mixed number?

   A. $\frac{5}{11}$

   B. $1\frac{1}{5}$

   C. $1\frac{6}{5}$

   D. $2\frac{1}{5}$

2. **M4N6.a.** Which model shows a fraction equivalent to the fraction shown in the model below?

   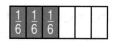

   A. | $\frac{1}{4}$ | $\frac{1}{4}$ | $\frac{1}{4}$ | |

   B. | $\frac{1}{4}$ | $\frac{1}{4}$ | | |

   C. | $\frac{1}{12}$ | $\frac{1}{12}$ | $\frac{1}{12}$ | $\frac{1}{12}$ | $\frac{1}{12}$ | $\frac{1}{12}$ |

   D. | $\frac{1}{8}$ | $\frac{1}{8}$ | $\frac{1}{8}$ | |

3. **M4N6.c.** What number does the following model show?

   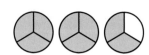

   A. $3\frac{2}{3}$

   B. $2\frac{2}{3}$

   C. $2\frac{1}{3}$

   D. $1\frac{2}{3}$

NUMBERS AND OPERATIONS

4. **M4N6.c.** Marcia lives $3\frac{1}{2}$ miles from Valdosta, Georgia. Which fraction is equivalent to $3\frac{1}{2}$?

   A. $\frac{3}{2}$

   B. $\frac{4}{2}$

   C. $\frac{7}{2}$

   D. $\frac{6}{1}$

5. **M4N6.c.** Calvin used $\frac{4}{3}$ cups of milk in a recipe. How many cups of milk did he use?

   A. $4\frac{1}{3}$

   B. $3\frac{1}{4}$

   C. $1\frac{1}{3}$

   D. $1\frac{1}{4}$

6. **M4N6.a.** Use the picture to find an equivalent fraction for $\frac{6}{9}$.

   A. $\frac{1}{3}$

   B. $\frac{1}{2}$

   C. $\frac{3}{6}$

   D. $\frac{2}{3}$

Cumulative CRCT Test Prep

GEOMETRY

7. **M4G3.b.** What ordered pair names point D in the coordinate system below?

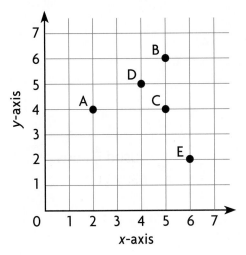

A. (5,4)

B. (4,5)

C. (4,4)

D. (5,5)

8. **M4G1.a.** A folded square napkin looks like this drawing.

How can you classify the figure the folded napkin forms?

A. a right triangle

B. an acute triangle

C. an obtuse triangle

D. an equilateral triangle

MEASUREMENT

9. **M4M2.a.** What is the measure of angle XYZ?

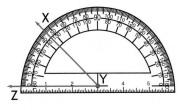

A. 145°

B. 135°

C. 45°

D. 40°

10. **M4M2.a.** The measure of each angle on the triangle below is 60°.

Which of the following angles measures less than 60°?

A.

B.

C.

D. ←——→

11. **M4M2.b.** The minute hand on a clock rotates 180° in one half hour. What type of a rotation is this?

A. a full rotation

B. a half rotation

C. a quarter rotation

D. a whole rotation

Add and Subtract Fractions and Mixed Numbers

≡FAST FACT • SCIENCE

Lemurs are primates that are native to the island of Madagascar. The Duke University Primate Center in Durham, North Carolina, is home to over 250 lemurs, representing 21 different species.

INVESTIGATION The pictograph shows the amounts of dry food that researchers feed some species of lemurs each day. How much dry food is each species of lemur given each day? How much dry food would each species of lemur be given each day if each 🍲 were $\frac{1}{2}$ cup? $\frac{1}{3}$ cup?

Using Data

LEMURS' DAILY DIETS

Mongoose lemur	🍲 🍲 🍲
Ring-tailed lemur	🍲 🍲 🍲 🍲
Crowned lemur	🍲 🍲 🍲
Grey gentle lemur	🍲

Key: Each 🍲 = $\frac{1}{4}$ cup of dry food.

CHECK WHAT YOU KNOW

Use this page to help you review and remember important skills needed for Chapter 15.

✓ EQUIVALENT FRACTIONS

Write two equivalent fractions for each picture.

1.

2.

3.

✓ MIXED NUMBERS

Write a mixed number for each picture.

4.

5.

6.

✓ MIXED NUMBERS AND IMPROPER FRACTIONS

Rename each fraction as a mixed number and each mixed number as a fraction.

7. $\frac{5}{3}$ 8. $2\frac{2}{5}$ 9. $\frac{9}{2}$ 10. $3\frac{1}{3}$ 11. $\frac{21}{5}$ 12. $5\frac{3}{4}$

VOCABULARY POWER

REVIEW

fraction [frak'shən] *noun*

The word *fraction* comes from the Latin word *frangere,* which means "to break." Another English word with the same root is *fractured,* which means "broken." Explain how a *fraction* can represent a piece of a "broken" whole.

PREVIEW

like fractions

 GO ON-LINE   www.harcourtschool.com/mathglossary

Add Like Fractions

M4N6.b. Add and subtract fractions and mixed numbers with common denominators. (Denominators should not exceed twelve.) *also* **M4P4.a., M4P4.b., M4P5.c.**

 Learn

A STEP AT A TIME Pam walked $\frac{1}{4}$ mile to Lori's house. Then, the two girls walked together $\frac{2}{4}$ mile to pottery class. How far did Pam walk in all?

Like fractions are fractions with the same denominator. You can add like fractions by using fraction bars or drawings.

One Way Use fraction bars.

Find $\frac{1}{4} + \frac{2}{4}$.

STEP 1

Start with one of the $\frac{1}{4}$ fraction bars.

$\frac{1}{4}$

STEP 2

Line up two more $\frac{1}{4}$ fraction bars. Count the $\frac{1}{4}$ fraction bars. $\frac{1}{4} + \frac{2}{4} = \frac{3}{4}$

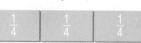

So, Pam walked $\frac{3}{4}$ mile.

Another Way Use drawings.

At pottery class, Pam and Lori divided a block of clay into 8 equal pieces. Pam used 2 pieces of the clay, and Lori used 3 pieces. What fraction of the block of clay did they use?

STEP 1

Draw a rectangle divided into 8 equal parts. Model $\frac{2}{8}$ by shading 2 of the parts.

STEP 2

Add $\frac{3}{8}$ by shading 3 more of the parts. There are 5 parts shaded.

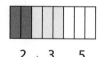

$\frac{2}{8} + \frac{3}{8} = \frac{5}{\blacksquare}$

STEP 3

There are 8 equal parts, so the denominator stays the same. Write the sum of the numerators over the denominator.

$\frac{2}{8} + \frac{3}{8} = \frac{5}{8}$

So, Pam and Lori used $\frac{5}{8}$ of the block of clay.

Add Numerators

What if Pam walked $\frac{3}{10}$ mile from class to the library and $\frac{7}{10}$ mile home? How far did Pam walk?

You also can add fractions with like denominators by adding the numerators.

Distance to the library		Distance home		Total distance	
↓		↓		↓	
$\frac{3}{10}$	+	$\frac{7}{10}$	=	$\frac{10}{10}$	← Add the numerators.
					← The denominator stays the same.

So, Pam walked a total of 1 mile.

Examples

Ⓐ $\frac{2}{10} + \frac{6}{10}$

$\frac{2}{10} + \frac{6}{10} = \frac{8}{10}$

Another name for $\frac{8}{10}$ is $\frac{4}{5}$.

$\frac{8}{10} = \frac{4}{5}$

Ⓑ $\frac{3}{8} + \frac{5}{8}$

$\frac{3}{8} + \frac{5}{8} = \frac{8}{8}$

Write the sum as a whole number.

$\frac{8}{8} = 1$

Ⓒ $\frac{2}{6} + \frac{5}{6}$

$\frac{2}{6} + \frac{5}{6} = \frac{7}{6}$

Write the sum as a mixed number.

$\frac{7}{6} = \frac{6}{6} + \frac{1}{6} = 1\frac{1}{6}$

MATH IDEA To add like fractions, add the numerators. Use the same denominator as in the like fractions.

Technology Link

More Practice: Harcourt Mega Math Fraction Action, *Fraction Flare-Up*, Level G

▶ **Check**

1. **Explain** why you add only the numerators when adding like fractions.

Find the sum.

2.

$\frac{2}{5} + \frac{1}{5}$

3. $\frac{4}{10} + \frac{3}{10}$

4. $\frac{1}{12} + \frac{4}{12}$

5. $\begin{array}{r} \frac{1}{2} \\ +\frac{1}{2} \\ \hline \end{array}$

6. $\begin{array}{r} \frac{3}{4} \\ +\frac{1}{4} \\ \hline \end{array}$

7. $\begin{array}{r} \frac{4}{8} \\ +\frac{2}{8} \\ \hline \end{array}$

8. $\begin{array}{r} \frac{1}{3} \\ +\frac{1}{3} \\ \hline \end{array}$

LESSON CONTINUES ▶

Find the sum.

9.

$$\frac{1}{8} + \frac{3}{8}$$

10.

$$\frac{1}{10} + \frac{4}{10}$$

11.

$$\frac{4}{6} + \frac{3}{6}$$

12. $\frac{2}{6} + \frac{4}{6}$

13. $\frac{3}{4} + \frac{2}{4}$

14. $\frac{3}{7} + \frac{4}{7}$

15. $\frac{2}{3} + \frac{2}{3}$

16. $\frac{2}{9} + \frac{4}{9}$

17. $\frac{5}{8} + \frac{3}{8}$

18. $\frac{5}{6} + \frac{4}{6}$

19. $\frac{1}{10} + \frac{7}{10}$

20.
$$\frac{3}{12}$$
$$+\frac{5}{12}$$

21.
$$\frac{9}{12}$$
$$+\frac{10}{12}$$

22.
$$\frac{3}{10}$$
$$+\frac{7}{10}$$

23.
$$\frac{3}{3}$$
$$+\frac{1}{3}$$

ALGEBRA For 24–31, find the value of □.

24. $\frac{7}{10} + \frac{2}{\square} = \frac{9}{10}$

25. $\frac{5}{\square} + \frac{3}{\square} = 1$

26. $\frac{5}{\square} + \frac{3}{\square} = \frac{8}{12}$

27. $\frac{4}{\square} + \frac{3}{\square} = \frac{7}{9}$

28. $\frac{\square}{4} + \frac{\square}{4} = \frac{2}{4}$

29. $\frac{1}{7} + \frac{2}{\square} = \frac{3}{\square}$

30. $\frac{3}{8} + \frac{3}{8} = \frac{\square}{4}$

31. $\frac{4}{\square} + \frac{3}{\square} = \frac{7}{11}$

32. **Vocabulary Power** The word *denominator* comes from a Latin word meaning "to name." Explain how the denominator helps name a fraction.

33. **Write About It** Describe how you could make a model from an egg carton to find the sum $\frac{3}{12} + \frac{5}{12}$. Solve.

34. **REASONING** The three identical jars at the right have pottery glaze. Will all the pottery glaze fit into one of the jars? Explain.

35. **What's the Error?** Allen says the sum $\frac{3}{5} + \frac{2}{5}$ is $\frac{5}{10}$. Describe his error. Write the correct answer.

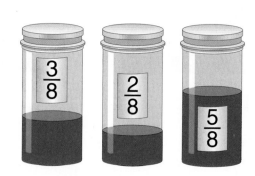

36. Each lap around a track is $\frac{1}{4}$ mile. Leslie walked 1 lap around the track on Saturday and 2 laps around the track on Sunday. How far did Leslie walk on Saturday and Sunday, in miles?

37. During cooking class, a loaf of bread was sliced into 9 equal pieces. Wendy, Peter, and Jack each got $\frac{1}{9}$ of the loaf. What fraction of the total loaf did they get altogether? How many pieces is this?

Maintain Skills

38. Use the decimal model to find $0.4 + 0.3$.

39. Measure the length of the barrette to the nearest centimeter.

CRCT Test Prep

40. **M4A1.b.** Evie had 30 pens. She gave $\triangle$ pens to Toby. Which expression shows how many pens Evie has left? (p. 46)

A. $\triangle - 30$ C. $30 \div \triangle$

B. $30 + \triangle$ D. $30 - \triangle$

41. **M4N6.c.** What is the mixed number for $\frac{11}{4}$? (p. 300)

A. $1\frac{1}{4}$ C. $3\frac{1}{4}$

B. $2\frac{3}{4}$ D. $11\frac{1}{4}$

Problem Solving   Thinker's Corner

ESTIMATE FRACTION SUMS You can use benchmarks to estimate fraction sums.

Estimate the sum $\frac{3}{8} + \frac{7}{8} + \frac{1}{8}$.

Use a number line to round fractions to a benchmark of 0, $\frac{1}{2}$, or 1.

$$\frac{3}{8} \quad + \quad \frac{7}{8} \quad + \quad \frac{1}{8}$$
$$\downarrow \qquad\quad \downarrow \qquad\quad \downarrow$$
$$\frac{1}{2} \quad + \quad 1 \quad + \quad 0 \quad = 1\frac{1}{2}$$

So, $\frac{3}{8} + \frac{7}{8} + \frac{1}{8}$ is about $1\frac{1}{2}$.

Benchmarks

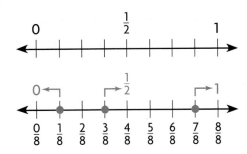

Round each fraction to its nearest benchmark.

Estimate each sum, and give the benchmarks you used. Then find the actual sum, and compare it to the estimate to determine whether your answer is reasonable.

1. $\frac{1}{6} + \frac{4}{6}$ **2.** $\frac{3}{8} + \frac{5}{8}$ **3.** $\frac{7}{12} + \frac{4}{12} + \frac{1}{12}$ **4.** $\frac{5}{6} + \frac{1}{6} + \frac{3}{6}$

Subtract Like Fractions

M4N6.b. Add and subtract fractions and mixed numbers with common denominators. (Denominators should not exceed twelve.) *also* M4P3.a., M4P3.b., M4P3.c., M4P3.d., M4P5, M4P5.b., M4P5.c.

Quick Review

Write another name for each fraction.

1. $\frac{3}{6}$ **2.** $\frac{14}{21}$

3. $\frac{6}{24}$ **4.** $\frac{8}{40}$

5. $\frac{8}{12}$

▶ **Explore**

How can you subtract two fractions with like denominators?

MATERIALS fraction bars

Activity Use fraction bars to find $\frac{5}{6} - \frac{3}{6}$.

One Way Take away fraction bars.

STEP 1	STEP 2	STEP 3
Line up 5 of the $\frac{1}{6}$ bars. 	Take away 3 of the $\frac{1}{6}$ bars. 	Count the $\frac{1}{6}$ bars left. There are two $\frac{1}{6}$ bars left.

Another Way Compare two groups of fraction bars.

STEP 1	STEP 2	STEP 3
Line up 5 of the $\frac{1}{6}$ bars. 	Line up 3 of the $\frac{1}{6}$ bars. 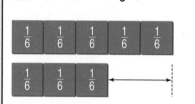	Find the difference between the rows of bars. The difference is two $\frac{1}{6}$ bars.

So, $\frac{5}{6} - \frac{3}{6} = \frac{2}{6}$, or $\frac{1}{3}$.

Try It

Find the difference.

a. $\frac{7}{8} - \frac{2}{8}$ **b.** $\frac{8}{12} - \frac{6}{12}$

c. $\frac{5}{10} - \frac{2}{10}$ **d.** $\frac{3}{4} - \frac{2}{4}$

I have $\frac{7}{8}$ and $\frac{2}{8}$. What is the difference?

You can draw pictures to subtract like fractions.

Example Use a drawing to find $\frac{7}{8} - \frac{3}{8}$.

STEP 1	STEP 2	STEP 3
Draw a rectangle divided into 8 equal parts. Model $\frac{7}{8}$ by shading 7 of the parts. 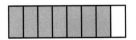	Subtract $\frac{3}{8}$ by crossing out 3 of the shaded parts. There are 4 shaded parts not crossed out. 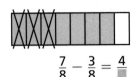 $\frac{7}{8} - \frac{3}{8} = \frac{4}{\blacksquare}$	The denominator stays the same. Write the difference over the denominator. $\frac{7}{8} - \frac{3}{8} = \frac{4}{8}$ Another name for $\frac{4}{8}$ is $\frac{1}{2}$. $\frac{4}{8} = \frac{1}{2}$

So, $\frac{7}{8} - \frac{3}{8} = \frac{1}{2}$.

• Find the difference in the numerators of $\frac{7}{8} - \frac{3}{8}$. How does this answer compare to the numerator of the difference, $\frac{4}{8}$, found in the Example?

MATH IDEA To subtract like fractions, use fraction bars, draw a picture, or subtract the numerators. Use the same denominator as you do when adding like fractions.

Technology Link
More Practice: Harcourt Mega Math Fraction Action, *Fraction Flare-Up*, Level H

▶ **Practice and Problem Solving**

Use fraction bars or draw a picture to find the difference.

1. $\frac{3}{5} - \frac{1}{5}$ 2. $\frac{8}{10} - \frac{1}{10}$ 3. $\frac{9}{9} - \frac{1}{9}$ 4. $\frac{11}{12} - \frac{5}{12}$

Find the difference.

5. $\frac{5}{8} - \frac{4}{8}$ 6. $\frac{6}{10} - \frac{2}{10}$ 7. $\frac{4}{6} - \frac{1}{6}$ 8. $\frac{5}{8} - \frac{2}{8}$

9. In a survey, $\frac{4}{10}$ of the students chose an animal as a mascot. The rest chose a cartoon character. What fraction of the students chose a cartoon character? Explain.

Maintain Skills

10. What is the value of the digit 9 in the number 25,943.7?

11. $595 \div 5$ 12. $438 \div 2$

CRCT Test Prep

13. **M4N4.b.** Hannah can fit 32 names on each page of the school directory. She has 416 names. How many pages does she need? (p. 232)

A. 12   B. 13   C. 14   D. 17

Add and Subtract Mixed Numbers

M4N6.b. Add and subtract fractions and mixed numbers with common denominators. (Denominators should not exceed twelve.) *also* **M4P5, M4P5.b.**

Quick Review

1. $\frac{1}{4} + \frac{2}{4}$ 2. $\frac{1}{3} + \frac{2}{3}$

3. $\frac{2}{5} + \frac{1}{5}$ 4. $\frac{4}{6} - \frac{1}{6}$

5. $\frac{5}{8} - \frac{3}{8}$

▶ Learn

DINNER TIME Susan is helping prepare fruit for the animals at the primate center. She has mixed $2\frac{2}{4}$ cups of banana slices with $1\frac{1}{4}$ cups of apple slices. How much fruit has she prepared?

Example 1

Add. $2\frac{2}{4} + 1\frac{1}{4}$

STEP 1

Draw a picture for each mixed number. Add the fractions first.

$$
\begin{array}{r}
2\frac{2}{4} \\
+1\frac{1}{4} \\
\hline
\frac{3}{4}
\end{array}
$$

STEP 2

Then add the whole numbers.

$$
\begin{array}{r}
2\frac{2}{4} \\
+1\frac{1}{4} \\
\hline
3\frac{3}{4}
\end{array}
$$

So, Susan has prepared $3\frac{3}{4}$ cups of fruit.

More Examples

Ⓐ $\begin{array}{r} 2\frac{1}{3} \\ +2\frac{1}{3} \\ \hline 4\frac{2}{3} \end{array}$

Ⓑ $\begin{array}{r} \frac{3}{5} \\ +1\frac{4}{5} \\ \hline 1\frac{7}{5} \end{array}$ $= 1 + 1\frac{2}{5} = 2\frac{2}{5}$

MATH IDEA When you add mixed numbers, add the fractions first, and then add the whole numbers.

Subtract Mixed Numbers

Subtracting mixed numbers is similar to adding mixed numbers.

Susan has $3\frac{5}{8}$ cups of dry food. She gives $2\frac{1}{8}$ cups to a group of ring-tailed lemurs. How much dry food does she have left?

Example 2

Subtract. $3\frac{5}{8} - 2\frac{1}{8}$

STEP 1

Draw a model for the first mixed number. Subtract the fractions first.

$$\begin{array}{r} 3\frac{5}{8} \\ -2\frac{1}{8} \\ \hline \frac{4}{8} \end{array}$$

STEP 2

Then subtract the whole numbers.

$$\begin{array}{r} 3\frac{5}{8} \\ -2\frac{1}{8} \\ \hline 1\frac{4}{8}, \text{ or } 1\frac{1}{2} \end{array}$$

So, Susan has $1\frac{1}{2}$ cups of dry food left.

More Examples

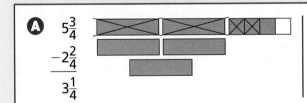

A
$$\begin{array}{r} 5\frac{3}{4} \\ -2\frac{2}{4} \\ \hline 3\frac{1}{4} \end{array}$$

B
$$\begin{array}{r} 2\frac{9}{12} \\ -2\frac{3}{12} \\ \hline \frac{6}{12}, \text{ or } \frac{1}{2} \end{array}$$

Check

1. **Explain** how you can check to be sure your answer to a subtraction problem is correct.

Technology Link

More Practice: Harcourt Mega Math The Number Games, *Tiny's Think Tank*, Level W

Find the sum or difference.

2. $\begin{array}{r} 2\frac{1}{4} \\ +3\frac{3}{4} \\ \hline \end{array}$

3. $\begin{array}{r} 4\frac{3}{5} \\ +1\frac{3}{5} \\ \hline \end{array}$

4. $\begin{array}{r} 2\frac{3}{5} \\ -1\frac{1}{5} \\ \hline \end{array}$

5. $\begin{array}{r} 2\frac{5}{6} \\ -1\frac{3}{6} \\ \hline \end{array}$

LESSON CONTINUES

Find the sum or difference.

6. $3\frac{1}{3}$
   $+2\frac{1}{3}$

7. $4\frac{3}{4}$
   $-1\frac{1}{4}$

8. $5\frac{1}{4}$
   $+1\frac{2}{4}$

9. $3\frac{5}{6}$
   $-2\frac{2}{6}$

10. $6\frac{10}{12}$
    $-2\frac{4}{12}$

11. $8\frac{1}{6}$
    $+1\frac{5}{6}$

12. $5\frac{8}{10}$
    $-3\frac{3}{10}$

13. $7\frac{2}{9}$
    $+4\frac{8}{9}$

14. $4\frac{3}{6}$
    $+2\frac{4}{6}$

15. $4\frac{2}{2}$
    $-3\frac{1}{2}$

16. $8\frac{7}{10}$
    $+7\frac{2}{10}$

17. $4\frac{6}{8}$
    $-1\frac{2}{8}$

18. $3\frac{5}{6} - 1\frac{4}{6}$

19. $5\frac{3}{8} + 1\frac{5}{8}$

20. $6\frac{5}{8} - 3\frac{2}{8}$

21. $7\frac{9}{12} + 4\frac{2}{12}$

22. $5\frac{3}{5} + 4\frac{2}{5}$

23. $12\frac{8}{10} - 8\frac{2}{10}$

24. $6\frac{5}{6} - 1\frac{2}{6}$

25. $1\frac{2}{8} + 3\frac{3}{8}$

26. $6\frac{1}{8} + 2\frac{5}{8}$

27. $7\frac{3}{5} - 1\frac{3}{5}$

28. $5\frac{1}{3} + 6\frac{2}{3}$

29. $9\frac{3}{4} - 9\frac{1}{4}$

ALGEBRA For 30–33, find the value of $\triangle$.

30. $3\frac{6}{8} + 5\frac{2}{8} = \triangle$

31. $9\frac{6}{10} + 11\frac{\triangle}{10} = 20\frac{9}{10}$

32. $8\frac{\triangle}{5} - 2\frac{2}{5} = 6\frac{2}{5}$

33. $7\frac{4}{6} - 4\frac{1}{6} = 3\frac{3}{6}$, or $3\frac{1}{\triangle}$

USE DATA For 34–36, use the table.

34. What is the total area of the enclosures for the zebras and the giraffes?

35. How much larger is the zebras' enclosure than the lions' enclosure?

36. **? What's the Question?** Two mixed numbers are $1\frac{1}{4}$ and $2\frac{1}{4}$. The answer is $3\frac{1}{2}$.

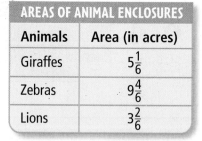

AREAS OF ANIMAL ENCLOSURES	
Animals	**Area (in acres)**
Giraffes	$5\frac{1}{6}$
Zebras	$9\frac{4}{6}$
Lions	$3\frac{2}{6}$

37. ≡FAST FACT • SCIENCE A ring-tailed lemur's tail is about $15\frac{1}{8}$ inches long. Its head and body are about $11\frac{6}{8}$ inches long. How long is a ring-tailed lemur in all?

38. Draw pictures to represent the mixed numbers $3\frac{1}{4}$ and $1\frac{1}{2}$. Explain how to redraw the second mixed number so you could add them together.

Maintain Skills

39. Find the area of the rectangle on the grid.

40. 8×63 **41.** 60×90

CRCT Test Prep

42. M4G1.a. What type of triangle is shown below? (p. 274)

A. isosceles   C. right
B. acute   D. obtuse

Problem Solving THINKER'S CORNER 💡

RENAMING TO SUBTRACT   Sometimes you need to rename a whole number when subtracting mixed numbers.

Enid is hiking a trail that is $2\frac{1}{3}$ miles long. So far, she has hiked $\frac{2}{3}$ mile. How much farther does she need to hike to reach the end of the trail?

• Model $2\frac{1}{3}$ using two whole bars and one $\frac{1}{3}$ bar.

 $2\frac{1}{3}$

• To subtract $\frac{2}{3}$, rename 1 whole with three $\frac{1}{3}$ bars.

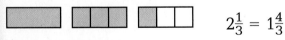 $2\frac{1}{3} = 1\frac{4}{3}$

• Subtract $\frac{2}{3}$.

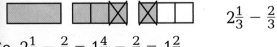 $2\frac{1}{3} - \frac{2}{3}$

So, $2\frac{1}{3} - \frac{2}{3} = 1\frac{4}{3} - \frac{2}{3} = 1\frac{2}{3}$.

Enid needs to hike $1\frac{2}{3}$ more miles to reach the end of the trail.

Use fraction bars to subtract.

1. $3\frac{1}{4} - \frac{3}{4}$ **2.** $5\frac{1}{3} - \frac{2}{3}$ **3.** $1\frac{3}{8} - \frac{7}{8}$ **4.** $2 - \frac{5}{6}$

Problem Solving Skill
Choose the Operation

M4P1.c. Apply and adapt a variety of appropriate strategies to solve problems. *also* **M4N6.b., M4P1.a., M4P1.b., M4P1.d., M4P3.a., M4P3.b., M4P3.c., M4P3.d.**

UNDERSTAND ⟩ **PLAN** ⟩ **SOLVE** ⟩ **CHECK**

WANT SOME FLIES WITH THAT? Gorillas and chimpanzees have similar diets in the wild. These tables show the makeup of each animal's diet.

Study the data. Then read Problems A and B.

GORILLA DIET	
Leaves, Seeds	$\frac{1}{6}$
Insects	$\frac{1}{6}$
Fruits	?

CHIMPANZEE DIET	
Leaves, Seeds	?
Insects	$\frac{1}{12}$
Fruits	$\frac{8}{12}$

A. What fraction of a gorilla's diet is made up of leaves and seeds and insects?

B. How much more of a chimpanzee's diet is made up of fruits than of insects?

MATH IDEA Before you solve a problem, read it carefully, and think about how the numbers are related. Then decide which operation is needed to solve the problem.

Talk About It

• Discuss how you would solve Problems A and B. Then solve.

• What operation would you use to find the fraction of a chimpanzee's diet that is made up of fruits and insects? Explain how you know.

• What operation would you use to find how much greater a fraction of its diet insects are for a gorilla than for chimpanzee? Explain how you know.

• What fraction of a gorilla's diet is made up of fruits? What fraction of a chimpanzee's diet is made up of leaves and seeds? Copy and complete the tables.

Problem Solving Practice

Write the operation. Then solve the problem.

1. Mei ate $\frac{1}{12}$ of the watermelon, and Billy ate $\frac{2}{12}$. What fraction of the watermelon did they eat?

2. Michelle practiced the piano for $\frac{5}{6}$ hour, and Seth practiced for $\frac{3}{6}$ hour. How much longer did Michelle practice than Seth?

For a science report on apes, Lloyd says that he wrote $\frac{2}{4}$ page more than Mary and Bob combined. Mary wrote $\frac{3}{4}$ page, and Bob wrote $1\frac{1}{4}$ pages. How many pages did Lloyd write?

3. Which expression could you use to solve the problem?

   A $\left(\frac{5}{4} - \frac{3}{4}\right) - \frac{2}{4}$ C $\left(\frac{5}{4} - \frac{3}{4}\right) + \frac{2}{4}$

   B $\left(\frac{3}{4} + \frac{5}{4}\right) + \frac{2}{4}$ D $\left(\frac{5}{4} + \frac{3}{4}\right) - \frac{2}{4}$

4. Which is NOT an answer to the question?

   F $\frac{10}{4}$ H $2\frac{2}{4}$

   G $\frac{6}{4}$ J $2\frac{1}{2}$

Mixed Applications

USE DATA For 5–7, use the graph.

Mr. Smith measured the amount of rainfall for five days. The measurements are shown on the graph.

5. What was the difference in the rainfall amounts on Friday and on Monday?

6. Find the total amount of rainfall for the five days.

7. **MULTISTEP** Was the total rainfall for the first two days greater than the rainfall amount on Friday? Explain.

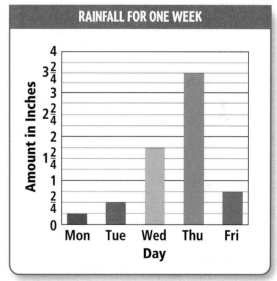

8. **MULTISTEP** Arjun spent 3 of his 8 quarters at the store. He gave a friend 2 quarters. What fraction of his quarters does he have left?

9. Write About It Explain how you know what operation to use when solving a word problem.

10. **REASONING** Find a number that could come next in the sequence. $0, \frac{1}{2}, 1, \frac{3}{2}, 2, \frac{5}{2}, \blacksquare$. Write a rule.

11. Find the value for ▲ that makes the equation true.

    $$▲ \times 3{,}000 = 360{,}000$$

Extra Practice

Set A (pp. 310–313)

Find the sum.

1. $\frac{1}{8} + \frac{5}{8}$ 2. $\frac{2}{6} + \frac{1}{6}$ 3. $\frac{4}{12} + \frac{5}{12}$ 4. $\frac{3}{10} + \frac{4}{10}$

5. $\frac{1}{4} + \frac{2}{4}$ 6. $\frac{2}{7} + \frac{3}{7}$ 7. $\frac{2}{10} + \frac{5}{10}$ 8. $\frac{4}{10} + \frac{6}{10}$

9. $\frac{4}{8} + \frac{2}{8}$ 10. $\frac{7}{12} + \frac{5}{12}$ 11. $\frac{4}{5} + \frac{3}{5}$ 12. $\frac{8}{12} + \frac{2}{12}$

13. $\frac{4}{5} + \frac{2}{5}$ 14. $\frac{6}{7} + \frac{1}{7}$ 15. $\frac{5}{8} + \frac{1}{8}$ 16. $\frac{3}{4} + \frac{3}{4}$

17. $\frac{3}{10} + \frac{2}{10}$ 18. $\frac{5}{12} + \frac{8}{12}$ 19. $\frac{5}{6} + \frac{5}{6}$ 20. $\frac{2}{3} + \frac{2}{3}$

21. There was $\frac{2}{3}$ cup of milk left in the refrigerator after Robbie used $\frac{1}{3}$ cup of milk in his oatmeal. How much milk was in the refrigerator before Robbie ate his oatmeal?

22. On Monday, $\frac{3}{10}$ inch of snow fell in Leigh's yard. On Tuesday, $\frac{7}{10}$ inch of snow fell. How much snow fell in all?

Set B (pp. 316–319)

Find the sum or difference.

1. $4\frac{2}{5}$ $+3\frac{1}{5}$ 2. $3\frac{2}{4}$ $+3\frac{3}{4}$ 3. $2\frac{1}{3}$ $+4\frac{1}{3}$ 4. $3\frac{5}{9}$ $+4\frac{4}{9}$

5. $3\frac{2}{10}$ $+6\frac{3}{10}$ 6. $8\frac{1}{2}$ $+7\frac{1}{2}$ 7. $5\frac{2}{3}$ $-4\frac{1}{3}$ 8. $8\frac{8}{12}$ $-5\frac{3}{12}$

9. $5\frac{4}{6}$ $-1\frac{3}{6}$ 10. $7\frac{4}{5}$ $-3\frac{2}{5}$ 11. $4\frac{5}{10}$ $-3\frac{2}{10}$ 12. $3\frac{3}{4}$ $-1\frac{1}{4}$

13. Joseph fed his dogs. Brewster got $2\frac{1}{4}$ cups of dry dog food, and Beatrice got $1\frac{1}{4}$ cups of dry dog food. How much dry dog food was used altogether?

14. Sam's book report is $3\frac{4}{8}$ pages long. Mary's book report is $2\frac{2}{8}$ pages long. Whose report is longer? How many pages longer?

Review/Test

 CHECK VOCABULARY AND CONCEPTS

Choose the best term from the box.

1. Fractions that have the same denominator are _?_. (p. 310)

2. The fractions $\frac{2}{5}$ and $\frac{4}{5}$ have like _?_. (p. 310)

3. Add like fractions by adding the _?_ and using the same denominator. (p. 310)

 CHECK SKILLS

Find the sum. (pp. 310–313, 316–319)

4. $\frac{2}{8} + \frac{5}{8}$

5. $\frac{2}{3} + \frac{1}{3}$

6. $\frac{1}{12} + \frac{4}{12}$

7. $\frac{2}{10} + \frac{6}{10}$

8. $3\frac{1}{4}$
   $+12\frac{3}{4}$

9. $2\frac{2}{3}$
   $+1\frac{2}{3}$

10. $2\frac{1}{4}$
    $+8\frac{2}{4}$

11. $7\frac{6}{8}$
    $+5\frac{3}{8}$

Find the difference. (pp. 314–315, 316–319)

12. $\frac{5}{8} - \frac{2}{8}$

13. $\frac{3}{4} - \frac{1}{4}$

14. $\frac{5}{5} - \frac{2}{5}$

15. $\frac{10}{12} - \frac{3}{12}$

16. $5\frac{8}{12}$
    $-2\frac{5}{12}$

17. $3\frac{3}{5}$
    $-\ \frac{2}{5}$

18. $9\frac{5}{8}$
    $-7\frac{3}{8}$

19. $2\frac{11}{12}$
    $-2\frac{5}{12}$

Find the sum or difference. (pp. 310–313, 314–315, 316–319)

20. $\frac{5}{9} - \frac{1}{9}$

21. $\frac{2}{5} + \frac{2}{5}$

22. $3\frac{1}{3} + 2\frac{1}{3}$

23. $8\frac{5}{6} - 4\frac{4}{6}$

 CHECK PROBLEM SOLVING

Write the operation(s). Then solve the problem. (pp. 320–321)

24. Justin had $1\frac{7}{8}$ pounds of ground beef. He used $1\frac{1}{8}$ pounds to make a meat loaf and $\frac{3}{8}$ pound for a hamburger. How much ground beef does he have left?

25. Ed worked $2\frac{3}{4}$ hours, and Tom worked $3\frac{1}{4}$ hours. Find the total time they worked.

Chapter CRCT Test Prep

NUMBERS AND OPERATIONS

1. **M4N6.b.** Fred rode his bike $\frac{4}{12}$ mile from his house to Jean's house. He and Jean then rode $\frac{5}{12}$ mile to the mall. How far did Fred ride from his house to the mall?

   A. $\frac{3}{4}$ miles

   B. $\frac{9}{24}$ miles

   C. $\frac{1}{3}$ miles

   D. $\frac{1}{12}$ miles

2. **M4N6.b.** Find the sum.

$$5\frac{3}{5} + 4\frac{2}{5}$$

   A. $1\frac{1}{5}$

   B. 9

   C. $9\frac{1}{2}$

   D. 10

3. **M4N6.b.** Which sum equals $1\frac{3}{8}$?

   A. $\frac{6}{8} + \frac{7}{8}$

   B. $\frac{5}{8} + \frac{7}{8}$

   C. $\frac{4}{8} + \frac{7}{8}$

   D. $\frac{4}{8} + \frac{9}{8}$

NUMBERS AND OPERATIONS

4. **M4N6.b.** The Wallaces lived in Macon for $5\frac{3}{4}$ years. Then they moved to Augusta. They lived there for $2\frac{2}{4}$ years before moving to Atlanta. How much longer did they live in Macon than in Augusta?

   A. $7\frac{5}{4}$ years more

   B. $7\frac{1}{4}$ years more

   C. $3\frac{5}{4}$ years more

   D. $3\frac{1}{4}$ years more

5. **M4N6.b.** The combined area of Jordan's living room and dining room is $11\frac{7}{9}$ square yards. What could be the area of each room?

   A. living room: $4\frac{5}{9}$ square yards
      dining room: $6\frac{2}{9}$ square yards

   B. living room: $6\frac{6}{9}$ square yards
      dining room: $5\frac{2}{9}$ square yards

   C. living room: $5\frac{2}{9}$ square yards
      dining room: $6\frac{5}{9}$ square yards

   D. living room: $15\frac{1}{9}$ square yards
      dining room: $4\frac{6}{9}$ square yards

6. **M4N6.b.** Find the difference.

$$\frac{11}{12} - \frac{9}{12}$$

   A. $\frac{2}{24}$

   B. $\frac{1}{6}$

   C. $1\frac{2}{3}$

   D. 2

Cumulative CRCT Test Prep

DATA ANALYSIS

Use the bar graph below to answer question 7.

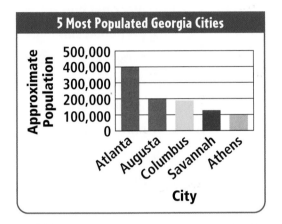

5 Most Populated Georgia Cities

Approximate Population: 500,000 / 400,000 / 300,000 / 200,000 / 100,000 / 0

City: Atlanta, Augusta, Columbus, Savannah, Athens

7. **M4D1.b.** What conclusion can you make based on the data in the graph?

A. Atlanta has twice as many people as Augusta.

B. Athens has half as many people as Savannah.

C. Columbus' population is more than the population of Savannah and Athens combined.

D. Augusta has twice as many people as Savannah.

8. **M4D1.c.** In May, 17 dogs were adopted from Pet Pals. In June, 23 dogs were adopted. In July, 26 were adopted. Which type of graph would be BEST to show these data?

A. line graph

B. pictograph

C. bar graph

D. double-bar graph

ALGEBRA

9. **M4A1.b.** Kia and her sisters had 6 boxes of juice. They drank 4 of them and then bought some more. Which expression shows the number of boxes they have now if □ represents the number of boxes they bought?

A. $\square - (6 + 4)$

B. $6 + (\square - 4)$

C. $(4 - \square) + 6$

D. $(6 - 4) + \square$

10. **M4A1.a.** What rule is shown in the table below?

INPUT	OUTPUT
38	32
25	19
19	13
12	6
7	1

A. Add 6.

B. Multiply by 2.

C. Subtract 6.

D. Divide by 2.

11. **M4A1.c.** What is the value of $(\triangle - 8) + 4$ if $\triangle = 12$?

A. 24

B. 16

C. 12

D. 8

GPS/CRCT Vocabulary

ELA4R3 The student understands and acquires new vocabulary and uses it correctly in reading and writing.

VOCABULARY

- point
- line
- ray
- line segment
- plane
- protractor
- degree(°)
- rotation
- diagonal line
- perpendicular
- congruent
- parallel
- rhombus
- trapezoid
- quadrilateral
- cube
- parallelogram
- rectangular prism
- proper fraction
- mixed fraction
- improper fraction

CONCEPT MATCH

MATERIALS *For each group of four* Vocabulary Cards, 21 index cards

- Work in a group of four. Make a set of picture cards or example cards for the terms.

- Mix up the vocabulary cards, and give each group member an equal number of cards. Mix up the picture/example cards, and place them face-up on the table.

- Match each of your vocabulary cards with its picture/example card.

- When everyone has finished, mix up your vocabulary cards. Pass them to the person on your left, and repeat the activity.

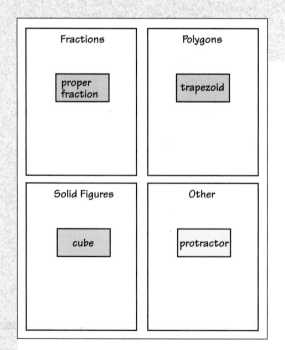

Fractions	Polygons
proper fraction	trapezoid

Solid Figures	Other
cube	protractor

MATH WORD WORK

MATERIALS *For each group* Vocabulary Cards, drawing paper

- Work with a group.

- On a sheet of drawing paper, draw 4 large rectangles, and label them *Fractions, Polygons, Solid Figures,* and *Other.*

- Take turns placing one of the vocabulary cards in the proper category.

CUT IT OUT

MATERIALS *For each student* construction paper, magazines, scissors, glue, crayons or markers

- Look through magazines for a picture or photograph that contains several geometric shapes.

- Cut out the picture or photograph, and glue it onto the center of the construction paper.

- Look at the vocabulary terms in the box on page 326. Find something in your picture or photograph that shows the vocabulary term, and circle it. Draw an arrow from the circle to the blank part of your paper, and write the vocabulary term so that the arrow points to it.

- Find as many objects as you can, but try to find at least four things that represent vocabulary terms.

WRITE ABOUT IT

- Choose any two vocabulary terms from the box on page 326.

- Write one sentence that includes both terms, but leave a blank line in place of each term. The sentence should show that you understand the mathematical meaning of each term.

- Trade papers with a partner, and complete each other's sentences. When you both have finished, check each other's work.

- Repeat the activity using three vocabulary terms.

- Try choosing more words and writing a short paragraph.

To measure the _____ of an angle, use a _____ .

Georgia Tasks

M4G1.c. Examine and classify quadrilaterals (including parallelograms, squares, rectangles, trapezoids, and rhombi). *also* **M4P4.c., M4P5, M4P5.b.**

SS4E1b. explain how *price incentives* affect people's behavior and choices.

Task A

PICTURE THIS

Many different geometric shapes can be seen outside the High Museum of Art in Atlanta. Often, when figures are shown in a photograph, they appear slightly different from how they are in real life.

a. Find something in the photo that looks like a quadrilateral. Trace the shape on tracing paper. How do you think it might appear in real life? Do you think it would be the same shape as your tracing? Explain.

b. There are many parallel and perpendicular lines shown in the photo. Create a picture using as many parallel and perpendicular lines as you can. You can also use curves. Describe the types of shapes that are in your picture.

Task B

SHARE YOUR PIZZA

Curtis, Joe, Sara, and Laura have a coupon for one free pizza at the Pizza Palace. They all want the same number of slices.

a. Tell which size pizza they should order. Explain your answer.

b. Write a fraction that names how much of the pizza will be left after each person eats 1 slice. Write an equivalent fraction for that amount.

c. Should the friends order the same size pizza if Laura decides she does not want any pizza? Explain.

PIZZA PALACE MENU

Size	Servings
Personal	4 slices
Small	6 slices
Medium	8 slices
Large	12 slices
Jumbo	16 slices

Maintain/Preview

Maintain

Measure the angle. Then classify the angle. (pp. 256–259)

1.

2.

3.

Classify the triangle or quadrilateral. (pp. 274–275, 276–279)

4.

5.

6.

Write an equivalent fraction. (pp. 296–297)

7. $\frac{3}{9}$

8. $\frac{7}{14}$

9. $\frac{4}{16}$

10. $\frac{15}{25}$

Add or subtract. (pp. 310–313, 314–315, 316–319)

11. $\frac{3}{6} + \frac{1}{6}$

12. $\frac{7}{12} - \frac{3}{12}$

13. $3\frac{7}{8} - 2\frac{6}{8}$

14. $9\frac{3}{5} + 4\frac{1}{5}$

15. Meghan has $6\frac{3}{5}$ yards of lace. Write $6\frac{3}{5}$ as an improper fraction. (pp. 300–303)

16. How many faces, edges, and vertices does a rectangular prism have? (pp. 282–285)

Preview

Choose ounces or pounds to measure the weight. (Chapter 16)

1.

2.

3.

4.

5.

6.

7.

8.

9.

Customary and Metric Measurement

Grizzly Bear

Cardinal

Raccoon

Ostrich

≡FAST FACT •
SCIENCE When animals walk through soft soil, they often leave tracks. People can look at the tracks and tell what type of animal has been there. For example, tracks with four toes on the front foot and five on the hind foot were made by a rodent.

Using Data
ANIMAL TRACKS

Track	Animal	Length
	Ostrich	14 cm
	Grizzly Bear	18 cm
	Cardinal	3 cm
	Raccoon	8 cm

INVESTIGATION Which animal has the largest track? the smallest? Measure your foot to the nearest centimeter. How does it compare to the tracks? Measure your foot using customary units. What unit of measure did you use?

CHECK WHAT YOU KNOW

Use this page to help you review and remember important skills needed for Chapter 16.

✓ MEASURE TO THE NEAREST INCH AND HALF INCH

Measure the length of each to the nearest inch.

1.

2.

Measure the length of each to the nearest $\frac{1}{2}$ inch.

3.

4.

✓ MEASURE TO THE NEAREST CENTIMETER

Measure the length of each object to the nearest centimeter.

5.

6.

7.

VOCABULARY POWER

REVIEW

measure [mezh′ər] *noun*

When *measure* is used as a noun, it means "a unit used for comparison." When used as a verb, it means "to find the size, quantity, amount, time, or degree of." Name some tools used for measuring.

PREVIEW

weight   foot (ft)

ounce (oz)   yard (yd)

pound (lb)   mile (mi)

ton (T)   millimeter

gram (g)   centimeter

kilogram (kg)   decimeter

linear units   meter

inch (in.)   kilometer

ON-LINE

www.harcourtschool.com/mathglossary

Length: Choose the Appropriate Unit

Concepts/Skill to Maintain Length. *also* M4P1.c.

► Learn

MEASURE UP! Have you ever wondered just how far you rode your bike or walked? You can use nonstandard units such as one rotation of the bike pedals and the length of your shoe, or you can use standard units such as miles and yards.

HANDS ON

Activity 1 MATERIALS: tape measure or yardstick

- Estimate and measure the distance from your desk to the classroom door, using your foot as the unit of measure. Record your estimate and the actual distance. Compare your results with your classmates' results.

- Estimate and measure the same distance in feet, using a tape measure or yardstick. Record your estimate and the actual distance. Compare your results with your classmates' results.

- How does your estimate compare to the distance you found by using a tape measure or yardstick?

Linear units are used to measure length, width, height, and distance. Understanding the sizes of different standard linear units will help you choose the appropriate units of measure to use.

Equivalent Measures
1 foot (ft) = 12 inches (in.)
1 yard (yd) = 3 feet
1 mile (mi) = 1,760 yards, or 5,280 feet

Examples

A An **inch (in.)** is about the length of your thumb from the first knuckle to the tip.

1 in.

Smaller objects, such as pencils or nails, are measured in inches.

B A **foot (ft)** is about the length of a sheet of paper.

A person's height or the length of a room is measured in feet.

1 ft

C A **yard (yd)** is about the length of a baseball bat.

1 yd

The length of a football field is measured in yards.

D A **mile (mi)** is about the distance you can walk in 20 minutes.

The distance a person travels in a car is measured in miles.

1 mi

More About Linear Units

At the Minnesota State Fair, large vegetables are lined up so judges can decide which vegetable is the biggest. The judges use string to compare the large vegetables.

You can use indirect measurement to compare the length of one object to the length of another.

Activity 2

MATERIALS: 2 apples, 2 pieces of string, scissors

- Use a string to find the distance around the first apple. Measure horizontally around the apple at its largest part.
- Cut or mark the string to show the distance around the apple.
- Then measure the second apple, using another piece of string.
- Compare the strings. How do the two apples compare?

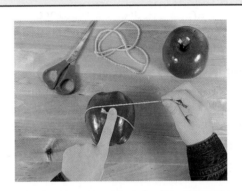

 Check

Technology Link

More Practice: Harcourt Mega Math Ice Station Exploration, *Linear Lab*, Level E

1. **Explain** how you can decide what linear unit to use.

Choose the most reasonable unit of measure. Write *in., ft, yd,* or *mi.*

2. The width of a book is about 8 ? .

3. The length of a car is about 14 ? .

4. Yesterday Jordan ran 3 ? .

5. The length of a license plate is about 1 ? .

6. The width of my thumb is about 1 ? .

7. The length of 15 football fields is about 1 ? .

Name the greater measurement.

8. 2 yd or 2 mi

9. 16 ft or 16 in.

10. 32 in. or 32 yd

11. 24 in. or 24 mi

12. 3 ft or 3 yd

13. 56 mi or 56 yd

LESSON CONTINUES

Choose the most reasonable unit of measure.
Write *in., ft, yd,* **or** *mi.*

14. The distance from New York to Los Angeles is 2,794 _?_.

15. The length of the playground is 22 _?_.

16. The length of a goldfish is about 3 _?_.

17. The door of your classroom is about 1 _?_ wide.

18. The width of my notebook is about 10 _?_.

19. The height of a desk is about 2 _?_.

Name the greater measurement.

20. 400 ft or 400 yd

21. 10 in. or 10 ft

22. 20 yd or 20 mi

Name the lesser measurement.

23. 10 yd or 10 ft

24. 128 in. or 128 yd

25. 30 in. or 30 ft

USE DATA For 26–29, use the table.

26. Compare the lengths of the cars. Write the types of cars in order from shortest to longest.

27. How many inches longer is the longest car compared to the shortest car?

28. The garage in Jim's house is 228 inches long. If Jim buys a sedan, will his car fit in his garage? Explain.

AVERAGE CAR LENGTHS (from bumper to bumper)	
Type of Car	**Length (in inches)**
Coupe	175
Sedan	215
SUV	206
Station Wagon	198

29. 📓 **Write About It** Explain why you think car makers describe the lengths of their cars in inches rather than in feet or yards.

30. MULTISTEP Karen bought 3 yards of lace for $2 per yard and 2 yards of fabric for $6 per yard. She gave the clerk a $20 bill. How much change did she receive?

31. Liz took a trip from Tifton, Georgia, to Huntsville, Alabama. Which unit of measure would you use to describe the distance between these two cities?

32. Measure the length of your math book by using the length of your thumb from the first knuckle to the tip. How many thumb lengths is it? How many inches is it?

33. Think about how long a yard is. Then estimate in yards the distance from the school office to your classroom. Choose a tool and a unit, and measure the distance. Record your estimate and measurement.

34. ✒ **Write a problem** about choosing a customary unit of measure to solve a problem.

Maintain Skills

35. What is the length of the paper clip to the nearest inch?

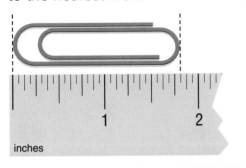

inches

CRCT Test Prep

36. M4N6.b. Haki rode $2\frac{5}{6}$ miles on his bike on Monday and $1\frac{1}{6}$ miles on Tuesday. How many more miles did he ride on Monday than on Tuesday? (p. 316)

A. 4 mi

B. $2\frac{2}{3}$ mi

C. $2\frac{1}{6}$ mi

D. $1\frac{2}{3}$ mi

Problem Solving Thinker's Corner 💡

MEASURING TOOLS Whenever you need to measure an object or a distance, you should choose the appropriate tool according to the size of the object or the distance.

What tools could you use to measure the distance from your house to your school?

TOOLS
Distances greater than 1 yard:
• Odometer: mile
• Pedometer: foot, mile
• Measuring wheel: foot
Lengths less than 1 foot:
• Ruler: inch
Lengths greater than 1 foot:
• Tape measure: inch, foot, yard
• Yardstick: inch, foot, yard
• Folding rule: inch, foot, yard

pedometer   measuring wheel   odometer

You could use a pedometer, a measuring wheel, or an odometer.

Give an example of an object or a distance you would measure by using the tool.

1. ruler

2. tape measure

3. odometer

4. measuring wheel

5. pedometer

6. yardstick

Measure Fractional Parts

Concepts/Skill to Maintain Length. *also* M4P3.a., M4P3.b., M4P3.c., M4P3.d., M4P4.a., M4P4.b., M4P5.b., M4P5.c.

▶ **Learn**

LEAF LESSON Mary collected and classified leaves for her science project. Part of her assignment was to measure each leaf to the nearest $\frac{1}{2}$ inch and $\frac{1}{4}$ inch.

Fractional units, such as $\frac{1}{2}$ inch and $\frac{1}{4}$ inch, are used to measure lengths that are between two whole units.

Measuring to the nearest fractional unit is similar to rounding a number.

Examples

A   Measure to the nearest $\frac{1}{2}$ inch.

The length is closer to 2 in. than to $1\frac{1}{2}$ in.
So, the leaf's length is about 2 in.

B   Measure to the nearest $\frac{1}{4}$ inch.

The length is closer to $1\frac{3}{4}$ in. than to 2 in.

So, the leaf's length is about $1\frac{3}{4}$ in.

1. **Explain** how to find the $\frac{1}{2}$-inch marks and the $\frac{1}{4}$-inch marks on a ruler.

Measure to the nearest $\frac{1}{2}$ inch. Then measure to the nearest $\frac{1}{4}$ inch.

2.

3.

▶ **Practice and Problem Solving** Extra Practice, page 350, Set B

Measure to the nearest $\frac{1}{2}$ inch. Then measure to the nearest $\frac{1}{4}$ inch.

4.

5.

Use a ruler. Draw a line for each length.

6. 2 in.

7. $1\frac{1}{2}$ in.

8. $3\frac{3}{4}$ in.

9. $5\frac{1}{4}$ in.

USE DATA For 10–11, use the picture.

10. Find the length of the rock to the nearest inch and nearest $\frac{1}{2}$ inch.

11. Find the length of the fossilized leaf in the rock to the nearest inch.

12. **Vocabulary Power** *Inch* comes from the Latin word *uncia*. A uncia was a unit of length $\frac{1}{12}$ of the length of the Roman unit called a *pes*. How is the uncia similar to the inch?

13. ✏️ **Write About It** Could you measure an object to the nearest $\frac{1}{4}$ in. and get a measurement that is a whole number? Explain.

14. Each side of a square patio is 10 feet long. Starting at one corner, there is a plant every 2 feet around the border of the patio. How many plants are around the patio?

Maintain Skills

15. Add. 0.6 + 0.8

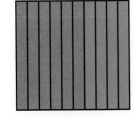 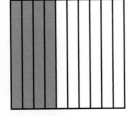

CRCT Test Prep

16. **M4N7.b.** Find the value of the expression. (p. 130)

$$15 - (5 \times 2)$$

A. 5

B. 10

C. 20

D. 25

Customary Weight

 M4M1.a. Use standard and metric units to measure the weight of objects. *also* M4M1.b., M4M1.c., M4P2.a., M4P2.b., M4P2.c., M4P5.c.

Quick Review

Multiply each number by 16.

1. 8   **2.** 10

3. 6   **4.** 5

5. 14

 Learn

HOW HEAVY? How would you describe the weight of a toy car? the weight of a real car?

Weight is the measure of how heavy an object is. The customary units for measuring weight are **ounce (oz)**, **pound (lb)**, and **ton (T)**.

VOCABULARY

weight	pound (lb)
ounce (oz)	ton (T)

One toy car weighs about 1 oz.

One remote-control car weighs about 1 lb.

Equivalent Weights
16 ounces (oz) = 1 pound (lb)
2,000 pounds (lb) = 1 ton (T)

One real car weighs about 1 T.

HANDS ON

Activity   **MATERIALS:** spring scale, 5 classroom objects
Choose 5 classroom objects that you can weigh with your scale.

STEP 1

Make a table. Estimate the weight of each object in ounces or pounds. Record the object and estimated weight.

OBJECT	ESTIMATE	ACTUAL
?	■	■

STEP 2

Weigh each object. Record each actual weight in your table. Compare your actual measurement to your estimate.

• Are your estimates reasonable?
• What tool do you think is used to measure the weight of a car?

Reasonable Unit of Weight

Marlon got a check-up. He wants to know how much he weighs. Will the doctor tell his weight in ounces, pounds, or tons?

The most reasonable unit of weight is usually the greatest unit that is not greater than what is being weighed.

Marlon weighs more than *1 ounce* and more than *1 pound*. He does not weigh more than *1 ton*. The greatest unit that is not greater than Marlon's weight is the *pound*.

So, the doctor will tell Marlon's weight in pounds.

Examples

A What is the most reasonable unit of weight for an airplane?

Think: An airplane weighs more than *1 ounce*, more than *1 pound*, and more than *1 ton*.

So, the most reasonable unit of weight is the ton.

B What is the most reasonable unit of weight for a pen?

Think: A pen weighs more than *1 ounce* but less than *1 pound* or *1 ton*.

So, the most reasonable unit of weight is the ounce.

▶ Check

1. Explain how to determine the most reasonable unit for measuring the weight of a baseball.

Choose the more reasonable measurement.

2. 15 oz or 15 lb

3. 1 lb or 1 T

4. 14 oz or 14 lb

5. 1 oz or 1 lb

6. 16 oz or 16 lb

7. 3 lb or 3 T

Choose the most reasonable unit of weight. Write *a, b,* or *c*.

8.

a. ounce
b. pound
c. ton

9.

a. ounce
b. pound
c. ton

LESSON CONTINUES

Estimate, and then find the actual weight of each object.

10. your math book

11. a shoe

Practice and Problem Solving ⟩ Extra Practice, page 350, Set C

Choose the more reasonable measurement.

12. 5 lb or 5 T

13. 12 oz or 12 lb

14. 2 lb or 2 T

15. 80 oz or 80 lb

16. 3 oz or 3 T

17. 1 lb or 1 T

Choose the most reasonable unit of weight. Write *a, b,* or *c.*

18.

a. ounce
b. pound
c. ton

19.

a. ounce
b. pound
c. ton

Estimate, and then find the actual weight of each object.

20. your notebook

21. a pencil

22. a stapler

Compare. Write < or > for each ●.

23. 23 oz ● 23 T

24. 16 lb ● 16 oz

25. 3T ● 3 lb

USE DATA For 26–28, use the table.

26. Hanna mailed a 2-oz letter to her aunt and a 2-lb book to her friend. She sent both by express mail. How much did both cost?

27. **REASONING** Martin wants to send a 3-lb toy to his cousin Elijah and a 2-lb toy to Elijah's sister. Should he put both toys in one box or mail them separately? Explain.

28. Kevin's phone bill must be paid by tomorrow. The phone bill is $65.99. How much will it cost to pay the bill and mail Kevin's payment by express mail?

29. Write a problem about weight using the data in the table. Solve your problem.

EXPRESS MAIL RATES FOR POST OFFICE TO ADDRESSEE SERVICE	
Weight	**Cost**
Up to 8 ounces	$13.65
Over 8 ounces up to 2 pounds	$17.85
Up to 3 pounds	$21.05
Up to 4 pounds	$24.20
Up to 5 pounds	$27.30
Up to 6 pounds	$30.40
Up to 7 pounds	$33.45
Up to 8 pounds	$34.75
Up to 9 pounds	$36.20
Up to 10 pounds	$37.50

30. MULTISTEP Jill's dog Bailey has been on a diet. He lost 2 lb a week for each of 4 weeks. Now he weighs 72 lb. How much did Bailey weigh before he went on the diet?

31. MULTISTEP Together, Beth and Sari's book bags weigh 25 lb. Beth's bag weighs 3 lb more than Sari's. How much does Sari's book bag weigh?

Maintain Skills

32. What is the value of the blue digit in 45,629?

33. Mira stocked 9 shelves with 16 boxes of cereal on each shelf. How many boxes of cereal did she stock?

34. What is the perimeter of the square?

16 in.

16 in. [ ] 16 in.

16 in.

CRCT Test Prep

35. **M4N6.b.** What is the sum $\frac{3}{5} + \frac{3}{5}$?
(p. 310)

A. $1\frac{1}{5}$ C. $\frac{4}{5}$

B. 1 D. $\frac{6}{10}$

36. **M4N4.a.** What is the quotient $968 \div 54$? (p. 232)

A. 16 r4   C. 17 r14

B. 17 r9   D. 17 r50

Problem Solving LINKUP...to Science

The chart below provides information about some animals that live in Georgia. Some of the units of measure are missing from the chart.

ANIMAL	FACTS	PICTURE
Sherman's fox squirrel	They live in Georgia and Florida, weigh about 3 _____, and are about 30 _____ long.	
Feral hogs	Feral hogs are domestic hogs that now live in the wild. Some feral hogs are very large and can weigh over 1 _____.	
Gopher tortoise	This is Georgia's official state reptile. It can weigh up to 15 _____ and live for 50 years.	

1. Copy the facts from the chart. Use the pictures and what you know about units of weight and length to complete the facts.

2. Research two more Georgia animals. Make a chart like the one above for the animals you found.

Metric Length

Concepts/Skill to Maintain Length.
also **M4P4.a., M4P4.b.**

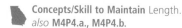
Learn

HOW LONG? HOW SHORT? The western pygmy-blue butterfly is one of the smallest butterflies. Measure the width of its wingspan to the nearest centimeter using a metric ruler.

The wingspan of this butterfly is between 2 and 3 centimeters. To the nearest centimeter, the wingspan is 2 centimeters.

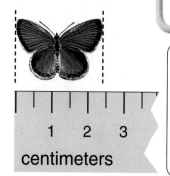

1   2   3
centimeters

You can use different metric units to measure length or distance.

VOCABULARY

millimeter (mm)   **centimeter (cm)**

decimeter (dm)   **meter (m)**

kilometer (km)

Equivalent Measures

1 centimeter (cm) = 10 millimeters (mm)

1 decimeter (dm) = 10 centimeters

1 meter (m) = 1,000 millimeters

1 meter = 10 decimeters

1 kilometer (km) = 1,000 meters

A **millimeter (mm)** is about the thickness of a dime.	A **centimeter (cm)** is about the width of your index finger.	A **decimeter (dm)** is about the width of an adult's hand.	A **meter (m)** is about the width of a door.
		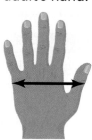	

HANDS ON

Activity 1   MATERIALS: centimeter ruler, meterstick

• Estimate, and then measure the lengths of 5 objects in your classroom to the nearest millimeter, centimeter, or meter. Record the estimates and actual measurements in a table.

• How did you estimate the length of each object?

• Order the objects you measured from least to greatest length.

Object	Unit of Measure	Estimate	Measurement
1.			
2.			
3.			

Greater Lengths

Activity 2

MATERIALS: centimeter ruler, meterstick

Now measure your desktop.

- Choose a unit of measure. Record all the linear measurements of your desktop to the nearest centimeter or meter.

- Compare your results to your classmates' results. Are the measurements of your desktops the same? If not, why not?

Mrs. Chen's class is taking a bus to the zoo. She wants to know how far the zoo is from the school. What unit of measure should she use?

Technology Link

More Practice: Harcourt Mega Math Ice Station Exploration, *Linear Lab,* Levels I and J

Longer distances and lengths can be measured in kilometers. A **kilometer (km)** is about the length of 10 football fields.

So, Mrs. Chen should measure the distance from the school to the zoo in kilometers.

MATH IDEA The millimeter, centimeter, meter, and kilometer are metric units of length or distance.

▶ Check

1. **Estimate** and measure the length of a poster or bulletin board in your classroom. Then explain how you decided what unit of measure to use.

Use a centimeter ruler or a meterstick to measure each item. Write the measurement and unit of measure used.

2. length of a thumbtack   3. length of a stapler   4. length of a classroom

Choose the most reasonable unit of measure. Write *mm, cm, m,* or *km.*

5.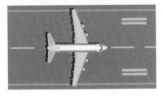

The length of an airport runway is about 3 _?_.

6.

The length of a baseball bat is about 1 _?_.

7.

The length of a key is about 5 _?_.

Use a centimeter ruler or a meterstick to measure each item. Write the measurement and unit of measure used.

8. length of a pencil

9. width of a poster

10. length of a chalkboard

Choose the most reasonable unit of measure. Write *mm, cm, m,* or *km*.

11.

The height of the table is about 76 _?_ .

12.

The length of the worm is about 10 _?_ .

13.

The length of the car is about 4 _?_ .

14. distance between two cities

15. height of a maple tree

16. thickness of a string

Compare. Write < or > for each ●.

17. 98 cm ● 98 m

18. 100 m ● 100 km

19. 87 mm ● 87 cm

Use a metric ruler. Draw a line for each length.

20. 20 centimeters

21. 35 millimeters

22. 123 millimeters

For 23–24, use the ruler to find the distance.

23. between point A and point B

24. between point B and point D

25. **MULTISTEP** Hudson ran a 5-kilometer race. Use the table to find how many minutes he ran in all.

HUDSON'S RACE	
Kilometer	**Time (each kilometer)**
1 and 2	5 min
3, 4, and 5	6 min

26. Tell whether the width of your notebook, your teacher's desk, and your desk are *about a meter, less than a meter,* or *more than a meter.* Then order the widths from greatest to least.

27. **REASONING** Cary's broken ruler begins at the 16-cm mark. If she draws a 7-cm line beginning at the 16-cm mark, at which mark will she stop?

28. Five students are 149 centimeters, 151 centimeters, 139 centimeters, 152 centimeters, and 144 centimeters tall. How much taller is the tallest student than the shortest student?

29. In the first 3 weeks of their science project, Lea's plant grew 197 millimeters, and Stacy's plant grew 211 millimeters. How much more did Stacy's plant grow than Lea's?

Maintain Skills

30. 432 ÷ 6   **31.** 57 × 8

32. What is the value of the blue digit in 5,683?

33. Zoe's classroom has a total of 35 desks. Each row has 7 desks in it. How many rows of desks are there?

CRCT Test Prep

34. **M4N4.a.** Greg has some nickels in one pocket and 4 dimes in the other. He has a total of 65¢. How many nickels does Greg have in his pocket? (p. 134)

A. 25   C. 7
B. 10   D. 5

Problem Solving LiNKUP ... to Reading

STRATEGY • USE GRAPHIC AIDS Some maps show distances with metric units. In many countries, distances from one city to another city are measured in kilometers. A map scale shows how distances on a map compare to actual distances. This scale shows 1 centimeter = 32 kilometers.

Use the scale to find the actual distance from Paris to Clermont.

Using a centimeter ruler, measure the length between the cities on the map. The length is about 2 centimeters. Since there are 32 kilometers in each centimeter, multiply 2 by 32.

So, 2 lengths × 32 kilometers = 64 kilometers.

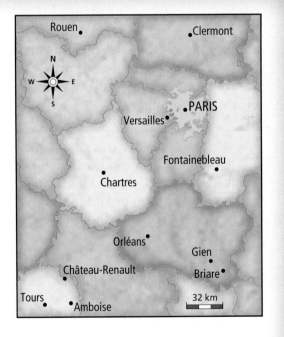

Estimate the distances in centimeters. Then use the scale to find the actual distances.

1. Tours to Versailles

2. Gien to Paris

3. Chartres to Château-Renault

4. Briare to Tours

5

HANDS ON

Metric Weight

M4M1.b. Know units used to measure weight (gram, kilogram, ounce, pound, and ton). *also* **M4M1.a., M4M1.c., M4P2.a., M4P2.b., M4P2.c., M4P3.a., M4P3.b., M4P3.c., M4P3.d., M4P5.c.**

▶ **Explore**

Weight is the measure of how heavy an object is. Metric units of weight are the **gram (g)** and the **kilogram (kg)**.

The weight of a dollar bill or a small paper clip is about 1 gram.

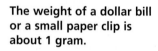

The weight of a baseball bat is about 1 kilogram.

Activity

Use a spring scale to find the weight of other objects.

STEP 1

Find the weight of each of 5 objects. Make a table. Estimate the weight of each object in grams or kilograms. Record the object and the estimated weight in the table.

OBJECT	ESTIMATE	ACTUAL
1.		
2.		
3.		
4.		
5.		

STEP 2

Weigh each object. Record the actual measurements to the nearest gram or kilogram in your table.

• Explain how to order the items you measured from least to greatest in weight.

Try It

Measure the weight.

a. a stapler
b. a box of crayons

We have a spring scale. Will the stapler weigh more than or less than 1 kilogram?

You can compare weights using < and >.

Equivalent Weight
1 kg = 1,000 g

Examples

A Compare. 6 kg ● 6 g
Think: There are 1,000 g in 1 kg.

So, 6 kg > 6 g.

B Compare. 50 g ● 50 kg
Think: There are 1,000 g in 1 kg.

So, 50 g < 50 kg.

▶ Practice and Problem Solving

Choose the more reasonable measurement.

1.

1 g or 1 kg

2.

20 g or 200 g

3.

10 g or 10 kg

4.

40 kg or 4,000 kg

USE DATA For 5–6, use the bar graph.

5. Find the vegetable whose sales increased from Day 1 to Day 2. How many more kilograms were sold on Day 2 than on Day 1?

6. Find the total weight of the vegetables sold during the two days.

7. REASONING The total weight of two backpacks is 20 pounds. One backpack is 2 pounds less than twice the weight of the other backpack. What is the weight of each backpack?

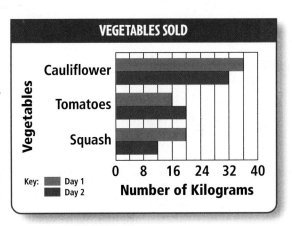

VEGETABLES SOLD

Cauliflower

Tomatoes

Squash

Vegetables

0   8   16   24   32   40
Number of Kilograms

Key: ▬ Day 1
▬ Day 2

Maintain Skills

Find the perimeter.

8.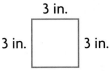
3 in.
3 in.   3 in.
3 in.

9.
2 cm
6 cm   6 cm
2 cm

CRCT Test Prep

10. **M4N4.a.** There are 256 cookies to be placed on 8 platters. How many cookies will be on each platter?

(p. 214)

A. 22   C. 32
B. 23   D. 37

6 Problem Solving Strategy
Make a Diagram

M4P5. Students will represent mathematics in multiple ways. *also* **M4P1.a., M4P1.b., M4P1.c., M4P1.d., M4P3.a., M4P3.b., M4P3.c., M4P3.d.**

PROBLEM Darrell and Charles each caught a fish while deep-sea fishing. The two fish have a weight of 10 kilograms. The weight of Charles's fish is 1 kilogram more than twice the weight of Darrell's fish. What is the weight of each fish?

UNDERSTAND

- What are you asked to find?
- What information will you use?

PLAN

- What strategy can you use to solve the problem?
  You can *make a diagram*.

SOLVE

- How can you use the strategy to solve the problem?
  Make a diagram showing the relationship between the weights of the two fish.

Charles's fish	▪ kg	▪ kg	1 kg	} Total weight
Darrell's fish	▪ kg			} is 10 kilograms.

Subtract 1 kilogram from 10 kilograms to find the sum of the three equal parts. $10 - 1 = 9$

Divide the sum by 3 to find the value of each part. $9 \div 3 = 3$

Each part is 3 kilograms, so Darrell's fish has a weight of 3 kilograms, and Charles's fish has a weight of $3 + 3 + 1$, or 7 kilograms.

CHECK

- What other strategy could you use?

Make a diagram to solve.

1. Val, Brent, and Don caught a total of 24 fish. Val caught 4 more fish than Brent. Don caught twice as many fish as Brent. How many fish did each catch?

For 2–3, use this information. Matt's dog is 15 centimeters longer than Michael's dog. Derek's dog is 9 centimeters longer than twice the length of Michael's dog. Michael's dog is 30 centimeters long.

2. What should you do to find the length of Matt's dog?
   A Subtract 15 cm from the length of Derek's dog.
   B Add 15 cm to the length of Derek's dog.
   C Subtract 15 cm from the length of Michael's dog.
   D Add 15 cm to the length of Michael's dog.

3. What are the lengths of Matt's, Michael's, and Derek's dogs in centimeters?
   F 18 cm; 30 cm; 15 cm
   G 45 cm; 30 cm; 69 cm
   H 45 cm; 30 cm; 60 cm
   J 180 cm; 30 cm; 150 cm

Mixed Strategy Practice

USE DATA For 4–5, use the table.

4. The Martins went fishing for the weekend. They rented a fishing boat for 4 hours. They also rented 3 fishing poles and bought one bucket of bait. How much money did the Martins spend?

Lakeside Fish Camp
Open Daily at 10 A.M.
Boat Rental.............. $25 per hour
Fishing Pole Rental..... $4 per day
Bucket of Bait............. $5 each

5. The Kells arrived at the Lakeside Fish Camp when it opened. They spent 4 hours fishing, $\frac{1}{2}$ hour eating lunch, and $1\frac{1}{2}$ hours driving home from the camp. At what time did they get home?

6. Jay and Norma work as fishing guides. They each work every other day. If Norma works this Saturday, who will work on the Saturday 4 weeks from this Saturday? Who will work on the Saturday 7 weeks from now?

7. Felipe has a piece of bamboo that is 540 centimeters long. To make 2 fishing poles, he shortened it by 60 centimeters and cut it in half. How long is each fishing pole?

8. ✏️ **Write a problem** that can be solved by making a diagram. Exchange problems with a classmate and solve.

Extra Practice

Set A (pp. 332–335)

**Choose the most reasonable unit of measure.
Write *in., ft, yd,* or *mi.*

1. The length of my foot is about 8 _?_.

2. The height of my dog is about 3 _?_.

3. The width of my room is 4 _?_.

Name the greater measurement.

4. 15 ft or 15 yd

5. 300 mi or 300 ft

6. 39 in. or 39 yd

Set B (pp. 336–337)

Estimate to the nearest inch. Then measure to the nearest $\frac{1}{4}$ inch.

1.

2.

Estimate to the nearest $\frac{1}{2}$ inch. Then measure to the nearest $\frac{1}{8}$ inch.

3.

4.

Set C (pp. 338–341)

Choose the more reasonable measurement.

1. 50 lb or 50 T

2. 12 oz or 12 lb

3. 10 lb or 10 T

Set D (pp. 342–345)

**Choose the most reasonable unit of measure.
Write *mm, cm, m,* or *km.*

1. The width of a book is about 22 _?_.

2. The length of a marker is about 13 _?_.

3. The height of a desk is about 1 _?_.

Compare. Write < or > for each ●.

4. 750 m ● 750 mm

5. 20 cm ● 20 km

6. 2 cm ● 2 mm

Review/Test

CHECK VOCABULARY AND CONCEPTS

Choose the best term from the box.

1. Units used to measure length, width, height, and distance are ? units. (p. 332)

2. The customary units for weight are ?, ?, and ?. (p. 338)

Vocabulary

foot	ton
linear	yard
mile	millimeter
ounce	centimeter
pound	meter

✓ CHECK SKILLS

Choose the most reasonable unit of measure.
Write *in., ft, yd,* or *mi.* (pp. 332–335)

3. The height of a desk is about 3 ?.

4. The length of a bus route is about 10 ?.

5. The width of a door is about 36 ?.

Name the greater measurement. (pp. 332–335, 338–341, 342–345)

6. 300 yd or 300 ft

7. 40 cm or 40 m

8. 4 T or 4 lb

9. Measure to the nearest $\frac{1}{4}$ inch. (pp. 336–337)

10. Measure to the nearest centimeter. (pp. 342–345)

Choose the most reasonable unit of measure. Write *mm, cm, m, km, g,* or *kg.* (pp. 342–345, 346–347)

11. the weight of a pin

12. the length of a swimming pool

13. the width of a fingernail

CHECK PROBLEM SOLVING

Solve. (pp. 348–349)

14. The weight of a box of cookies is 60 grams. The weight of a box of crackers is 3 grams more than twice the weight of the box of cookies. What is the weight of the box of crackers?

15. Karl's grandmother bought 72 inches of ribbon. She cut the ribbon into two pieces. One piece is 6 inches longer than twice the length of the other piece. What is the length of each piece of ribbon?

Chapter CRCT Test Prep

MEASUREMENT

1. **M4M1.b.** What is the most reasonable unit of measure for the weight of a large dog?

A. pound

B. ton

C. gram

D. ounce

2. **M4M1.a.** Which object pictured below weighs about 1 ton?

A.

B.

C.

D.

3. **M4M1.c.** Which of the following is the LEAST measure of weight?

A. 1 pound

B. $\frac{1}{2}$ pound

C. 1 ton

D. 1 ounce

MEASUREMENT

4. **M4M1.b.** What is the most reasonable measurement for the weight of the school bus?

A.   5 grams

B.   5 kilograms

C. 5,000 grams

D. 5,000 kilograms

5. **M4M1.a.** Christopher bought a bag of apples that weighs 4 kilograms. Which of the following objects weighs about the same as the bag of apples?

A.

B.

C.

D.

6. **M4M1.c.** Which of the following correctly compares one measurement to another?

A. 20 kilograms < 20 grams

B. 5 grams < 5 kilograms

C. 1 kilogram > 10 kilograms

D. 1 gram > 1 kilogram

Cumulative CRCT Test Prep

NUMBERS AND OPERATIONS

Use the table below to answer question 7.

Distances Between Selected Cities in Georgia to the Nearest Mile	
Cities	**Distance**
Macon to Atlanta	76
Savannah to Atlanta	225
Augusta to Atlanta	139
Macon to Savannah	161
Augusta to Savannah	111

7. **M4N2.d.** The Marleys drove from Atlanta to Macon to Savannah. The Johnsons drove from Atlanta to Augusta to Savannah. About how many miles in all did the family who drove the greater distance travel?

   A. about 250 miles

   B. about 240 miles

   C. about 160 miles

   D. about 10 miles

8. **M4N1.b.** Georgia has an area of fifty-nine thousand, four hundred forty-one square miles. What is this number in standard form?

   A. 594,401

   B. 590,441

   C. 59,441

   D. 59,401

GEOMETRY

9. **M4G1.a.** Which triangle can be classified as an acute triangle?

   A.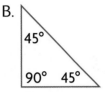
   60° 105° 15°

   B.
   45° 90° 45°

   C.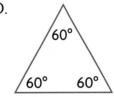
   140° 20° 20°

   D.
   60° 60° 60°

10. **M4G1.d.** Which statement is ALWAYS true about a rhombus and a rectangle?

    A. It has 4 equal sides.

    B. It has 4 right angles.

    C. It has 2 pairs of parallel sides.

    D. It has 4 pairs of parallel sides.

11. **M4G2.c.** What figure can you make by folding this pattern?

    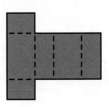

    A. a cube

    B. a rectangular prism

    C. a hexagonal prism

    D. a triangular prism

Perimeter and Area of Plane Figures

≡FAST FACT • ART You're flying in an airplane over fields in Eudora, Kansas. You look down and see a huge vase filled with sunflowers! This image was made by artist Stan Herd. Using materials such as crops, rocks, and mounds of soil, he designs huge pictures that cover from $\frac{1}{4}$ acre to 160 acres. To make the *Sunflower Field*, he planted 10,000 sunflowers.

INVESTIGATION How could you estimate the area of just the vase? Each square on the grid stands for 1 acre.

Using Data
SUNFLOWER FIELD BY STAN HERD

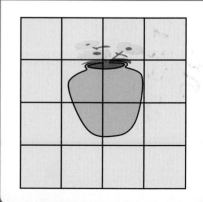

CHECK WHAT YOU KNOW

Use this page to help you review and remember important skills needed for Chapter 17.

FIND PERIMETER

Count to find the perimeter of each figure.

1. 　　2. 　　3. 　　4.

FIND AREA

Count to find the area of each figure in square units.

5. 　　6. 　　7. 　　8.

EXPRESSIONS WITH VARIABLES

Find the value of the expression.

9. $6 + 2 + \star$ if $\star = 6$　　10. $3 + \square + 5$ if $\square = 4$　　11. $\triangle + 16 + 8$ if $\triangle = 7$

12. $4 + \triangle + 4 + 8$ if $\triangle = 8$　13. $3 + 3 + 2 + \square$ if $\square = 2$　14. $5 + \star + 3 + 6$ if $\star = 9$

15. $4 \times \square$ if $\square = 5$　　16. $7 \times \triangle$ if $\triangle = 3$　　17. $\star \times 6$ if $\star = 2$　　18. $2 \times \square$ if $\square = 12$

19. $3 \times \triangle$ if $\triangle = 2$　　20. $6 \times \star$ if $\star = 7$　　21. $\square \times 5$ if $\square = 8$　　22. $9 \times \triangle$ if $\triangle = 11$

VOCABULARY POWER

REVIEW

square [skwâr] *noun*

Square is the root of the word *squadron*, which originally meant "a square array of soldiers." How does this help you understand the term, *square unit*?

PREVIEW

perimeter

formula

area

GO ON-LINE

www.harcourtschool.com/mathglossary

Find Perimeter

Concepts/Skill to Maintain Perimeter
also M4A1.b., M4A1.c., M4N7.b., M4P5.c.

▶ Learn

MEASURING MATH **Perimeter** is the distance around a figure. You can use what you know about units of length to help you estimate and measure perimeter.

HANDS ON

Activity **MATERIALS:** customary and metric rulers

STEP 1

Copy the table. Estimate the perimeter of the cover of your math book in centimeters. Record your estimate.

STEP 2

Measure the length of each side to the nearest centimeter. Then add the lengths of the sides to find the perimeter.

STEP 3

Choose two other objects in your classroom to measure. Choose the most appropriate unit of measure for each object. Estimate the perimeter and then measure it.

PERIMETER			
Object	Unit	Estimate	Measure
math book	cm		

- How do your measurements compare to your estimates?

- How did you decide which unit to use to measure each object?

Examples Find the perimeter.

A Add the lengths of the sides.

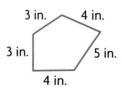

3 in. + 4 in. + 5 in. + 4 in. + 3 in. = 19 in.
The perimeter is 19 inches.

B Add the lengths of the sides.

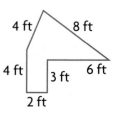

4 ft + 4 ft + 8 ft + 6 ft + 3 ft + 2 ft = 27 ft
The perimeter is 27 feet.

Use a Formula to Find Perimeter

The amusement park has a safety fence around its carousel. What is the perimeter of the fence?

You can use a **formula**, or mathematical rule, to find perimeter. Since the carousel's safety fence has 5 sides, use a formula that has 5 variables.

P = sum of the length of the sides

$P = a + b + c + d + e$

Use a letter as a variable to represent the length of each side.

$P = 14 + 17 + 13 + 15 + 16$

$P = 75$

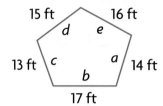

So, the perimeter of the safety fence is 75 feet.

You can use a formula to find the perimeter of a rectangle and of a square.

Polygon	Perimeter	Formula
rectangle	Perimeter = length + width + length + width	$P = l + w + l + w$
	or	or
	Perimeter = 2 × length + 2 × width	$P = (2 \times l) + (2 \times w)$
square	Perimeter = side + side + side + side	$P = s + s + s + s$
	or	or
	Perimeter = 4 × side	$P = 4 \times s$

More Examples

C

7 in.
5 in.   5 in.
7 in.

Use the formula.
$P = (2 \times l) + (2 \times w)$
$P = (2 \times 7) + (2 \times 5)$
$P = 14 + 10$
$P = 24$
The perimeter is 24 inches.

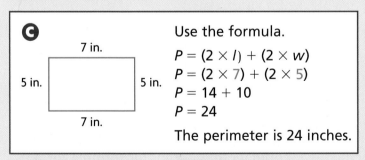

D

3 ft
3 ft

Use the formula.
$P = 4 \times s$
$P = 4 \times 3$
$P = 12$
The perimeter is 12 feet.

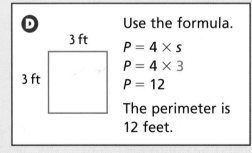

▶ Check

1. **Estimate** the perimeter of your desk in inches. Then measure the perimeter to the nearest $\frac{1}{4}$ inch, and compare the measurement to your estimate.

LESSON CONTINUES ▶

Find the perimeter.

2.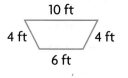
14 m
7 m
15 m

3.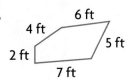
6 ft
4 ft
2 ft
5 ft
7 ft

4.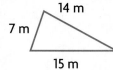
12 in.
3 in.

5.
9 cm
9 cm

Find the perimeter.

6.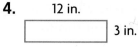
10 ft
4 ft   4 ft
6 ft

7.
12 in.
12 in.   12 in.
12 in.

8.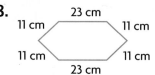
23 cm
11 cm   11 cm
11 cm   11 cm
23 cm

9.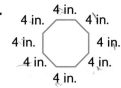
4 in.
4 in.   4 in.
4 in.   4 in.
4 in.   4 in.
4 in.

10.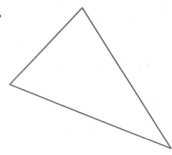
2 yd
4 yd
7 yd
3 yd
6 yd

11.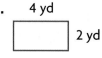
11 m
4 m   5 m
10 m   15 m
15 m

12.
4 cm
2 cm 1 cm
3 cm   5 cm
3 cm

13.
15 yd   11 yd
7 yd
21 yd   24 yd
32 yd

Use a formula to find the perimeter.

14.
12 yd
9 yd

15.
11 cm
11 cm

16.
4 yd
2 yd

17.
13 m
13 m

Measure with a ruler to find the perimeter.

18.

19.

20.

21. REASONING An equilateral triangle and a square each have a perimeter of 24 inches. Draw each figure.

22. Write About It Explain how you could write a perimeter formula for an equilateral triangle.

23. **?** What's the Question? A quadrilateral has sides with lengths of 4 feet, 5 feet, 8 feet, and 10 feet. The answer is 27 feet.

24. REASONING The perimeter of a rectangle is 26 centimeters. The length is 8 centimeters. What is the width?

25. MULTISTEP The Wegners are putting a fence around their yard. Their rectangular yard is 60 feet wide by 24 feet long. If each 6-foot panel costs $21, how much will the fence cost?

26. Vocabulary Power *Perimeter* comes from the Greek root words *peri* meaning "around" and *metron* meaning "measure." In your own words, write a definition for *perimeter*.

Maintain Skills

27. What is the value of the digit 6 in 50,607?

28. Find the area of the rectangle.

29. What unit of measure would you use for the distance from Atlanta to Augusta?

30. 123
        $\times$ 7

31. 84 ÷ 3

CRCT Test Prep

32. **M4M1.a.** What is the most reasonable unit of measure for the weight of a granola bar? (p. 346)

A. meter   C. kilogram

B. gram   D. centimeter

33. **M4N6.a.** Jan and Jon have the same part of their homework left to do. Jan still has $\frac{1}{4}$ left. How much does Jon have left? (p. 296)

A. $\frac{2}{4}$ C. $\frac{2}{8}$

B. $\frac{2}{6}$ D. $\frac{1}{8}$

Problem Solving LiNKUP . . . to Architecture

Interior designers use wallpaper to decorate rooms. This table can be used to estimate the number of rolls of wallpaper needed to cover the walls of a room.

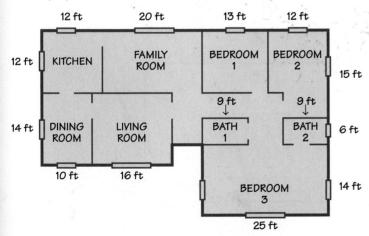

WALLPAPER TO COVER WALLS		
Room Perimeter (in feet)	Rolls Needed	
	8-ft walls	10-ft walls
25–32	4	5
33–40	5	7
41–48	6	8
49–56	7	9
57–64	8	10
65–72	9	11
73–80	10	13

USE DATA For 1–4, use the floor plan and the wallpaper table to find the number of rolls of wallpaper needed for each room.

1. bedroom 1 with 8-foot walls

2. dining room with 10-foot walls

3. kitchen with 8-foot walls

4. family room with 10-foot walls

2 Find Area

Concepts/Skill to Maintain Area
also M4A1.b., M4A1.c., M4P5.b., M4P5.c.

▶ **Learn**

ROW BY ROW Area is the number of square units needed to cover a surface. Mr. Jones is putting 1-square-foot tiles on the shower wall of his bathroom. Estimate the number of tiles he needs to cover the wall.

Think: How many squares are in each row? about 6 squares

How many rows are needed? about 8 rows

$6 \times 8 = 48$

So, Mr. Jones needs about 48 1-square-foot tiles to cover the area of the shower wall.

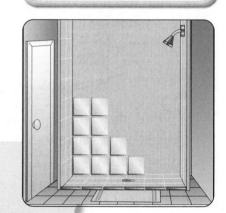

Example

One Way You can count square units to find the area.

STEP 1	STEP 2	STEP 3
Using a centimeter ruler and grid paper, draw a rectangle 7 cm long and 5 cm wide.	Count the number of squares. 7 cm 5 cm ⬜ 5 cm 7 cm	Record your answer in square units. Area: 35

Another Way You can use multiplication.

To find the area of a rectangle, multiply the length by the width.
Area: length × width
Area: 7×5
Area: 35

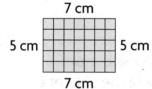

So, the area is 35 sq cm.

• How is using an array similar to using multiplication to find the area of the rectangle above?

• Describe situations in which someone might need to find area.

Divide Figures into Parts

What is the area of this figure?

It is easier to find the area of some figures by dividing them into rectangles first.

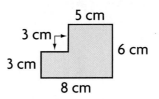

Example

STEP 1

Divide the figure into two rectangles.

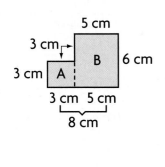

STEP 2

Find the area of each part.

Figure A

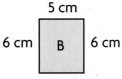

Area: length × width
Area: 3 × 3
Area: 9

The area is 9 sq cm.

Figure B

5 cm

6 cm | B | 6 cm

5 cm

Area: length × width
Area: 5 × 6
Area: 30

The area is 30 sq cm.

STEP 3

Add the areas together to find the total area of the figure.

9 + 30 = 39

So, the total area is 39 sq cm.

• Discuss why you can multiply the length of the side of a square by itself to find the area of the square.

Technology Link

More Practice: Harcourt Mega Math Ice Station Exploration, *Polar Planes*, Levels Q and R

▶ Check

1. **Draw** this figure, and show one way to divide it into rectangles so you can find the area.

Find the area.

2.

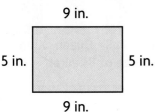

3.

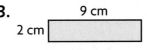

4.

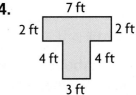

LESSON CONTINUES ▶

Find the area.

5.
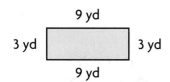
9 yd
3 yd   3 yd
9 yd

6.
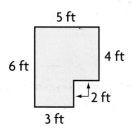
4 in.
4 in.   4 in.
4 in.

7.
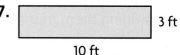
3 ft
10 ft

8.
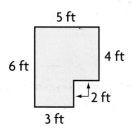
5 ft
6 ft   4 ft
2 ft
3 ft

9.
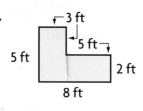
3 ft
5 ft
5 ft
2 ft
8 ft

10.
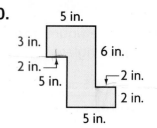
5 in.
3 in.   6 in.
2 in.
5 in.   2 in.
2 in.
5 in.

 ALGEBRA   **Find the unknown length.**

11.

9 yd
?
Area: 45 sq yd

12.
9 ft
?
Area: 81 sq ft

13.
10 cm
?
Area: 70 sq cm

**Use a centimeter ruler to measure each figure.
Find the area and perimeter.**

14.

15.

USE DATA For 16–17, use the bar graph. The
length of each blanket is 90 inches.

16. What is the difference in area between a full
blanket and a twin blanket?

17. What is the difference in area between a
king blanket and a queen blanket?

18. **? What's the Question?** The school
yard has an area of 90 sq ft set aside for
hopscotch. The length of the section is 10 ft.
The answer is 9 ft.

19. ✎ **Write About It** One bulletin board is a
rectangle. Another is a square. Explain how
16 square pictures could cover either one.

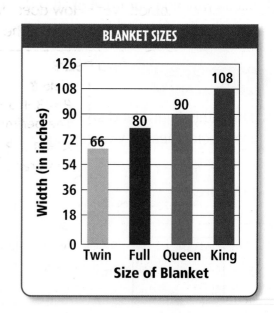

BLANKET SIZES

Width (in inches)

126
108   108
90   90
80
72   66
54
36
18
0

Twin   Full   Queen   King
Size of Blanket

20. MULTISTEP Andrea's living room is 4 yards wide. The perimeter is 20 yards. What is the area?

21. Don is putting carpet in a room that measures 14 ft by 12 ft. How many square feet of carpet does he need?

22. REASONING The area of a rectangle is 48 square inches. The length of the sides of the rectangle are whole numbers. What are the possible lengths of the sides of the rectangle?

23. ≡**FAST FACT** • **SOCIAL STUDIES**
The largest U.S. flag, the Superflag, is 505 ft by 255 ft. It travels to events around the country. It takes at least 700 people to unfurl the flag. What is its perimeter?

Maintain Skills

24. Use the model to subtract 0.6 − 0.2.

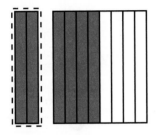

CRCT Test Prep

25. **M4N7.b.** What is the value of the expression? (p. 130)

$$8 \times 3 + 4$$

A. 56   **B.** 28   **C.** 20   **D.** 15

26. **M4A1.b.** Which expression shows 36 cookies divided into a number of bags, □? (p. 128)

A. □ ÷ 36   **C.** 36 ÷ □
B. 36 − □   **D.** □ + 36

Problem Solving   THiNker's Corner 💡

COMBINED FIGURES Look at the drawing of Carl's farm. It is divided into a rectangle and a square. Will he need more fencing to enclose the two fields separately or to enclose the combined field? How does the total area of the two fields compare to the area of the combined field?

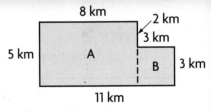

TWO FIELDS		COMBINED FIELD
Field A $P = 8 + 5 + 8 + 5 = 26$ The perimeter is 26 km. $A = 8 \times 5 = 40$ The area is 40 sq km.	**Field B** $P = 3 + 3 + 3 + 3 = 12$ The perimeter is 12 km. $A = 3 \times 3 = 9$ The area is 9 sq km.	$P = 8 + 2 + 3 + 3 + 11 + 5 = 32$ The perimeter is 32 km. Add the areas together to find the area of the combined field. $A = 40 + 9 = 49$ The area is 49 sq km.
Total Area = 40 + 9 = 49 sq km		

Since 26 km + 12 km, or 38 km, is greater than 32 km, he will need more fencing to enclose the two fields separately than the combined field. The areas are equal.

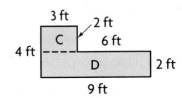

Use the figure at the right. Find the combined and divided perimeters and areas.

Relate Area and Perimeter

M4P5.a. Create and use representations to organize, record, and communi-cate mathematical ideas. *also* **M4P2.a., M4P2.b., M4P2.d., M4P3.b., M4P5.b.**
Concepts/Skill to Maintain Area and Perimeter

▶ **Learn**

AREA VS. PERIMETER Two figures can have the same area but different perimeters, or different areas but the same perimeter.

HANDS ON

MATERIALS: square tiles, grid paper

Activity 1

Copy each figure using square tiles. Use grid paper to record your work. Then find the area and perimeter of each figure.

Ⓐ	Ⓑ	Ⓒ	Ⓓ

• Compare and contrast figures A and B.

• Compare and contrast figures C and D.

Activity 2 Show a rectangle that has the same area as rectangle R but a different perimeter. You may use square tiles to model.

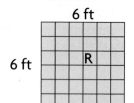

6 ft

6 ft

R

Area = 36 sq ft
Perimeter = 24 ft

One possible rectangle:

9 ft

4 ft

Area = 36 sq ft
Perimeter = 26 ft

• Describe the difference between area and perimeter.

▶ **Check**

1. **Draw** two figures that have different perimeters but the same area. Use grid paper.

2. **Draw** two figures that have different areas but the same perimeter. Use grid paper.

For 3–8, find the area and perimeter of each figure.
Then draw another figure that has the same perimeter
but a different area.

3. 7 ft

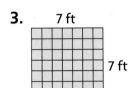

7 ft

4. 10 cm

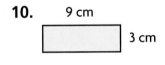

4 cm   4 cm

10 cm

5. 5 cm

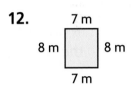

5 cm

6. 9 in.

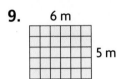

4 in.

7. 9 cm

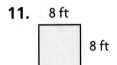

10 cm   10 cm

9 cm

8.

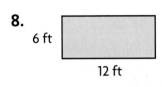

6 ft

12 ft

For 9–12, find the area and perimeter of each figure.
Then draw another figure that has the same area but
a different perimeter.

9. 6 m

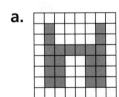

5 m

10. 9 cm

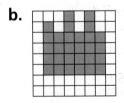

3 cm

11. 8 ft

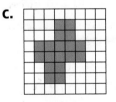

8 ft

12. 7 m

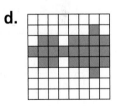

8 m   8 m

7 m

For 13–14, use figures a–d.

13. Which of the figures below have the
same area but different perimeters?

14. Which of the figures below have the
same perimeter but different areas?

a.   **b.**

c.   **d.**

15. Write a problem about the
square floor of a tree house that is
8 feet on each side.

16. REASONING The area of a rectangular
garden is 24 square feet. Give four
possible perimeters of the garden.

Maintain Skills

17. 47×20 **18.** 70×18

19. $938 \div 3$ **20.** $521 \div 7$

21. Which is longer, a wire that is 10 feet
long or a wire that is 10 yards long?

CRCT Test Prep

22. ◖ **M4M1.a.** What is the most
reasonable unit of measure for the
weight of a bowling ball? (p. 338)

A. ounce   C. ton

B. pound   D. gram

Problem Solving Strategy
Look for a Pattern

M4P1.a. Build new mathematical knowledge through problem solving.
also M4A1.a., M4P1.b., M4P1.c., M4P2, M4P3.a., M4P3.b., M4P3.c.,
M4P3.d., M4P5.b., M4P5.c.
Concepts/Skill to Maintain Area and Perimeter

Quick Review

1. 99 ÷ 11   **2.** 360 ÷ 15

3. 504 ÷ 14   **4.** 132 ÷ 12

5. 700 ÷ 35

PROBLEM Mr. Jiminez wants to build different-size storage buildings, so he drew plans for the buildings. Some of the buildings will be twice as long as others but will have the same width. He wants to know how the areas of the buildings are related. How do the areas change?

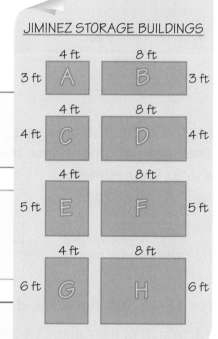

JIMINEZ STORAGE BUILDINGS

UNDERSTAND

- What are you asked to find?
- What do you know?

PLAN

- What strategy can you use to solve the problem?

  You can *look for a pattern* to solve the problem.

SOLVE

- How can you *look for a pattern* to solve the problem?

  Look for a pattern in the areas.

	LENGTH	WIDTH	AREA		LENGTH	WIDTH	AREA
Building A	4	3	12	Building C	4	4	16
Building B	8	3	24	Building D	8	4	32
Building E	4	5	20	Building G	4	6	24
Building F	8	5	40	Building H	8	6	48

The areas change from 12 to 24, 16 to 32, 20 to 40, and 24 to 48.

So, as the length of one side doubles, the area also doubles.

CHECK

- Explain how you can check your answer.

Look for a pattern, **and solve.**

Act It Out or Use Objects
Make a Picture or Diagram
Guess and Check
► **Use or Look for a Pattern**
Use Logical Reasoning
Make an Organized List
Use or Make a Table
Work Backwards

1. **What if** Mr. Jiminez wants to know how the areas of his storage buildings change when both sides are doubled? Make a table to show how the areas change. Explain.

2. Mr. Jiminez also wants to know what happens to the perimeters of his storage buildings when both sides are doubled. Make a table to show how the perimeters change. Explain.

Rectangular swimming pools come in different sizes. Use the table to find how the perimeters of the swimming pools are related.

3. How do the widths of the swimming pools change?

   A decrease by 20 ft
   B decrease by 30 ft
   C increase by 10 ft
   D increase by 20 ft

SWIMMING POOL SIZES

Pool	Length	Width	Perimeter
A	12 ft	20 ft	64 ft
B	12 ft	30 ft	84 ft
C	12 ft	40 ft	104 ft
D	12 ft	50 ft	124 ft

4. What pattern do you see in the perimeters of the swimming pools?

   F increase by 20 feet   **G** double in size   **H** decrease by 10 ft   **J** decrease by half

Mixed Strategy Practice

5. In a coordinate system, graph a rectangle with vertices (1,2), (6,2), (1,5), and (6,5). Then find the perimeter and area of the rectangle.

6. Three stickers cost 15¢. Six stickers cost 30¢, and 9 stickers cost 45¢. How much will 15 stickers cost? How much will 30 stickers cost?

7. Mark travels $14\frac{3}{4}$ miles to soccer practice. First, he travels $5\frac{1}{4}$ miles to pick up John, then $3\frac{3}{4}$ miles to pick up Harold, and finally $2\frac{1}{4}$ miles to pick up Frank. How many miles does Mark have left to travel to soccer practice?

8. ✎ **Write About It** Explain how to find the unknown length.

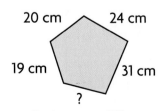

20 cm   24 cm
19 cm   31 cm
?
Perimeter = 115 cm

Extra Practice

Set A (pp. 356–359)

Find the perimeter.

1. 4 in., 2 in., 5 in., 3 in., 3 in., 7 in.

2. 14 in., 9 in., 9 in., 14 in.

3. 3 m, 3 m, 3 m, 3 m, 3 m

4. 9 yd, 6 yd, 2 yd, 7 yd

Use a formula to find the perimeter.

5. 11 mm, 11 mm

6. 9 in., 3 in.

7. 15 in., 6 in.

8. 9 cm, 9 cm

9. Mai walked around the perimeter of the playground 3 times. The rectangular playground is 25 meters long and 15 meters wide. How far did Mai walk?

Set B (pp. 360–363)

Find the area.

1. 3 in., 9 in.

2. 8 cm, 5 cm

3. 7 cm, 4 cm, 7 cm, 4 cm, 3 cm, 3 cm

4. 5 ft, 3 ft, 1 ft, 4 ft, 7 ft, 6 ft

5. Mandy's class is painting a mural on a wall. The wall is 6 feet high and 4 feet wide. What is the area of the wall?

Set C (pp. 364–365)

Find the area and perimeter of each figure. Then draw another figure that has the same area but a different perimeter.

1.

2.

3. 7 cm, 5 cm

4. 6 in., 7 in., 6 in., 7 in., 14 in., 12 in.

5. Debbie's living room ceiling measures 16 feet by 14 feet. What are the area and perimeter of the ceiling?

Review/Test

✓ CHECK VOCABULARY AND CONCEPTS

Choose the best term from the box.

1. You can use a mathematical rule, or _?_, to find the perimeter of a figure. (p. 357)

2. The number of square units needed to cover a surface is its _?_. (p. 360)

3. Two figures can have different areas but the same _?_. (p. 364)

✓ CHECK SKILLS

Find the perimeter. (pp. 356–359)

4. 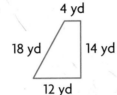 4 in. 5 in. 4 in. 5 in. 6 in. 6 in.

5. 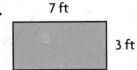 4 yd, 18 yd, 14 yd, 12 yd

6.  4 m, 3 m, 4 m, 5 m, 3 m, 6 m

7. 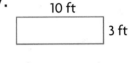 10 ft, 3 ft

Find the area. (pp. 360–363)

8. 20 m, 10 m

9. 7 ft, 3 ft

10. 4 ft, 4 ft

Find the area and perimeter of each figure. Then draw another figure that has the same perimeter but a different area. (pp. 364–365)

11. 5 in., 5 in.

12. 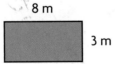 8 m, 3 m

13. 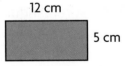 12 cm, 5 cm

✓ CHECK PROBLEM SOLVING

Solve. (pp. 366–367)

14. Mr. Walker's front porch is 6 feet by 8 feet. He wants to double the length and the width of his porch. How will the area of the porch change?

15. Jacey's garden is 7 feet long and 5 feet wide. She wants to double both the length and width. How will the perimeter of the garden change?

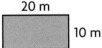

Cumulative CRCT Test Prep

ALGEBRA

1. **M4A1.c.** Which expression can be used to find the area of a rectangle whose sides are 8 centimeters and 5 centimeters?

   A. $2 \times 8 \times 5$

   B. $(2 \times 8) + (2 \times 5)$

   C. 8×5

   D. $8 + 5 + 8 + 5$

2. **M4A1.c.** Which expression can be used to find the perimeter of the rectangle?

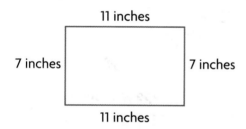

11 inches

7 inches   7 inches

11 inches

   A. $2 \times 7 \times 11$

   B. $(2 \times 7) + (2 \times 11)$

   C. 7×11

   D. $2 \times 7 + 11$

3. **M4A1.a.** A rectangular vegetable garden is 10 feet long and 6 feet wide. A flower garden is twice as long and half as wide. Which statement is true?

   A. The areas are the same.

   B. The perimeters are the same.

   C. The area of the vegetable garden is twice the area of the flower garden.

   D. The perimeter of the vegetable garden is twice the perimeter of the flower garden.

GEOMETRY

4. **M4G2.c.** Which of the following is a pattern for a cube?

   A.
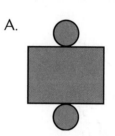

   B.
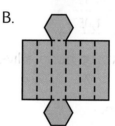

   C.
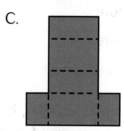

   D.
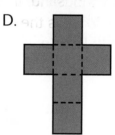

5. **M4G3.a.** Tatum graphed the points (1,3), (4,3), and (1,6) in a coordinate system. What point should she plot next if she wants the points to be the vertices of a square?

   A. (3,1)

   B. (3,4)

   C. (4,6)

   D. (6,1)

Cumulative CRCT Test Prep

NUMBERS AND OPERATIONS

6. **M4N2.d.** The table below shows the populations of several small towns in Georgia.

Selected Georgia Populations	
Town	**Population**
Alamo	1,943
Baxley	4,150
Lakeview	4,820
Comer	1,052

About how many more people live in Baxley than in Alamo?

A. about 1,000 more

B. about 2,000 more

C. about 3,000 more

D. about 4,000 more

7. **M4N1.b.** College Park, Georgia, has a population of twenty thousand, three hundred eighty-two. What is the population of College Park in standard form?

A.   20,382

B.   23,820

C. 20,000,082

D. 20,300,382

8. **M4N4.d.** Which quotient is the same as 3,600 ÷ 9?

A. 36 ÷ 9

B. 360 ÷ 9

C. 360 ÷ 90

D. 3,600 ÷ 9

DATA ANALYSIS

9. **M4D1.d.** Seldon asked his friends about their favorite TV programs. There were 12 votes for the news, 8 for cartoons, 19 for sports, and 10 for comedy. He displayed the data in this bar graph.

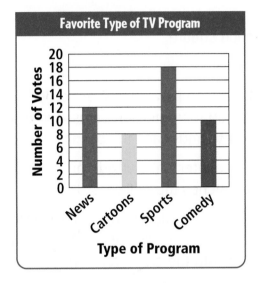

What information is missing?

A. one vote for sports

B. one vote for cartoons

C. two votes for sports

D. two votes for cartoons

10. **M4D1.c.** What type of graph would be the BEST to display data about the temperature of a liquid as it was heated during an experiment?

A. pictograph

B. bar graph

C. double-bar graph

D. line graph

GPS/CRCT Vocabulary

ELA4R3 The student understands and acquires vocabulary and uses it correctly in reading and writing.

THREE IN A ROW

MATERIALS *For each group* Definition Cards, counters

- Make a 3-by-3 grid for yourself. Write a vocabulary term in each square.

- Work with a group.

- Choose one player to be the caller. The caller mixes up the definition cards. The caller picks one card and reads the definition aloud.

- Put a counter on your grid on top of the word that matches the definition.

- Play until one player covers three words—across, down, or diagonally. The winner trades places with the caller, and everyone plays again.

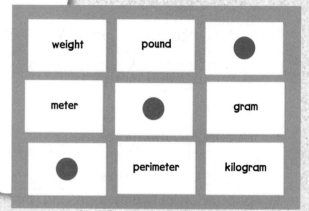

MATH WORD WORK

MATERIALS *For each pair* grid paper

- Cut out a 10-by-10 grid. Choose four vocabulary terms to make a crossword puzzle.

- Write the words lightly in pencil across or down in the grid. Make sure one letter of each word crosses another word. Shade the empty squares in the grid.

- Number each word. Then write a clue for each word. Your clue can be a sentence or an example.

- Erase the words from the puzzle. Trade puzzles with another pair of students. Solve each other's puzzle.

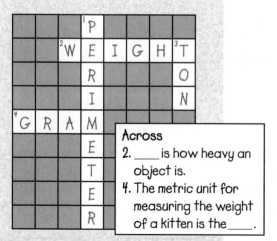

Across
2. ____ is how heavy an object is.
4. The metric unit for measuring the weight of a kitten is the ____.

I'M A POET, AND I KNOW IT

- Work with a partner. Choose one of the units of measure. Write a short poem that has your unit of measure as the theme. Do not use the unit in your poem. You can draw a picture for your poem.

- Trade poems with another pair of students. Try to figure out the unit of measure in the other pair's poem.

> Red apple, green apple,
> It doesn't matter to me.
> I like to eat one every day.
> I wonder how much it weighs?
>
> The theme is "ounces" or "grams."

CHOOSE THE UNIT

MATERIALS *For each group* index cards

- Take five index cards. Write each unit of weight on an index card. Write the abbreviation, too.

ounce (oz)   **pound (lb)**   **ton (t)**

gram (g)   **kilogram (kg)**

- Take turns naming a classroom object or something else that is familiar. Everyone in the group holds up the card that shows the best unit to use to measure the weight of the object. You can go around the group more than once.

- Repeat with the other four units of weight.

Georgia Tasks

M4P1.a. Build new mathematical knowledge through problem solving. *also* **M4P1.b., M4P1.c., M4P1.d., M4P4.c.**

Concepts/Skill to Maintain Area

SS4H3 The student will explain the factors that shaped British colonial America.

Task A

TRUSTEE GARDEN

In 1734, James Oglethorpe established the Trustee Garden near Savannah. The area of the garden was about 10 acres. It was a model garden for medical plants and a place to experiment with crops that might be exported to England. The Trustee gardeners experimented with mulberry trees, orange trees, olive trees, and grapevines.

▲ **James Oglethorpe**

a. An acre is 4,840 square yards. What could be the dimensions of an acre that is rectangular in shape? Explain how you found your answer.

b. Mulberry trees need at least 15 feet between each tree. How many mulberry trees could be planted in a plot of ground 100 feet by 30 feet? Explain how you found your answer.

▲ **Planning the city of Savannah, around 1733**

Task B

ON THE EDGE

Tina earns extra money in the spring by putting lawn edging around her neighbors' gardens. The table shows how many feet of edging she will need for each neighbor.

The garden center sells edging in rolls of 10.5 feet and 15 feet.

a. Tina decided to buy the 10.5-foot rolls of edging. How many rolls will she need to buy? Explain how you know.

b. How could Tina buy the edging in different-sized rolls to have the least amount left over?

EDGING FOR NEIGHBORS	
Neighbor	**Length**
Mrs. Jones	9 ft
Mr. Morgan	6.5 ft
Mr. Rodriguez	11.25 ft
Ms. O'Donnell	8.75 ft

Maintain/Preview

Maintain

Choose the more appropriate unit of measure. (pp. 332–335, 338–341)

1.

7 in. or 7 ft

2.

2 oz or 2 lb

Choose the greater measurement. (pp. 338–341, 346–347)

3. 3 oz or 3 T

4. 4 kg or 4 g

5. 8 lb or 8 oz

Find the perimeter. (pp. 356–359)

6.

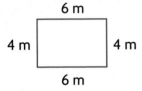

6 m · 4 m · 4 m · 6 m

7.

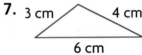

3 cm · 4 cm · 6 cm

8.

7 in. · 2 in. · 4 in. · 8 in. · 4 in. · 5 in.

Find the area. (pp. 360–363)

9.

8 ft · 3 ft · 3 ft · 8 ft

10.

6 cm · 6 cm · 6 cm · 6 cm

11.

7 yd · 3 yd · 2 yd · 5 yd · 4 yd · 3 yd

Preview

Write the decimal for the shaded part. (Chapter 18)

1.

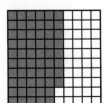

2.

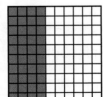

3.

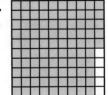

4.

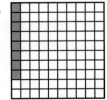

Round the number to the nearest hundred. (Chapter 19)

5. 526

6. 1,432

7. 891

8. 2,904

Find the product. (Chapter 20)

9. 14×7

10. 29×32

11. 56×80

12. 93×28

Understand Decimals

≡FAST FACT • SOCIAL STUDIES In July 1968, Chicago hosted 1,000 athletes in the first international Special Olympics Games. Now the Special Olympics reaches more than 1.5 million children and adults with disabilities, in over 180 countries.

INVESTIGATION The table lists the times in a 100-meter dash at a recent Special Olympics competition. Run the 100-meter dash with your classmates. Use a stopwatch to record times to the nearest hundredth of a second. Make a table comparing everyone's times.

Using Data

100-METER DASH TIMES (in seconds)			
20.18	21.35	22.40	21.03
23.86	20.88	20.07	21.63

Use this page to help you review and remember
important skills needed for Chapter 18.

✓ MODEL FRACTIONS

Write the fraction for the shaded part.

1.
2.
3.
4.

✓ DECIMALS AND MONEY

Write the name of the coin that is described.

5. 0.1 of a dollar is a _?_ .

6. 0.01 of a dollar is a _?_ .

Write a decimal for the money amount.

7. two dollars and fifteen cents

8. three dollars and twelve cents

✓ FRACTIONS WITH DENOMINATORS OF 10 AND 100

Write a fraction for each.

9. five tenths

10. nine hundredths

11. fifty-three hundredths

Complete to show equivalent fractions.

12. $\frac{6}{10} = \frac{\blacksquare}{100}$

13. $\frac{1}{10} = \frac{\blacksquare}{100}$

14. $\frac{9}{10} = \frac{\blacksquare}{100}$

VOCABULARY POWER

REVIEW

greater than (>) [grā•tər ᵗʰan] *adjective*

The symbol > first was used in a
mathematics publication in 1631. Other
symbols also were used to show "greater
than," even into the 1700s. Make up your
own symbol for "greater than." Explain
how the symbol could be useful in
comparing two numbers.

PREVIEW

decimal

decimal point

equivalent decimals

 www.harcourtschool.com/mathglossary

Relate Fractions and Decimals

M4N5.a. Understand decimals are part of the base-ten system.
also M4N1.a., M4N1.b., M4P4.c.

Quick Review

Draw a model for each.

1. $\frac{3}{10}$ 2. $\frac{7}{10}$ 3. $\frac{9}{10}$

4. $\frac{15}{100}$ 5. $\frac{4}{100}$

VOCABULARY

decimal

decimal point

▶ **Learn**

BATTER UP! A decimal is a number with one or more digits to the right of the decimal point . Decimals are part of the base-ten system. Each place value is ten times the place value to its right.

Understanding fractions that have a denominator of 10 or 100 will help you understand decimals.

Fraction:	$\frac{1}{1}$	$\frac{1}{10}$	$\frac{1}{100}$
Decimal:	1	0.1	0.01
Read:	one	one tenth	one hundredth

Gina plays on a Little League team. Gina scored 14 of her team's 100 runs this year. In the past three games, she was at bat 10 times and had 6 hits.

Example Gina had 6 hits out of 10 tries at bat.

Model	**Fraction**	**Decimal**
	Write: $\frac{6}{10}$	Write: 0.6
	Read: six tenths	Read: six tenths

Gina scored 14 of her team's 100 runs this year.

Model	**Fraction**	**Decimal**
	Write: $\frac{14}{100}$	Write: 0.14
	Read: fourteen hundredths	Read: fourteen hundredths

So, Gina got a hit $\frac{6}{10}$, or 0.6, of her times at bat recently and scored $\frac{14}{100}$, or 0.14, of her team's runs this year.

Read and Write Decimals

Decimals, like whole numbers, can be written in standard form, word form, and expanded form. Look at these numbers on the place-value chart.

Examples

Ones	.	Tenths	Hundredths
0	.	8	
0	.	1	2

Standard Form	Word Form	Expanded Form
0.8	eight tenths	0.8
0.12	twelve hundredths	$0.1 + 0.02$

You can write a decimal for a fraction that has a denominator other than 10 or 100. First write the fraction using a denominator of 10 or 100.

Example

What decimal shows the same amount as $\frac{1}{2}$?

$$\frac{1}{2} = \frac{1 \times 5}{2 \times 5} = \frac{5}{10} \qquad \frac{5}{10} = 0.5$$

So, $\frac{1}{2}$ shows the same amount as 0.5.

A number line divided into 100 equal parts can be used to model fractions and decimals that show the same amount in tenths or hundredths.

$$\frac{25}{100}$$

$\frac{0}{100}$ $\frac{10}{100}$ $\frac{20}{100}$ $\frac{30}{100}$ $\frac{40}{100}$ $\frac{50}{100}$ $\frac{60}{100}$ $\frac{70}{100}$ $\frac{80}{100}$ $\frac{90}{100}$ $\frac{100}{100}$

0   0.1   0.2 ↑ 0.3   0.4   0.5   0.6   0.7   0.8   0.9   1
         0.25

So, the decimal 0.25 shows the same amount as $\frac{25}{100}$, or $\frac{1}{4}$.

LESSON CONTINUES ▶

Technology Link

More Practice: Harcourt Mega Math Fraction Action, *Fraction Flare-Up*, Level N, and *Number Line Mine*, Level N

1. **Explain** how the tenths model is different from the hundredths model.

Write the decimal and fraction shown by each model or number line.

2.

3.

4.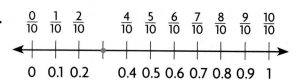

▶ **Practice and Problem Solving** (Extra Practice, page 394, Set A)

Write the decimal and fraction shown by each model or number line.

5.

6.

7.

8.

9.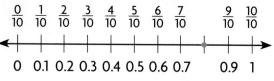

10.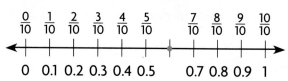

Write each fraction as a decimal. Use a model to help you.

11. $\frac{8}{10}$

12. $\frac{7}{10}$

13. $\frac{60}{100}$

14. $\frac{25}{100}$

15. $\frac{4}{100}$

16. $\frac{32}{100}$

17. $\frac{1}{5}$

18. $\frac{2}{100}$

19. $\frac{2}{4}$

20. $\frac{4}{5}$

21. $\frac{5}{10}$

22. $\frac{3}{5}$

23. $\frac{47}{100}$

24. $\frac{7}{100}$

25. $\frac{9}{10}$

ALGEBRA Find the missing number or digit to write each fraction as a decimal.

26. $\frac{\blacksquare}{10} = 0.70$

27. $\frac{75}{\blacksquare} = 0.75$

28. $\frac{\blacksquare}{100} = 0.20$

29. $\frac{\blacksquare}{10} = 0.4$

30. $\frac{5}{\blacksquare} = 0.5$

Write the decimal two other ways.

31. 0.1

32. $0.4 + 0.07$

33. 0.4

34. 8 tenths

35. **MULTISTEP** For three weeks, a theater sold $9,500 worth of tickets per week. For each of the next 2 weeks, the theater sold $7,200 worth of tickets per week. What were the total ticket sales?

36. **Write About It** Aline walked $\frac{3}{4}$ mile to school. Dave walked 0.75 mile to school. Aline said she walked farther than Dave. Is she correct? Explain.

USE DATA For 37–39, use the graph.

37. The graph shows how Pepe spends 100 minutes of baseball practice. He spends $\frac{28}{100}$ of the time running bases. What decimal is this?

38. Write a decimal to show what part of the total time is spent on warm-ups.

39. **Write a problem** about the time Pepe spends fielding and throwing.

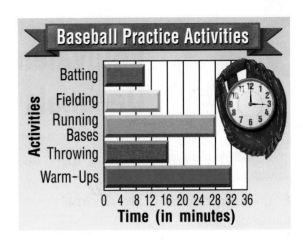

Baseball Practice Activities

Activities: Batting, Fielding, Running Bases, Throwing, Warm-Ups

Time (in minutes): 0 4 8 12 16 20 24 28 32 36

Maintain Skills

40. What is the perimeter of the rectangle?

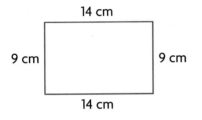

14 cm

9 cm   9 cm

14 cm

CRCT Test Prep

41. **M4N6.b.** Tamara lives $2\frac{7}{8}$ miles from school. Tia lives $1\frac{5}{8}$ miles from school. How much farther from school does Tamara live than Tia? (p. 316)

A. $4\frac{4}{8}$ miles   C. $1\frac{2}{8}$ miles

B. $2\frac{2}{8}$ miles   D. $1\frac{1}{8}$ miles

Problem Solving   Thinker's Corner

REASONING You can use a meterstick to model decimal numbers.

meter (m)	decimeter (dm) *Deci* means "tenths."	centimeter (cm) *Centi* means "hundredths."
1.0 meter	1 decimeter = 0.1, or $\frac{1}{10}$, meter.	1 centimeter = 0.01, or $\frac{1}{100}$, meter.

Write 3.26 meters as meters + decimeters + centimeters.

3.26 in expanded form is $3 + 0.2 + 0.06$.

0.2 meter = 2 decimeters   0.06 meter = 6 centimeters

So, 3.26 meters = 3 meters + 2 decimeters + 6 centimeters.

Complete.

1. $\frac{4}{10}$ m = ■ dm   2. 0.23 m = ■ cm   3. $\frac{9}{100}$ m = ■ cm

4. 4.52 m = 4 m + ■ dm + ■ cm   5. 0.51 m = ■ m + ■ dm + ■ cm

 HANDS ON

Equivalent Decimals

M4N5.b. Understand the relative size of numbers and order two digit decimals. *also* **M4P3.a., M4P3.b., M4P3.c., M4P3.d., M4P5, M4P5.a., M4P5.b., M4P5.c.**

▶ **Explore**

Equivalent decimals are decimals that name the same number.

Use models and paper folding to find equivalent decimals. Are 0.2 and 0.20 equivalent decimals?

VOCABULARY

equivalent decimals

MATERIALS tenths and hundredths models; markers

Activity

STEP 1

Shade 0.2 of the tenths model and 0.20 of the hundredths model.

0.2

two tenths
2 out of 10

0.20

twenty hundredths
20 out of 100

STEP 2

Fold 0.2 of the tenths model and 0.20 of the hundredths model. Then compare the models.

0.2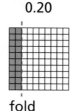

fold

0.20

fold

The folded parts of the models are the same size.

So, 0.2 and 0.20 are equivalent decimals.

Try It

Use a tenths model and a hundredths model. Are the two decimals equivalent? Write *equivalent* or *not equivalent*.

a. 0.50 and 0.6   **b.** 0.3 and 0.30

c. 0.70 and 0.75   **d.** 0.8 and 0.80

How do these models show whether 0.50 and 0.6 are equivalent?

▶ Connect

Felipe said that $0.30 is 3 tenths of a dollar. Lea said that $0.30 is 30 hundredths of a dollar. Who was correct?

Example   Compare the models.

Felipe used a tenths model to show
$0.30 = 3 tenths.

0.3 of a dollar

Each column is equal to 0.1, or one tenth, of a dollar.

Lea used a hundredths model to show
$0.30 = 30 hundredths.

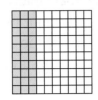

0.30 of a dollar

Each square is equal to 0.01, or one hundredth, of a dollar.

The two models show that 3 tenths of a dollar is equal to 30 hundredths of a dollar. So, both Felipe and Lea are correct.

• How else can $0.30 be read?

▶ Practice and Problem Solving

Are the two decimals equivalent? Write *equivalent* or *not equivalent*.

1. 0.7 and 0.70

2. 0.04 and 0.4

3. 0.9 and 0.09

4. 0.28 and 0.82

5. 0.17 and 0.07

6. 0.1 and 0.10

Write an equivalent decimal for each. You may use decimal models.

7. 0.8

8. 0.7

9. 0.90

10. 0.2

11. 0.5

12. 0.10

13. 0.40

14. 0.6

15. MENTAL MATH Erin's family plants a garden on 0.5 acre of their land. Write an equivalent decimal for this amount.

16. ✎ **Write About It** Make a model to show that 0.8 and 0.80 are equivalent. Explain your model.

Maintain Skills

17. 90 × 16

18. 276 ÷ 3

19. Which digit is in the tens place of the number 34,571.9?

CRCT Test Prep

20. **M4N6.b.** What is the sum $\frac{5}{9} + \frac{4}{9}$?
(p. 310)

A. $\frac{1}{9}$

B. $\frac{9}{18}$

C. 1

D. 9

LESSON 3

Relate Mixed Numbers and Decimals

M4N1.b. Equate a number's word name, its standard form, and its expanded form. *also* M4N1.a., M4P4.a., M4P4.b.

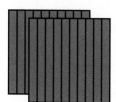
ANNA'S BANANAS Plantains, a variety of banana, grow in Mexico. Anna bought two and three tenths pounds of plantains at the store. How can you write this weight as a mixed number and as a decimal?

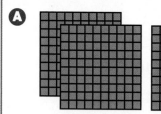

Mixed Number: $2\frac{3}{10}$

Decimal: 2.3

Read: two and three tenths

So, write the weight as $2\frac{3}{10}$, or 2.3, pounds.

• **What if** Anna also bought $3\frac{4}{10}$ pounds of peanuts? What decimal would a decimal scale show for that amount?

▲ There are 300 varieties of bananas worldwide.

Examples

Ⓐ

Mixed Number: $2\frac{46}{100}$

Decimal: 2.46

Read: two and forty-six hundredths

Ⓑ

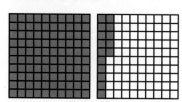

Mixed Number: $1\frac{15}{100}$

Decimal: 1.15

Read: one and fifteen hundredths

• **REASONING** How can you write four and eight hundredths as a mixed number and as a decimal?

Technology Link

More Practice: Harcourt Mega Math Fraction Action *Number Line Mine*, Level O, *Fraction Flare-Up*, Level M

384

Read and Write Decimals

Decimals greater than 1 can be written in standard form, word form, and expanded form. Look at these numbers in the place-value chart.

Picnic Day

Examples

Tens	Ones	.	Tenths	Hundredths
	9	.	7	
6	5	.	4	1

Standard Form	Word Form	Expanded Form
9.7	nine and seven tenths	9 + 0.7
65.41	sixty-five and forty-one hundredths	60 + 5 + 0.4 + 0.01

More Examples

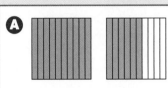

A

Standard Form: 1.6
Expanded Form: 1 + 0.6
Word Form: one and six tenths
Mixed Number: $1\frac{6}{10}$

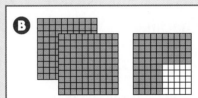

B

Standard Form: 2.75
Expanded Form: 2 + 0.7 + 0.05
Word Form: two and seventy-five hundredths
Mixed Number: $2\frac{75}{100}$

▶ Check

1. **Explain** how you can use a number line or a decimal model to relate mixed numbers and decimals.

Write a decimal and mixed number for each decimal model. Then write the word form and the expanded form.

2.

3.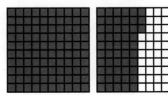

4.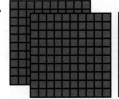

LESSON CONTINUES ▶

Write a decimal and mixed number for each decimal model.
Then write the word form and the expanded form.

5.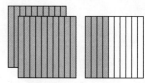

6.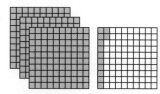

7.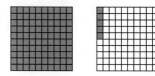

8.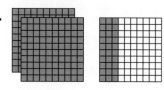

9.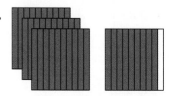

10.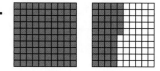

Write a mixed number or decimal.

11. 11.50

12. $9\frac{25}{100}$

13. 7.25

14. $4\frac{2}{10}$

15. 7.7

16. $4\frac{40}{100}$

17. 8.06

18. 16.3

19. $27\frac{6}{10}$

20. $6\frac{50}{100}$

21. $7\frac{16}{100}$

22. 6.85

23. $1\frac{9}{10}$

24. 3.48

25. $20\frac{1}{100}$

26. MULTISTEP Kerri went to the store with $100. She spent $22 on a shirt, $12 on a hat, and $45 on a pair of lawn chairs for her parents. How much money did Kerri have left?

27. Lance spent twenty-four dollars and eighteen cents on a lock for his bike. Write this amount in standard form and in expanded form.

28. Vocabulary Power Numbers such as $1\frac{1}{2}$ and $2\frac{3}{5}$ are called *mixed numbers*. In what way is a mixed number "mixed"?

29. Name two mixed numbers and two decimals between 4.25 and 4.50.

30. ❔ **What's the Error?** Kris wrote the mixed number $2\frac{7}{10}$ in two ways, shown at the right. Describe her error. Write the correct answer.

31. Keith swam 1.25 kilometers. His brother swam 1.7 kilometers. Write each distance as a mixed number.

> Kris
> two and seven tenths
> 2 + 0.07

32. MULTISTEP Tasha buys 16 posters. Each poster costs $3. If she gives the cashier $60, how much is her change?

33. Sumi ran 10.75 miles. Larry ran $10\frac{4}{5}$ miles. Who ran farther? Explain.

Maintain Skills

34. There are 30 students in art class. If up to 4 students can sit at each table, what is the least number of tables needed?

35. Find the number of square units in the area of the square.

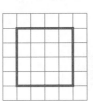

CRCT Test Prep

36. **M4G1.a.** Which of the following triangles can be classified as an acute triangle? (p. 274)

A. ▷

B. △

C. ◹

D. ◺

Problem Solving — THiNKER'S CORNER

USING A NUMBER LINE Eric is $5\frac{1}{2}$ feet tall. Jack is 5.75 feet tall. Sarah is taller than Eric but shorter than Jack. What is a possible height for Sarah?

You can use a number line to name a decimal and an equivalent mixed number between $5\frac{1}{2}$ and 5.75.

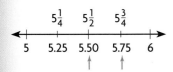

Think: The decimal equivalent of $5\frac{1}{2}$ is 5.50.

Find a decimal between 5.50 and 5.75. Then write it as an equivalent mixed number.

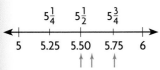

One decimal between 5.50 and 5.75 is 5.60.

$$5.60 = 5\frac{60}{100} = 5\frac{6}{10} = 5\frac{3}{5}$$

Sarah's height could be 5.60, or $5\frac{3}{5}$, feet.

Use a number line to find a decimal and equivalent mixed number between each of the following pairs of numbers.

1. $2\frac{1}{4}$ and 2.5

2. $3\frac{3}{5}$ and 3.8

3. 4.25 and $4\frac{3}{10}$

Compare and Order Decimals

 M4N5.b. Understand the relative size of numbers and order two digit decimals. *also* **M4P5.b., M4P5.c.**

Quick Review

Write an equivalent decimal for each.

1. 0.50   **2.** 0.60

3. 0.1   **4.** 0.20

5. 0.9

▶ Learn

TUNNEL TRAVEL The Brooklyn-Battery Tunnel in New York is 1.73 miles long. The E. Johnson Memorial Tunnel in Colorado is 1.70 miles long. Which tunnel is longer?

Example You can use a number line, a place-value chart, or a decimal model to compare decimals.

Use a number line.

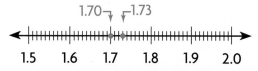

Since 1.73 is to the right of 1.70, 1.73 > 1.70.

Use a place-value chart.

ONES	.	TENTHS	HUNDREDTHS
1	.	7	3
1	.	7	0

1 = 1   7 = 7   3 > 0

Think: Line up the decimal points. Compare the digits, beginning with the greatest place value.

Since 3 > 0, 1.73 > 1.70.

Use a decimal model.

Think: Compare the number of shaded squares.

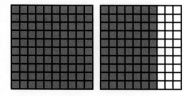

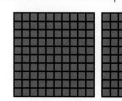

1.70   1.73

Since the model for 1.73 has 3 more shaded squares, 1.73 > 1.70.

So, the Brooklyn-Battery Tunnel is longer.

> **Remember**
>
> On a number line, the numbers to the right are greater than the numbers to the left.

Order Decimals

One Way   Use a number line to order decimals.
Order 9.4, 9.63, and 9.27 from greatest to least.

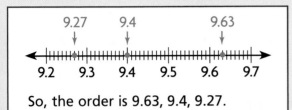

So, the order is 9.63, 9.4, 9.27.

Another Way   Use place value to order decimals. Order 1.23, 0.98, and 1.28 from least to greatest.

STEP 1	STEP 2	STEP 3
Line up the decimal points. Compare the digits in the greatest place. 1.23 ↓ 0.98 0 < 1 ↓ 1.28 Since 0 < 1, 0.98 is the least.	Compare the tenths. 1.23 ↓ 2 = 2 1.28 There are the same number of tenths.	Compare the hundredths. 1.23 ↓ 3 < 8 1.28 So, the order from least to greatest is 0.98, 1.23, 1.28.

• **What if** you wanted to write the decimals from greatest to least? How would doing so change the order?

Example

Order 0.81, 0.6, 0.65 from least to greatest.

0.81		**Think:** 8 > 6, so 0.81 is the greatest.
↓		
0.6	0.60	0.6 is equivalent to 0.60.
↓	↓	0.65 is equivalent to 0.65.
0.65	0.65	0 < 5, so 0.6 is the least.

The order from least to greatest is 0.6, 0.65, 0.81.

LESSON CONTINUES

1. **Explain** how you can use decimal models to help you compare decimals.

Compare. Write <, >, or = for each ⬤.

2. 0.45 ⬤ 0.35   **3.** 0.5 ⬤ 0.7   **4.** $0.03 ⬤ $0.30   **5.** 5.4 ⬤ 5.24

6. 1.03 ⬤ 1.30   **7.** 0.89 ⬤ 0.98   **8.** 0.2 ⬤ 0.20   **9.** $1.35 ⬤ $1.37

Use the number line to order the decimals from *least* to *greatest.*

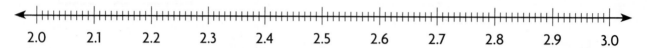

2.0   2.1   2.2   2.3   2.4   2.5   2.6   2.7   2.8   2.9   3.0

10. 2.01, 2.10, 2.2, 2.02   **11.** 2.7, 2.67, 2.76, 2.6

▶ **Practice and Problem Solving**   Extra Practice, page 394, Set C

Compare. Write <, >, or = for each ⬤.

12. 0.82 ⬤ 0.93   **13.** $0.81 ⬤ $0.18   **14.** 0.5 ⬤ 0.51   **15.** 0.20 ⬤ 0.02

16. 1.0 ⬤ 1.02   **17.** 0.60 ⬤ 0.6   **18.** $2.31 ⬤ $2.63   **19.** 0.74 ⬤ 0.53

Use the number line above to order the decimals from *least* to *greatest.*

20. 2.01, 2.11, 2.13, 2.10   **21.** 2.23, 2.45, 2.32, 2.5   **22.** 2.94, 2.49, 2.4, 3.00

Order the decimals from *greatest* to *least.*

23. $1.04, $4.11, $0.41, $1.40   **24.** 0.96, 1.06, 0.9, 1.6

25. 4.08, 4.3, 4.80, 4.03   **26.** 2.00, 2.71, 2.09, 2.97

27. 0.08, 8.6, 8.06, 0.86   **28.** 1.70, 1.03, 1.37, 1.07

29. ❓ **What's the Question?** Wes has $4 more than June. Debbie has $7 less than Wes. June has $5. The answer is $2.

30. Compare the decimals 0.8 and 0.2 using < or >. Then explain how you can use a number line to find the difference between them.

31. **REASONING** Which of these numbers has the same value as the digit 7 in the number 136.07?

70, 7, 0.7, 0.07

32. **REASONING** List all the possible digits for the missing digit.

12.34 < 12.■6 < 12.77

USE DATA For 33–35, use the table.

33. What was the time for the fastest runner? What was the time for the slowest runner?
    HINT: The least time is the fastest.

34. Mia also ran the 50-yard dash. Her time was 6.48 seconds. Order the times from least to greatest.

35. Keisha ran the 50-yard dash in 6.43 seconds. Compare her time to Jessica's time. Who was faster?

50-YARD DASH

Runner	Time (in seconds)
Lisa	6.50
Jessica	6.45
Kelly	6.40

Maintain Skills

36. Use the model to find the difference 0.9 − 0.6.

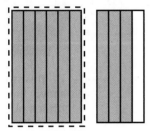

CRCT Test Prep

37. **M4M1.b.** Which unit of measure is the most reasonable for the weight of a table? (p. 338)

    A. ounce   C. foot
    B. pound   D. ton

38. **M4G1.d.** Which quadrilateral has only one pair of parallel sides? (p. 276)

    A. trapezoid   C. rhombus
    B. rectangle   D. parallelogram

Problem Solving Thinker's Corner

A-MAZE-ING REASONING

MATERIALS: Decimal Maze worksheet

1. On the worksheet, trace a path through the maze from A to B. For each step, move to a number of greater value.

2. On the worksheet, trace a path through the maze from C to D. For each step, move to a number of lesser value.

3. Then, using the blank maze on the worksheet, make your own maze. Try to make your path the only possible way to get through the maze. Give your maze to a partner to solve.

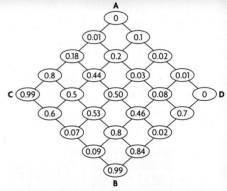

Problem Solving Strategy
Use Logical Reasoning

M4P1.a. Build new mathematical knowledge through problem solving. *also* **M4P1.b., M4P1.c., M4P1.d., M4P2.a., M4P2.b., M4P2.c., M4P2.d., M4P3.a., M4P3.b., M4P3.c.**

PROBLEM Miss Epps used a stopwatch to time Max, Jenna, and Dalia in a race. The times were 25.15 sec, 30.50 sec, and 34.10 sec. Jenna was slower than Dalia. A boy came in second. Who came in first, second, and third?

UNDERSTAND

• What are you asked to find?

• What information will you use?

PLAN

• What strategy can you use to solve the problem?

Use logical reasoning to determine the order in which the students finished.

▲ **This stopwatch shows thirteen and fifteen hundredths seconds.**

SOLVE

• How can you use the strategy?

Organize what you know in a table. Show all the possibilities.

Ⓐ A boy came in second.

Max is the only boy, so he must have the middle time. No two people have the same time, so there can be only one *yes* in each row and column.

	25.15	30.50	34.10
Max	NO	YES	NO
Dalia		NO	
Jenna		NO	

Ⓑ Jenna was slower than Dalia.

Since 34.10 sec is slower than 25.15 sec, Dalia's time must be 25.15 sec.

	25.15	30.50	34.10
Max	NO	YES	NO
Dalia	YES	NO	NO
Jenna	NO	NO	YES

So, Dalia was first, Max was second, and Jenna was third.

CHECK

• What other strategy could you use?

Problem Solving Practice

Use logical reasoning and solve.

1. **What if** after the race, Max, Dalia, and Jenna were thirsty? One person had a sports drink. The winner chose juice, and another person had water. Max does not like sports drinks. What did each person drink?

Strategies

Act It Out or Use Objects

Make a Picture or Diagram

Guess and Check

Use or Look for a Pattern

▶ **Use Logical Reasoning**

Make an Organized List

Use or Make a Table

Work Backwards

Problem Solving

The temperatures last week were 85°F, 75°F, 77°F, 83°F, and 81°F. Monday was the hottest day, and Thursday was the coolest. Wednesday was cooler than Friday but warmer than Tuesday.

2. On which day was the temperature 83°F?
   - **A** Monday
   - **B** Tuesday
   - **C** Wednesday
   - **D** Friday

3. What was the temperature on Wednesday?
   - **F** 75°F
   - **G** 77°F
   - **H** 81°F
   - **J** 85°F

Mixed Strategy Practice

4. Tim earns $4.00 an hour mowing lawns. He worked $2\frac{1}{4}$ hours on Saturday and $2\frac{3}{4}$ hours on Sunday. How much did he earn?

5. What two numbers come next in this pattern? Explain.

   32, 28, 23, 17, ,

6.

   1   2   3

   If this pattern continues, how many squares will be in the 7th figure? Explain.

7.   ?

   Look at the pattern. Describe the pattern. Draw the next figure.

8. Each side of a square blanket is 60 inches long. If Sue sews a 6-inch border along each edge of the blanket, what would be the perimeter of the blanket?

9. Bruno, David, and Zack are out for breakfast. The waiter brings eggs and bacon, pancakes, and cereal to their table. Bruno needs syrup, and David does not like meat. Who gets which order?

10. Write the greatest and least four-digit decimals expressed to hundredths without a zero in the hundredths place.

Extra Practice

Set A (pp. 378–381)

Write the decimal and fraction shown by each model or number line.

1.

2.

3.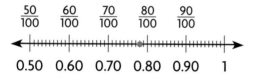

$\frac{50}{100}$ $\frac{60}{100}$ $\frac{70}{100}$ $\frac{80}{100}$ $\frac{90}{100}$

0.50   0.60   0.70   0.80   0.90   1

Write each fraction as a decimal.

4. $\frac{2}{10}$ 5. $\frac{33}{100}$ 6. $\frac{8}{100}$ 7. $\frac{9}{10}$ 8. $\frac{84}{100}$

9. Patty has $\frac{3}{10}$ of a dollar. How much money does she have?

Set B (pp. 384–387)

Write a mixed number or decimal.

1. 6.5   2. $7\frac{1}{4}$ 3. 1.5   4. 3.75   5. 8.25

6. 9.75   7. $5\frac{1}{2}$ 8. 2.3   9. 8.07   10. 4.80

Write the decimal in word form, expanded form, and as a mixed number.

11. 3.04   12. 1.57   13. 2.4   14. 1.01   15. 13.26

Set C (pp. 388–391)

Compare. Write <, >, or = for each ●.

1. 0.30 ● 0.3   2. 5.67 ● 6.75   3. 3.60 ● 3.06   4. 1.2 ● 1.20

Order the decimals from *least* to *greatest.*

5. 0.19; 0.21; 0.91; 0.12

6. $4.35; $3.45; $4.53; $3.54

7. 0.05; 0.57; 5.7; 0.75

8. 6.02; 2.6; 2.06; 0.62

9. Juan ran 1.65 miles during track practice, and Evan ran 1.68 miles. Who ran the greater distance?

Review/Test

✓ CHECK VOCABULARY AND CONCEPTS

Choose the best term from the box.

Vocabulary

decimal
decimal point
equivalent decimals

1. A number with one or more digits to the right of the decimal point is a __?__. (p. 378)

2. Decimals that name the same number are __?__. (p. 382)

✓ CHECK SKILLS

Write each fraction as a decimal. (pp. 378–381)

3. $\frac{6}{10}$

4. $\frac{1}{100}$

5. $\frac{9}{25}$

6. $\frac{48}{100}$

Write an equivalent decimal for each. (pp. 382–383)

7. 0.60

8. 0.9

9. 0.4

10. 0.50

Write a mixed number or a decimal. (pp. 384–387)

11. $6\frac{79}{100}$

12. $1\frac{67}{100}$

13. $3\frac{5}{100}$

14. 8.16

Write the decimal in word form, expanded form, and as a mixed number.

15. 4.9

16. 1.03

17. 3.58

18. 42.67

Compare. Write <, >, or = for each ●. (pp. 388–391)

19. 0.71 ● 0.63

20. 0.56 ● 0.83

21. 2.6 ● 2.61

Order the decimals from *greatest* to *least*. (pp. 388–391)

22. 1.23, 2.23, 1.32, 0.89, 2.03

23. 3.06, 3.97, 3.61, 3.8

✓ CHECK PROBLEM SOLVING

Solve. (pp. 392–393)

24. May, Peg, Lon, and Tim each bought a gift. The gifts cost $9.57, $8.64, $9.32, and $8.97. May's gift cost more than Tim's but less than Lon's. Lon's cost more than Peg's. Tim's gift cost $8.97. Name each child and the price of his or her gift.

25. Four runners ran a mile in 6.52 min, 7.20 min, 6.59 min, and 7.16 min. Elena finished after Lara but before Nick. Jan ran the fastest. List the runners, with their times, from first through fourth place.

 Chapter CRCT Test Prep

NUMBERS AND OPERATIONS

1. **M4N5.a.** Josh has read $\frac{4}{10}$ of his book for his book report. Which decimal number shows the part of the book Josh has read?

 A. 0.4

 B. 0.25

 C. 0.2

 D. 0.14

2. **M4N5.b.** The table shows how far each family lives from the library.

How Far from the Library?	
Family	**Distance**
Chung	0.7 mile
Hall	0.77 mile
Jones	0.70 mile
Roho	7.0 miles

 Which two families live the same distance from the library?

 A. Chung and Hall

 B. Hall and Roho

 C. Jones and Roho

 D. Chung and Jones

3. **M4N1.b.** Which is NOT another way of writing fifteen hundredths?

 A. 0.15

 B. 0.1 + 0.05

 C. 1,500

 D. $\frac{15}{100}$

NUMBERS AND OPERATIONS

Use the table below to answer question 4.

January Precipitation	
City	**Precipitation**
Atlanta, GA	5.0 inches
Jackson, MS	5.7 inches
Birmingham, AL	5.50 inches
Portland, OR	5.10 inches

4. **M4N5.b.** What is the order of the cities from least to greatest amount of precipitation in January?

 A. Portland, Atlanta, Jackson, Birmingham

 B. Atlanta, Portland, Birmingham, Jackson

 C. Portland, Atlanta, Birmingham, Jackson

 D. Atlanta, Portland, Jackson, Birmingham

5. **M4N5.b.** Dawn and four friends had lunch together. Dawn paid $5.08 for her lunch. John's lunch cost $5, Ray's lunch cost $5.80, Carter's lunch cost $5.18, and Rosa's lunch cost $5.20. Who had the lunch that cost less than Dawn's lunch?

 A. John

 B. Ray

 C. Carter

 D. Rosa

Cumulative CRCT Test Prep

ALGEBRA

6. M4A1.a. Phil drew a rectangle that is 5 inches long and 2 inches wide. Ravi drew a rectangle with the same length but twice as wide. Which statement is TRUE about the rectangles?

A. The areas are the same.

B. The perimeters are the same.

C. The area of Ravi's rectangle is twice the area of Phil's rectangle.

D. The perimeter of Ravi's rectangle is twice the perimeter of Phil's rectangle.

7. M4A1.b. A number of books, ★, are put equally into 4 boxes. Which expression shows this situation?

A. ★ ÷ 4

B. 4 ÷ ★

C. ★ × 4

D. 4 × ★

8. M4A1.c. What is the value of 7 × △ if △ = 7?

A. 7

B. 14

C. 49

D. 77

9. M4A1.c. Which value of □ makes the statement true?

$$3 + 8 = \square + 5$$

A. 3

B. 6

C. 8

D. 11

GEOMETRY

10. M4G1.a. How can you classify the triangle below according to the measure of its angles?

A. right triangle

B. acute triangle

C. scalene triangle

D. obtuse triangle

11. M4G3.b. Which building is located at (2,4) in the coordinate system below?

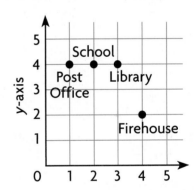

A. School

B. Post Office

C. Library

D. Firehouse

12. M4G1.c. Which figure has opposite sides that are parallel and four right angles?

A. a rhombus

B. a trapezoid

C. a parallelogram

D. a rectangle

Add and Subtract Decimals

≡FAST FACT • SCIENCE The first weather station in Alaska was established in Anchorage in 1915. December is the snowiest month in Anchorage, with an average snowfall of 14.8 inches.

INVESTIGATION The graph below shows the annual snowfall for 5 years in Anchorage. Use base-ten blocks or paper strips to model the annual snowfall for each year. Then find the difference between the greatest and the least amounts shown.

Owl snow sculpture in Alaska

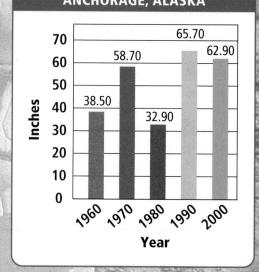

Using Data

ANNUAL SNOWFALL IN ANCHORAGE, ALASKA

Year	Inches
1960	38.50
1970	58.70
1980	32.90
1990	65.70
2000	62.90

CHECK WHAT YOU KNOW

Use this page to help you review and remember important skills needed for Chapter 19.

✓ MODEL DECIMALS

Write the decimal for the shaded part.

1.   **2.**   **3.**   **4.**

✓ DECIMAL PLACE VALUE

Write the value of the blue digit in each decimal.

5. 0.13   **6.** 0.45   **7.** 4.37   **8.** 0.68

9. 89.05   **10.** 0.74   **11.** 0.56   **12.** 35.2

✓ ROUND WHOLE NUMBERS

Round to the nearest hundred and the nearest ten.

13. 145   **14.** 281   **15.** 764   **16.** 115

17. 405   **18.** 327   **19.** 575   **20.** 391

VOCABULARY POWER

REVIEW

decimal [deˈsə•məl] *noun*

Decimal begins with the prefix *deci-,* which means "one tenth." Based on what you know about decimals, explain why the prefix *deci-* helps you understand what a decimal is.

 www.harcourtschool.com/mathglossary

Round Decimals

M4N2.c. Understand the meaning of rounding a decimal to the nearest whole number. *also* **M4P2, M4P2.a., M4P2.d., M4P3.a., M4P3.b., M4P3.c., M4P3.d.**

SNOW TREK Lisa and some friends went cross-country skiing. They covered 4.2 miles.

Round 4.2 to the nearest whole number.

One Way Use a number line.

4.2

```
  4                   5
```

4.2 is between 4 and 5, but it is closer to 4.

Another Way Use the rounding rules.

Look at the tenths place.   4.2

Since 2 < 5, the digit 4 stays the same.

So, 4.2 rounded to the nearest whole number is 4.

Remember

Rounding Rules:
• Find the place to which you want to round.
• Look at the digit to its right.
• If that digit is less than 5, the digit in the rounding place stays the same.
• If that digit is 5 or more, the digit in the rounding place is increased by 1.

Example

Round $17.65 to the nearest dollar.

Use the rounding rules.

Look at the tenths place. $17.65

Since 6 > 5, the digit 7 is increased by 1.

So, $17.65 rounds to $18.

• What amounts of money would round to $6?

MATH IDEA Decimals can be rounded using a number line or the rounding rules.

1. **Explain** how to use a number line to round 3.4 to the nearest whole number.

Round each number to the nearest whole number or dollar.

2. 2.2	3. 1.8	4. $16.98	5. 7.35	6. $9.57
7. 4.5	8. $5.45	9. 8.3	10. 6.82	11. $21.89

▶ **Practice and Problem Solving** (Extra Practice, page 414, Set A)

Round each number to the nearest whole number or dollar.

12. 5.84	13. 3.18	14. $1.43	15. $7.71	16. $36.52
17. 13.68	18. 49.27	19. 27.64	20. $83.54	21. $54.91
22. 10.07	23. 61.9	24. 5.81	25. 9.4	26. $24.59

27. Round 5.26 and 5.62 to the nearest whole number, and compare.

28. **REASONING** For what digits will 43.■5 round to 44?

29. David bought a jacket on sale for $32.49. To the nearest ten dollars, how much did David's jacket cost?

30. What are the least and greatest numbers in tenths that round to 2?

31. **REASONING** James paid $5.82 for a paint set. He told Pete the cost was about $6.00. Was $6.00 a reasonable rounded amount? Explain.

32. **? What's the Question?** The population of Georgia is about 8.2 million people. The answer is 8 million people.

Maintain Skills

33. Find the length of the safety pin to the nearest centimeter.

34. Find the length of the ribbon to the nearest inch.

CRCT Test Prep

35. **M4G3.b.** What is the ordered pair for point A in this coordinate system? (p. 82)

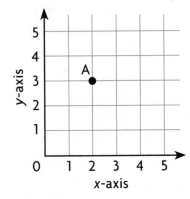

A. (4,3)   C. (2,4)
B. (4,2)   D. (2,3)

Estimate Decimal Sums and Differences

M4N2.d. Represent the results of computation as a rounded number when appropriate and estimate a sum or difference by rounding numbers. *also* M4N7.d., M4P2.a., M4P2.b., M4P2.d., M4P3, M4P3.a., M4P3.b., M4P3.c., M4P3.d., M4P5.b., M4P5.c.

Quick Review

1. $58 + 72$ **2.** $130 + 45$

3. $216 + 194$ **4.** $125 - 32$

5. $1,089 - 59$

Learn

PACK YOUR BAGS! The table shows the three countries that had the most visitors in 2000. Altogether, about how many people traveled to these countries?

Estimate by rounding to the nearest whole number.

74.5	→	75
52.7	→	53
+48.5	→	49
		177

- Line up the decimal points.
- Round to the nearest whole number.

So, altogether about 177 million travelers visited France, the United States, and Spain in 2000.

A travel magazine showed that in New Orleans, Louisiana, each traveler spent an average of $82.98 per day. In Paris, France, it was an amount equal to $97.55. About how much more did each traveler spend in Paris per day?

Estimate by rounding to the nearest dollar.

$97.55	→	$98
−$82.98	→	−$83
		$15

- Line up the decimal points.
- Round to the nearest dollar.

So, each traveler spent about $15 more per day in Paris.

- Name some situations in which you might need only an estimated sum or difference.

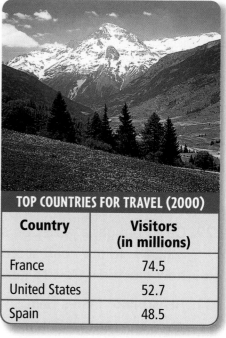

TOP COUNTRIES FOR TRAVEL (2000)

Country	Visitors (in millions)
France	74.5
United States	52.7
Spain	48.5

▲ **Spring meadow, France**

Check

1. Explain how you would determine whether a total cost of $19.48 is reasonable for a travel book that costs $12.99 and a poster that costs $6.49.

Estimate the sum or difference.

2. $24.76
    +$ 5.21

3.   5.25
    +7.06

4.   2.31
   −1.23

5. $7.80
   −$2.07

6.   17.13
   +19.78

Practice and Problem Solving Extra Practice, page 414, Set B

Estimate the sum or difference.

7. $2.8 - 0.5$ **8.** $\$21.06 - \$4.11$ **9.** $1.07 + 1.54$ **10.** $2.93 + 2.54$

11. $3.59 - 3.37$ **12.** $7.99 - 1.93$ **13.** $7.12 + 7.71$ **14.** $\$11.99 + \$10.58$

Estimate to compare. Write $<$ or $>$ for each ●.

15. $12.85 - 8.02$ ● $15.95 - 9.99$ **16.** $82.85 + 3.70$ ● $96.20 - 11.04$

USE DATA For 17–19, use the graph.

17. MULTISTEP Ann rode the north and south trails. Carly rode the east and west trails. To the nearest mile, about how many more miles did Ann ride than Carly?

18. Brett and Rob rode all four bike trails. To the nearest mile, how far did each ride?

19. REASONING Trudy wants to ride a bike trail with a distance greater than $1\frac{1}{2}$ miles. Which trails could Trudy choose?

20. Vocabulary Power When you *round* a number such as 5.28 to the nearest whole number, you change the number. Explain how rounding a number changes it.

21. MULTISTEP Pam bought a bike helmet for $22.29, a light for $21.79, and a backpack for $21.99, including tax. Estimate the total cost and the change she should receive from $70.00.

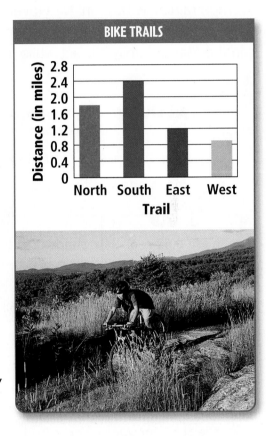

BIKE TRAILS

Distance (in miles): North, South, East, West — Trail

Maintain Skills

For 22–23, write the value of the blue digit.

22. 50,982   **23.** 43,081

24. What is the area of the rectangle in square units?

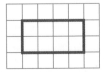

CRCT Test Prep

25. **M4A1.a.** What rule can be used to extend the pattern? (p. 52)

In	15	24	29
Out	7	16	

A. Add 8.
B. Add 9.
C. Subtract 8.
D. Subtract 9.

LESSON

3 Add Decimals

M4N5.c. Add and subtract both one and two digit decimals.
also M4P3.a., M4P3.b., M4P3.c., M4P3.d., M4P4.c., M4P5.

 Learn

SLIGHT CHANCE OF RAIN The Marco family will
be in Tucson, AZ, in November and December. The
average rainfall is 0.62 in. for November and
0.94 in. for December. How many inches of rainfall
can the Marco family expect while in Tucson?

Activity   **MATERIALS:** decimal models, color pencils

Add. 0.62 + 0.94   Estimate. 1 + 1 = 2

Use decimal models to find 0.62 + 0.94.

STEP 1	STEP 2
Shade 0.62 red.	Shade 0.94 blue. Find the sum. 0.62 + 0.94 = 1.56

The answer of 1.56 is close to the estimate of 2, so the
answer is reasonable.

So, the total amount of expected rainfall is 1.56 inches.

MATH IDEA You can add decimals the same way you
add whole numbers if you line up the decimal points first.

Examples

A
```
  0.41   ← Line up the decimal points.
+ 0.36
  0.77   Place the decimal point in the sum.
```

B
```
    1
  $4.26
+ $0.54
  $4.80
```

C
```
  1 1
  5.06
+ 3.98
  9.04
```

• Which examples can be solved using mental math? Explain.

404

▲ Tucson, Arizona

Quick Review
1. $1.10 + $0.25
2. $0.85 + $0.20
3. $3.05 + $0.45
4. $7.03 + $0.05
5. $0.75 + $0.25

1. Make a model to find the sum $1.42 + 0.55$. Draw a picture of your model.

Find the sum. Estimate to check.

2. $0.8 + 0.1$ **3.** $0.6 + 2.5$ **4.** $3.72 + 5.03$ **5.** $0.69 + 4.23$

> **Practice and Problem Solving**   Extra Practice, page 414, Set C

Find the sum. Estimate to check.

6. $0.9 + 0.5$ **7.** $1.66 + 0.32$ **8.** $0.36 + 2.28$ **9.** $\$5.61 + \$2.69$

10. $\begin{array}{r} 0.73 \\ +0.49 \end{array}$ **11.** $\begin{array}{r} \$7.05 \\ +\$0.95 \end{array}$ **12.** $\begin{array}{r} 1.89 \\ +1.54 \end{array}$ **13.** $\begin{array}{r} 24.91 \\ +21.70 \end{array}$ **14.** $\begin{array}{r} \$49.99 \\ +\$71.99 \end{array}$

Write the letter of the model that matches each problem. Solve.

a.   b.   c.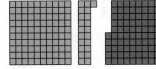

15. $1.21 + 0.85$ **16.** $0.4 + 0.9$ **17.** $0.43 + 0.57$

 **ALGEBRA**   **Use mental math to find the missing addend.**

18. $\blacksquare + 5.25 = 9.5$ **19.** $1.1 + 0.6 + \blacksquare = 1.8$ **20.** $1.11 + \blacksquare = 2.22$

USE DATA For 21–22, use the table.

21. MULTISTEP How many more inches of snow fell in the first three months of 2001 than in 2002?

22. ≡**FAST FACT** • **SCIENCE** The record snowfall for January in Pittsburgh is 40.2 inches. Is this amount greater than or less than the total amount of snowfall for the first 3 months of 2001 and 2002? by how much?

SNOWFALL IN PITTSBURGH, PA (in inches)		
	2001	2002
January	13.7	10.0
February	2.7	6.4
March	8.0	4.0

Maintain Skills

23. Stamps are sold in booklets containing 20 stamps. How many stamps are in 7 booklets?

CRCT Test Prep

24. M4N7.b. What is the value of $24 + 8 \div 4$? (p. 130)

A. 36   B. 26   C. 12   D. 2

LESSON
4 Subtract Decimals

M4N5.c. Add and subtract both one and two digit decimals.
also M4P2.a., M4P2.b., M4P2.c., M4P2.d., M4P5, M4P5.b., M4P5.c.

Quick Review

1. $3.50 − $1.00

2. $0.85 − $0.25

3. $1.20 − $0.90

4. $5.25 − $0.75

5. $0.89 − $0.10

> ## Learn

SMALL SITES One of the smallest countries in the world is Monaco, with an area of 1.8 square kilometers. Central Park in New York City has an area of 3.2 square kilometers. How much larger is Central Park than Monaco?

Activity **MATERIALS:** decimal models, color pencils, scissors

Subtract. 3.2 − 1.8   **Estimate.** 3 − 2 = 1

Take-Away Model Use decimal models.

STEP 1

Show 3.2 by shading decimal models.

STEP 2

Take away 18 tenths. 14 tenths are left.

18 tenths = 1.8

3.2 − 1.8 = 1.4

The answer of 1.4 is close to the estimate of 1, so the answer is reasonable. So, Central Park is 1.4 square kilometers larger than Monaco.

▲ **The Principality of Monaco**

Technology Link

More Practice: Harcourt Mega Math The Number Games, *Tiny's Think Tank*, Level L

Examples

A 2.3 − 1.4

$$\begin{array}{r} 1 \overset{13}{\cancel{}} \\ 2.\cancel{3} \\ -1.4 \\ \hline 0.9 \end{array}$$

Line up the decimal points.

Place the decimal point in the difference.

B $18.56 − $4.93

$$\begin{array}{r} 7\;\;15 \\ \$18.\cancel{5}\cancel{6} \\ -\$\;\;4.93 \\ \hline \$13.63 \end{array}$$

C 84.63 − 26.57

$$\begin{array}{r} 7\,14\;\;\;5\,13 \\ 8\cancel{4}.\cancel{6}\cancel{3} \\ -26.57 \\ \hline 58.06 \end{array}$$

1. **Explain** how regrouping to subtract decimals is similar to regrouping to subtract whole numbers.

Find the difference. Estimate to check.

2. 0.8
   −0.5

3. $20.82
   −$ 7.71

4. 22.3
   −11.9

5. 3.42
   −0.24

6. 2.91
   −1.68

▶ **Practice and Problem Solving** Extra Practice, page 414, Set D

Find the difference. Estimate to check.

7. 0.9
   −0.2

8. $6.93
   −$0.54

9. 1.6
   −0.8

10. 41.97
    −10.38

11. $52.72
    −$21.28

12. 2.45
    −2.38

13. 3.51
    −1.27

14. 4.768
    −2.993

15. 16.70
    − 5.17

16. 5.08
    −2.22

17. $7.89 − $4.37

18. 9.84 − 3.87

19. 8.2 − 6.9

20. $29.53 − $18.98

21. 9.12 − 3.07

22. 4.23 − 2.81

23. 13.20 − 11.49

24. 9.53 − 4.10

 **ALGEBRA** **Use mental math to find the missing digits.**

25. 2.■
   −■.1
   ─────
    1.2

26. ■.5
   −4.■
   ─────
    0.2

27. 6.■
   −■.6
   ─────
    5.1

28. ■.8
   −7.■
   ─────
    3.5

29. **REASONING** The difference of two 3-digit decimal numbers is 1.34. One number has a 6 in the ones and hundredths places. The other has a 6 in the tenths place. What are the two numbers?

31. **MULTISTEP** Molly has saved $600 for a trip to France with the French Club. She needs twice that amount plus $50 more. How much does the trip cost?

30. **?** **What's the Error?** Josh made this model for 4.6 − 2.9 = 1.7. Describe his error. Draw a correct model.

Maintain Skills

32. Which is taller, a tree that is 3 feet tall or a tree that is 3 yards tall?

CRCT Test Prep

33. **M4N1.b.** Which number is 7 tenths? (p. 378)

A. 0.07   B. 0.7   C. 7   D. 70

Add and Subtract Decimals and Money

> M4N5.c. Add and subtract both one and two digit decimals. *also* M4N2.d., M4P5.b., M4P5.c.

Quick Review

Compare. Write <, >, or = for each ●.

1. 47.5 ● 4.81 **2.** 3.2 ● 2.3

3. 0.75 ● 0.72 **4.** 2.8 ● 2.84

5. 9.9 ● 9.90

▶ Learn

RAIN, RAIN, GO AWAY! Danny is doing a report on Iowa weather. Des Moines receives about 33 inches of rain each year. Use the table to find the total average rainfall from April through June.

Example 1

Add. 3.21 + 3.96 + 4.18

Estimate. 3 + 4 + 4 = 11

STEP 1

Line up the decimal point and place value of each number.

```
  3.21
  3.96
+ 4.18
```

STEP 2

Add as you do with whole numbers. Place the decimal point in the sum.

```
  1 1
  3.21
  3.96
+ 4.18
 11.35
```

AVERAGE RAINFALL (DES MOINES, IA)

Month	Amount of Rain (in inches)
April	3.21
May	3.96
June	4.18

Since the answer of 11.35 is close to the estimate of 11, the answer is reasonable. So, the total average rainfall is 11.35 inches.

Example 2

Danny's report includes information about the highest recorded monthly rainfall. Use the tables. About how much greater was the record rainfall for April through June than the total average rainfall for the same three months?

HIGHEST RECORDED RAINFALL (DES MOINES, IA)

Month and Year	Amount of Rain (in inches)
April 1976	7.76
May 1996	11.08
June 1881	15.79

Add. 7.76 + 11.08 + 15.79

```
 11  2
   7.76
 11.08
+15.79
 34.63
```

34.63 rounded to the nearest whole number is 35.

11.35 rounded to the nearest whole number is 11.

35 − 11 = 26

So, the record rainfall was about 26 inches greater than the total average rainfall for April through June.

Equivalent Decimals

Sometimes one number has more decimal places after the decimal point than the other. Write equivalent decimals with the same number of decimal places before adding or subtracting.

Andrea goes to the store to buy a sun visor that costs $12.56. She gives the cashier $20. How much change should she receive?

Example

Subtract. $20 − $12.56   **Estimate.** $20 − $13 = $7

STEP 1

Line up the decimal points. Place zeros to the right of the decimal point so that each number has the same number of digits after the decimal point.

$$\begin{array}{r} \$2\,0\,.\,0\,0 \\ -\,\$1\,2\,.\,5\,6 \\ \hline \end{array}$$

STEP 2

Subtract as you do with whole numbers. Place the decimal point in the difference.

$$\begin{array}{r} \overset{9\quad\ 9}{\overset{1\ 10\ 10 10}{\$2\,0\,.\,0\,0}} \\ -\,\$1\,2\,.\,5\,6 \\ \hline \$\ \ 7\,.\,4\,4 \end{array}$$

So, Andrea will receive $7.44 in change.

- How much change should Andrea receive if she gives the cashier $20.01? Why would she do this?

More Examples

A $25 − $16.33

$$\begin{array}{r} \overset{14\quad\ 9}{\overset{1\ 4\ 10 10}{\$2\,5\,.\,0\,0}} \\ -\,\$1\,6\,.\,3\,3 \\ \hline \$\ \ 8\,.\,6\,7 \end{array}$$

B $32 + $57.89

$$\begin{array}{r} \$3\,2\,.\,0\,0 \\ +\,\$5\,7\,.\,8\,9 \\ \hline \$8\,9\,.\,8\,9 \end{array}$$

C 57.68 − 38.56

$$\begin{array}{r} \overset{4\ 17}{5\,7}\,.\,6\,8 \\ -\,3\,8\,.\,5\,6 \\ \hline 1\,9\,.\,1\,2 \end{array}$$

 You can also use a calculator to add and subtract decimals.

```
25 − 16.33 =
            8.67
```

LESSON CONTINUES ▶

Technology Link

More Practice: Harcourt
Mega Math The Number
Games *Buggy Bargains*,
Levels F, G, and I

1. **Explain** why zeros are sometimes placed to the right of the decimal points of numbers.

Find the sum or difference. Estimate to check.

2. $21 – $10.20   3. 5.4 + 0.39   4. $13 + $9.12   5. 15.03 – 9.6

▶ **Practice and Problem Solving**   Extra Practice, page 414, Set E

Find the sum or difference. Estimate to check.

6. 9.5
   +2.52

7. 6.4
   −2.26

8. $3
   −$1.39

9. 3.8
   +4.07

10. $21.28
    −$ 8

11. 43.8
    + 1.73

12. $7
    −$3.18

13. 5.3
    −2.87

14. 56.12
    − 8

15. 16.2
    + 9.5

16. $6.99 + $2.09   17. 1.3 − 0.4   18. 18.7 − 5.94   19. $65 − $30.50

20. 56.83 − 0.67   21. $1.34 + $12.09   22. 41.36 − 7.89   23. 69.4 + 7.82

24. 4.5 + 19 + 6.03   25. 14.4 + 19 + 7.74   26. $45 + $31.50 + $20

 **Find the missing number.**

27. 2.51 − 0.8 = ▇   28. 2.32 − 1.6 = ▇   29. ▇ − 0.90 = 0.2

30. 3.02 − ▇ = 1.31   31. 0.9 + 2.25 = ▇   32. ▇ + 0.52 = 1.12

33. Ernie wants to buy an MP3 player that costs $199. Last week, Ernie saved $77.80 from his paycheck. This week, he saved $86.25. About how much more money does he need to buy the MP3 player?

34. Mindy is picking up some photo prints that cost $12.75 and batteries for her camera that cost $5.19. About how much change will she receive from a $20 bill?

35. **? What's the Error?** Maria added 3.16, 1.04, and 0.07 and got a sum of 42.7. Describe her error. Write the correct answer.

36. Write a problem using addition or subtraction in which the answer is $9.21.

37. Alex went to the store with $10 and left the store with $5.98. He bought milk, eggs, and bread. The milk was $1.49, and the eggs were $0.89. How much was the bread?

38. Trevor scored 2 home runs in a college baseball game. Use the diagram to find how many feet Trevor ran to score the 2 home runs.

39. Will is walking to the ball field, which is 2.3 kilometers from his home. He has walked 0.8 kilometer. How much farther must he walk?

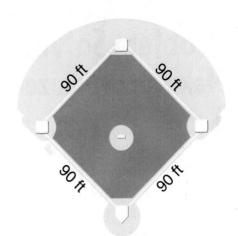

Maintain Skills

40. What is the value of the digit 8 in 83,192.5?

41. Shari does 30 jumping jacks each day. How many jumping jacks does she do in 7 days?

CRCT Test Prep

42. **M4G1.c.** Which quadrilateral has four congruent sides? (p. 276)

A. parallelogram
B. rhombus
C. trapezoid
D. rectangle

Problem Solving THiNKer's CorNer

BENCHMARK DECIMALS

Rounding decimals to benchmarks, such as 0, 0.5, and 1, on a number line can help you estimate sums and differences.

Josh and Maya went on a nature walk to collect different types of leaves for science class. During the first hour, they walked 0.46 mi. During the second hour, they walked 0.85 mi. About how many miles did they walk?

Estimate. $0.46 + 0.85$

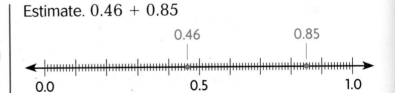

$0.46 \rightarrow 0.5$ 0.46 is between 0 and 0.5 but closer to 0.5.

$+0.85 \rightarrow \underline{1.0}$ 0.85 is between 0.5 and 1 but closer to 1.

$ 1.5$

So, Josh and Maya walked about 1.5 miles.

Use a number line and benchmark decimals to estimate each sum or difference.

1. $0.55 + 0.32$ **2.** $0.79 - 0.53$ **3.** $0.33 + 0.55$ **4.** $0.89 - 0.41$ **5.** $0.08 + 0.64$

Problem Solving Strategy
Make an Organized List

 M4P1.a. Build new mathematical knowledge through problem solving. *also* M4N5.c., M4P1.b., M4P1.c., M4P1.d., M4P3.a., M4P3.b., M4P3.c., M4P3.d.

PROBLEM Marcia is visiting Georgia and wants to buy some pecans, for which Georgia is famous. She has two $5 bills, four $1 bills, 3 quarters, 3 dimes, and 5 nickels. How many different sets of equivalent bills and coins can she use to buy a 5-pound bag of Georgia pecans that costs $10.25?

UNDERSTAND

- What are you asked to find?
- What information will you use?

PLAN

- What strategy can you use to solve the problem?
  You can *make an organized list* to find sets of bills and coins with a value of $10.25.

SOLVE

- How can you use the strategy to solve the problem?
  Make an organized list that shows equivalent sets of money.

$5 Bills	$1 Bills	Quarters	Dimes	Nickels
2		1		
2			2	1
2			1	3
2				5
1	4	3	3	4

So, there are 5 equivalent sets.

CHECK

- How can you decide whether your answer is correct?

Strategies

Act It Out or Use Objects

Make a Picture or Diagram

Guess and Check

Use or Look for a Pattern

Use Logical Reasoning

▶ **Make an Organized List**

Use or Make a Table

Work Backwards

Problem Solving

1. What if Marcia buys the pecans at a different stand that charges $9.75 for 5 pounds of pecans. What different equivalent sets of bills and coins can she use?

2. Georgia is also known for its peaches. Greg has three $1 bills, 6 quarters, 3 dimes, and 2 nickels. What equivalent sets of bills and coins can he use to buy 3 pounds of peaches for $3.75?

Shawn wants to buy a pound of pecans for $2.75.
He has two $1 bills, 6 quarters, 3 dimes, and 6 nickels.

3. Shawn wants to keep one of his $1 bills and as many coins as he can. Which combination of bills and coins should he use?

A one $1 bill, 2 quarters, 5 nickels

B one $1 bill, 6 quarters, 2 dimes, 1 nickel

C one $1 bill, 5 quarters, 3 dimes, 4 nickels

D two $1 bills, 3 quarters

4. If Shawn pays with the fewest total number of coins and bills that he can, which coins will he have left?

F 6 quarters, 3 dimes, 6 nickels

G 4 quarters, 2 dimes, 5 nickels

H 3 quarters, 3 dimes, 6 nickels

J 3 quarters, 2 dimes, 4 nickels

Mixed Strategy Practice

5. Pedro has only nickels and dimes. Which 10 coins can he use to buy a bag of fruit snacks for $0.65?

6. Kendra has $4.25 left after spending $2.95 for a sandwich and $1.75 for a glass of milk for lunch. How much did Kendra have before she bought lunch?

7. Tiffany has one $10 bill, three $5 bills, four $1 bills, 6 quarters, and 6 dimes. In how many different ways can she pay the exact amount for a rice cooker that costs $19.50?

8. ✏️ **Write a problem** in which you must use the following bills and coins: two $1 bills, 3 quarters, 5 dimes, 4 nickels. Solve your problem.

9. Roz has $11 more than Fred. Together they have $37. How much money does each have?

Extra Practice

Set A (pp. 400–401)

Round each number to the nearest whole number.

1. 9.30   **2.** $5.79   **3.** $8.65   **4.** 4.53   **5.** $3.49

6. $8.93   **7.** 4.57   **8.** 16.89   **9.** 39.47   **10.** $7.65

Set B (pp. 402–403)

Estimate the sum or difference.

1.	2.	3.	4.	5.
$2.80	2.35	2.35	$23.47	18.92
+$2.30	+1.19	−0.91	−$14.96	+39.45

Set C (pp. 404–405)

Find the sum. Estimate to check.

1.	2.	3.	4.	5.
10.29	$15.98	6.41	7.98	6.29
+33.46	+$12.04	+7.23	+2.31	+8.88

6. 0.31 + 4.57   **7.** 4.87 + 8.13   **8.** 7.5 + 8.3   **9.** 5.76 + 2.18

10. Bob went to the store. He bought oranges for $1.32, juice for $1.48, and eggs for $1.10. How much money did he spend?

Set D (pp. 406–407)

Find the difference. Estimate to check.

1.	2.	3.	4.	5.
2.56	13.28	$11.27	$75.43	67.30
−1.38	− 3.53	−$ 7.55	−$18.63	−31.72

6. $0.78 − $0.51   **7.** 5.94 − 5.76   **8.** $9.49 − $6.23   **9.** $7.65 − $1.85

Set E (pp. 408–411)

Find the sum or difference. Estimate to check.

1.	2.	3.	4.	5.
$13.95	22.49	$26.00	74.3	14.28
+$21.76	+14.3	−$18.94	− 6.79	+ 8.5

6. 16.3 + 1.09   **7.** $8 − $3.78   **8.** 3.7 − 1.99   **9.** 46 − 3.05

Review/Test

✓ CHECK VOCABULARY AND CONCEPTS

Choose the best term from the box.

Vocabulary

decimal points
equivalent decimals
tenths

1. When adding or subtracting decimals, first line up the ? . (pp. 404, 406)

2. 0.6 and 0.60 are ? since they are different names for the same amount. (p. 409)

✓ CHECK SKILLS

Round each number to the nearest whole number or dollar. (pp. 400–401)

3. 8.29   **4.** $4.68   **5.** $9.76   **6.** 3.49

7. 7.69   **8.** $19.95   **9.** 1.63   **10.** 14.83

11. 22.56   **12.** $8.48   **13.** 5.09   **14.** $39.88

Estimate the sum or difference. (pp. 402–403)

15. $\begin{array}{r} 1.29 \\ +3.46 \end{array}$ **16.** $\begin{array}{r} \$5.98 \\ +\$9.04 \end{array}$ **17.** $\begin{array}{r} 16.10 \\ +87.25 \end{array}$ **18.** $\begin{array}{r} 14.33 \\ -\ 4.65 \end{array}$

19. 4.88 + 6.32   **20.** $13.85 − $7.55   **21.** 21.15 − 8.72   **22.** 11.82 + 3.38

Find the sum or difference. Estimate to check. (pp. 404–405, 406–407, 408–411)

23. 5.7 + 8.4   **24.** $9.61 + $0.81   **25.** 16.3 + 9.74

26. $3.67 − $0.59   **27.** 23.1 − 5   **28.** $78.41 − $42.83

29. 1.94 + 0.8   **30.** 42.51 + 22.4   **31.** 20 − 8.68

✓ CHECK PROBLEM SOLVING

Make an organized list to solve. (pp. 412–413)

32. A bag of peanuts costs $2.35. What different combinations of bills and coins can you use to pay the exact amount if you have two $1 bills, 5 quarters, 3 dimes, and 3 nickels?

33. Vera has two $5 bills, four $1 bills, 5 quarters, 8 dimes, and 1 nickel. In how many different ways can she use the bills and coins to pay exactly $10 for a birthday cake?

Chapter CRCT Test Prep

NUMBERS AND OPERATIONS

1. **M4N2.c.** Malcolm's new dog weighs 28.2 pounds. How much does his dog weigh to the nearest pound?

    A. 30 pounds

    B. 29 pounds

    C. 28 pounds

    D. 27 pounds

2. **M4N2.d.** The Appalachian Trail runs through Georgia. The table shows how far Stan hiked along the trail each day for 4 days.

Day	Distance
Thursday	2.8 miles
Friday	3.1 miles
Saturday	4.2 miles
Sunday	4.9 miles

    About how far did Stan hike over the four days?

    A. about 13 miles

    B. about 15 miles

    C. about 17 miles

    D. about 19 miles

3. **M4N5.c.** Chatsworth, GA, has an area of 4.74 square miles. Ellijay, GA, has an area of 2.68 square miles. How much larger is Chatsworth than Ellijay?

    A. 7.42 square miles larger

    B. 6.32 square miles larger

    C. 2.14 square miles larger

    D. 2.06 square miles larger

NUMBERS AND OPERATIONS

4. **M4N5.c.** Alan bought a sandwich for $5.25 and a drink. He paid with a $10 bill. He received $3.25 in change. How much did his drink cost?

    A. $1.00

    B. $1.25

    C. $1.50

    D. $2.00

5. **M4N5.c.** A pair of Speed X Sneakers costs $59.95 at Sports Haven. The same pair of sneakers costs $4.75 more at Sneaker Warehouse. How much do the sneakers cost at Sneaker Warehouse?

    A. $55.20

    B. $55.30

    C. $63.70

    D. $64.70

6. **M4N2.d.** According to the U.S. Census taken in the year 2000, the population of Los Angeles, CA, is about 3.7 million, and the population of Chicago, IL, is about 2.9 million. About how many people live in these two cities?

    A. about 5 million people

    B. about 6 million people

    C. about 7 million people

    D. about 12 million people

Cumulative CRCT Test Prep

DATA ANALYSIS

7. **M4D1.a.** Jason made a bar graph to show how many points each of the starters made during a basketball game.

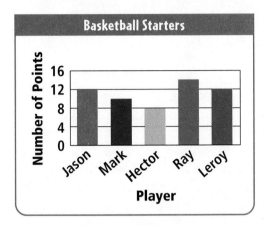

Which data set shows how many points each starter made?

A. Jason: 12; Mark: 9; Hector: 8; Ray: 13; Leroy: 12

B. Jason: 12; Mark: 10; Hector: 8; Ray: 14; Leroy: 12

C. Jason: 12; Mark: 10; Hector: 8; Ray: 16; Leroy: 12

D. Jason: 12; Mark: 11; Hector: 10; Ray: 13; Leroy: 12

8. **M4D1.c.** What type of graph would BEST display the number of cans that the fourth-grade boys and the fourth-grade girls collected for a recycling project?

A. line graph

B. bar graph

C. double-bar graph

D. pictograph

MEASUREMENT

9. **M4M2.a.** What is the measure of the angle?

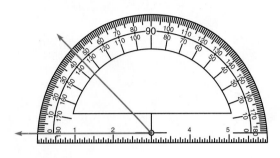

A. 135°

B. 90°

C. 45°

D. 15°

10. **M4M2.b.** Which rays show a half rotation?

A.

B.

C.

D.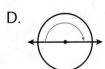

Multiply Decimals by Whole Numbers

≡**FAST FACT** • SOCIAL STUDIES The Appalachian Trail is one of the most famous hiking trails in the United States. It runs 2,174 miles from Maine through Georgia. The Georgia part of the trail is 79 miles long. But if you prefer to hike shorter distances, Georgia also has many other hiking trails you might enjoy.

INVESTIGATION Rich has walked a total of 2.4 miles on some of the Georgia trails. On which trails did he walk? How many times did he walk each trail?

The path to Anna Ruby Falls is paved. The path follows Smith Creek and has benches for resting along the way.

Using Data

HIKING TRAILS IN GEORGIA		
Trail	**County**	**Length**
Cherokee Quarry Trail	Lincoln	0.5 mi
Anna Ruby Falls Trail	White	0.8 mi
Songbird Trail	Murray	0.6 mi
Horse Trough Falls Trail	White and Union	0.3 mi
Helton Creek Falls Trail	Union	0.4 mi

CHECK WHAT YOU KNOW

Use this page to help you review and remember important skills needed for Chapter 20.

MULTIPLICATION PATTERNS

Find the product.

1. 8×100 **2.** 6×200 **3.** 9×20 **4.** 4×80

5. 15×100 **6.** $18 \times 1{,}000$ **7.** 31×10 **8.** 44×100

9. 2×500 **10.** $6 \times 3{,}000$ **11.** 7×40 **12.** 3×800

13. 28×100 **14.** $72 \times 1{,}000$ **15.** 19×10 **16.** $53 \times 1{,}000$

MULTIPLY BY A 1-DIGIT NUMBER

Find the product.

17. $\begin{array}{r} 32 \\ \times\ 5 \\ \hline \end{array}$ **18.** $\begin{array}{r} 51 \\ \times\ 7 \\ \hline \end{array}$ **19.** $\begin{array}{r} 74 \\ \times\ 3 \\ \hline \end{array}$ **20.** $\begin{array}{r} 40 \\ \times\ 2 \\ \hline \end{array}$

21. $\begin{array}{r} 56 \\ \times\ 5 \\ \hline \end{array}$ **22.** $\begin{array}{r} 61 \\ \times\ 8 \\ \hline \end{array}$ **23.** $\begin{array}{r} 93 \\ \times\ 8 \\ \hline \end{array}$ **24.** $\begin{array}{r} 82 \\ \times\ 2 \\ \hline \end{array}$

25. $\begin{array}{r} 314 \\ \times\ 2 \\ \hline \end{array}$ **26.** $\begin{array}{r} 132 \\ \times\ 6 \\ \hline \end{array}$ **27.** $\begin{array}{r} 405 \\ \times\ 3 \\ \hline \end{array}$ **28.** $\begin{array}{r} 421 \\ \times\ 9 \\ \hline \end{array}$

29. $\begin{array}{r} 643 \\ \times\ 4 \\ \hline \end{array}$ **30.** $\begin{array}{r} 510 \\ \times\ 7 \\ \hline \end{array}$ **31.** $\begin{array}{r} 823 \\ \times\ 5 \\ \hline \end{array}$ **32.** $\begin{array}{r} 518 \\ \times\ 2 \\ \hline \end{array}$

VOCABULARY POWER

REVIEW

hundredth [hun′•drədth] *adjective* or *noun*

One whole can be divided into 100 equal parts, or 100 hundredths. One dollar can be divided into hundredths. What is another name for one hundredth of one dollar?

www.harcourtschool.com/mathglossary

Multiply Decimals

M4N5.d. Model multiplication and division of decimals by whole numbers. *also* M4P3.a., M4P3.b., M4P3.d., M4P5, M4P5.a., M4P5.b., M4P5.c.

▶ Explore

Walt loves to hike along the Helton Creek Falls Trail in Union County, GA. The trail is 0.4 mile long. If Walt hikes the entire trail every Saturday for 3 Saturdays, how far will he have hiked in all?

Activity 1

Make a model to find $3 × 0.4$.

STEP 1

Use tenths models. Shade 0.4, or 4 tenths, three times. Use a different color each time.

STEP 2

Count the number of shaded tenths. There are 12 shaded tenths. 12 tenths is equivalent to 1 whole and 2 tenths.

So, $0.4 × 3 = 1.2$.

So, Walt will have hiked 1.2 miles in all for the 3 Saturdays.

- How many decimal places are in the factors of $0.4 × 3$? How many are in the product?

- What materials would you need to model $0.45 × 3$? Describe what you would do.

Technology Link

More Practice: Harcourt Mega Math The Number Games, *Buggy Bargains*, Level J

Try It

Make a model to find the product.

a. $2 × 0.7$

b. $3 × 0.9$

c. $2 × 0.25$

d. $4 × 0.15$

How many more tenths need to be shaded to show 3 × 4 tenths?

Connect

You can write a multiplication sentence for your model.

Activity 2
Find 2×0.24.

STEP 1

Model

Use a hundredths model. Shade 0.24, or 24 hundredths, two times. Use a different color each time. Count the number of shaded hundredths. There are 48 shaded hundredths.

STEP 2

Record

$$\begin{array}{r} 0.24 \\ \times\ \ 2 \\ \hline 0.48 \end{array}$$

- Multiply as with whole numbers. $(24 \times 2 = 48)$
- Use the model to place the decimal point.
  $2 \times 0.24 = 48$ hundredths, which is 0.48.

So, $2 \times 0.24 = 0.48$.

Practice and Problem Solving

Make a model to find each product.

1. 2×0.4
2. $\$5 \times 0.6$
3. 3×0.7
4. 5×0.5

5. 2×0.65
6. $3 \times \$0.75$
7. 5×0.08
8. $2 \times \$0.09$

USE DATA For 9–11, use the table.

Walt will buy some supplies for his next hike.

9. MULTISTEP How much more will 3 packs of trail mix cost than 2 bottles of bug repellent?

10. Walt has $5. Can he buy 6 mini-flashlights for himself and his friends? Explain.

11. ✎ **Write a problem** that can be solved using the data in the table and multiplication of a decimal and a whole number. Solve your problem.

HIKING SUPPLIES	
Supply	**Cost**
Trail Mix	$0.89 per pack
Mini-Flashlight	$0.95 each
Bug Repellent	$0.75 per 2-oz bottle

Maintain Skills

12. 67×8
13. $75 \div 5$

14. What is the value of the blue digit in the number 56,741?

CRCT Test Prep

15. ⬤ **M4N5.b.** Which decimals are listed in order from least to greatest? (p. 388)

A. 1.23, 1.8, 1.09
B. 1.09, 1.8, 1.23
C. 1.8, 1.23, 1.09
D. 1.09, 1.23, 1.8

Algebra: Mental Math: Multiplication Patterns

M4N7.d. Use mental math and estimation strategies to compute.
also M4N5.e., M4P1.a., M4P1.b., M4P1.c., M4P1.d., M4P2.a.,
M4P2.b., M4P2.c., M4P2.d., M4P3.a., M4P3.b., M4P3.c., M4P3.d.

Quick Review

1. 32×10

2. 532×10

3. 76×100

4. 410×100

5. $98 \times 1{,}000$

▶ **Learn**

MONEY MATTERS A dime is 0.1 of a dollar. Luis saves one dime each day. How much will Luis have after 1,000 days?

Example
What is $0.1 \times 1{,}000$?

Look for a pattern.

$0.1 \times 1 = 0.1$

$0.1 \times 10 = 1.$ ← The decimal point moves one place to the right.

$0.1 \times 100 = 10.$ ← The decimal point moves two places to the right.

$0.1 \times 1{,}000 = 100.$ ← The decimal point moves three places to the right.

So, if Luis saves 1 dime each day for 1,000 days, he will have 100 dollars.

• How many dimes will Luis have saved when he has 10 dollars?

 MATH IDEA The number of zeros in the whole number factor is the same as the number of places the decimal point moves to the right.

More Examples

Ⓐ $\$0.25 \times 1 = \$0.25$

$\$0.25 \times 10 = \$2.50$

$\$0.25 \times 100 = \$25$

$\$0.25 \times 1{,}000 = \$250$

Ⓑ $0.08 \times 1 = 0.08$

$0.08 \times 10 = 0.8$

$0.08 \times 100 = 8$

$0.08 \times 1{,}000 = 80$

REASONING How is multiplying a decimal by 100 the same as multiplying a whole number by 100?

1. **Explain** why the product 0.25×100 has two digits but the product 0.08×100 has only 1 digit.

Use mental math to complete each pattern.

2. $1 \times 0.6 = 0.6$
   $10 \times 0.6 = 6$
   $100 \times 0.6 = \square$
   $1,000 \times 0.6 = 600$

3. $\$0.05 \times 1 = \$0.05$
   $\$0.05 \times 10 = \square$
   $\$0.05 \times 100 = \$5$
   $\$0.05 \times 1,000 = \$50$

4. $1 \times 0.15 = 0.15$
   $10 \times 0.15 = 1.5$
   $100 \times 0.15 = 15$
   $1,000 \times 0.15 = \square$

▶ **Practice and Problem Solving** ⬤ Extra Practice, page 428, Set A

Use mental math to complete each pattern.

5. $1 \times 0.2 = 0.2$
   $10 \times 0.2 = 2$
   $100 \times 0.2 = 20$
   $1,000 \times 0.2 = \square$

6. $\$0.80 \times 1 = \$0.80$
   $\$0.80 \times 10 = \square$
   $\$0.80 \times 100 = \$80$
   $\$0.80 \times 1,000 = \$800$

7. $1 \times 0.04 = 0.04$
   $10 \times 0.04 = 0.4$
   $100 \times 0.04 = \square$
   $1,000 \times 0.04 = 40$

Use mental math to multiply.

8. 0.75×100

9. $0.01 \times 1,000$

10. 0.67×10

11. 0.07×100

USE DATA For 12–13, use the table.

BLOCK	HEIGHT
	0.05 m
	0.2 m
	0.15 m

12. What is the height of a block tower that has 100 red blocks stacked one on top of the other?

13. **MULTISTEP** Jenny built two 2-meter towers using different color blocks for each. Only one color was used in each tower. What color blocks did she use? How many blocks are in each tower?

14. **? What's the Error?** Mel says that 1,000 nickels are worth more than 1,000 quarters because 1,000 nickels are $500, but 1,000 quarters are only $250.

15. **Vocabulary Power** A decimal has a dot called the *decimal point*. Explain why decimals have a decimal point.

Maintain Skills

16. Barry is building a fence around his pool. How much fencing does Barry need?

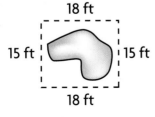

18 ft
15 ft   15 ft
18 ft

CRCT Test Prep

17. ⬤ M4N5.b. Which of the following is TRUE? (p. 388)

    A. $0.97 < 0.79$ C. $0.6 = 0.60$
    B. $0.08 > 0.10$ D. $0.9 = 0.09$

18. ⬤ M4M1.c. Which of the following is the GREATEST weight? (p. 338)

    A. 20 ounces C. 15 pounds
    B. 15 ounces D. 15 tons

Multiply Decimals by Whole Numbers

 M4N5.e. Multiply and divide both one and two digit decimals by whole numbers. *also* **M4N2.d., M4P2.b., M4P2.c., M4P2.d., M4P3.a., M4P3.b., M4P3.c., M4P3.d.**

▶ Learn

EGGSACTLY! Eggs are one of the main products produced on Georgia farms. A typical jumbo egg weighs about 0.15 lb. Eggs are usually sold by the dozen, in a carton of 12 eggs. About how much will one dozen jumbo eggs weigh?

▲ An egg's classification depends on its weight.

Example Find 0.15×12.

STEP 1	**STEP 2**
Multiply as with whole numbers.	Find the total number of decimal places in the factors. Place the decimal point that number of places from the right in the product.

STEP 1

Multiply as with whole numbers.

$$\begin{array}{r} 0.15 \\ \times\ \ 12 \\ \hline 30 \\ +\ 150 \\ \hline 180 \end{array}$$

STEP 2

$$\begin{array}{rl} 0.15 & \text{2 decimal places in this factor} \\ \times\ \ 12 & \text{0 decimal places in this factor} \\ \hline 30 & \\ +\ 150 & \\ \hline 1.80 & \text{2 decimal places in the product} \end{array}$$

So, one dozen jumbo eggs will weigh about 1.8 lb.

- Why can the solution to the problem be written as 1.8 lb instead of as 1.80 lb?

More Examples

A Find 8×0.9.

$8 \times 0.9 = 7.2$

There is 1 decimal place in the factor, so there is 1 decimal place in the product.

B Round the product $\$0.51 \times 32$ to the nearest dollar.

$$\begin{array}{rl} \$0.51 & \text{2 decimal places} \\ \times\ \ \ 32 & \text{0 decimal places} \\ \hline 102 & \\ +153 & \\ \hline \$16.32 & \text{2 decimal places in the product} \end{array}$$

The product is about $16. $16.32 rounded to the nearest dollar is $16.

REASONING Is $6 \times 0.5 = 0.3$ correct? Explain.

▶ Check

1. Explain how the product of any whole number and a decimal less than 1 is related to the whole number.

Count the decimal places to place the decimal point in the product.

2.
$$\begin{array}{r} 18 \\ \times 0.5 \\ \hline 9\,0 \end{array}$$

3.
$$\begin{array}{r} 56 \\ \times 0.08 \\ \hline 4\,4\,8 \end{array}$$

4.
$$\begin{array}{r} 0.85 \\ \times\quad 9 \\ \hline 7\,6\,5 \end{array}$$

5.
$$\begin{array}{r} \$0.45 \\ \times\quad 24 \\ \hline \$1\,0\,8\,0 \end{array}$$

Find the product.

6. $8 \times \$0.12$ **7.** 26×0.06 **8.** 0.62×9 **9.** 0.8×19

▶ Practice and Problem Solving   Extra Practice, page 428, Set B

Count the decimal places to place the decimal point in the product.

10.
$$\begin{array}{r} 16 \\ \times 0.4 \\ \hline 6\,4 \end{array}$$

11.
$$\begin{array}{r} 48 \\ \times 0.05 \\ \hline 2\,4\,0 \end{array}$$

12.
$$\begin{array}{r} \$0.92 \\ \times\quad 7 \\ \hline \$6\,4\,4 \end{array}$$

13.
$$\begin{array}{r} 0.27 \\ \times\quad 16 \\ \hline 4\,3\,2 \end{array}$$

Find the product.

14. 4×0.9 **15.** 7×0.04 **16.** 0.12×9 **17.** $0.43 \times \$7$

18. 18×0.28 **19.** 24×0.05 **20.** $\$0.74 \times 14$ **21.** 0.32×48

USE DATA For 22–23, use the shopping list.

22. MULTISTEP Roast beef costs $5 per lb, and ham costs $4 per lb. To the nearest dollar, how much will the roast beef and ham cost?

Cold Cuts to Buy	
Ham	0.25 lb
Swiss Cheese	0.32 lb
Roast Beef	0.75 lb

23. **Write a problem** that can be solved using the data in the list. Solve your problem.

Maintain Skills

24. What is the area of the sandbox if each unit equals 1 foot?

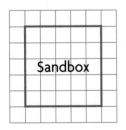

Sandbox

25. What digit is in the ten thousands place in the number 32,745.8?

26. $75 \div 9$ **27.** $523 \div 5$

28. Which is longer, a dog's leash that is 4 feet long or a dog's leash that is 4 yards long?

CRCT Test Prep

29. **M4N6.b.** Alec ate $\frac{1}{8}$ of an apple pie. Rico ate $\frac{3}{8}$ of the same pie. What fraction of the pie did they eat altogether? (p. 310)

A. $\frac{3}{16}$ C. $\frac{3}{8}$

B. $\frac{4}{16}$ D. $\frac{4}{8}$

30. **M4N6.a.** Which fraction is equivalent to $\frac{1}{3}$? (p. 296)

A. $\frac{3}{9}$ C. $\frac{3}{15}$

B. $\frac{3}{12}$ D. $\frac{4}{24}$

Problem Solving Skill
Evaluate Reasonableness of Answers

M4N5.e. Multiply and divide both one and two digit decimals by whole numbers. *also* **M4P1.a., M4P1.b., M4P1.c., M4P1.d., M4P2.a., M4P3.a., M4P3.b., M4P3.c., M4P3.d., M4P5.b., M4P5.c.**

Quick Review

1. 3.4 + 5.6

2. $2.37 + $5.89

3. 5.23 + 6.78

4. 12.6 − 7.5

5. $15 − $7.86

UNDERSTAND ⟩ **PLAN** ⟩ **SOLVE** ⟩ **CHECK**

FRUIT IS GOOD FOOD Willard's Produce has a chart that shows the average weight of each type of fruit sold at the fruit stand. What is the weight of 6 peaches from Willard's Produce?

Which is the more reasonable answer?

a. Rita's answer is 18.6 lb.

b. Julia's answer is 1.86 lb.

AVERAGE WEIGHT	
Fruit	**Weight**
Apple	0.55 lb
Orange	0.62 lb
Peach	0.31 lb
Grapefruit	0.92 lb

 MATH IDEA   If you estimate before solving a problem, you can compare your answer to the estimate. If your answer is close to your estimate, then your answer is reasonable.

Estimate. 0.31×6

Think: Is 0.31 *less than, about,* or *greater than* $\frac{1}{2}$?

$\frac{1}{2} = 0.5$, so 0.31 is *less than* $\frac{1}{2}$.

0.31×6 is *less than* $\frac{1}{2}$ of 6.

$\frac{6}{2} = 3$. So, $0.31 \times 6 < 3$. The answer will be less than 3.

You can multiply to check.

$$\begin{array}{r} 0.31 \\ \times 6 \\ \hline 1.86 \end{array}$$ $1.86 < 3$

So, Julia's answer of 1.86 lb is the more reasonable one.

Remember

To find $\frac{1}{2}$ of a number, you can divide the number by 2.

Talk About It

• Why is it helpful to estimate to see whether an answer is reasonable?

• Why is Rita's answer not reasonable for the problem?

• How do you know that Julie's answer is reasonable for the problem?

1. Fruit needs rain to grow well. Rain is expected to fall at a rate of 0.6 inch every hour for the next 6 hours. Erik says this means there will be 36 inches of rain. Ben says it means there will be 3.6 inches. Which is the more reasonable amount? Explain.

2. **What if** the temperature dropped and it started to snow at a rate of 0.25 inch per hour? Which is the more reasonable prediction for the amount of snow that would fall in 4 hours, 10 inches or 1 inch? Explain.

Last week, it rained for two days in a row. About 0.2 inch of rain fell every hour.

3. Which is the best estimate of the amount of rain that fell during the first 24 hours?

   A more than 12 inches
   B less than 12 inches
   C exactly 12 inches
   D more than 24 inches

4. About how much rain fell during the first 24 hours?

   F about 48 inches
   G about 24 inches
   H about 4.8 inches
   J about 2.4 inches

Mixed Applications

USE DATA For 5–7, use the graph.

5. **MULTISTEP** Robert bought 2 granola bars and a yogurt. How much did the three snacks cost in all?

6. Amber paid for her apple with a $5 bill. How much change did she receive?

7. **REASONING** Suppose you had $2 to spend on snacks. Which snacks could you buy so that you would spend exactly $2?

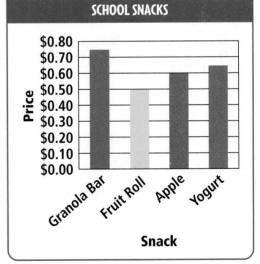

8. Josie lives 0.3 mile from school. Last week, Josie walked to and from school on Monday, Tuesday, Thursday, and Friday. How many miles did Josie walk?

Extra Practice

Set A (pp. 422–423)

Use mental math to complete each pattern.

1. $1 \times 0.7 = 0.7$
$10 \times 0.7 = 7$
$100 \times 0.7 = 70$
$1{,}000 \times 0.7 = \square$

2. $\$0.30 \times 1 = \$0.30$
$\$0.30 \times 10 = \square$
$\$0.30 \times 100 = \$30$
$\$0.30 \times 1{,}000 = \$300$

3. $1 \times 0.01 = 0.01$
$10 \times 0.01 = 0.1$
$100 \times 0.01 = \square$
$1{,}000 \times 0.01 = 10$

4. $1 \times 0.12 = 0.12$
$10 \times 0.12 = 1.2$
$100 \times 0.12 = 12$
$1{,}000 \times 0.12 = \square$

5. $\$0.50 \times 1 = \$0.50$
$\$0.50 \times 10 = \square$
$\$0.50 \times 100 = \$50$
$\$0.50 \times 1{,}000 = \$500$

6. $1 \times 0.95 = 0.95$
$10 \times 0.9 = 9.5$
$100 \times 0.95 = \square$
$1{,}000 \times 0.95 = 950$

Use mental math to multiply.

7. 0.4×100 **8.** $0.06 \times 1{,}000$ **9.** 0.37×10 **10.** 0.08×100

11. 0.9×10 **12.** 0.04×100 **13.** $0.42 \times 1{,}000$ **14.** 0.07×10

15. 0.18×100 **16.** $0.12 \times 1{,}000$ **17.** 0.30×10 **18.** $\$0.87 \times 10$

Set B (pp. 424–425)

Count the decimal places to place the decimal point in the product.

1. $\begin{array}{r} 18 \\ \times 0.5 \\ \hline 9\,0 \end{array}$ **2.** $\begin{array}{r} \$\ 52 \\ \times 0.07 \\ \hline \$3\,6\,4 \end{array}$ **3.** $\begin{array}{r} 0.86 \\ \times\ \ \ 6 \\ \hline 5\,1\,6 \end{array}$ **4.** $\begin{array}{r} 0.25 \\ \times\ \ 18 \\ \hline 4\,5\,0 \end{array}$

5. $\begin{array}{r} 70 \\ \times 0.9 \\ \hline 6\,3 \end{array}$ **6.** $\begin{array}{r} 85 \\ \times 0.06 \\ \hline 5\,1\,0 \end{array}$ **7.** $\begin{array}{r} 0.18 \\ \times\ \ \ 5 \\ \hline 9\,0 \end{array}$ **8.** $\begin{array}{r} \$0.59 \\ \times\ \ \ \ 40 \\ \hline \$2\,3\,6\,0 \end{array}$

Find the product.

9. 4×0.6 **10.** 3×0.09 **11.** $\$0.18 \times 4$ **12.** 0.38×5

13. $\$82 \times 0.28$ **14.** 50×0.06 **15.** 0.78×35 **16.** 0.7×97

17. A large egg weighs about 0.12 lb. About how much do 2 dozen large eggs weigh?

18. Mario's dog gained 0.75 pound each week for 8 weeks. How much did his puppy gain in all?

19. Crystal bought 6 notebooks. Each notebook cost $0.88. How much did she spend in all?

20. Tron made a string of 30 beads. Each bead is 0.85 inch long. How long is a string of all 30 beads?

Review/Test

✓ CHECK VOCABULARY AND CONCEPTS

Choose the best term from the box.

Vocabulary

tenths
hundredths
decimal places
decimal points

1. 0.02 can be read as 2 ? . (p. 420)

2. To place a decimal in the product, count the number of ? in the factors. (p. 424)

3. 0.6 stands for 6 ? . (p. 420)

✓ CHECK SKILLS

Use mental math to multiply. (pp. 422–423)

4. 0.9×100

5. 0.02×10

6. 0.48×10

7. $0.13 \times 1{,}000$

8. 0.05×100

9. $\$0.75 \times 100$

Count the decimal places to place the decimal point in the product. (pp. 424–425)

10.
$$\begin{array}{r} 12 \\ \times 0.6 \\ \hline 7\,2 \end{array}$$

11.
$$\begin{array}{r} 81 \\ \times 0.09 \\ \hline 7\,2\,9 \end{array}$$

12.
$$\begin{array}{r} \$0.79 \\ \times\ \ \ 14 \\ \hline \$1\,1\,0\,6 \end{array}$$

13.
$$\begin{array}{r} 0.05 \\ \times\ \ 84 \\ \hline 4\,2\,0 \end{array}$$

Find the product.

14. 8×0.5

15. 6×0.04

16. $\$0.45 \times 5$

17. 0.28×9

18. $\$55 \times 0.55$

19. 80×0.04

20. 0.92×75

21. 0.8×87

✓ CHECK PROBLEM SOLVING

Solve. For 22–23, use the table. (pp. 426–427)

22. Charlie wants to buy 6 pencils. He estimates that they will cost less than $3. Is he correct? Explain.

23. Holly says that 8 folders will cost $12. Gayle says that they will cost $1.20. Whose answer is more reasonable? Why?

24. Which is a more reasonable answer for 0.56×12, 67.2 or 6.72? Why?

25. Which product is about 34, 0.15×68 or 0.6×68? How can you tell?

SCHOOL SUPPLIES	
Supply	**Cost**
Pen	$0.35
Pencil	$0.12
Notebook	$0.75
Folder	$0.15

Chapter CRCT Test Prep

NUMBERS AND OPERATIONS

1. **M4N5.e.** Over the last three months, Glenn saved 100 quarters. How much money did he save in quarters?

   A. $300

   B. $250

   C. $25

   D. $2.50

2. **M4N5.d.** Which model shows how to multiply 2×0.8?

   A.

   B.

   C.

   D.

   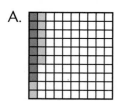
   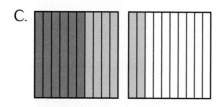
   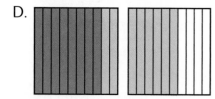

3. **M4N5.e.** When Joy first planted her tomato seedling, it was 0.4 inch tall. It grew ten times as much as that height in a month. How much did the seedling grow?

   A.   0.04 inch

   B.   4 inches

   C.   40 inches

   D. 400 inches

NUMBERS AND OPERATIONS

4. **M4N5.e.** The table below shows the number of tickets needed for rides at the fair.

Ride Admissions	
Ride	**Tickets Needed**
Bumper Cars	3
Roller Coaster	5
Loop-D-Loop	4
Ferris Wheel	2

   If each ticket costs $0.75, how much will it cost to ride the roller coaster two times?

   A. $2.50

   B. $3.75

   C. $7.50

   D. $10.00

5. **M4N5.e.** Six kittens each weigh 0.65 pound. What is their total weight?

   A.   3.6 pounds

   B.   3.9 pounds

   C. 36 pounds

   D. 39 pounds

6. **M4N5.e.** Quartz is the official gem of Georgia. Darren has 5 pieces of quartz. Each piece weighs 0.25 pound. How much quartz does Darren have in all?

   A.   1.25 pounds

   B.   2.5 pounds

   C. 12.5 pounds

   D. 25 pounds

Cumulative CRCT Test Prep

MEASUREMENT

7. M4M1.b. What is the most reasonable unit of measure for the weight of a desktop computer?

A. gram

B. pound

C. ounce

D. ton

8. M4M2.b. The minute hand on a clock rotates 180° in 30 minutes. What type of rotation is this?

A. full rotation

B. half rotation

C. quarter rotation

D. whole rotation

9. M4M1.c. Which expression correctly compares one unit of weight to another?

A. 6 ounces < 6 pounds

B. 1 ton < 1 pound

C. 3 pounds < 3 ounces

D. 7 pounds > 7 tons

ALGEBRA

10. M4A1.a. What pattern do you see in the areas of the gardens?

Garden	Length (feet)	Width (feet)	Area (square feet)
A	10	6	60
B	10	7	70
C	10	8	80
D	10	9	90

A. an increase of 1 foot

B. an increase of 1 square foot

C. an increase of 10 feet

D. an increase of 10 square feet

11. M4A1.a. What is the rule used in the table?

IN	OUT
63	55
54	46
45	37
36	☐
27	19

A. Add 9.

B. Add 6.

C. Subtract 8.

D. Subtract 4.

12. M4A1.b. Natalie is 5 years older than her sister, Margie. Which expression shows how old Natalie is? Let ☐ stand for Margie's age.

A. $5 - ☐$

B. $☐ - 5$

C. $5 \times ☐$

D. $☐ + 5$

Divide Decimals by Whole Numbers

≡FAST FACT • SPORTS In 1996, the Summer Olympic Games were held in Atlanta, GA. Since the modern Olympic Games began, the winning time in the men's 100-meter freestyle swimming race has decreased by 34 seconds from 1 minute 22.2 seconds in 1896 to 48.17 seconds in 2004.

Using Data

100-METER SWIMMING TIMES

Bar graph titled "100-Meter Swimming Times" showing Seconds (0–70) on the vertical axis and Swimmer on the horizontal axis:
- Eduardo: 63
- Julian: 51
- Cody: 59
- David: 68
- Jehan: 60

INVESTIGATION A 100-meter swimming race consists of swimming two lengths of an Olympic-sized pool. During the race, a swimmer swims both lengths at about the same rate. Look at the graph. How long did it take each swimmer to swim just 1 meter? 10 meters? What patterns do you see?

CHECK WHAT YOU KNOW

Use this page to help you review and remember
important skills needed for Chapter 21.

MULTIPLICATION AND DIVISION PATTERNS

Complete the pattern.

1. $3 \times 5 = 15$ $15 \div 5 = 3$ **2.** $400 \times 6 = 2{,}400$ $24 \div 6 = 4$
       $30 \times 5 = 150$ $150 \div 5 = 30$ $40 \times 6 = 240$ $240 \div 6 = 40$
       $300 \times 5 = \blacksquare$ $1{,}500 \div 5 = \blacksquare$ $4 \times 6 = \blacksquare$ $2{,}400 \div 6 = \blacksquare$

DECIMAL MODELS

Write the decimal shown by each model.

3.   **4.** 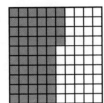   **5.**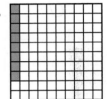

DIVISION

Divide.

6. $6\overline{)42}$ **7.** $9\overline{)72}$ **8.** $4\overline{)48}$ **9.** $7\overline{)63}$

10. $3\overline{)120}$ **11.** $5\overline{)250}$ **12.** $8\overline{)824}$ **13.** $6\overline{)222}$

14. $224 \div 4$ **15.** $336 \div 8$ **16.** $783 \div 9$ **17.** $190 \div 5$

VOCABULARY POWER

REVIEW

zero [zē′rō] *noun*

In mathematics, *zero* means "none." In everyday life, there are
other words people use to mean *zero*, such as *love* in tennis or
a duck in the British game of cricket. Ask your friends and family
what words they use for *zero,* and make a list of those words.

 www.harcourtschool.com/mathglossary

Divide Decimals

HANDS ON

M4N5.d. Model multiplication and division of decimals by whole numbers.
also **M4A1.b., M4P2.a., M4P2.b., M4P2.c., M4P2.d., M4P3.a., M4P3.b., M4P3.c., M4P3.d., M4P5, M4P5.a., M4P5.b., M4P5.c.**

Quick Review

1. 45 ÷ 9   **2.** 56 ÷ 8
3. 63 ÷ 7   **4.** 320 ÷ 4
5. 540 ÷ 6

MATERIALS tenths and hundredths models; markers; scissors

▶ Explore

LUNCH TIME Amanda bought 0.6 pound of turkey at the deli. She will make 3 turkey sandwiches and put the same amount of turkey in each. How much turkey will each sandwich have?

Activity 1

Divide. 0.6 ÷ 3
Make a model to show how many are in each group.

STEP 1	STEP 2	STEP 3
Shade 0.6 of a tenths model.	Use scissors to cut apart the 6 tenths to be divided.	Place an equal number of tenths in 3 groups. Each group has 2 tenths.
	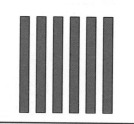	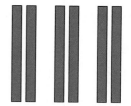

• How many groups did you make?

• How many are in each group?

So, each sandwich will have 0.2 pound of turkey.

⚡ **MATH IDEA** Using models can help you with the division of decimals.

Try It

Make a model to solve each problem.

a. 0.4 ÷ 2

b. 0.8 ÷ 4

c. 0.9 ÷ 3

d. 0.6 ÷ 2

How many tenths strips should we put in each group to show 0.4 ÷ 2?

Sometimes, to divide a decimal number less than 1 by a whole number, you have to exchange the tenths for hundredths.

Activity 2
Divide 0.2 by 5.

STEP 1	STEP 2	STEP 3	STEP 4
Shade 0.2 of a tenths model.	Exchange the 2 tenths for 20 hundredths.	Divide the hundredths into 5 equal-sized groups. Each group has 4 hundredths.	Write a number sentence to model what you have done. $0.2 \div 5 = 0.04$

 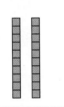

▶ **Practice and Problem Solving**

Write a number sentence for each model.

1.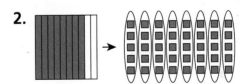

2.

Make a model to divide.

3. $0.6 \div 4$ 4. $0.24 \div 2$ 5. $0.12 \div 6$ 6. $0.3 \div 3$

7. $0.2 \div 4$ 8. $0.9 \div 3$ 9. $0.4 \div 4$ 10. $0.32 \div 4$

11. $0.16 \div 4$ 12. $0.63 \div 7$ 13. $0.14 \div 2$ 14. $0.28 \div 7$

15. Dennis wants to cut a 0.42-meter piece of rope into 6 equal pieces. How many cuts must he make? How long will each piece be?

16. **REASONING** How can this pattern help you understand decimal division?

$80 \div 4 = 20$
$8 \div 4 = 2$
$0.8 \div 4 = 0.2$

Maintain Skills

17. Larry baked 4 batches of cookies. There were 24 cookies in each batch. How many cookies did Larry bake in all?

CRCT Test Prep

18. **M4N7.d.** What is the BEST estimate for $3,841 + 2,155$? (p. 36)

A. 5,000   C. 6,000
B. 5,500   D. 6,500

Algebra: Mental Math: Division Patterns

M4N5.e. Multiply and divide both one and two digit decimals by whole numbers. *also* **M4A1.b., M4N7.d., M4P1.a., M4P1.b., M4P1.c., M4P1.d., M4P3.a., M4P3.b., M4P3.c., M4P4.a.**

▶ Learn

EATS LIKE A BIRD   A hummingbird can eat 0.3 gram of sap or insects in one hour. If a hummingbird eats the same amount from each of 6 trees, how much does it eat from each tree in one hour?

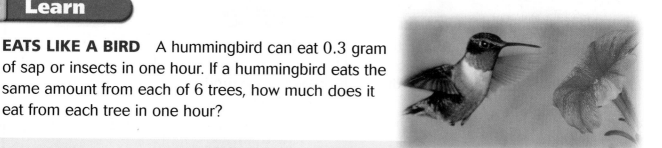

Example

Find $0.3 \div 6$.

You can use a pattern to find the quotient.	
$30 \div 6 = 5$	Begin with a basic fact.
$3 \div 6 = 0.5$	Use the basic fact to find the first decimal quotient.
$0.3 \div 6 = 0.05$	Continue the pattern.

So, a hummingbird eats 0.05 gram from each tree.

More Examples

A $20 \div 4 = 5$ ←basic fact	**B** $18 \div 6 = 3$ ←basic fact	**C** $12 \div 3 = 4$ ←basic fact
$2 \div 4 = 0.5$	$1.8 \div 6 = 0.3$	$1.2 \div 3 = 0.4$
$0.2 \div 4 = 0.05$	$0.18 \div 6 = 0.03$	$0.12 \div 3 = 0.04$

MATH IDEA If the divisor does not change, the quotient decreases as the dividend decreases.

▶ Check

1. Explain how to find the quotient $0.48 \div 8$ by using a basic fact and a pattern.

Copy and complete each pattern.

2. $40 \div 8 = $ ■
  $4 \div 8 = $ ■
  $0.4 \div 8 = $ ■

3. $28 \div 4 = $ ■
  $2.8 \div 4 = $ ■
  $0.28 \div 4 = $ ■

4. $16 \div 4 = $ ■
  $1.6 \div 4 = $ ■
  $0.16 \div 4 = $ ■

Copy and complete each pattern.

5. $20 \div 2 = \blacksquare$
$2 \div 2 = \blacksquare$
$0.2 \div 2 = \blacksquare$

6. $42 \div 6 = \blacksquare$
$4.2 \div 6 = \blacksquare$
$0.42 \div 6 = \blacksquare$

7. $35 \div 7 = \blacksquare$
$3.5 \div 7 = \blacksquare$
$0.35 \div 7 = \blacksquare$

8. $45 \div 5 = \blacksquare$
$4.5 \div 5 = \blacksquare$
$0.45 \div 5 = \blacksquare$

9. $64 \div 8 = \blacksquare$
$6.4 \div 8 = \blacksquare$
$0.64 \div 8 = \blacksquare$

10. $32 \div 8 = \blacksquare$
$3.2 \div 8 = \blacksquare$
$0.32 \div 8 = \blacksquare$

ALGEBRA **Copy and complete each table. Use mental math and patterns.**

11. Divide by 5.

400	40	4	0.4
80	$\blacksquare$	$\blacksquare$	$\blacksquare$

12. Divide by 6.

480	48	4.8	0.48
$\blacksquare$	$\blacksquare$	$\blacksquare$	$\blacksquare$

13. Divide by 8.

560	$\blacksquare$	5.6	0.56
$\blacksquare$	7	$\blacksquare$	$\blacksquare$

14. Divide by 3.

270	27	$\blacksquare$	$\blacksquare$
$\blacksquare$	$\blacksquare$	0.9	0.09

Complete each pair of problems.

15. $0.54 \div 9 = 0.06$, $0.06 \times 9 = \blacksquare$

16. $0.21 \div 7 = 0.03$, $\blacksquare \times 7 = 0.21$

17. $0.2 \div 5 = 0.04$, $0.04 \times 5 = \blacksquare$

18. $0.6 \div 3 = 0.2$, $0.2 \times 3 = \blacksquare$

19. REASONING The overall body length of a male hummingbird is about 0.07 m. If its total length is about twice its wingspan, how would you find its wingspan? What is the wingspan?

20. MULTISTEP Mike paid $\$0.50$ for a whistle and a box of birdseed bags. The whistle cost $\$0.14$, and there were 6 bags of birdseed in the box. How much did each bag of birdseed cost?

21. Vocabulary Power In business, a *dividend* is an amount of money paid to shareholders out of a company's earnings. Explain how a dividend in business is similar to a dividend in a division problem.

22. ? What's the Error? Leonard wrote the quotient $0.15 \div 5$ as 0.3. Explain and correct his error.

Maintain Skills

23. What is the value of the digit 6 in the number $9{,}624.1$?

24. Damian drove from Waycross, GA, to Valdosta, GA. Did he drive 61 miles or 61 yards?

CRCT Test Prep

25. **M4N7.b.** What is the value of the expression? (p. 130)

$$2 + 4 \times 2$$

A. 14

C. 12

B. 13

D. 10

3 Divide Decimals by Whole Numbers

 M4N5.e. Multiply and divide both one and two digit decimals by whole numbers. *also* **M4P3.a., M4P3.d.**

▶ **Learn**

SHE'S NOT ALL WET   Kimberly swam 0.64 mile while practicing for the Olympic trials. She swam the same distance during each of 4 periods. How far did she swim each period?

Find $0.64 \div 4$.

One Way You can use patterns.

$64 \div 4 = 16$
$6.4 \div 4 = 1.6$
$0.64 \div 4 = 0.16$

Technology Link

More Practice: Harcourt Mega Math The Number Games, *Buggy Bargains*, Levels M and N

So, Kimberly swam 0.16 mile each period.

Another Way Use paper and pencil.

Divide 0.84 by 3. Write $3\overline{)0.84}$.

STEP 1

Divide as though the decimal point were not there.

$$\begin{array}{r} 28 \\ 3\overline{)0.84} \\ -6 \\ \hline 24 \\ -24 \\ \hline 0 \end{array}$$

STEP 2

Place the decimal point in the quotient directly above the decimal point in the dividend.

$$\begin{array}{r} 0.28 \\ 3\overline{)0.84} \\ -6 \\ \hline 24 \\ -24 \\ \hline 0 \end{array}$$

Write a zero in the ones place of the quotient.

STEP 3

Multiply to check your work.

$$\begin{array}{r} {}^{2} \\ 0.28 \\ \times 3 \\ \hline 0.84 \end{array}$$

⚡**MATH IDEA** Use the method that seems to make the most sense for the problem you are solving: models, patterns, or paper and pencil.

1. **Explain** why the quotient will always be less than 1 when you divide a decimal less than 1 by a whole number.

Divide. Multiply to check.

2. $5\overline{)0.25}$ 3. $3\overline{)0.63}$ 4. $6\overline{)0.72}$ 5. $2\overline{)0.1}$

▶ **Practice and Problem Solving** Extra Practice, page 442, Set B

Divide. Multiply to check.

6. $2\overline{)0.14}$ 7. $3\overline{)0.96}$ 8. $4\overline{)0.24}$ 9. $7\overline{)0.35}$

10. $9\overline{)0.72}$ 11. $5\overline{)0.85}$ 12. $5\overline{)0.4}$ 13. $5\overline{)\$0.45}$

14. $0.42 \div 3$ 15. $0.7 \div 2$ 16. $\$0.87 \div 3$ 17. $0.08 \div 8$

18. $\$0.36 \div 4$ 19. $0.30 \div 5$ 20. $0.56 \div 8$ 21. $\$0.76 \div 4$

USE DATA For 22–24, use the table.

22. If a year on Mercury is divided into 4 seasons, what part of an Earth year is one season?

23. What part of an Earth year does Venus need to complete one half of its trip around the sun?

24. About how many times as long is a year on Venus than on Mercury?

PLANETARY YEARS	
Planet	**Length of a Year**
Mercury	0.24 Earth year
Venus	0.62 Earth year

25. ✏ **Write About It** How can knowing that $0.16 \div 4 = 0.04$ help you find the quotients $0.32 \div 4$ and $0.16 \div 2$?

26. ❓ **What's the Error?** Chloë divided 0.20 by 4 and wrote the quotient as 0.5. Explain and correct her error.

Maintain Skills

27. Use the model to find the sum $0.3 + 0.5$.

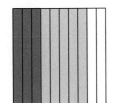

CRCT Test Prep

28. M4N6.b. Nadia had $6\frac{1}{4}$ pounds of cans to recycle. She collected another $5\frac{3}{4}$ pounds. How many pounds did she collect in all? (p. 316)

A. 11 pounds
B. $11\frac{1}{4}$ pounds
C. 12 pounds
D. $12\frac{1}{4}$ pounds

Problem Solving Strategy
Use a Table

 M4P1.a. Build new mathematical knowledge through problem solving.
also **M4N5.e., M4P1.a., M4P1.b., M4P1.c., M4P1.d., M4P3.a., M4P3.b., M4P3.c., M4P3.d.**

PROBLEM   Some animals run very fast but only for short distances. The table shows how far some animals can run in several minutes. Which animals can run more than one-half mile in 1 minute?

RUNNING ANIMALS	
Animal	**Distance in 3 Minutes**
Elephant	1.26 miles
Lion	2.4 miles
Rabbit	1.74 miles
Zebra	2.01 miles

UNDERSTAND

- What are you asked to find?

- What information will you use?

PLAN

- What strategy can you use to solve the problem?

  You can *use a table* to solve the problem.

SOLVE

- How can you use the strategy to solve the problem?

  List the animals in the table from slowest to fastest. Then divide each distance by 3. A rabbit, a zebra, and a lion can run more than one-half mile in 1 minute.

RUNNING ANIMALS		
Animal	**Distance in 3 Minutes**	**Distance in 1 Minute**
Elephant	1.26 miles	1.26 ÷ 3 = 0.42 mile
Rabbit	2.4 miles	2.4 ÷ 3 = 0.8 mile
Zebra	1.74 miles	1.74 ÷ 3 = 0.58 mile
Lion	2.01 miles	2.01 ÷ 3 = 0.67 mile

CHECK

- How can you check your answer?

Strategies

Act It Out or Use Objects
Make a Picture or Diagram
Guess and Check
Use or Look for a Pattern
Use Logical Reasoning
Make an Organized List
▶ **Use or Make a Table**
Work Backwards

1. **What if** a house cat were added to the list of animals? It can run 1.5 miles in 3 minutes. How far can a house cat run in 1 minute? Would the house cat be included in the list of animals that can run more than one-half mile in 1 minute?

USE DATA For 2–5, use the table. Some of the world's smallest animals live on islands in the Caribbean Sea or in South America. The table shows their lengths.

2. Which animal is about half the length of the Jaragua lizard?

3. Which animal is about one seventh the length of the thread snake?

ANIMAL LENGTHS	
Animal	**Length (in inches)**
Jaragua lizard	0.63
Male bee hummingbird	2.2
Thread snake	4.25
Brazilian frog	0.33

4. A firecracker dwarf goby is a very small fish. It can be about 0.7 inch long. Which number sentence could you use to estimate about how many times as long a thread snake is than a dwarf goby?

   A $4.25 \times 0.7 = \square$
   B $4.25 + 0.7 = \square$
   C $4.25 \div 0.7 = \square$
   D $4.25 - 0.7 = \square$

5. Which operation would you use to estimate how much longer the largest animal shown in the table is than the smallest?

   F addition
   G subtraction
   H multiplication
   J division

Mixed Strategy Practice

6. The Chicago Zoo in Illinois has 208 species of animals. The Louisville Zoo in Kentucky has 14 species fewer than twice the number in the Chicago Zoo. How many species of animals are in the Louisville Zoo?

7. There are 14 endangered reptile species in the United States and 64 outside the United States. The number of threatened but not endangered species is 41 less than the endangered total. How many species are threatened?

8. A glass snake can separate its tail from its body to escape from danger. Its tail is about twice as long as the rest of its body. If a glass snake is 60 cm long, about how long is its tail?

9. A museum display case can hold any two of the following animal figures: frogs, lizards, snakes, and birds. How many different pairs of animal figures can be in a display?

Extra Practice

Set A (pp. 436–437)

Copy and complete each pattern.

1. $10 \div 2 = \blacksquare$
$1 \div 2 = \blacksquare$
$0.1 \div 2 = \blacksquare$

2. $12 \div 4 = \blacksquare$
$1.2 \div 4 = \blacksquare$
$0.12 \div 4 = \blacksquare$

3. $36 \div 6 = \blacksquare$
$3.6 \div 6 = \blacksquare$
$0.36 \div 6 = \blacksquare$

4. $21 \div 3 = \blacksquare$
$2.1 \div 3 = \blacksquare$
$0.21 \div 3 = \blacksquare$

5. $63 \div 7 = \blacksquare$
$6.3 \div 7 = \blacksquare$
$0.63 \div 7 = \blacksquare$

6. $32 \div 4 = \blacksquare$
$3.2 \div 4 = \blacksquare$
$0.32 \div 4 = \blacksquare$

7. $56 \div 8 = \blacksquare$
$5.6 \div 8 = \blacksquare$
$0.56 \div 8 = \blacksquare$

8. $8 \div 2 = \blacksquare$
$0.8 \div 2 = \blacksquare$
$0.08 \div 2 = \blacksquare$

9. $60 \div 3 = \blacksquare$
$6 \div 3 = \blacksquare$
$0.6 \div 3 = \blacksquare$

Copy and complete each table. Use mental math and patterns.

10. Divide by 4.

200	20	2	0.2
50	$\blacksquare$	$\blacksquare$	$\blacksquare$

11. Divide by 6.

300	30	3	0.3
$\blacksquare$	$\blacksquare$	$\blacksquare$	$\blacksquare$

Set B (pp. 438–439)

Divide. Multiply to check.

1. $2\overline{)0.8}$ **2.** $5\overline{)0.3}$ **3.** $4\overline{)0.68}$ **4.** $6\overline{)0.42}$

5. $8\overline{)\$0.64}$ **6.** $9\overline{)0.63}$ **7.** $3\overline{)0.48}$ **8.** $7\overline{)0.49}$

9. $0.6 \div 2$ **10.** $0.9 \div 6$ **11.** $\$0.44 \div 4$ **12.** $0.78 \div 3$

13. $\$0.50 \div 5$ **14.** $0.7 \div 5$ **15.** $0.84 \div 7$ **16.** $0.39 \div 3$

17. Sara had 0.48 kilogram of raisins. She divided the raisins into 6 packages that each weighed the same. How many kilograms of raisins were in each package?

18. Lex bought 0.6 pound of cheese. He made 4 sandwiches with the same amount of cheese in each sandwich. How much cheese did he use in each sandwich?

19. At King Elementary, the 6 fourth-grade classes collected 0.24 ton of newspaper to recycle. If each class collected the same amount, how much did each class collect?

20. Ursula paid $0.95 for 5 pencils. How much did each pencil cost?

Review/Test

✔ CHECK CONCEPTS

Write a division sentence for each model. (pp. 434–435)

1.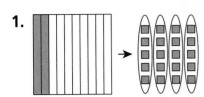

2.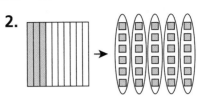

Make a model to divide. (pp. 434–435)

3. 0.4 ÷ 4   **4.** 0.18 ÷ 2   **5.** 0.12 ÷ 3   **6.** 0.9 ÷ 3

7. 0.35 ÷ 5   **8.** 0.54 ÷ 9   **9.** 0.20 ÷ 4   **10.** 0.42 ÷ 3

11. 0.24 ÷ 3   **12.** 0.64 ÷ 4   **13.** 0.66 ÷ 6   **14.** 0.45 ÷ 5

✔ CHECK SKILLS

Divide. Multiply to check. (pp. 438–439)

15. 3)0.15   **16.** 2)0.38   **17.** 2)0.24   **18.** 9)0.45

19. 0.36 ÷ 3   **20.** $0.27 ÷ 9   **21.** 0.4 ÷ 8   **22.** 0.95 ÷ 5

23. 0.8 ÷ 5   **24.** $0.63 ÷ 7   **25.** 0.3 ÷ 6   **26.** 0.06 ÷ 3

27. 0.4 ÷ 8   **28.** 0.08 ÷ 4   **29.** $0.56 ÷ 7   **30.** 0.84 ÷ 6

✔ CHECK PROBLEM SOLVING

For 31–33, use the table. (pp. 440–441)

31. What is the cost of one grapefruit at Abbot's?

32. How much more does 1 grapefruit cost at Edward's than at Canton Farms?

33. Alex bought some grapefruits at one of the stores shown in the table. Later he bought 6 grapefruits for $0.96 at a farm stand. Each grapefruit at the farm stand cost $0.10 less than each grapefruit at the store. At which store did he shop?

GRAPEFRUITS	
Store	**Price**
Abbot's	3 for $0.78
Canton Farms	4 for $0.96
Edward's	2 for $0.50

Chapter CRCT Test Prep

NUMBERS AND OPERATIONS

1. **M4N5.e.** Melody and Lamar earned $0.90 in all from recycling bottles. They shared the money equally. How much did each get?

   A. $0.18

   B. $0.45

   C. $1.80

   D. $4.50

2. **M4N5.d.** What division problem does the model show?

   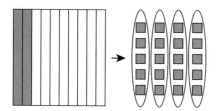

   A. $5 \div 0.2 = 25$

   B. $4 \div 0.2 = 20$

   C. $0.2 \div 5 = 0.04$

   D. $0.2 \div 4 = 0.05$

3. **M4N5.e.** Ina can get 4 photos printed for $0.60. How much does each print cost?

   A. $0.15

   B. $0.24

   C. $1.50

   D. $2.40

NUMBERS AND OPERATIONS

4. **M4N7.d.** Use the pattern to find the quotient $0.48 \div 8$.

   $$48 \div 8 = 6$$
   $$4.8 \div 8 = 0.6$$
   $$0.48 \div 8 = \square$$

   A. 0.006

   B. 0.06

   C. 0.6

   D. 6.0

5. **M4N5.e.** A wooden dowel is 0.76 foot long. Andrew cuts the dowel into 4 equal pieces. How long is each piece?

   A. 1.9 feet

   B. 0.9 foot

   C. 0.19 foot

   D. 0.09 foot

6. **M4N5.e.** Harry's five notebooks weigh a total of 0.45 pound. How much does each notebook weigh?

   A. 9 pounds

   B. 0.9 pound

   C. 0.90 pound

   D. 0.09 pound

Cumulative CRCT Test Prep

DATA ANALYSIS

Use the bar graph below to answer question 7.

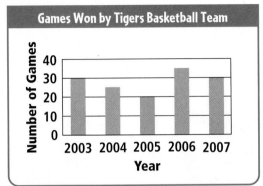

Games Won by Tigers Basketball Team

7. **M4D1.c.** How would the bars on the graph change if the scale of the graph had an interval of 5 instead of 10?

A. The bars would be longer.

B. The bars would be shorter.

C. There would be fewer bars.

D. There would be more bars.

Use the bar graph below to answer question 8.

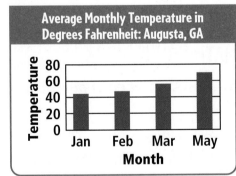

Average Monthly Temperature in Degrees Fahrenheit: Augusta, GA

8. **M4D1.d.** Nan wanted to show the temperatures from January through May. What data is missing from her graph?

A. January: 44°

B. April: 63°

C. May: 70°

D. June: 77°

GEOMETRY

9. **M4G3.b.** The coordinate system shows the location of four students' desks. What ordered pair names the location of Kendra's desk?

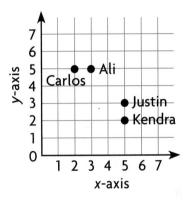

A. (3,4)

B. (5,3)

C. (2,5)

D. (5,2)

10. **M4G3.a.** Who lives in the house located at (1,4) in the coordinate system shown below?

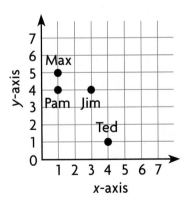

A. Ted

B. Max

C. Pam

D. Jim

GPS/CRCT Vocabulary

ELA4R3 The student understands and acquires vocabulary and uses it correctly in reading and writing.

MATH WORD RIDDLES

MATERIALS *For each group*
Vocabulary Cards, 3 index cards

- Work with a group.

- On the index cards, write a riddle for each of the vocabulary terms.

- Exchange sets of riddle cards with another group. Match each riddle with a vocabulary term.

- Compare the riddles that each group wrote for each of the terms.

Equivalent Decimals

0.4 = 0.40

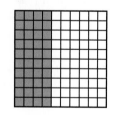

=

Equivalent decimals are two or more decimals that name the same amount.

MATH WORD WORK

MATERIALS *For each pair* poster board

- Work with a partner. Choose a vocabulary term. Create a poster to illustrate your term

- Include a definition, examples, and models.

- Share your poster with the class. Make a bulletin board display of all the posters.

SCRAMBLED SENTENCES

MATERIALS *For each group* index cards, markers

• In your own words, write a sentence using one or more of the vocabulary terms.

• Write each word of the sentence on an index card. Use a different color marker for each word.

• Mix up your cards. Exchange cards with another group member. Take turns unscrambling the cards and reading the sentences aloud.

• Trade your cards with a different group member, and play again.

DECIMAL MAZE

MATERIALS *For each student* grid paper

• Make an 8-by-8 grid. Choose a vocabulary term. Write each letter of your term in a square that touches another square so that if forms a path through the grid. Label the square with the first letter START. Label the square with the last letter FINISH.

• Fill in the empty squares with any other letters you wish.

• Trade mazes with a classmate.

• Trace the path through your classmate's maze to reveal the vocabulary term.

D	D	E	C	M	N	D	E
D	C	E	I	E	M	A	D
M	E	C	L	A	D	A	E
E	C	I	M	L	A	I	L
C	D	I	M	E	D	N	M
M	A	D	M	I	M	D	E
A	E	A	N	D	M	L	A
C	L	A	L	I	D	A	E

Start (left of second row)

Finish (below grid)

Georgia Tasks

M4N5.c. Add and subtract both one and two digit decimals.
also **M4N7.d., M4P1.b.**

S4E4. Students will analyze weather charts/maps and collect weather data to predict weather events and infer patterns and seasonal changes.

SS4E2 The student will identify the elements of a *personal budget* and explains why personal *spending* and *saving* decisions are important.

Task A

WEATHER CHECK

You can learn to be a meteorologist at the University of Georgia at Athens. A meteorologist predicts the weather by studying weather patterns.
The students in Mrs. Brewer's class are studying weather. They are using rain gauges to measure rainfall.

a. The students measured the rainfall outside their classroom for two months. During the first month, they recorded a total rainfall of 6.29 inches. There were five rainstorms. The amounts for the first four storms were 0.50, 1.21, 0.75, and 2.63 inches. How much rain fell during the fifth storm?

b. During the second month, rainfall amounts were 0.25, 1.63, 0.32, and 2.0 inches. How does the rainfall for the two months compare?

Task B

SAVING MONEY

Mina wants to buy a telescope. The telescope costs $197.98. Mina gets an allowance of $15.00 per week.

a. Mina plans to save $0.75 each day out of her allowance. About how many weeks will it take to save enough money to buy the telescope? Explain how you found your answer.

b. Mina wants to buy the telescope 3 months from now. Is that a reasonable goal? Why or why not?

Maintain/Preview

Maintain

Compare. Write <, >, or = for each ●. (pp. 388–391)

1. 0.26 ● 0.62   **2.** 0.19 ● 0.91   **3.** 0.40 ● 0.4   **4.** 0.82 ● 0.79

Estimate the sum or difference. (pp. 402–403)

5. 28.5   **6.** $47.66   **7.** 58.72   **8.** $7.54
   +34.6   +$88.16   −38.9   −$1.03

Add or subtract. (pp. 408–411)

9. 0.52   **10.** 7.92   **11.** $9.28   **12.** 46.03
   +0.61   −5.43   +$5.83   −18.92

Multiply or divide. (pp. 424–425, 438–439)

13. 5×0.18 **14.** 0.62×7 **15.** $\$0.95 \div 5$ **16.** $0.56 \div 4$

17. Nan spent $0.68 on each of 7 colored pencils. How much did she spend in all? (pp. 424–425)

18. Frank spent $6.28 on notebooks, $4.19 on pens, and $15.88 on a book. How much did he spend in all? (pp. 408–411)

Preview

Find the value of the blue digit. (Grade 5)

1. 3,672   **2.** 249,125   **3.** 1,864,324   **4.** 8,667,259

Compare. Write <, >, or = for each ●. (Grade 5)

5. 529 ● 952   **6.** 603 ● 630   **7.** 819 ● 788   **8.** 356 ● 356

Multiply. (Grade 5)

9. 82×10 **10.** 510×10 **11.** 10×298 **12.** 634×10

Divide. (Grade 5)

13. $15\overline{)390}$ **14.** $42\overline{)259}$ **15.** $78\overline{)810}$ **16.** $55\overline{)220}$

17. A bookstore received 24 cartons of books. Each carton held 16 books. How many books did the bookstore receive in all?

18. Keisha has 351 buttons in her collection. She places 13 buttons on each display card. How many display cards does she need for her buttons?

GEORGIA CRCT HANDBOOK

The tips and the problems on the following pages will help you succeed on the CRCT.

Tips for Success on the GEORGIA CRCT H2

Before working on the CRCT Practice problems and before taking the CRCT, sharpen your test-taking skills by reviewing these pages. Here you can find tips such as how to understand the directions and how to check your work.

CRCT Practice H6

The problems in this section cover the five performance standards of the Georgia Performance Standards curriculum. Use these problems to build your test-taking skills and to prepare for CRCT success.

OTHER RESOURCES

Table of Measures H36

All the important measures used in this book are in this table.
If you've forgotten exactly how many feet are in a mile, this table
will help you.

Glossary H37

This glossary will help you speak and write the language of
mathematics. Use the glossary to check the definitions of
important terms.

Index H48

Use the index when you want to review a topic. It lists the page
numbers where the topic is taught.

Tips for Success on the **Georgia CRCT**

Being a good test-taker is like being a good problem solver. When you answer test questions, you are solving problems. Remember to **UNDERSTAND, PLAN, SOLVE,** and **CHECK.**

UNDERSTAND

Read the problem.

- Look for math terms, and recall their meanings.
- Reread the problem, and think about the question.
- Use the details in the problem and the question.

1. Twenty students signed up for a new club. Six more girls than boys signed up. How many boys signed up?

   A. 16   C. 7

   B. 13   D. 4

TIP! **Understand the problem.**
Six more girls than boys is the difference between the number of girls and boys. So, find two numbers with a difference of 6 whose sum is 20. The number of boys will be the lesser number. The answer is **C.**

- Each word is important. Missing a word or reading it incorrectly could cause you to get the wrong answer.
- Pay attention to words that are all CAPITAL letters and words like *estimate, about, round, best,* or *least to greatest.*

2. Skates cost $219. Kent rounded the price to the nearest hundred dollars. Abby rounded to the nearest ten dollars. Which statement is TRUE?

   A. Kent's amount and Abby's amount are the same.

   B. Kent's amount is $20 less than Abby's amount.

   C. Kent's amount is $10 less than Abby's amount.

   D. Kent's amount is $10 more than Abby's amount.

TIP! **Look for important words.**
The words *rounded* and *true* are important words. Kent and Abby each rounded the price to a different place value. Round the price as Kent and Abby did. Then compare your rounded amounts to each answer choice to determine which one is true. The answer is **B.**

Think about how you can solve the problem.

- Can you solve the problem with the information given?
- Pictures, charts, tables, and graphs might have the information you need.
- You may need to recall information not given.
- The answer choices might have information you need.

3. The table shows the types of CDs Paul has in his collection.

My CD Collection	
Type of Music	Number of CDs
Rock	15
Country	11
Classical	3
Folk	7

Paul received 4 folk music CDs as birthday gifts. Of which types of CDs does he now have the same number in his collection?

A. rock and classical

B. country and rock

C. classical and folk

D. country and folk

TIP! **Get the information you need.**
Use the table to find how many of each type of CD Paul has now. Then find the two types of CDs that have the same number. The answer is **D**.

- You might need to write a number sentence and solve it.
- Some problems have two steps or more.
- You might need to look at relationships rather than compute.
- If the path to the solution isn't clear, choose a problem-solving strategy, and use it to solve the problem.

4. Roberto has $38, which is $2 more than twice the amount Janet has. How much money does Janet have?

A. $14

B. $18

C. $40

D. $78

TIP! **Decide on a plan.**
Use the strategy *work backwards*. Start with Roberto's $38. When you work backwards, each operation will be opposite to what is in the problem. *$2 more* means add $2, so you would subtract $2. *Twice the amount* means multiply by 2, so you would divide by 2. The answer is **B**.

Follow your plan, working logically and carefully.

- Estimate your answer. Are any answer choices unreasonable?
- Use reasoning to find the most likely choices.
- Be sure you completed all steps needed to solve the problem.
- If your answer does not match any of the answer choices, check the numbers you used. Then check your computation.

5. The coordinate system shows the location of some points.

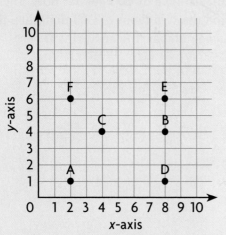

Which set of points forms a right triangle when connected?

A. A, F, E   C. A, D, E, F

B. A, D, C   D. A, D, B, C

TIP! Eliminate choices.
You can eliminate choices C and D because they do not form triangles. Only answer choices A and B form triangles. Since A has a right angle, it is a right triangle. The answer is **A**.

- If your answer still does not match, look for another form of the number, such as a decimal instead of a fraction.
- If answer choices are given as pictures, look at each one by itself while you cover the other three.
- Read answer choices that are statements, and relate them to the problem one by one.
- Change your plan if it isn't working. Try a different strategy.

6. Which statement is TRUE?

   A. A rhombus is also a parallelogram.

   B. A parallelogram is also a rectangle.

   C. A trapezoid is also a parallelogram.

   D. A rectangle is also a square.

TIP! Choose the answer.
Read each statement to decide whether it is true. If you aren't sure which is true, think about the properties of rhombuses, trapezoids, parallelograms, squares, and rectangles. The answer is **A**.

Take time to catch your mistakes.

- Be sure you answered the question asked.
- Be sure your answer fits the information in the problem.
- Check for important words you might have missed.
- Be sure you used all the information you needed.
- Check your computation by using a different method.
- Draw a picture when you are unsure of your answer.

7. What number is inside the triangle, inside the square, and is an improper fraction?

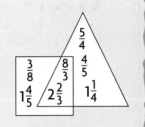

A. $\frac{3}{8}$

B. $\frac{4}{5}$

C. $2\frac{2}{3}$

D. $\frac{8}{3}$

TIP! **Check your work.**
Look at your answer choice. Does it match all the descriptions given in the problem? If not, look for important words you might have missed. The answer is **D**.

Don't Forget!

Before the test

- Listen to the teacher's directions, and read the instructions.
- Write down the ending time if the test is timed.
- Know where and how to mark your answers.
- Know whether you should write on the test page or use scratch paper.
- Ask any questions you might have before the test begins.

During the test

- Work quickly but carefully. If you are unsure how to answer a question, leave it blank, and return to it later.
- If you cannot finish on time, look over the questions that are left. Answer the easiest ones first. Then go back to answer the others.
- Fill in each answer space carefully. Erase completely if you change an answer. Erase any stray marks.
- Be sure the answer number matches the question number, especially if you skip a question.

✔ NUMBERS AND OPERATIONS

1. **M4N1.a.** Compare the digits to find the change in value.

   364,210 to 384,210

   A. increased by 200

   B. increased by 2,000

   C. increased by 20,000

   D. increased by 200,000

2. **M4N1.b.** Georgia is the twenty-first largest state in the United States. Its area is 58,876 square miles. What is the word name for 58,876?

   A. fifty-eight million, eight hundred seventy-six

   B. fifty-eight million, eight hundred seventy-six thousand

   C. five hundred eighty-eight thousand, seventy-six

   D. fifty-eight thousand, eight hundred seventy-six

3. **M4N7.b.** What is the value of the expression?

   $$18 - (7 - 3)$$

   A. 10

   B. 14

   C. 22

   D. 28

4. **M4N4.a.** Kara bought 32 flowers to make 8 bouquets. She put the same number of flowers in each bouquet. How many flowers are in each bouquet?

   A. 3

   B. 4

   C. 6

   D. 24

5. **M4N7.d.** Each school bus holds 34 students. The school will use 18 buses for a field trip. What is the BEST estimate of the number of students going on the trip?

   A. 50

   B. 60

   C. 600

   D. 5,000

Study and Review	
Item	Lesson Pages
1	2–3
2	4–5
3	46–49
4	114–117
5	174–175

✓ NUMBERS AND OPERATIONS

6. **M4N7.d.** The population of Locust Grove, GA, is 2,322, and the population of Stockbridge, GA, is 9,853. What is the MOST reasonable estimate of the difference in population of these two towns if you use rounding to estimate?

A.   800

B. 8,000

C. 12,000

D. 13,000

7. **M4N3.** For a 7-day trip, Kim budgeted $95 per day for food. How much did she budget in all?

A. $545

B. $655

C. $665

D. $725

8. **M4N5.d.** Which of the following multiplication problems does the model show?

A. 2 × 8 = 16

B. 8 × 0.2 = 1.6

C. 2 × 0.8 = 0.16

D. 2 × 0.8 = 1.6

Use the table below for question 9.

Walking to School	
Student	**Number of Blocks to and from School**
Kim	12
Sean	8
Bonnie	11
Xavier	9

9. **M4N4.a.** Which student walks 60 blocks to and from school each week?

A. Kim

B. Sean

C. Bonnie

D. Xavier

10. **M4N7.b.** What is the value of the expression?

$$125 - (16 \times 3)$$

A.   77

B. 106

C. 112

D. 327

Study and Review	
Item	**Lesson Pages**
6	36–39
7	152–155
8	420–421
9	118–119
10	128–129

✓ NUMBERS AND OPERATIONS

11. **M4N7.b.** Use the order of operations to find the value of the expression.

$$9 \times 2 + 6 \div 3$$

A. 8

B. 13

C. 16

D. 20

12. **M4N3.** Victoria Bryant State Park contains 475 acres. Mistletoe State Park has 4 times as many acres as Victoria Bryant. How many acres are in Mistletoe State Park?

A. 120 acres

B. 479 acres

C. 1,900 acres

D. 19,000 acres

13. **M4N4.b.** What is the quotient?

$$481 \div 12$$

A. 40

B. 40 r1

C. 410

D. 401

14. **M4N6.c.** Which of the following improper fractions is equal to $1\frac{2}{5}$?

A. $\frac{12}{5}$

B. $\frac{7}{5}$

C. $\frac{5}{7}$

D. $\frac{5}{12}$

15. **M4N7.c.** Which number sentence shows how to compute 6×23 using the Distributive Property?

A. $6 \times (20 + 3) = (6 \times 20) + (6 \times 3) = 120 + 18 = 138$

B. $6 \times 20 \times 3 = 360$

C. $6 + (20 \times 3) = 6 + 60 = 66$

D. $(6 \times 20) + 3 = 120 + 3 = 123$

16. **M4N6.b.** Use the model to find $\frac{2}{6} + \frac{3}{6}$.

| $\frac{1}{6}$ | $\frac{1}{6}$ | | $\frac{1}{6}$ | $\frac{1}{6}$ | $\frac{1}{6}$ |

A. $\frac{1}{6}$

B. $\frac{5}{12}$

C. $\frac{5}{6}$

D. 1

17. **M4N5.e.** Oliver has 56 quarters in his piggy bank. How much money does he have altogether?

A. $0.14

B. $1.40

C. $14.00

D. $140.00

Study and Review	
Item	Lesson Pages
11	130–131
12	156–159
13	240–241
14	300–303
15	170–171
16	310–313
17	424–425

✓ NUMBERS AND OPERATIONS

18. (M4N6.b.) Paul has a piece of shelving that is $18\frac{3}{5}$ feet long. He cuts off a piece that is $12\frac{2}{5}$ feet long. How long is the piece that is left over?

A. $6\frac{1}{5}$ feet

B. $7\frac{1}{5}$ feet

C. 30 feet

D. 31 feet

19. (M4N5.a.) What is the decimal for the model shown below?

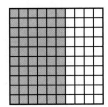

A. 0.06

B. 0.4

C. 0.6

D. 6.0

20. (M4N5.c.) Linda bought a box of cereal for $4.48 and milk for $2.75. She gave the clerk $10. How much change did she receive?

A. $2.77

B. $3.77

C. $7.23

D. $17.23

Use the table below for question 21.

Person	Weight of Fish
Jenna	3.8 pounds
Rob	4.1 pounds
Jamil	3.58 pounds
Michelle	4.06 pounds

21. (M4N5.b.) Jenna and her friends entered a fishing contest at Lake Blue Ridge. What are the weights of the fish they caught in order from least to greatest?

A. 4.1, 4.06, 3.58, 3.8

B. 3.58, 3.8, 4.06, 4.1

C. 3.8, 3.58, 4.1, 4.06

D. 3.58, 3.8, 4.1, 4.06

22. (M4N5.e.) Kendra purchased 6 packages of cheese. Each package weighed 0.75 pound. What was the total weight of the 6 packages?

A. 0.75 pound

B. 4.20 pounds

C. 4.50 pounds

D. 6.75 pounds

Study and Review	
Item	Lesson Pages
18	316–319
19	378–381
20	408–411
21	388–391
22	424–425

✓ NUMBERS AND OPERATIONS

23. **M4N2.d.** When Chris visited Augusta, he spent $21.48 on a poster and $17.88 on other souvenirs. What is the BEST estimate of the amount he spent on the poster and souvenirs?

A. $3

B. $15

C. $39

D. $360

24. **M4N5.e.** Mario paid $0.96 for 8 pencils. How much did each pencil cost?

A. $0.12

B. $0.14

C. $0.16

D. $0.18

25. **M4N1.a.** In 1790, the population of the United States was 3,929,214. What is the value of the blue digit in 3,929,214?

A. 9,000,000

B. 900,000

C. 90,000

D. 9,000

Use the table below for question 26.

State	Miles of Gulf Coastline
Alabama	53
Florida	770
Louisiana	397
Mississippi	44
Texas	367

26. **M4N2.a.** Rounded to the nearest hundred, which state has about 400 miles of Gulf coastline?

A. Florida

B. Louisiana

C. Mississippi

D. Alabama

27. **M4N4.c.** Juanita wants to bake 76 muffins. Her muffin tin holds a batch of 8 muffins. What is the LEAST number of batches she will need to bake?

A. 8

B. 9

C. 10

D. 11

Study and Review	
Item	**Lesson Pages**
23	402–403
24	438–439
25	6–9
26	32–35
27	208–211

28. **M4N7.b.** What is the value of the expression?

$$32 - (8 + 12)$$

A. 12

B. 14

C. 36

D. 52

29. **M4N7.d.** Use the basic fact and the number pattern to find $6,000 \times 30$.

$$6 \times 3 = 18$$
$$60 \times 30 = 1,800$$
$$600 \times 30 = 18,000$$

A.　　18,000

B.　　180,000

C.　1,800,000

D. 18,000,000

30. **M4N3.** There are 30 apples in each bag of large apples, 50 apples in each bag of medium apples, and 100 apples in each bag of small apples. A bakery purchased 20 bags of medium apples. How many apples did the bakery buy?

A.　　100

B.　　600

C.　1,000

D. 10,000

Use table below for question 31.

City	Elevation
Augusta	162 feet
Crawfordville	589 feet
Elberton	708 feet
Louisville	36 feet

31. **M4N7.d.** The elevation of the highest point in Georgia, Brasstown Bald, is about 8 times that of Crawfordville. About how high is Brasstown Bald?

A. 5,600 feet

B. 4,800 feet

C. 1,600 feet

D.　480 feet

32. **M4N4.b.** Find the quotient.

$$328 \div 50$$

A.　6 r28

B. 60 r8

C. 65 r3

D. 66

Study and Review	
Item	Lesson Pages
28	46–49
29	168–169
30	172–173
31	150–151
32	234–237

CRCT Practice

✓ NUMBERS AND OPERATIONS

33. **M4N3.** Every member of the chess club pays $38 in dues to help pay for trips to chess meets. If there are 46 members in the chess club, how much do they collect in dues?

A. $84

B. $350

C. $1,600

D. $1,748

34. **M4N6.b.** Selena ate $\frac{3}{8}$ of a pizza, and Will ate $\frac{4}{8}$ of the pizza. How much of the pizza did they eat in all?

A. $\frac{7}{8}$

B. $\frac{3}{4}$

C. $\frac{1}{2}$

D. $\frac{1}{8}$

35. **M4N1.b.** Emily guessed the number of marbles in a jar to be 5,983. Karen guessed 100 more than Emily. What is the word form for Karen's guess?

A. five thousand, nine hundred, ninety-three

B. six thousand, eighty-three

C. six thousand, one hundred eighty-three

D. six thousand, nine hundred, eighty-three

Use the map below for question 36.

36. **M4N4.b.** The bicycle club rode from Tifton to Brunswick and back. They rode at a rate of 13 miles per hour. How long did the trip take?

A. 10 hours

B. 15 hours

C. 20 hours

D. 30 hours

37. **M4N5.e.** A snack at summer camp costs $0.75 per day. Grace is going to summer camp for 8 days. How much will she spend on snacks?

A. $4.56

B. $6.00

C. $7.85

D. $8.75

Study and Review	
Item	Lesson Pages
33	184–187
34	310–313
35	4–5
36	234–237
37	424–425

38. **M4N2.a.** Which of the following numbers would be rounded to 9,000 when rounded to the nearest hundred?

A. 8,933

B. 8,958

C. 9,286

D. 9,954

39. **M4N6.c.** Which of the following mixed numbers is equal to $\frac{11}{5}$?

A. $1\frac{1}{5}$

B. 2

C. $2\frac{1}{5}$

D. $2\frac{4}{5}$

Use the table below for question 40.

Item	Weight (in pounds)
Pork Chops	1.57
Ground Beef	1.08
Steak	1.75
Sausage	1.8

40. **M4N5.b.** Derek bought some meat at the butcher shop. Of which item did he buy the MOST?

A. pork chops

B. ground beef

C. steak

D. sausage

Use the table below for question 41.

Some Georgia Covered Bridges	
Name of Bridge	Length
Watson Mill	228.6 feet
Euharlee Creek	137.6 feet
Concord	131.7 feet
Poole's Mill	94.6 feet

41. **M4N5.c.** Georgia's covered bridges are very old. The Watson Mill Bridge was built in 1885. How much longer is the Watson Mill Bridge than the Concord Bridge?

A. 96.9 feet

B. 97.9 feet

C. 131 feet

D. 360.3 feet

42. **M4N1.a.** What is the value of the digit 9 in 8,239,461?

A. 900

B. 9,000

C. 900,000

D. 9,000,000

Study and Review	
Item	Lesson Pages
38	32–35
39	300–303
40	388–391
41	406–407
42	6–9

✔ **NUMBERS AND OPERATIONS**

43. **M4N1.b.** The Chattahoochee and Oconee forests cover 862,368 acres. What is the expanded form of 862,368?

   A. $8,000,000 + 60,000 + 2,000 + 300 + 60 + 8$

   B. $86,000 + 2,000 + 300 + 60 + 8$

   C. $800,000 + 60,000 + 2,000 + 368$

   D. $800,000 + 60,000 + 2,000 + 300 + 60 + 8$

44. **M4N7.a.** There will be 152 guests at a party. The guests will be seated at 19 tables. Which operation would you use to find the number of people that will be seated at each table?

   A. multiplication

   B. division

   C. addition

   D. subtraction

45. **M4N3.** Evan plans to read 68 pages in his book every day for 8 days. How many pages will he have read by the end of the 8 days?

   A. 544 pages

   B. 534 pages

   C. 76 pages

   D. 60 pages

Use the graph below for question 46.

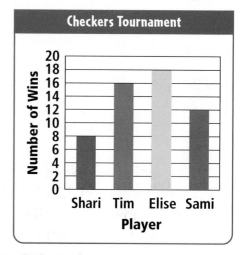

46. **M4N4.a.** How many times as many games as Shari did Tim win?

   A. 2

   B. 4

   C. 6

   D. 8

47. **M4N7.b.** Which expression has the value 49?

   A. $3 + 4 \times 7$

   B. $(58 - 18) \div 2$

   C. $58 - 18 \div 2$

   D. $8 \times 6 - (8 - 6)$

Study and Review	
Item	Lesson Pages
43	4–5
44	242–243
45	152–155
46	114–117
47	130–131

✓ NUMBERS AND OPERATIONS

48. **M4N7.d.** Tricia is packing 32 boxes of Georgia peaches. Each box holds 28 peaches. What is the BEST estimate of the number of peaches Tricia packs?

A. 60

B. 90

C. 600

D. 900

49. **M4N7.d.** During one week, birdwatchers counted 3,329 birds. During the following week, they counted 8,631 birds. What is the BEST estimate of the total number of birds counted?

A. 1,200

B. 3,000

C. 9,000

D. 12,000

50. **M4N4.d.** Which of the following division problems has the same answer as $1,920 \div 60$?

A. $192 \div 6$

B. $192 \div 60$

C. $1,920 \div 6$

D. $19,200 \div 60$

51. **M4N1.a.** What is the value of the blue digit in the number 56,391.48?

A. 0.03

B. 3

C. 30

D. 300

52. **M4N7.c.** Which number sentence shows how to compute 7×19 using the Distributive Property?

A. $7 \times 10 \times 9 = 630$

B. $7 \times (10 + 9) = (7 \times 10) + (7 \times 9) = 70 + 63 = 133$

C. $7 + (10 \times 9) = 7 + 90 = 97$

D. $7 \times 10 + 9 = 70 + 9 = 79$

53. **M4N6.b.** Jay mowed $\frac{3}{10}$ of the lawn before school and mowed $\frac{5}{10}$ of the lawn after school. How much of the lawn did he mow?

A. $\frac{8}{10}$

B. $\frac{1}{2}$

C. $\frac{8}{20}$

D. $\frac{1}{5}$

54. **M4N2.d.** What is the BEST estimate for the sum $23.48 + 35.71$?

A. 50

B. 55

C. 60

D. 70

Study and Review	
Item	Lesson Pages
48	174–175
49	36–39
50	230–231
51	4–5
52	170–171
53	310–313
54	402–403

✓ NUMBERS AND OPERATIONS

55. **M4N7.b.** Use the order of operations to find the value of the expression.

$$8 \times 9 - 6 \div 3$$

A. 6

B. 22

C. 56

D. 70

56. **M4N4.a.** A car dealer has 8 new cars ready to test drive. There are 864 people who want to drive the cars. If all the cars are driven the same number of times, how many times will each car be driven?

A.　18

B.　108

C.　180

D. 1,080

57. **M4N3.** Each person in a school relay race is going to run 128 meters. If there are four people on a relay team, how long is the race?

A.　32 meters

B. 128 meters

C. 256 meters

D. 512 meters

58. **M4N5.b.** Mark and his friends spent a day exploring the Trackrock Archaeological Area. They measured some petroglyphs and recorded the following measurements: 10.3 centimeters, 8.82 centimeters, 10.03 centimeters, and 8.29 centimeters. What are the measurements in order from least to greatest?

A. 10.3, 10.03, 8.82, 8.29

B. 10.3, 10.03, 8.29, 8.82

C. 8.29, 8.82, 10.03, 10.3

D. 8.29, 8.82, 10.3, 10.03

59. **M4N5.e.** Bill bought 8 packs of flower seeds. Each one cost $0.49. How much did he spend in all?

A. $3.92

B. $4.02

C. $4.98

D. $8.49

Study and Review	
Item	Lesson Pages
55	130–131
56	216–219
57	156–159
58	388–391
59	424–425

60. ⬛ **M4N2.d.** Ed wants to mail 3 packages. One weighs 8.2 pounds, another weighs 12.8 pounds, and the third weighs 14.71 pounds. What is the BEST estimate of the total weight of all three packages?

A. 8 pounds

B. 26 pounds

C. 36 pounds

D. 55 pounds

61. ⬛ **M4N5.e.** Marcia bought 0.75 pound of roast beef. She made 3 sandwiches and put the same amount of roast beef in each. How much roast beef was in each sandwich?

A. 0.5 pound

B. 0.25 pound

C. 0.15 pound

D. 0.05 pound

62. ⬛ **M4N1.b.** In 1994, three million people used the Internet. Most of them lived in the United States. What is the standard form of the number three million?

A.   3,000

B.   300,000

C.   3,000,000

D. 3,000,000,000

Use the table below for question 63.

Appalachian Trail Hike	
Day	**Distance**
Monday	12.6 miles
Tuesday	11.8 miles
Wednesday	15.7 miles
Thursday	8.2 miles

63. ⬛ **M4N5.c.** Robin went for a 4-day hike on the Appalachian Trail in Georgia. How far did she hike in all?

A. 47.3 miles

B. 48.2 miles

C. 48.3 miles

D. 48.4 miles

64. ⬛ **M4N4.a.** Jeannie wrote 24 thank-you notes to the people who gave her birthday presents. If Jeannie wrote 6 notes per hour, how long did it take her to write the notes?

A. 2 hours

B. 4 hours

C. 6 hours

D. 8 hours

Study and Review	
Item	**Lesson Pages**
60	402–403
61	438–439
62	6–9
63	404–405
64	114–117

✓ NUMBERS AND OPERATIONS

65. **M4N6.a.** Which of the following are two equivalent fractions for the picture?

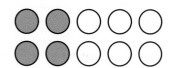

A. $\frac{10}{4}$ and $\frac{5}{2}$

B. $\frac{3}{5}$ and $\frac{6}{10}$

C. $\frac{2}{3}$ and $\frac{4}{6}$

D. $\frac{2}{5}$ and $\frac{4}{10}$

66. **M4N7.d.** Use the basic fact and the number pattern to find $8 \times 60,000$.

$$8 \times 6 = 48$$
$$8 \times 60 = 480$$
$$8 \times 600 = 4,800$$

A.   4,800

B.   48,000

C.   480,000

D. 4,800,000

67. **M4N3.** The main kitchen for the school district makes 120 pizzas each day to serve in the schools. If each pizza is cut into 8 slices, how many slices of pizza does the school district serve each day?

A.   15

B.   128

C.   960

D. 9,600

Use the table below for question 68.

State	Acres of Forest
Florida	16.3 million
Georgia	24.4 million
Alabama	23.0 million
Arkansas	18.8 million

68. **M4N5.b.** Which list of states shows the number of acres of forest in order from least to greatest?

A. Florida, Georgia, Alabama, Arkansas

B. Florida, Arkansas, Alabama, Georgia

C. Florida, Arkansas, Georgia, Alabama

D. Georgia, Alabama, Arkansas, Florida

69. **M4N2.a.** Rounded to the nearest hundred, there are about 900 students in Armando's school. How many students could be in Armando's school?

A. 842

B. 871

C. 952

D. 977

Study and Review	
Item	Lesson Pages
65	296–297
66	168–169
67	156–159
68	388–391
69	32–35

70. (M4N3.) The drama club plans to raise money by selling sweatshirts for $18 each. They ordered 75 sweatshirts that cost $7 each. How much money will they raise if they sell all the sweatshirts?

A. $126

B. $545

C. $825

D. $1,350

71. (M4N6.b.) Sheila has $\frac{11}{12}$ pound of sliced turkey. She uses $\frac{9}{12}$ pound making lunch. How much turkey does she have left?

A. $\frac{2}{12}$ pound

B. $\frac{1}{4}$ pound

C. $\frac{1}{2}$ pound

D. $1\frac{8}{12}$ pounds

72. (M4N5.c.) How much more does a burger cost than a turkey wrap?

Burger	$4.25
Turkey wrap	$3.70
Hot dog	$1.60

A. $7.25

B. $1.55

C. $1.10

D. $0.55

Use the table below for question 73.

Flower Order	
Type	Number Ordered
Daffodils	156
Roses	432
Tulips	336

73. (M4N4.b.) A florist in Macon plans to make bouquets of 12 roses for Valentine's Day. How many bouquets of roses can he make with his order?

A. 8

B. 30

C. 36

D. 42

74. (M4N2.c.) Randy wants to round 75.82 to the nearest whole number. Which statement is TRUE?

A. The digit in the tens place will increase.

B. The digit in the ones place will increase.

C. The digit in the ones place will stay the same.

D. The digit in the ones place will decrease.

Study and Review	
Item	Lesson Pages
70	184–187
71	314–315
72	408–411
73	234–237
74	400–401

✔ **NUMBERS AND OPERATIONS**

75. **M4N6.c.** Which of the following is $\frac{12}{9}$ written as a mixed number?

   A. $1\frac{2}{9}$

   B. $1\frac{3}{9}$

   C. $\frac{4}{3}$

   D. $2\frac{3}{9}$

76. **M4N6.a.** Which of the following are two equivalent fractions for the picture below?

   A. $\frac{3}{6}$ and $\frac{6}{12}$

   B. $\frac{1}{6}$ and $\frac{2}{12}$

   C. $\frac{1}{3}$ and $\frac{2}{6}$

   D. $\frac{1}{2}$ and $\frac{3}{6}$

77. **M4N2.d.** Clara spent $35.78 on a bike helmet and $42.20 on shoes. What is the BEST estimate of how much she spent in all?

   A. $10

   B. $30

   C. $40

   D. $80

78. **M4N1.b.** What is the standard form for three hundred thousand, twenty-nine?

   A.   329

   B.   3,029

   C. 300,029

   D. 329,000

Use the table below for question 79.

Lengths of Trails in Elachee Nature Science Center	
Trail	**Length**
Ed Dodd	0.75 mile
Geiger	1 mile
West Lake	2.6 miles
East Lake	1.8 miles

79. **M4N5.c.** Ryan hiked the West Lake Trail, and Elias hiked the Ed Dodd Trail. How much farther than Elias did Ryan hike?

   A. 0.8 mile

   B. 0.85 mile

   C. 1.85 miles

   D. 3.35 miles

80. **M4N5.b.** Which pair shows equivalent decimals?

   A. 0.12, 0.21

   B. 0.5, 0.05

   C. 0.4, 0.24

   D. 0.7, 0.70

Study and Review	
Item	**Lesson Pages**
75	300–303
76	296–297
77	402–403
78	4–5
79	406–407
80	382–383

✔ MEASUREMENT

1. **M4M1.a.** Westville is a living history museum near Lumpkin, GA, that has a blacksmith. Blacksmiths make shoes for horses. What is the MOST reasonable weight for a horseshoe?

   A.   1 ounce

   B.   1 pound

   C. 100 pounds

   D.   1 ton

2. **M4M1.c.** Which of the following statements is TRUE?

   A. 4 tons < 4 ounces

   B. 4 pounds < 4 ounces

   C. 4 pounds < 4 tons

   D. 4 ounces > 4 tons

3. **M4M1.a.** Which object weighs about 1 gram?

   A.

   B.

   C.

   D.

4. **M4M1.a.** Which of the following animals would most likely have its weight measured in ounces?

   A.

   B.

   C.

   D.

5. **M4M1.b.** Which of the following units is NOT used to measure weight?

   A. ounce

   B. ton

   C. pound

   D. yard

✓ MEASUREMENT

6. **M4M1.a.** Which object weighs more than 1 kilogram?

A.

B.

C.

D.

Use the figure below for question 7.

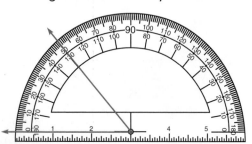

What is the measure of

9. **M4M2.b.** What is the measure of a half rotation?

A. 45°

B. 90°

C. 180°

D. 360°

10. **M4M1.a.** Jeremy needs a photo of something that weighs about 1,000 kilograms. Which photo should he choose?

A.

B.

C.

D.
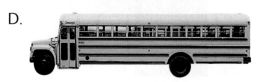

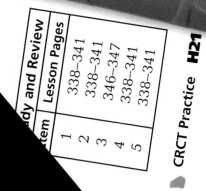

✓ GEOMETRY

1. **M4G1.a.** Which of the following triangles is a right triangle?

A.

B.

C.

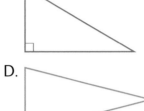

D.

2. **M4G1.a.** Which of the following types of triangle has an angle that is greater than a right angle?

A. obtuse triangle

B. right triangle

C. acute triangle

D. equilateral triangle

3. **M4G1.b.** Which of the quadrilaterals below has sides that are ALWAYS perpendicular?

A. rhombus

B. parallelogram

C. trapezoid

D. rectangle

4. **M4G1.b.** Which figure has exactly 1 pair of parallel sides?

A.

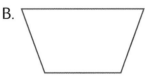

B.

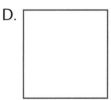

C.

D.

5. **M4G1.d.** Which quadrilateral is NOT a parallelogram?

A. rectangle

B. rhombus

C. square

D. trapezoid

Study and Review	
Item	Lesson Pages
1	274–275
2	274–275
3	276–279
4	276–279
5	276–279

✓ GEOMETRY

6. (M4G1.c.) Which figure is a square?

A.

B.

C.

D.

7. (M4G1.c.) Which figure is a trapezoid with 2 congruent sides?

A.

B.

C.

D.

8. (M4G1.c.) Which statement does NOT describe every rectangle?

A. It is a parallelogram.

B. It has 4 right angles.

C. The opposite sides are congruent.

D. It has 4 congruent sides.

9. (M4G2.a.) How many more vertices does a cube have than a rectangular prism?

A. 0

B. 2

C. 6

D. 8

10. (M4G2.a.) Which statement BEST describes the faces of a cube?

A. 2 rectangles and 4 squares

B. 6 rectangles

C. 6 squares

D. 2 triangles and 4 rectangles

11. (M4G2.b.) Which of the following statements BEST describes the relationship between the opposite faces of a rectangular prism?

A. They are perpendicular.

B. They are parallel.

C. They intersect.

D. They are squares.

Study and Review	
Item	**Lesson Pages**
6	276–279
7	276–279
8	276–279
9	282–285
10	282–285
11	282–285

✓ GEOMETRY

12. **M4G2.a.** Which shapes can form the faces of a rectangular prism?

   A. squares only

   B. rectangles only

   C. rectangles and circles

   D. rectangles and triangles

13. **M4G2.c.** Which pattern could be folded to make a cube?

   A.
   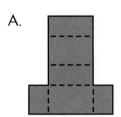

   B.
   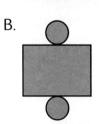

   C.
   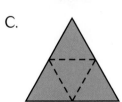

   D.
   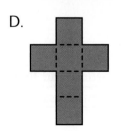

Use the rectangular prism below for question 14.

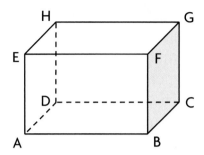

14. **M4G2.b.** Which two edges on the rectangular prism are parallel?

   A. $\overline{AB}$ and $\overline{EF}$

   B. $\overline{AB}$ and $\overline{BC}$

   C. $\overline{FG}$ and $\overline{GH}$

   D. $\overline{AD}$ and $\overline{GC}$

15. **M4G2.a.** Which shapes can form the faces of a cube?

   A. rectangles only

   B. squares only

   C. rectangles and squares

   D. rectangles and triangles

Study and Review	
Item	**Lesson Pages**
12	282–285
13	286–287
14	282–285
15	282–285

✔ GEOMETRY

16. **M4G3.a.** Angela graphed the points in the coordinate system shown below. She wants to graph another point to make a rectangle. Which ordered pair should she graph next?

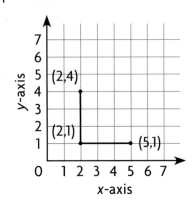

A. (2,5)

B. (4,5)

C. (5,4)

D. (4,1)

17. **M4G3.b.** Which ordered pair names point Q in the coordinate system shown below?

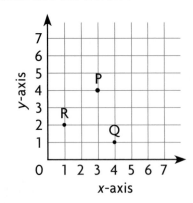

A. (1,2)

B. (4,1)

C. (1,4)

D. (3,4)

18. **M4G3.c.** Which point is located at (2,5) in the coordinate system shown below?

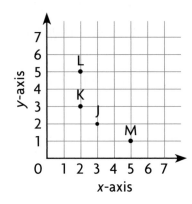

A. J

B. K

C. L

D. M

19. **M4G1.a.** Which type of triangle has an angle that measures exactly 90°?

A. an acute triangle

B. an equilateral triangle

C. an obtuse triangle

D. a right triangle

Study and Review	
Item	**Lesson Pages**
16	82–83
17	82–83
18	82–83
19	274–275

✓ GEOMETRY

20. **M4G1.a.** Which triangle is an obtuse triangle?

A.

B.

C.

D.

21. **M4G2.a.** Which of the following statements is NOT true?

A. A cube has the same number of faces as a rectangular prism.

B. A cube and a rectangular prism each have 6 congruent faces.

C. A cube has the same number of edges as a rectangular prism.

D. A cube has the same number of vertices as a rectangular prism.

22. **M4G1.d.** Which of the following quadrilateral has 4 congruent sides and no right angles?

A. parallelogram

B. square

C. rectangle

D. rhombus

23. **M4G3.a.** Brad graphed the point in the coordinate system shown below. He wants to graph another point 2 units to the right and 1 unit down from the first point. What ordered pair gives the location of the second point?

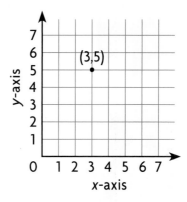

A. (3,5)

B. (1,4)

C. (5,4)

D. (2,1)

Study and Review	
Item	Lesson Pages
20	274–275
21	282–285
22	276–279
23	82–83

✓ GEOMETRY

24. **M4G2.c.** Which pattern folds to make a triangular prism?

A.

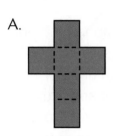

B.

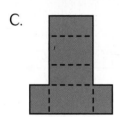

C.

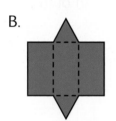

D.

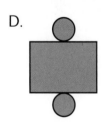

25. **M4G3.c.** Which point is located at (0,4) in the coordinate system shown below?

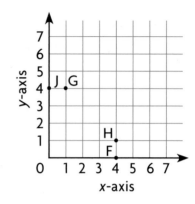

A. F

B. G

C. H

D. J

26. **M4G1.b.** Which quadrilateral has 2 pairs of parallel congruent sides and 4 right angles?

A. square

B. parallelogram

C. rhombus

D. trapezoid

Study and Review	
Item	Lesson Pages
24	286–287
25	82–83
26	276–279

✓ ALGEBRA

1. **M4A1.c.** Six people were at the park and then three left. Which expression can be used to find how many people are in the park now?

   A. $6 - 3$

   B. $6 + 3$

   C. 6×3

   D. $6 \div 3$

2. **M4A1.b.** Lana had 6 fish in her aquarium. Then she got some more fish. Let ☐ represent the number of new fish. Which expression shows the number of fish Lana has in her aquarium now?

   A. $☐ - 6$

   B. $6 + ☐$

   C. $6 - ☐$

   D. $6 \times ☐$

3. **M4A1.a.** What rule can be used to find the missing number in the pattern below?

In	6	13	23	37	48
Out	14	21	31		56

   A. Add 7.

   B. Add 8.

   C. Subtract 7.

   D. Subtract 8.

4. **M4A1.a.** Which table shows the following rule?

   Subtract 6.

   A.
In	3	7	10	12
Out	9	13	16	18

   B.
In	18	24	30	36
Out	3	4	5	6

   C.
In	9	12	15	20
Out	3	6	9	14

   D.
In	2	4	7	9
Out	12	24	42	54

5. **M4A1.a.** Which of the following is the rule for the table?

In	2	7	10	15
Out	6	11	14	19

   A. Add 4.

   B. Add 6.

   C. Subtract 4.

   D. Multiply by 3.

Study and Review	
Item	Lesson Pages
1	46–49
2	46–49
3	52–53
4	52–53
5	52–53

✔ ALGEBRA

6. **M4A1.b.** Brian found some shells. Tina found 3 times as many shells as Brian. Let □ represent the number of shells Brian found. Which expression shows how many shells Tina found?

A. 3 + □

B. 3 × □

C. □ ÷ 3

D. □ − 3

7. **M4A1.b.** Which expression matches the words below?

24 books divided equally among some classes

A. 24 × △

B. 24 ÷ △

C. △ ÷ 24

D. △ − 24

Use the table below for question 8.

In	Out
4	24
5	30
6	36
7	42

8. **M4A1.a.** What is the rule used in the table?

A. Add 20.

B. Add 10.

C. Multiply by 6.

D. Multiply by 8.

9. **M4A1.c.** What is the value of 8 × △ if △ = 4?

A. 2

B. 4

C. 11

D. 32

10. **M4A1.c.** What is the value of (9 + 7) − ★ if ★ = 2?

A. 5

B. 7

C. 14

D. 16

11. **M4A1.b.** Justine made 4 loaves of bread in the morning. In the afternoon, she made some more bread. Let □ represent the number of loaves Justine made in the afternoon. Which expression shows the total number of loaves of bread she made?

A. 4 + □

B. 4 − □

C. □ − 4

D. □ ÷ 4

Study and Review	
Item	Lesson Pages
6	132–133
7	132–133
8	136–137
9	132–133
10	46–49
11	46–49

✔ ALGEBRA

12. **M4A1.c.** Find the value of $9 + (\triangle - 2)$ if $\triangle = 5$.

A. 2

B. 6

C. 12

D. 16

13. **M4A1.a.** Which table shows the following rule?

Add 7.

A.
In	9	12	17	20
Out	2	5	10	13

B.
In	9	12	17	20
Out	14	17	22	25

C.
In	9	12	17	20
Out	12	17	20	24

D.
In	9	12	17	20
Out	16	19	24	27

14. **M4A1.b.** There are 18 children in Connie's karate class, but some are absent today. Let $\triangle$ represent the number of children absent. Which expression shows the number of children who showed up today?

A. $\triangle - 18$

B. $\triangle + 18$

C. $18 - \triangle$

D. $18 \div \triangle$

15. **M4A1.c.** What is the value of $48 \div \triangle$ if $\triangle = 8$?

A. 6

B. 7

C. 40

D. 56

16. **M4A1.a.** What rule can be used to find the missing number in the table below?

In	12	11	8	6	5
Out	24	22	16	12	

A. Add 12.

B. Multiply by 2.

C. Subtract 1.

D. Divide by 2.

17. **M4A1.b.** What number does the variable represent?

$$17 - \star = 9 + 5$$

A. 14

B. 12

C. 8

D. 3

Study and Review	
Item	Lesson Pages
12	46–49
13	52–53
14	46–49
15	132–133
16	136–137
17	50–51

✔ DATA ANALYSIS

1. **M4D1.d.** Taylor's quiz scores are 9, 8, 10, 9, 9, 7, 8, and 7. She made this graph to show her quiz scores.

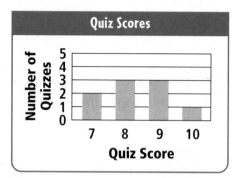

Which statement about Taylor's graph is TRUE?

A. The graph correctly shows the quiz scores.

B. There is an extra quiz score of 8 shown in the graph.

C. There is an extra quiz score of 9 shown in the graph.

D. The graph is missing a quiz score.

2. **M4D1.a.** A librarian made a pictograph to show how many books were checked out by each grade in one day. He used this key.

> **Key:** 📖 = 10 Books

How many symbols did he use to show that the fourth graders checked out 45 books?

A. $3\frac{1}{2}$

B. 4

C. $4\frac{1}{2}$

D. 45

3. **M4D1.b.** Derek made the following line graph to show how his puppy's weight changed from January through April.

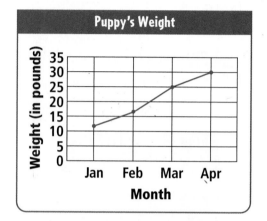

Which statement about Derek's graph is TRUE?

A. The puppy gained weight each month.

B. The puppy lost weight each month.

C. The puppy weighed more in January than in February.

D. The puppy did not gain any weight each month.

Study and Review	
Item	Lesson Pages
1	68–69
2	72–73
3	96–97

✓ DATA ANALYSIS

4. **M4D1.c.** The bar graph below shows the number of minutes Zane exercised each day from Monday through Thursday.

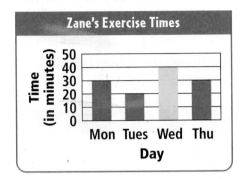

Which statement is TRUE?

A. If the interval were 1, the bars would be narrower.

B. If the interval were 5, the bars would be shorter.

C. If the interval were 20, the bars would be shorter.

D. If the interval were 2, the bars would be wider.

5. **M4D1.c.** Which data would be the BEST to display in a line graph?

A. weekly allowance of 10 students

B. favorite sport of students in a fourth-grade class

C. a baby's weight each month from birth to one year

D. most popular movie of students in an elementary school

6. **M4D1.a.** The table below shows the height of a plant Dani grew for a science project.

Plant Growth				
Week	1	2	3	4
Height (in inches)	3	7	9	12

She started to make a line graph of the data. What does Dani need to do to complete her graph?

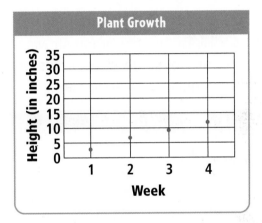

A. Plot additional points on the graph.

B. Connect the points on the graph.

C. Draw bars up to each point on the graph.

D. The graph is complete.

Study and Review	
Item	Lesson Pages
4	70–71
5	92–95
6	86–87

✓ DATA ANALYSIS

7. **M4D1.c.** What type of graph would be the BEST to display the number of visitors to the World of Coca-Cola in Atlanta, GA, each day for a week?

A. bar graph

B. double-bar graph

C. line graph

D. pictograph

8. **M4D1.a.** The bar graph shows the number of students with different belt colors in a karate class.

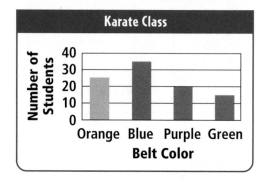

Which data set was used to make the bar graph?

A. orange 30, blue 40, purple 20, green 10

B. orange 20, blue 30, purple 20, green 10

C. orange 25, blue 35, purple 25, green 15

D. orange 25, blue 35, purple 20, green 15

9. **M4D1.d.** Scott surveyed his friends Manuel, Tino, Angelina, Francine, and Toby about the number of books each person read last month. He made the following bar graph to show his results.

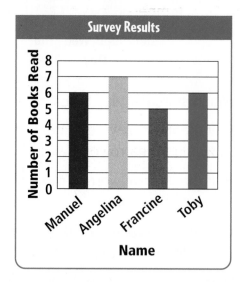

Which statement about Scott's graph is TRUE?

A. Data is missing from the graph.

B. Data is repeated in the graph.

C. None of Scott's friends read 5 books.

D. The graph correctly shows the data.

Study and Review	
Item	Lesson Pages
7	92–95
8	72–73
9	68–69

✓ DATA ANALYSIS

10. ▸ M4D1.c. Which data would be the BEST to display in a pictograph?

A. daily rainfall for 5 days

B. pets of students in a fourth grade class

C. attendance at 4 school basketball games

D. high temperature each hour for 6 hours

11. ▸ M4D1.b. The bar graph shows how far Raven rode her bike each week for 6 weeks.

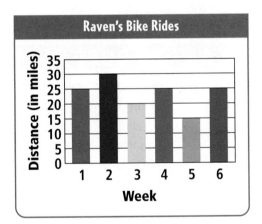

Which number shows the weekly distance that Raven rode most often?

A. 15

B. 20

C. 25

D. 30

12. ▸ M4D1.a. The table below shows the transportation choices of the fourth graders in Thea's school.

How We Get to School	
Method of Transportation	**Number of Students**
Walk	40
Bike	25
Bus	50
Car	30

Thea made a pictograph of the data shown in the table. What is wrong with Thea's pictograph?

How We Get to School	
Method of Transportation	**Number of Students**
Walk	👤👤👤👤👤
Bike	👤👤👤
Bus	👤👤👤👤👤
Car	👤👤👤

A. The key is missing.

B. There are not enough symbols.

C. There are too many symbols.

D. The title is missing.

Study and Review	
Item	**Lesson Pages**
10	92–95
11	88–91
12	72–73

TABLE OF MEASURES

METRIC

Length

1 centimeter (cm) = 10 millimeters (mm)
1 decimeter (dm) = 10 centimeters
1 meter (m) = 10 decimeters
1 kilometer (km) = 1,000 meters

Capacity

1 liter (L) = 1,000 milliliters (mL)
1 metric cup = 250 milliliters

Mass/Weight

1 gram (g) = 1,000 milligrams (mg)
1 kilogram (kg) = 1,000 grams

CUSTOMARY

Length

1 foot (ft) = 12 inches (in.)
1 yard (yd) = 3 feet, or 36 inches
1 mile (mi) = 1,760 yards, or 5,280 feet

Capacity

1 tablespoon (tbsp) = 3 teaspoons (tsp)
1 cup (c) = 8 fluid ounces (fl oz)
1 pint (pt) = 2 cups
1 quart (qt) = 2 pints
1 gallon (gal) = 4 quarts

Mass/Weight

1 pound (lb) = 16 ounces (oz)
1 ton (T) = 2,000 pounds

TIME

1 minute (min) = 60 seconds (sec)
1 hour (hr) = 60 minutes
1 day = 24 hours
1 week (wk) = 7 days
1 year (yr) = 12 months (mo), or about 52 weeks
1 year = 365 days
1 leap year = 366 days

MONEY

1 penny = 1 cent (¢)
1 nickel = 5 cents
1 dime = 10 cents
1 quarter = 25 cents
1 half dollar = 50 cents
1 dollar ($) = 100 cents

SYMBOLS

$\perp$	is perpendicular to	$<$	is less than	°	degree
$\parallel$	is parallel to	$>$	is greater than	°F	degrees Fahrenheit
$\overleftrightarrow{AB}$	line AB	$\leq$	is less than or equal to	°C	degrees Celsius
$\overrightarrow{AB}$	ray AB	$\geq$	is greater than or equal to	$^+8$	positive 8
$\overline{AB}$	line segment AB	$\approx$	is approximately equal to	$^-8$	negative 8
$\angle ABC$	angle ABC	$=$	is equal to	1:2	ratio of 1 to 2
$\triangle ABC$	triangle ABC	$\neq$	is not equal to	(2,3)	ordered pair (x,y)
				%	percent

FORMULAS

Perimeter of polygon = sum of length of sides
Perimeter of rectangle $P = (2 \times l) + (2 \times w)$
Perimeter of square $P = 4 \times s$

Area of rectangle $A = l \times w$
Volume of rectangular
prism $V = l \times w \times h$

Pronunciation Key

a	add, map	f	fit, half	n	nice, tin	p	pit, stop	yōō	fuse, few
ā	ace, rate	g	go, log	ng	ring, song	r	run, poor	v	vain, eve
â(r)	care, air	h	hope, hate	o	odd, hot	s	see, pass	w	win, away
ä	palm, father	i	it, give	ō	open, so	sh	sure, rush	y	yet, yearn
b	bat, rub	ī	ice, write	ô	order, jaw	t	talk, sit	z	zest, muse
ch	check, catch	j	joy, ledge	oi	oil, boy	th	thin, both	zh	vision,
d	dog, rod	k	cool, take	ou	pout, now	th	this, bathe		pleasure
e	end, pet	l	look, rule	ŏŏ	took, full	u	up, done		
ē	equal, tree	m	move, seem	ōō	pool, food	û(r)	burn, term		

ə the schwa, an unstressed vowel representing the sound spelled *a* in **a**bove, *e* in sick**e**n, *i* in poss**i**ble, *o* in mel**o**n, *u* in circ**u**s

Other symbols:
• separates words into syllables
′ indicates stress on a syllable

A

acute angle [ə•kyōōt′ ang′əl] An angle that measures greater than 0° and less than 90° (p. 257)
Example:

acute triangle [ə•kyōōt′ trī′ang•əl] A triangle with three acute angles (p. 274)
Example:

addend [a′dend] A number that is added to another in an addition problem
Example: 2 + 4 = 6;
 2 and 4 are addends.

addition [ə•di′shən] The process of finding the total number of items when two or more groups of items are joined; the opposite operation of subtraction

A.M. [ā•em′] The time between midnight and noon

analog clock [a′nəl•ôg kläk] A device for measuring time by moving hands around a circle for showing hours, minutes, and sometimes seconds
Example:

angle [ang′əl] A figure formed by two line segments or rays that share the same endpoint (p. 256)
Example:

area [âr′ē•ə] The number of square units needed to cover a surface (p. 360)
Example:

area = 9 square units

array [ə•rā′] An arrangement of objects in rows and columns

Associative Property of Addition [ə•sō′shē•ə•tiv prä′pər•tē əv ə•di′shən] The property that states you can group addends in different ways and still get the same sum
Example: 3 + (8 + 5) = (3 + 8) + 5

Associative Property of Multiplication [ə•sō′shē•ə•tiv prä′pər•tē əv mul•tə•plə•kā′shən] The property that states you can group factors in different ways and still get the same product (p. 108)
Example: 3 × (4 × 2) = (3 × 4) × 2

B

bar graph [bär graf] A graph that uses bars to show data

benchmark [bench′märk] A known number of things that helps you understand the size or amount of a different number of things (p. 10)

calendar [ka′lən•dər] A table that shows the days, weeks, and months of a year

centimeter (cm) [sən′tə•mē•tər] A metric unit for measuring length or distance (p. 342)
100 centimeters = 1 meter
Example:

1 centimeter

century [sen′chə•rē] A measure of time equal to 100 years

closed figure [klōzd fi′gyər] A figure that begins and ends at the same point
Examples:

Commutative Property of Addition
[kə•myoo′tə•tiv prä′pər•tē əv ədi′shən] The property that states that when the order of two addends is changed, the sum is the same
Example: 4 + 5 = 5 + 4

Commutative Property of Multiplication
[kə•myoo′tə•tiv prä′pər•tē əv mul•tə•plə•kā′shən] The property that states that when the order of two factors is changed, the product is the same (p. 108)
Example: 4 × 5 = 5 × 4

compatible numbers [kəm•pa′tə•bəl num′bərz] Numbers that are easy to compute mentally (pp. 31, 150)

cone [kōn] A solid, pointed figure that has a flat, round base (p. 282)
Example:

congruent [kən•groo′ənt] Having the same size and shape (p. 274)
Example:

coordinate grid [kō•ôr′də•nət grid] A grid formed by a horizontal line called the *x*-axis and a vertical line called the *y*-axis
Example:

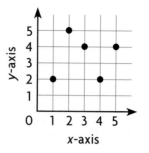

coordinate plane [kō•ôr′də•nət plān] A plane formed by two intersecting and perpendicular number lines called axes
Example:

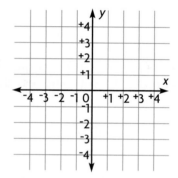

coordinate system [kō•ôr′də•nət sis′təm] A method for locating points using the coordinate plane (p. 82)

corner [kôr′nər] See *vertex.*

cube [kyoob] A solid figure with six congruent square faces (p. 282)
Example:

cup (c) [kup] A customary unit used to measure capacity
8 ounces = 1 cup

cylinder [si′lən•dər] A solid figure that is shaped like a can
Example:

D

data [dā′tə] Information collected about people or things

decade [de′kād] A measure of time equal to 10 years

decimal [de′sə•məl] A number with one or more digits to the right of the decimal point (p. 378)

decimal fraction [de′sə•məl frak′shən] See *decimal*.

decimal point [de′sə•məl point] A symbol used to separate dollars from cents in money amounts and to separate the ones and the tenths places in a decimal (p. 378)
Example: 6.4
⌐ decimal point

decimeter (dm) [de′sə•mē•tər] A metric unit for measuring length or distance (p. 342)
10 decimeters = 1 meter

degree (°) [di•grē′] The unit used for measuring angles and temperatures (p. 256)

degree Celsius (°C) [di•grē′ sel′sē•əs] A metric unit for measuring temperature

degree Fahrenheit (°F) [di•grē′ får′ən•hīt] A standard unit for measuring temperature

denominator [di•nä′mə•nā•tər] The number below the bar in a fraction that tells how many equal parts are in the whole (p. 294)
Example: $\frac{3}{4}$ ← denominator

diagonal line [di•a′gə•nəl līn] A line segment joining nonadjacent vertices of a polygon (p. 259)

difference [di′fər•əns] The answer to a subtraction problem (p. 28)

digit [di′jət] Any one of the ten symbols 0, 1, 2, 3, 4, 5, 6, 7, 8, or 9 used to write numbers

digital clock [di′jə•təl kläk] A clock that shows time to the minute using digits
Example:

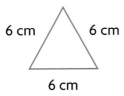

dimension [də•men′shən] A measure in one direction

Distributive Property [di•stri′byə•tiv prä′pər•tē] The property that states that multiplying a sum by a number is the same as multiplying each addend by the number and then adding the products (p. 108)
Example: 5 × (10 + 6) = (5 × 10) + (5 × 6)

dividend [di′və•dend] The number that is to be divided in a division problem
Example: 36 ÷ 6; 6)36; the dividend is 36.

divisible [də•vi′zə•bəl] Capable of being divided so that the quotient is a whole number and the remainder is zero
Example: 21 is divisible by 3.

division [də•vi′zhən] The process of sharing a number of items to find how many groups can be made or how many items will be in each group; the opposite operation of multiplication

divisor [də•vi′zər] The number that divides the dividend
Example: 15 ÷ 3; 3)15; the divisor is 3.

double-bar graph [du′bəl bär graf] A graph used to compare similar kinds of data (p. 80)
Example:

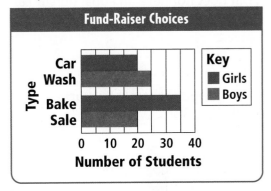

doubles [du′bəlz] Two addends that are the same number

E

edge [ej] The line segment where two or more faces of a solid figure meet (p. 283)
Example:

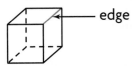

equilateral triangle [ē•kwə•la′tə•rəl trī′ang•əl] A triangle with 3 congruent sides (p. 274)
Example:

6 cm   6 cm

6 cm

equivalent [ē•kwiv′ə•lənt] Having the same value or naming the same amount

equivalent decimals [ē•kwiv′ə•lənt de′sə•məlz] Two or more decimals that name the same amount (p. 382)

equivalent fractions [ē•kwiv′ə•lənt frak′shənz] Two or more fractions that name the same amount (p. 296)
Example: $\frac{2}{4}$ and $\frac{1}{2}$ name the same amount.

estimate [es′tə•māt] *verb* To find an answer that is close to the exact amount

estimate [es′tə•mət] *noun* A number close to an exact amount

expanded form [ik•span′dəd fôrm] A way to write numbers by showing the value of each digit
Example: $253 = 200 + 50 + 3$

expression [ik•spre′shən] A part of a number sentence that has numbers and operation signs but does not have an equal sign (p. 46)

 F

face [fās] A polygon that is a flat surface of a solid figure (p. 282)
Example:

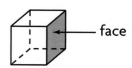

fact family [fakt fam′ə•lē] A set of related multiplication and division, or addition and subtraction, equations (p. 112)
Example: $7 \times 8 = 56$; $8 \times 7 = 56$;
$56 \div 7 = 8$; $56 \div 8 = 7$

factor [fak′tər] A number that is multiplied by another number to find a product

foot (ft) [fŏŏt] A customary unit used for measuring length or distance (p. 332)
1 foot = 12 inches

formula [fôr′myŏŏ•lə] A set of symbols that expresses a mathematical rule (p. 357)
Example: $P = (2 \times l) + (2 \times w)$

fraction [frak′shən] A number that names a part of a whole or part of a group (p. 294)

frequency [frē′kwen•sē] The number of times an event occurs (p. 65)

frequency table [frē′kwen•sē tā′bəl] A table that uses numbers to record data about how often something happens

 G

gallon (gal) [ga′lən] A customary unit for measuring capacity
4 quarts = 1 gallon

gram (g) [gram] A unit for measuring weight (p. 346)
1,000 grams = 1 kilogram

greater than (>) [grā′tər than] A symbol used to compare two quantities, with the greater quantity given first
Example: $6 > 4$

grid [grid] Evenly divided and equally spaced squares on a figure or flat surface

Grouping Property of Addition [grŏŏ′ping prä′pər•tē əv ə•di′shən] See *Associative Property of Addition.*

Grouping Property of Multiplication [grŏŏ′ping prä′pər•tē əv mul•tə•plə•kā′shən] See *Associative Property of Multiplication.*

 **H**

hexagon [hek′sə•gän] A polygon with six sides (p. 272)
Examples:

hexagonal prism [hek•sag′ə•nəl priz′əm] A solid figure that has two hexagonal bases and six rectangular faces (p. 282)
Example:

hour (hr) [our] A unit used to measure time;
60 minutes = 1 hour

hundredth [hən′drədth] One of one hundred equal parts
Example:

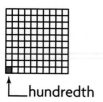
hundredth

Identity Property of Addition [i·den′tə·tē prä′pər·tē əv ə·di′shən] The property that states that when you add zero to any number, the sum is that number
Example: 0 + 16 = 16

Identity Property of Multiplication [i·den′tə·tē prä′pər·tē əv mul·tə·plə·kā′shən] The property that states that the product of any number and 1 is that number (p. 108)
Example: 9 × 1 = 9

improper fraction [im·prä′pər frak′shən] A fraction in which the numerator is greater than or equal to the denominator, such as $\frac{4}{3}$ or $\frac{5}{5}$ (p. 301)

inch (in.) [inch] A customary unit used for measuring length or distance (p. 332)
Example:

intersecting lines [in·tər·sek′ting līnz] Lines that cross each other at exactly one point (p. 262)
Example:

interval [in′tər·vəl] The distance between two numbers on the scale of a graph (p. 70)

inverse operations [in′vərs ä·pə·rā′shənz] Operations that undo each other; addition and subtraction are inverse operations; multiplication and division are inverse operations. (p. 112)
Example: 6 × 8 = 48 and 48 ÷ 6 = 8

isosceles triangle [i·sä′sə·lēz trī′ang·əl] A triangle with two congruent sides (p. 274)
Example:

10 in. /\ 10 in.

7 in.

Word History

When you look at the sides on an *isosceles* triangle, you see that two sides are congruent, or equal in length. The Greek root *iso-* means "same or equal," and *skelos* means "legs."

key [kē] The part of a map or graph that explains the symbols

kilogram (kg) [ki′lə·gram] A metric unit for measuring weight (p. 346)
1 kilogram = 1,000 grams

kilometer (km) [kə·lä′mə·tər] A metric unit for measuring length or distance (p. 343)
1,000 meters = 1 kilometer

less than (<) [les ᵗħan] A symbol used to compare two numbers, with the lesser number given first
Example: 3 < 7

like fractions [lik frak′shənz] Fractions with the same denominator (p. 310)

line [lin] An undefined term; description: A straight path of points in a plane that continues without end in both directions with no endpoints (p. 254)
Example:

S ────────── T

line graph [lin graf] A graph that uses a line to show how data change over a period of time (p. 84)
Example:

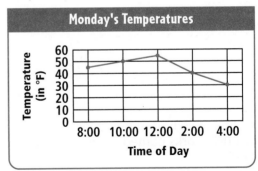

Monday's Temperatures

line segment [lin seg′mənt] A part of a line that includes two points called endpoints and all the points between them (p. 254)
Example:

A ────────── B

linear units [li′nē·ər yōō′nəts] Units that measure length, width, height, or distance (p. 332)

meter (m) [mē′tər] A metric unit for measuring length or distance (p. 342)
100 centimeters = 1 meter

mile (mi) [mīl] A customary unit for measuring length or distance (p. 332)
5,280 feet = 1 mile

millimeter (mm) [mi′lə•mē•tər] A metric unit for measuring length or distance (p. 342)
1 centimeter = 10 millimeters

millions [mil′yənz] The period after thousands (p. 6)

minute (min) [mi′nət] A unit to measure short amounts of time used
60 seconds = 1 minute

mixed fraction [mixt′ frak′shən] See *mixed number*.

mixed number [mikst nəm′bər] An amount given as a whole number and a fraction (p. 300)

multiple [mul′tə•pəl] The product of a given whole number and another whole number (p. 119)

multiplication [mul•tə•plə•kā′shən] A process used to find the total number of items in equal-size groups or to find the total number of items in a given number of groups when each group contains the same number of items; multiplication is the inverse of division.

multistep problem [mul′ti•step prä′bləm] A problem requiring more than one step to solve (p. 194)

number line [num′bər līn] A line with equally spaced tick marks named by numbers
Example:

numerator [noo′mə•rā•tər] The number above the bar in a fraction that tells how many parts of the whole or group are being considered (p. 294)

Example: $\frac{2}{3}$ ← numerator

obtuse angle [äb•toos′ ang′əl] An angle that measures greater than 90° and less than 180° (p. 257)
Example:

Word History

The Latin prefix *ob-* means "against." When combined with *-tuse* meaning "to beat," the word *obtuse* means "to beat against." This makes sense when you look at an obtuse angle because the angle is not sharp or acute. The angle has been beaten against and become blunt and rounded.

obtuse triangle [äb•toos′ trī′ang•əl] A triangle with one obtuse angle (p. 274)
Example:

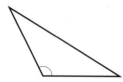

octagon [äk′tə•gän] A polygon with eight sides (p. 272)
Example:

open figure [ō′pən fi′gyər] A figure that does not begin and end at the same point
Examples:

order of operations [ôr′dər əv ä•pə•rā′shənz] A special set of rules that can be used to solve an expression with more than one operation (p. 130)

Order Property of Addition [ôr′dər prä′pər•tē əv ə•di′shən] See *Commutative Property of Addition*.

Order Property of Multiplication [ôr′dər prä′pər•tē əv mul•tə•plə•kā′shən] See *Commutative Property of Multiplication*.

M

N

O

ordered pair [ôr′dərd pâr] A pair of numbers used to locate a point on a coordinate grid; the first number tells how far to move horizontally, and the second number tells how far to move vertically. (p. 82)

origin [ôr′ə•jən] The point where the *x*-axis and the *y*-axis in the coordinate plane intersect, (0,0)

ounce (oz) [ouns] A customary unit for measuring weight (p. 338)
16 ounces = 1 pound

parallel [par′ə•lel] See *parallel lines.*

parallel lines [par′ə•lel linz] Lines in the same plane that never intersect and are always the same distance apart (p. 262)
Example:

Word History

Euclid, an early Greek mathematician, was one of the first to explore the idea for parallel lines. The prefix *para-* means "beside or alongside." This prefix helps you understand the meaning of the word *parallel*.

parallelogram [par•ə•lel′ə•gram] A quadrilateral whose opposite sides are parallel and congruent (p. 277)
Example:

parentheses [pə•ren′thə•sēz] The symbols used to show which operation or operations in an expression should be done first

partial product [pär′shəl prä′dəkt] A method of multiplying in which the ones, tens, and hundreds, are multiplied separately and then the products are added together

pentagon [pen′tə•gän] A polygon with five sides (p. 272)
Examples:

pentagonal prism [pen•tag′ə•nəl priz′əm] A solid figure that has two pentagonal bases and five rectangular faces (p. 282)
Example:

perimeter [pə•ri′mə•tər] The distance around a figure (p. 356)

period [pir′ē•əd] Each group of three digits separated by commas in a multidigit number
Example: 85,643,900 has three periods.

perpendicular [pər•pən•di′kyə•lər] See *perpendicular lines.*

perpendicular lines [pər•pən•di′kyə•lər linz] Two lines that intersect to form four right angles (p. 262)
Example:

pictograph [pik′tə•graf] A graph that uses pictures to show and compare information (p. 12)
Example:

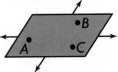

How We Get to School	
Walk	❀ ❀ ❀
Ride a Bike	❀ ❀ ❀ ❀
Ride a Bus	❀ ❀ ❀ ❀ ❀ ❀
Ride in a Car	❀ ❀

Key: Each ❀ = 10 students.

place value [plās val′yo͞o] Place value determines the value of a digit in a number, based on the location of the digit.

plane [plān] A flat surface that extends without end in all directions (p. 254)
Example:

plane figure [plān fi′gyər] A figure in a plane that is formed by lines that are curved, straight, or both

P.M. [pē•em′] The time between noon and midnight

point [point] An undefined term; description: An exact location in space (p. 254)

polygon [pä′lē•gän] A closed plane figure with straight sides; each side is a line segment. (p. 272)
Examples:

pound (lb) [pound] A customary unit for measuring weight (p. 338)
16 ounces = 1 pound

product [prä′dəkt] The answer to a multiplication problem (p. 164)

proper fraction [prä′pər frak′shən] A fraction in which the numerator is less than the denominator. (p. 294)
Examples: $\frac{3}{4}$ and $\frac{1}{2}$

protractor [prō′trak•tər] A tool for measuring the size of an angle (p. 256)

quadrilateral [kwä•drə•la′tə•rəl] A polygon with four sides (p. 272)

quart (qt) [kwôrt] A customary unit for measuring capacity
2 pints = 1 quart

quotient [kwō′shənt] The number, not including the remainder, that results from dividing (p. 208)
Example: 8 ÷ 4 = 2; 2 is the quotient.

ray [rā] A part of a line; it has one endpoint and continues without end in one direction. (p. 254)
Example:

rectangle [rek′tang•əl] A parallelogram with opposite sides that are congruent and with four right angles
Example:

rectangular prism [rek•tang′yə•lər pri′zəm] A solid figure in which all six faces are rectangles (p. 282)
Example:

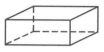

regroup [rē•grōōp′] To exchange amounts of equal value to rename a number
Example: 5 + 8 = 13 ones or 1 ten 3 ones

regular polygon [reg′yə•lər pä′lē•gän] A polygon that has sides that are the same length (p. 272)
Examples:

remainder [ri•mān′dər] The amount left over when a number cannot be divided equally

rhombus [räm′bəs] A parallelogram with four congruent sides (p. 277)
Example:

right angle [rīt ang′əl] An angle that forms a square corner and has a measure of 90° (p. 257)
Example:

90°

right triangle [rīt trī′ang•əl] A triangle with one right angle (p. 274)
Example:

rotation (turn) [rō•tā′shən] A movement of a figure to a new position by rotating the figure around a point (p. 260)
Example:

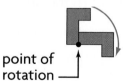

point of rotation

round [round] To replace a number with another number that tells about how many or how much (p. 32)

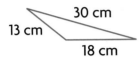

scale [skāl] A series of numbers placed at fixed distances on a graph to help label the graph (p. 70)

scalene triangle [skā′lēn trī′ang•əl] A triangle with no congruent sides (p. 274)
Example:

30 cm
13 cm
18 cm

schedule [ske′jōōl] A table that lists activities or events and the times they happen

second (sec) [se′kənd] A small unit of time 60 seconds = 1 minute

solid figure [sä′ləd fi′gyər] A three-dimensional figure

sphere [sfēr] A round object whose curved surface is the same distance from the center to all its points
Example:

square [skwâr] A parallelogram with 4 congruent sides and 4 right angles
Example:

square unit [skwâr yōō′nət] A unit of area with dimensions of 1 unit × 1 unit

standard form [stan′dərd fôrm] A way to write numbers by using digits
Example: 3,540 ← standard form

straight angle [strāt ang′əl] An angle whose measure is 180° (p. 257)
Example:

subtraction [səb•trak′shən] The process of finding how many are left when a number of items are taken away from a group of items; the process of finding the difference when two groups are compared; the opposite operation of addition

 sum [sum] The answer to an addition problem (p. 28)

survey [sûr′vā] A method of gathering information to record data (p. 64)

T

tablespoon (tbsp) [tā′bəl•spōōn] A customary unit used for measuring capacity 3 teaspoons = 1 tablespoon

tally table [ta′lē tā′bəl] A table that uses tally marks to record data

Word History

Some people keep score in card games by making marks on paper (||||). These marks are known as tally marks. The word *tally* is related to *tailor*, from the Latin *talea*, meaning "one who cuts." In early times, a method of keeping count was by cutting marks into a piece of wood or bone.

teaspoon (tsp) [tē′spōōn] A customary unit used for measuring capacity 1 tablespoon = 3 teaspoons

tenth [tenth] One of ten equal parts
Example:

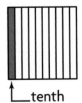
tenth

three-dimensional [thrē•də•men′shən•əl] Measured in three directions, such as length, width, and height (p. 282)
Example:

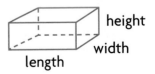
height
width
length

time line [tīm līn] A schedule of events or an ordered list of historic moments

ton (T) [tun′] A customary unit used to measure weight (p. 338)
2,000 pounds = 1 ton

trapezoid [tra′pə•zoid] A quadrilateral with exactly one pair of parallel sides (p. 277)
Example:

trends [trendz] On a graph, areas where the data increase, decrease, or stay the same over time (p. 84)

triangle [tri′ang•əl] A polygon with three sides (p. 272)
Example:

triangular prism [tri•an′gyə•lər pri′zəm] A solid figure that has two triangular bases and three rectangular faces (p. 282)
Example:

turn [tûrn] See *rotation.*

two-dimensional [tōō•də•men′shən•əl] Measured in two directions, such as length and width (p. 282)
Example:

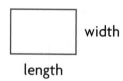
width

length

unlike fractions [un′lĭk frak′shənz] Fractions with different denominators

variable [vâr′ē•ə•bəl] A letter or symbol that stands for a number or numbers (p. 47)

Venn diagram [ven dī′ə•gram] A diagram that shows relationships among sets of things (p. 280)
Example:

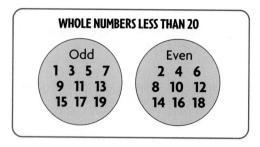

vertex [vûr′teks] The point at which two rays of an angle or two or more line segments meet in a plane figure, or where three or more edges meet in a solid figure; the top point of a cone (p. 256)
Example:

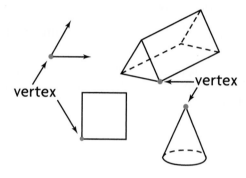
vertex   vertex

weight [wāt] The measure of how heavy an object is (p. 338)

whole number [hōl num′bər] One of the numbers 0, 1, 2, 3, 4...; the set of whole numbers goes on without end.

word form [wûrd fôrm] A way to write numbers by using words
Example: Sixty-two million, four hundred fifty-three thousand, two hundred twelve

x-axis [eks′ak′səs] The horizontal line in a coordinate system or on a coordinate plane (p. 82)

x-coordinate [eks′kō•ôr′də•nət] The first number in an ordered pair; it tells the distance to move horizontally (p. 82)

Y

y-axis [wī′ak′səs] The vertical line in a coordinate system or on a coordinate plane (p. 82)

y-coordinate [wī′kō·ôr′də·nət] The second number in an ordered pair; it tells the distance to move vertically. (p. 82)

yard (yd) [yärd] A customary unit for measuring length or distance (p. 332)
3 feet = 1 yard

 Z

Zero Property of Multiplication [zē′rō prä′pər·tē əv mul·tə·plə·kā′shən] The property that states that the product of 0 and any number is 0 (p. 108)
Example: $0 \times 8 = 0$

A

B

C

Z

Zero

   in addition, 40

   in division, 212, 216–219, 240–241

   in multiplication, 148, 157, 188

   in subtraction, 40–43

Zero Property

   of multiplication, 108–111

Photography Credits: Page Placement key: (t) top, (b) bottom, (c) center, (l) left, (r) right, (bg) background, (i) inset.

PHOTO CREDITS